An Introduction to Chinese Literature

中國文學概論

柳無忌著

Bloomington and London

AN
INTRODUCTION
TO
CHINESE
LITERATURE

Liu Wu-chi

INDIANA UNIVERSITY PRESS

The Chinese calligraphy has been written by Yi-t'ung Wang

cl. ISBN 0-253-33090-4   *pa. ISBN 0-253-33091-2*
Copyright © 1966 by Liu Wu-chi
Library of Congress catalog card number: 66-12729
Manufactured in the United States of America
3 4 5 6 7   80 79 78 77 76

Dedicated to My Father
LIU YA-TZU, 1887–1958
The Last Great Writer of Traditional
Chinese Poetry

Acknowledgments

I want to take this opportunity to thank all friends who have shown a kind interest in this work and who have helped in the preparation of the manuscript. In particular, my gratitude goes to the Bollingen Foundation in New York and to the Indiana University Foundation in Bloomington, Indiana, for grants-in-aid for the writing of the book. I am indebted to Mrs. Willard Church, a devoted friend of China and the Chinese, for her generous help and constant encouragement. I am deeply grateful to Mrs. Dorothy Wikelund, Assistant Editor, Indiana University Press, and to Professor J. L. Cranmer-Byng for having read the entire manuscript and offered many valuable suggestions. I am also greatly obliged to Mrs. Marjorie A. Barritt, Miss Rebecca Woodward, Mrs. Mardy Miller and Mrs. Grace Landers for their technical assistance.

Preface

To record in a single volume the development of a national literature at least 3,000 years old is an exigent and stimulating task. As the title indicates, this book is not a comprehensive history of Chinese literature, adequate treatment of which would require a work of no less scope than the *Cambridge History of English Literature*, but an introductory account with a specific objective.

My purpose is to meet the need of Western readers who have some curiosity about Chinese literature and who, after their interest has been aroused, may be induced to sample further its great works. Hence this book, almost like an anthology supplemented by commentary, includes a large amount of illustrative material from Chinese poetry and prose. In this respect it is fortunate that a number of Chinese masterworks, as listed in the "Guide to Further Readings" at the end of the book, have been translated into English, and that more and better translations are anticipated. While I have found it expedient to use my own renderings, which are as close to the original as possible, I owe a debt of gratitude to my predecessors for their labor of love.

Another feature of this *Introduction* is its emphasis on major writers and works, that I have discussed at some length within the limits imposed by the size of the book. This leaves little room for many authors who deserve a prominent place in Chinese literary history; it also necessitates the omission, reluctantly made, of such topics as the poetry of the Ming-Ch'ing period, informal essays of the late Ming era, and the late Ch'ing novel. On the other hand, it is evident that the great Classics, because of their long, profound influence on traditional literature, should be a significant part of this study. For instance, in appreciating Chinese poetry, some knowledge of the *Classic of Poetry* is essential since later poets continually echoed lines and phrases from it. To a lesser extent, the collection, *Songs of Ch'u*, as represented by the works of Ch'ü Yüan, is also a source of ideas and expressions which reoccur in later poetry. In prose, one can easily see how a monumental work of literary art such as

Ssu-ma Ch'ien's *Historical Records* became a model for later historical writings. Inspired by these and other classical works, Chinese writers attained new heights in the poetry and prose of the T'ang-Sung period, of which the readers are given here an adequate coverage in description and selections.

A fascinating story is inherent in the development of Chinese drama and fiction. The attraction lies both in the intrinsic literary merit of major novels and plays hitherto not fully recognized in the West, and in new information on them and insights gained in recent years. For this reason, as generous space is given them in the latter half of the book as to the great Classics in the first half. This departure from the traditional treatment of Chinese literature, though radical, is made deliberately to reveal to Western readers literary achievements of the Chinese in areas of which they may not have been aware. Some new material has also been introduced from my own research in drama and fiction. In this connection I must mention that the recent publication of several significant English language studies of Chinese fiction and poetry has advanced the cause of modern Sinology to such an extent that students of Chinese literature have now to include in their reading not only Chinese and Japanese but also Western language works. The present volume, however, though taking into consideration the fruits of Western scholarship, is based mainly on Chinese sources, particularly on the literary works themselves, from which I have derived while preparing this manuscript inexhaustible pleasure and inspiration.

All in all, the story of Chinese literature as told here is one of remarkable growth and essential continuity, each generation of writers enriching the common store with its own contribution. Unlike other ancient literatures, that of China is by no means static and stereotyped, as it has sometimes wrongly been supposed to be. It has been developing always, and if this development seems slow at times, it has been nonetheless steady. It is the author's hope that the following *Introduction* will give the nonspecialist some idea of the continuous progress and lasting splendor of Chinese literature, of its vast corpus and high attainments. This book is designed as a guide to a field that is so broad and fertile that the reader may be assured of many happy discoveries if he will continue to explore its various pathways.

LIU WU-CHI

Bloomington, Indiana

Contents

Plates

An Introduction to Chinese Literature

Introduction : Chinese Literature and Its Characteristics

Cataclysmic changes past and present notwithstanding, China is still a land which treasures its great traditions. Chinese culture, marked by antiquity, continuity, and constant renewal, has remained essentially homogeneous for at least three thousand years. As early as 1400 B.C., archaeological evidence indicates, the Chinese people had already a remarkable civilization supported by a well-advanced writing system and a fine technology of bronze casting and sericulture. During the incomparably long Chou dynasty, which lasted some eight hundred years—until the third century B.C.—much of ancient Chinese civilization, built upon a sociopolitical structure that closely resembled the feudal system in medieval Europe, was firmly established. This was the period of classical Chinese philosophy, in which great thinkers from the newly risen intellectual class vied with each other to win the minds of the rulers and the people alike. The brilliance of this philosophy was matched only by that of the poetry which flourished at about the same time in the Yellow River and Yangtze regions.

Chinese culture continued to develop for another two thousand years from the Han through the T'ang and Sung eras to the modern period. During the centuries, this culture remained almost unchallenged and basically unimpaired in the face of political disruptions and civil wars, changing dynasties, and the conquest of the country by non-Chinese ethnic groups from beyond the Great Wall: occupying North China for long periods were the Toba and the Tungus (fourth to sixth centuries), the Kitans and the Jurchens (tenth to thirteenth centuries), the Mongols (thirteenth to fourteenth centuries) and the Manchu (seventeenth to twentieth centuries), the whole country having been under the rule of the last two groups for a total of four hundred years. Instead of being destroyed by them, the Chinese culture made a tremendous impact on these alien groups, who were eventually assimilated by the Han-Chinese, thus replenishing with fresh blood the indigenous stock.

3

Other foreign influences also contributed to Chinese civilization. Buddhism, which was first brought to China from Central Asia, not only offered the Chinese a new attitude toward life and thought, but also stimulated their creativity in painting, sculpture, and literature. In our own period, Western science and technology have increased man's knowledge of the world and the universe; they have also brought to the Chinese an awareness of the inexorable laws of nature, the determining factors of social environment, and the need to cope with both. All these ideas are reflected in modern Chinese literature. Thus nourishment from abroad has sustained periodically the growth of Chinese culture, and prevented stagnation and decadence. While absorbing foreign influences, the Chinese have been able to keep intact their own culture, which has been constantly expanding and thriving.

Whatever native ingredients and alien elements entered into the melting pot of Chinese civilization, its main component has been essentially Confucianism, which consists of the teachings of Confucius, Mencius, and their followers in subsequent ages. Especially important among later scholars were the Neo-Confucianists of the Sung and Ming periods, who, in the typical eclectic manner in which Chinese thinkers formulated their teachings, instilled into Confucianism selected portions of Taoism and Buddhism. After that time, the Neo-Confucian teachings and interpretations of the Confucian classics became standard works of reference for candidates in the state examination, which required a knowledge of the Confucian doctrines. Since successful scholars were appointed to offices in the government and could look forward, if they were ambitious and clever enough, to climbing the bureaucratic ladder to positions of power and influence, the Confucian classics, which formed the literary basis of the examinations, became the most immediate concern of the would-be scholar-officials.

A practicable moral philosophy that teaches the rules of personal cultivation and the virtues of human relationship, Confucianism has molded the Chinese national character and pervaded every aspect of Chinese society, the family, literature and the arts. In a broad sense, much of Chinese literature is Confucian literature. The all-embracing influence of Confucianism worked in two ways: it affected the life and ideas of writers who followed the tradition, and of those who reacted against it. Generally speaking, Confucianism triumphed in times of peace and prosperity, but when the country was in disorder, Taoism and Buddhism took over, gaining a large following among the people. Similarly in a man's personal life, success strengthened his belief in the Confucian orthodoxy while disappointments bred in him a desire to wander astray to the other-worldliness of Buddhism and Taoism. It was the rebels from Confucianism who deviated from the norm and carved out new paths in literary fields. They found their inspiration sometimes abroad but oftener among the common people, whose spring of native wit and emotion replenished constantly the dwindling reservoir of literary sources and materials depleted by long periods of use.

The majority of Chinese writers, however, have been conformists to the grand Confucian tradition. To them, literature has been a vehicle for the communication of the aim of Confucian doctrine: to teach and influence people to be good. Thus there is always a moral lesson in a work of Chinese literature. In literary criticism, aesthetic excellence was considered secondary to moral soundness. In the course of centuries there had been built up a large body of moral treatises, exhortations and admonitions, and though modern critics tend to disparage them, their sway over the Chinese mind and conduct was great and lasting. Likewise, history was highly regarded for its moral and political import, the lessons of the past being held up as a mirror for the present and future. One of the four major divisions of a Chinese library, history ranked next to the Confucian classics in importance, above philosophy and belles-lettres. Enriched by a vast bulk of historical materials, Chinese literary writings abound in allusions to historical figures and events, a knowledge of which is even now a criterion for Chinese scholarship.

Influenced by Confucian ethics, the Chinese were especially strong in their sense of right and wrong, which naturally found expression in literature. This moral concern gave rise to the concept of poetic justice, which is as much Chinese as Greek. The idea that virtue is to be rewarded and vice punished was propagated by Confucian philosophers and embodied in the heavens and hells of the Buddhist and Taoist religions. The three great Chinese doctrines merged in the common belief in retribution, a popular tenet upheld by all and sundry whatever their philosophy or religion. This belief, amply demonstrated in literature, deterred the growth of anything like the Western concept of tragedy. Though a man may fall victim to the snares of fate and suffer from tragedies in real life, it would be the Chinese writer's duty to see to it that in literature's make-believe world sorrows are toned down and virtues are praised and duly recompensed. From the Chinese point of view it would be a blemish in a literary work not to give its readers a sense of satisfaction in the ultimate vindication and triumph of the good and virtuous.

All these considerations strengthened the Chinese belief in the pragmatic view of literature. Instead of being the mysterious or inscrutable Orientals represented by Westerners in their early reports on China, the Chinese were and are a practical people, have supported the down-to-earth teachings of Confucius, and created a literature whose main function is utilitarian rather than aesthetic. Brushing aside as worthless the concept of art for art's sake, Chinese writers pressed philosophy and history into the service of literature, not because of their contribution to knowledge and truth but because of their usefulness to humanity. Chinese literature itself was enriched by many types of utilitarian prose (official proclamations, memorials to the throne, prefaces and postscripts to books, eulogies and epitaphs), all written in a well-wrought style and serving as models of literary composition. Epistolary writing became a useful art cultivated by the men of letters. Besides beautiful descriptions of nature, literary accounts of travels often abound in human interest, sometimes illuminated by moral reflections and philosophical disquisitions on life. The use of an almost naturalistic narrative technique and the inclusion of rich details of materialistic life in the novel make it an archetype of realism as well as an indispensable source material for the study of traditional Chinese family and society. True to the storytelling tradition, the first person narrator performs the role of the readers' confidante, dispensing freely his advice and his words of wordly wisdom.

The writing of poetry, which has been generally regarded in the West as the most imaginative and loftiest of all literary forms, was in China a common, everyday undertaking of the intellectuals. Chinese poets, unlike some of their Western compeers who happily built their castles in the air, were on the whole earthbound and mundane. They were disturbed neither by poetic agonies and aesthetic aspirations, nor by the thrills of romantic excursions into the mind and the universe. Instead, they were content with weaving songs out of the materials of daily life and occupation. Almost every educated Chinese was a poet who turned out verses as fast as there was an occasion for them. And in China there were numerous occasions for poetry: court celebrations and religious festivities; weddings and funerals; garden parties, where the beauties of the peonies and chrysanthemums were felicitated; convivial feasts during which, after a generous flow of wine, companies were promoted, merged and dissolved; trips to scenic spots, where even the latent poetic talent would burst into bloom—these and a thousand and one other occasions, on which, no matter how trivial they seemed, poetry was the language that spoke understandingly and pleasurably to the heart.

The popularity of poetry is further attested by the inclusion of a vast number of poems in drama and fiction. Some of the early prose stories have a large mixture of poetry, and are called poetic tales. Chinese drama is almost exclusively poetic drama, the songs forming not only an integral part of the play but also its most important part. Critical acclaim was directed not so much to the plot, structure, and characterization of a play as to its poetry, which heightened the sentiments in the dialogue. A unique type of literature, the *fu* was evolved as a crossbreed between poetry and prose. In China there was little demarcation between the two forms, and much of Chinese literature, the best and most significant, was written in poetry.

One of the striking features of Chinese poetry is compactness, the most popular forms being four-line and eight-line poems, with five or seven words in each line. For the Chinese, brevity was the soul of poetry. Within this limited scope, fine workmanship became a major requirement for excellence, and each word was weighed carefully for artistic effect. There is an interesting though probably apocryphal story of the T'ang poet Li Po's making fun of his friend, Tu Fu, for the latter's painstaking efforts at writing poetry. One day, meeting Tu Fu on the top of a hill, Li Po was said to have accosted him in the following verse:

> How thin, wretchedly thin you have grown!
> Have you been suffering from poetry again?

Another story tells of the hard way in which Chia Tao, a later T'ang poet, settled a point of versification. Walking one day on the busy, crowded streets of metropolitan Ch'ang-an, Chia Tao was beating rhythm with a stick when he knocked down a front carrier of an official sedan. He had been debating whether he should use the word "push" or "knock" in the line

> The monk knocks at the moonlit door.

Thus, deeply immersed in thought, he began to push and knock until he inadvertently upset the official procession. Fortunately for Chia Tao, the great dignitary in the sedan chair was no other than the famous writer Han Yü. The latter not only forgave the distressed poet but also settled the poetic problem for him in favor of the word "knock." Since then the term "push and knock" has become synonymous with a writer's careful deliberation in literary compositions.

Music was another important asset of Chinese poetry. All its three major types, *shih*, *tz'u*, and *ch'ü*, were originally sung with accompaniment by music. Later, when music was weaned from poetry, a complicated prosody was evolved with definite rhyming schemes and tonal patterns. Though no longer set to music, Chinese poems were written to be read aloud, probably in much the same way as the Greek were. It was quite an experience to watch an old-fashioned scholar shaking his head and wagging his queue with a great deal of gusto and relish as he recited a poem, intoning every word in such a way as to bring out the best musical qualities of the verse he declaimed. This kind of poetry recitation, however, has become a lost art today.

Basing their creativity upon brevity, artistry, and music, Chinese poets managed to bring into being with the magic of words a fairyland of poetry. The commonplace which is transformed into the wonderful is not far to seek, for its like is here in all our little worlds: on the hearths of our homes, warm with friendship and family love, in the moon that smiles and the flowers that beckon to us, in the landscape paintings that re-create the beauty of nature in a series of pictorial images. Poetry too can keep us company when we are traveling in distant lands. Extremely nostalgic, the frequently exiled Chinese poets were unconsolable in their yearnings for their native land, strong in their expressions of domestic attachment, and insistent in their reminiscences of the golden age that had slipped away. All these sentiments are natural and ordinary enough, but in the voices of the poets they become poignantly beautiful in rhythmic utterances. The Chinese writers have performed the miracle of transforming the homely into the beautiful, of investing the trivia of daily life with a halo of poetry, or, rather, they have proved, in the words of a critic, that common sense, the most salutary and the most nearly universal sense, is also at the heart of the sense of beauty itself, quickened and yet sobered by the wistful warmth of humanity.

1 : From the Dawn of Chinese Language to the *Classic of Poetry*

Much of the early history of the Chinese language is wrapped in myth and legend. It is not known when or how the language originated, but it is possible to reconstruct the several stages of its development and the kind of literature that was first written in it. The earliest forms of Chinese writing, according to tradition, began at the time of the Yellow Emperor, who is supposed to have ruled some five thousand years ago. It is said that Ts'ang Chieh, his historiographer, first imitated markings left by birds and animals on the sand; from these markings evolved the earliest Chinese words. Though legendary, the story suggests what has come to be the accepted view—that in the beginning the Chinese characters were largely pictographic.

In the quasi-historical period, the Chinese language began to evolve, and by the time it appeared on the ritual bronze vessels and on the tortoise shells and ox bones used for divination purposes during the historical Yin dynasty (eighteenth to twelfth century B.C.), it was already a well-developed form capable of recording the oracular utterances of the deities as well as human activities and sentiments. This kind of writing, known as "shell-and-bone inscriptions," had almost all the characteristics of the modern Chinese language. Many of the Yin dynasty inscriptions have been deciphered and studied by modern scholars. Over two thousand words are known out of a vocabulary of about four thousand. The wealth of this language is impressive, and it indicates that the Chinese civilization of the Yin period must have been on a high level.[1]

In recording these inscriptions, the diviners would sometimes combine single words to form phrases and sentences. There were long passages like the following:

> Divined on the day of *kuei-mao*.*
> It is going to rain today.

* *Kuei* is the last of the ten celestial stems, and *mao* is the fourth of the twelve terrestrial branches. A combination of these cyclical characters indicates the hour, day, and year in the Chinese calendar.

9

> Is the rain going to come from the West?
> Is the rain going to come from the East?
> Is the rain going to come from the North?
> Is the rain going to come from the South?

Apparently, the Yin people were already making some kind of poetic effort.

Another source of knowledge of the early Chinese language is the bronze vessels that were cast in the same period. In form and craftsmanship, Yin bronzes are works of art which have not been surpassed in spite of our modern technology in metal-casting. The inscriptions on these vessels are similar to those on the bones and shells. Together, they reveal an interesting picture of the society and mores of an ancient people who made good use of the language by recording in it what they considered worthy of preservation for posterity.

A general idea of ancient China can also be obtained from some of the oldest Chinese writings, in which are found interesting details of the numerous activities of the early people, including their crude attempts at literary creation. But the authenticity of these writings is doubtful: if not entirely forged, they must have been revised and much embellished by later writers. The same is true of the ancient Chinese songs said to have been composed during the reign of certain legendary emperors whose very existence is questionable. Such being the case, these songs cannot be considered as the "fountainhead of ancient Chinese poetry." Nevertheless, available evidence suggests that the ancient Chinese, like most primitive people, had a great love for music and dancing, with which early Chinese poetry was closely allied.

The history of Chinese literature begins properly with the Confucian canon transmitted to posterity by China's greatest teacher, Confucius (551–479 B.C.). It represents the bulk of ancient Chinese literature of the Chou dynasty (twelfth to third century B.C.), which came after the Yin. During this period China entered the iron age and built up a flourishing agrarian civilization based on feudatory landholding. The Chou kingdom, which had its center of activity in the plains of the Yellow River, was divided into a number of loosely confederated states governed by feudal lords who owed allegiance to the king. The ruler of each state parceled out his fief among the lesser nobles, who turned the land over to the peasants for cultivation. The latter were attached to the household of the noble and served him as agricultural serfs.

In the Chou period, each feudal court, like the royal court, was staffed by diviners who advised the ruler on religious matters, historiographers who compiled state annals, and musicians and ritualists who performed elaborate ceremonies on state occasions. In the ruler's service were also tutors who initiated the young princes in the six arts, namely, music, ritual, writing, arithmetic, archery, and charioteering. If the traditional account of the upper Chinese society of the period is in any way reliable, Chou culture must have been well advanced. It was under these circumstances that the five Confucian books, comprised of the *Classic of Change*, the *Classic of History*, the *Classic of Poetry*, the *Record of Rites*, and the *Spring and Autumn*, were produced and preserved.

Originally, the *Classic of Change* was a manual of divination based upon eight trigrams (supposed to have been invented by Fu Hsi, a mythical emperor), which by this time had been multiplied to sixty-four hexagrams. It presumably underwent some revision in the hands of Confucius and his followers and has become in its present form a sort of metaphysical treatise. The *Record of Rites*, a later restoration of the original *Classic of Rites*, which was lost in the third century B.C., is a source book of ancient Chinese rites and court manners. In addition to rules and regulations, it contains many interesting anecdotes relating to these rules. The *Spring and Autumn*, generally believed to have been compiled by Confucius himself, is a chronicle of the principality of Lu, Confucius' native state, from 722 to 479 B.C. Written in the form of annals, it has brief entries and a concise, matter-of-fact style. Though historically and culturally significant, these three classics have little of the literary merit which is apparent in the other two.

In the *Classic of History* are found the best specimens of early Chinese prose. The book is a collection of edicts, proclamations, addresses, and other official documents of ancient China. While some of the supposedly earlier works may be spurious, much of early Chou history can be reconstructed from these documents. Though archaic in form, they are surprisingly interesting and revealing, once the language barrier is surmounted. As shown in the *Classic of History*, Chinese prose had made great progress since the days of the shell-and-bone inscriptions, and the way was paved for its achievement in the post-Confucian era.

From the literary point of view, however, most important is the *Classic of Poetry*, a unique anthology of Chinese poems of the Chou period. There are two theories as to how these poems were first collected. One theory holds that though stamped with the Confucian seal, the book had existed long before the time of Confucius, who was merely its transmitter. According to another account, there was a much larger collection—over three thousand ancient poems—from which he selected some three hundred for his own use. In this case, Confucius was credited with the role of a fastidious editor, who weeded out the duplicates, omitted many poems he considered unsuitable, and gave the ones chosen a sort of literary polish. The net result of his presumed labor is the present *Classic of Poetry*.

But the question remains where and how Confucius got these three hundred, not to mention three thousand, poems. Tradition asserts that he culled them from the library of the royal house and the archives of the feudal courts, to which he had access. It has been said that in the beginning of the Chou dynasty, the king used to send out officers to search the countryside for songs sung by the people. The songs were brought back to the court so that the king could learn firsthand the state of affairs in the feudal principalities: whether the people were satisfied with their rulers, or whether they suffered and complained. Apparently the Chinese had realized long ago that rather than to believe in the florid speeches of rulers and politicians, the best way to get honest public opinion was to listen to the words of poetry, which according to Chinese critics, "expresses earnest thought." Anyway this may explain how a large number of folk songs found their way into the Confucian anthology.

The *Classic of Poetry*, which now contains three hundred and five poems, has been conventionally divided into four sections as follows:

(1) 160 ballads of the state (*kuo-feng*) sung by the people of the various states;

(2) 74 minor festal songs (*hsiao-ya*) for festivities and entertainments given by the king;

(3) 31 greater festal songs (*ta-ya*) sung on state occasions such as the assembly of the feudal lords at the king's court;

(4) 40 hymns and eulogies (*sung*) sung at sacrifices to gods and ancestral spirits of the royal house.

The anthology seems to be almost evenly divided between folk poems in the first section and court poems in the other three sections.

Presumably, the *Classic of Poetry* was the text Confucius used to teach his students to give expression to their feelings and thoughts. In the master's own words, one idea dominates all the three hundred poems: it is "to keep the heart right."[2] He told his son that anyone who has not learned the poems "stands with his face right against the wall." On another occasion, he said, "If you do not study poetry, your language will not be polished."[3] Poetry having been an essential part of aristocratic education, rulers and diplomats, it has been observed, often used these poems to enrich their conversation and as a kind of diplomatic "feeler" to sound out another's intentions by noting his reaction to the poetic quotations. A diplomat would be disgraced who failed to recognize an allusion in a poem recited by his host and was at a loss for a reply.[4]

This being the case, it is curious that this classic anthology should consist of a large number of love poems sung by country lads and lasses. Indeed it is hard to fathom how the poetic effusions of a lovelorn girl, for instance, could be used as a model of polite language to be studied by young nobles and intellectuals. To reconcile this paradox, Chinese scholars since the Han dynasty have tried ingeniously to explain the love poems as allegorical and to make out the yearnings of love as yearnings of the people for their rulers or vice versa.

This theory has now been generally discounted. But in fact, some of these poems do permit a number of interpretations, the Chinese language being flexible and loose in syntax, and the meaning of a word or phrase capable of being construed in various ways. To illustrate this point, the poem, "How Goes the Night" (No. 182), is translated here literally as follows:

> How goes the night?
> The night has not ended;
> The light is from the torches in the courtyard:
> The *chün-tzu* has (have) arrived,
> His (their) harness bells tinkling.
>
> How goes the night?
> The night is not yet gone;
> Bright are the torches in the courtyard:
> The *chün-tzu* has (have) arrived,
> His (their) harness bells clinking.
>
> How goes the night?
> The night approaches dawn;
> Blazing are the torches in the courtyard;
> The *chün-tzu* has (have) arrived,
> I (we) see his (their) banners.

According to the traditional Chinese interpretation, the poem, one of the minor festal songs, describes the king's anxiety to be punctual at his morning audience — "And now my lords will soon be here."[5] But the poem can also be construed differently as describing (a) a noble "lord" eager to greet his beloved friend;[6] (b) a wife or attendant welcoming the return of "my lord";[7] (c) court ladies or attendants expecting the arrival of "the lord."[8] The confusion is caused chiefly by the word "*chün-tzu*" (princely man or lord), which can be singular or plural, and to which can be assigned any article or personal pronoun.

In another poem (No. 211), the content of the following verses becomes strikingly different in two separate English translations:

> Here comes the Descendant,
> With his wife and children,
> Bringing dinner to the southern acres.
> The labourers come to take good cheer,
> Break off a morsel here, a morsel there,
> To see what tastes good.[9]

and

> The descendant comes; through their wives and children he sends food to (the men in) those southern acres; the inspector of the fields comes and is pleased; he thrusts aside his attendants and (himself) tastes whether it is good or not.[10]

Such cases abound, and it is sometimes baffling to determine the correct meaning of these poems.

But whatever differences of interpretation there may have been regarding individual poems, taken as a whole the book constitutes a valuable anthology of ancient poetry. No matter whether these poems were used by the king to study the conditions in his vassal states, by Confucius to elevate the mind and purify the language of his students, or whether some of these are simple folk songs that belonged to the peasant serfs, there is little doubt that the anthology offers the best available material for a study of the Chou people's mores.

The life of the early Chinese aristocrat is shown graphically in these poems. They tell of solemn audiences held by the king as well as of feasts and carousals at night in the royal clan hall. The following has been called "the world's earliest drinking song":

> Soaking wet is the dew;
> Without the sun it dries not.
> Long, long we drink at night.
> Do not return home until drunk!
>
> Soaking wet is the dew
> On yonder thick grass.
> Long, long we drink at night,
> In the clan hall, until all's over.[11]

There are many other songs of drinking and feasting, of music and dancing in the palace courtyard: songs of blind musicians who play the little drum and big drum, the tambourine, the music stone, the staff, the clapper, and the pipes and flutes;[12] songs of dancing by a big tall man, "strong as a tiger," with a flute in his left hand and a pheasant feather in his right, his face red as if smeared with ochre.[13]

There are descriptions of war chariots in which the lord went out fighting and hunting. Each of these chariots was drawn by four lusty stallions, which pranced along as the noble charioteer held in his one hand the six reins and in the other a trident spear with a silvered butt or a tiger-skin quiver with its two unstrung bows.[14] Thus arrayed, the lord went to the battlefield with tortoise-and-snake banners, ox-tail banners, falcon banners, or dragon banners fluttering in the wind;[15] or to the hunting ground with bells tinkling and greyhounds baying:

14

> The hounds, with double bells;
> That man, so handsome and kind.
>
> The hounds, with double rings;
> That man, so handsome and fair.
>
> The hounds, with double hoops;
> That man, so handsome and strong.[16]

The game the hunters took home consisted mostly of foxes, badgers, deer, stags, and wild oxen. The hunters also killed the little boar and the big rhinoceros so that their meat could be served to the guests to accompany cups of sweet wine.[17]

Some folk poets, however, looked at hunting and war from a different point of view. Peasants themselves, they complained repeatedly of conscription and military service. Sometimes the tone of the poem though restrained was bitter:

> Long ago, when we marched,
> The millet was just flowering.
> Now when we come back,
> Snow has covered the road.
> The king's service brings many hardships;
> We have no time to rest or to stay.
> Do we not yearn to go home?
> But we fear the bamboo tablets.[18]

On these bamboo tablets were written the king's conscription orders. At other times, the complaint was bold and more direct:

> We are not rhinos, nor tigers,
> But we have to roam in those wilds.
> Alas! We men on the march,
> Morning and night without rest![19]

The peasants also had grievance for their hard-working life that contributed not so much to their own welfare as to the prosperity and enjoyment of the idle, rich, and noble:

> Chop, chop, we cut the sandalwood
> And lay it on the river bank,
> The water so clear and rippling.
> If we did not sow and reap,
> How could you bring in three hundred
>   stack-yards of grain;
> If we did not chase and hunt,
> How could one see all these badgers
>   hanging in your courtyard?
> Indeed, that lord,
> He eats not the food of idleness![20]

These poems also provide a detailed account of Chinese ancestral rites, which had their beginning in prehistorical times and by the Chou period were already formalized. One of the poems, "Thick Grows the Star-Thistle,"[21] describes a thanksgiving offering in a noble household at harvest time. Here in due order are told the numerous preparations for this solemn rite: the purification of the oxen and sheep, the flaying and boiling of the victims, the arrangement of foodstands, the ordering of the various dishes for guests and visitors by the lady of the house, and then the quaffing of the wine cup among the guests as healths and pledges went the round. After these preliminaries, the sacrifice began. The sacrificer was a "pious grandson," a young heir of the house, whose role was to impersonate the ancestors to whom the offering was made. He was "the dead one," or literally, "the corpse," because into him the spirits entered at the sacrifice. During the ceremony, he went to his seat of honor and there he remained until the sacrifice was performed and "the spirits were all drunk." Then he was escorted away amidst a flourish of bells and drums. In the meantime, a private feast was spread in an inner apartment for the male members of the family, such as the uncles, brothers, and cousins of the sacrificer. After being satiated with wine, food, and music, they all bowed their heads and pronounced their blessings on the master of the house, thereby bringing the sacrifice to a happy conclusion.

A different aspect of Chinese life, the rural society with its manifold activities, is presented in another group of poems. A good example is "The Seventh Month."[22] This has been called the "Farmer's Calendar" because it gives a detailed account of farming life and occupations in different seasons, such as plowing, silkworm culture and weaving, hunting, housework, reaping and harvesting, provision of food and wine, cutting and storing of ice, and harvest feasting and drinking to the health of the lord.

The poem, "Clearing Away the Weeds and Shrubs,"[23] presents a good description of Chinese farming. First, the land has to be cleared of thickets and weeds for plowing:

> In a thousand pairs they weed,
> In wet lands, along raised paths.

They sow the hundred grains, each seed containing life. Then the blades begin to sprout and grow into fine plants. In good years the reaping and harvesting gladden the eyes:

> And then they reap—a bountiful harvest;
> Piled high are the grain stacks,
> Myriads, many myriads and millions,

> To make wine, make sweet wine,
> As offering to ancestors and ancestresses,
> For fulfillment of the hundred rites.

The poem ends with an invocation to the glory of the state and peace for the elders.

During slack seasons when not working in the fields the peasants found time to enjoy themselves on many festival occasions, which provided the young with opportunities for courtship and mating. It has sometimes been said that the Chinese did not write love poems. This statement, however, has to be modified in view of the *Classic of Poetry* which, as we have seen, contains a large number of love songs.[24] They are characterized by a simplicity of language and genuineness of emotion found only among the unsophisticated people of the countryside; on the other hand, the themes and contents of these poems are manifold and varied. Some describe, for instance, the jollities of two bands of young people dancing and lovemaking from the opposite banks of a stream.[25] Courtship is facilitated by an exchange of gifts:

> She threw me a quince;
> In return I gave her a girdle-gem.
> Not that I have requited her gift,
> But that we would love forever.
>
> She threw me a peach;
> In return I gave her a greenstone.
> Not that I have requited her gift,
> But that we would love forever.
>
> She threw me a plum;
> In return I gave her a jetstone.
> Not that I have requited her gift,
> But that we would love forever.[26]

The lover's gift may consist only of a reed and a blade of grass, nevertheless it is precious because of the giver:

> Lovely is the modest girl.
> She awaits me at the corner of the wall—
> I love her, but do not see her;
> I scratch my head, not knowing what to do.
>
> Pretty is the modest girl.
> She gave me a red reed;
> The red reed is bright,
> But I delight in the beauty of the girl.

From the pasture she brought me a young blade,
Truly beautiful and rare.
No, it is not only that you are beautiful,
You are the gift of a beautiful girl![27]

In both language and content, this poem of an enamored youth treasuring his lover's gift has parallels in English poetry—a fact that underlines the universality of literature, transcending both time and place.

There are also poems of romantic love, of tryst and assignation. Some of these are perfect little gems like the following:

The willows at the eastern gate,
Their leaves are so profuse;
At dusk we were to meet,
And now the morning star is bright.

The willows at the eastern gate,
Their leaves are so lush;
At dusk we were to meet,
And now the morning star glitters.[28]

In another poem, the language is more direct and the expression more outspoken:

I beg you, Chung-tzu,
Do not leap into my homestead;
Do not break my willow trees!
Not that I care about them,
But I am afraid of my parents.
Chung I dearly love,
But of my parents' words,
Indeed I am afraid.

I beg you, Chung-tzu,
Do not leap over my wall;
Do not break my mulberry trees!
Not that I care about them,
But I am afraid of my elder brothers.
Chung I dearly love,
But of my brothers' words,
Indeed I am afraid.

I beg you, Chung-tzu,
Do not leap into my garden;
Do not break my sandalwood trees!
Not that I care about them,
But I am afraid of people's gossip.
Chung I dearly love,
But of people's gossip,
Indeed I am afraid.[29]

There are also songs of frustration, disappointment, and lamentation. One of these describes the exasperation of a marriageable girl as she waits impatiently for suitors who are laggard in wooing her:

> The plums are falling—
> There are only seven.
> For the gentlemen who court me,
> Lucky is the time.
>
> The plums are falling—
> There are only three.
> For the gentlemen who court me,
> Now is the time.
>
> The plums are falling—
> In a basket I've gathered them all.
> For the gentlemen who court me,
> Speak while there is time.[30]

Of the following two songs, the first depicts an anguished girl:

> Blue, blue is your collar;
> Sad, sad is my heart.
> Though I have not gone to you,
> Why do you send no news?
>
> Blue, blue is your girdle-gem;
> Sad, sad is my mind.
> Though I have not gone to you,
> Why do you not come?
>
> Leisurely and pleasure-seeking,
> On the watch tower by the city wall—
> A day without seeing you
> Is as long as three months.[31]

and the second a tormented youth:

> The moon rises, how bright!
> The lovely one, how beautiful!
> How gentle and graceful!
> My heart is grieved.
>
> The moon rises, how glittering!
> The lovely one, how pretty!
> How gentle and tender!
> My heart is saddened.
>
> The moon rises, how brilliant!
> The lovely one, how splendid!
> How gentle and fair!
> My heart is tormented.[32]

19

Sometimes nature conspires with man to bring pain to the lovelorn:

> The wind and the squall:
> He looked at me, then laughed;
> He jested and laughed with scorn.
> In my heart I am grieved.
>
> The wind and the dust storm:
> Graciously he promised to come,
> But neither came nor went away.
> Long, long I think of him.
>
> The wind and the darkened sky:
> All day long the sky was black.
> I lie awake and there is no sleep;
> I yearn and then I gasp.
>
> The sky was overcast with clouds:
> Boom, boom, the thunder roared.
> I lie awake and there is no sleep;
> I yearn and keep yearning.[33]

On another occasion, the neglected girl conceals her sorrow and bravely challenges the arrogant lover:

> You, artful lad,
> Will not speak with me,
> Yet, because of you,
> Shall I refuse to eat?
>
> You, artful lad,
> Will not eat with me.
> Yet, because of you,
> Shall I refuse to rest?[34]

There is also the tragedy of love told in an unaffected, vivid and poignant narrative:

> In the wilds there is a dead doe;
> In white rushes it is wrapped.
> There was a girl longing for spring;
> A fine gentleman seduced her.
>
> In the woods there are tree stumps;
> In the wilds lies a dead deer,
> Wrapped and bound with white rushes.
> There was a girl fair as jade.
>
> "Ah, not so hasty, not so rough!
> Do not move my girdle kerchief;
> Do not make the dog bark."[35]

Unique among these folk love poems is the following, which tells a complete and sustained story with consummate art:

> A simple rustic you seemed,
> Carrying cloth to barter for silk.
> But you did not come to buy silk;
> You came to plot for me.
> I saw you off, wading the river Ch'i
> As far as Tun-ch'iu.
> "It is not that I'd put off the date,
> But no good go-between you have.
> Pray, do not be angry;
> Autumn is the time to meet again."
>
> I climbed that ruined wall
> To look towards Fu-kuan.
> I did not see Fu-kuan;
> My tears flowed in streams.
> After I had seen Fu-kuan,
> How I laughed and talked!
> "You've consulted the shell and the stalk,*
> And there is nothing inauspicious.
> Come with your carriage
> And carry me away and my goods."
>
> Before shedding from the mulberry tree,
> How glossy green the leaves are!
> Alas, you turtle dove,
> Eat not the mulberries!
> Alas, you women,
> Do not dally with men!
> When a man dallies,
> He will still be excused;
> But when a woman dallies,
> No pardon will she have.
>
> The mulberry leaves have fallen,
> All yellow and sere.
> Since I came to you,
> Three years I have eaten poverty.
> The waters of the Ch'i are full;
> They wet the curtains of the carriage.
> The woman remains constant,
> But the man has altered his ways:
> He is lacking in faith
> And changeable in his conduct.

---

* The use of the milfoil stalk for divination purposes was a Chou innovation whereas the use of the tortoise shell had its origin earlier in Yin.

Three years I was your wife,
I never tired of household chores.
Early I rose and late I went to sleep;
Not a morning was I without work.
First you found fault with me,
Then treated me with violence.
My brothers, not knowing this,
Jeered and laughed at me.
Quietly I brood over it
And myself I pity.

Together with you I was to grow old;
Old, it has made me wretched!
The Ch'i, at least, has its banks,
And the swamp, its shores.
At the feast of the "tufted hair,"
We talked and laughed gaily.
You pledged solemnly your troth,
Little recking that it would be broken.
No, I never thought that it could be broken
And that this should be the end.[36]

The "tufted hair" in the last stanza is literally the "tied horns," worn by boys and girls before marriage and is used here to mean "the young people."

The examples quoted above will give the reader some idea of the pleasures which await him in the *Classic of Poetry*. But to enjoy these poems to the full one should read many of them, because only then will one catch their generally happy mood. In spite of a few poems about hardship and sorrow, these songs which belong to the morning of Chinese civilization have a freshness and spontaneity, a confidence in life which Chinese poetry never again quite recaptures. Like the *Border Ballads* in English they carry their own music and vitality through the ages, taking the reader back among the feudal courts and the country people of ancient China.

The merits of this remarkable anthology are manifold. First, the poems therein set an example for all later Chinese poetry in metrical form and rhyming device. The pattern of four-word verse created by these early poets is flexible and variable enough to admit extra words and particles that make the lines less monotonous. The use of repetitions and refrains, particularly in the ballads of the state, not only underlies their folk nature but also relates them in form to the songs and ballads of other peoples. Second, though composed three thousand years ago and tinged with archaism, they sound on the whole surprisingly modern and refreshing. The language is direct, poignant, rich in similes and metaphors.

22

Third, these poems initiate a realistic tradition in Chinese poetry and leave to posterity a wealth of human and social information. While not noted for description of nature, which is presented rather for its symbolic meaning and kinship with man than for its own beauty, they give nevertheless a long list of birds, beasts, and flowers that has attracted the attention of critics ever since Confucius.[37]

Most important of all, the *Classic of Poetry* is unique in content among the poetic compositions of the ancient world. It is much broader in scope than the Vedas and the Psalms, its themes not being limited to religious matters and pious sentiments. It is unlike the Homeric epics in that instead of war and adventure, it sings, in the words of an English poet, "some more humble lay,/ Familiar matter of to-day,/ Some natural sorrow, loss, or pain,/ That has been, and may be again." Very few anthologies can compare with the *Classic of Poetry* in expressing so spontaneously, so simply, and so intimately the voice and feelings of the common people. Indeed, only in this collection of early Chinese songs can one find such a vivid and truthful picture of their activities, manners, customs, and beliefs, their joys and sorrow, their festivities and tragedies—the stuff of which great literature is made.

2 : Ch'ü Yüan, Father of Chinese Poetry

The *Classic of Poetry* was the literary product of the people who dwelt on the central plains of the Yellow River, the cradle of ancient Chinese civilization. In the early days, the regions south of the Yellow River were inhabited by tribes under the overlordship of the Chou nobles. Gradually, these southern states began to loom large on the scene and to play a prominent role in Chinese politics. Among them, the most important was the state of Ch'u (in Hupeh and neighboring provinces). Lying on the banks of another great river, the Yangtze, Ch'u was the mightiest state in the South and also the most advanced in culture. Thus in the fifth and fourth centuries B.C., there existed in China two cultural centers. Besides the Yellow River civilization represented by the Confucian classics, there was also the Yangtze civilization which produced the *Songs of Ch'u (Ch'u Tz'ŭ)*, another important anthology of ancient Chinese poetry.[1]

The mountains, streams, and forests of the South were fertile ground for legends and myths. Whereas Chinese history had its beginning in the North, and the sage-emperors and dynastic rulers of antiquity appeared first in the northern Confucian literature, Chinese mythology found a favorable climate for development in the South. For one thing, the Yangtze people did not have to eke out a meager existence in harsh surroundings; they were blessed by the bounties of nature, which enabled them to lead a life of comparative ease and to indulge in dreams of the romantic and the supernatural. These traits gave rise to a type of civilization quite different from that of the North.

The South produced a number of poets of whom the best known are Ch'ü Yüan and Sung Yü. It is believed that Sung Yü was a follower of Ch'ü Yüan and probably his student. Their poems, together with those of later imitators, have been collected in the *Songs of Ch'u*. This anthology is different in content from the *Classic of Poetry* in that its songs are more lyrical in nature and romantic in spirit. They have also a different rhythm and music, and a verse form characterized by rhymed lines of irregular length and the constant recurrence of certain particles. These

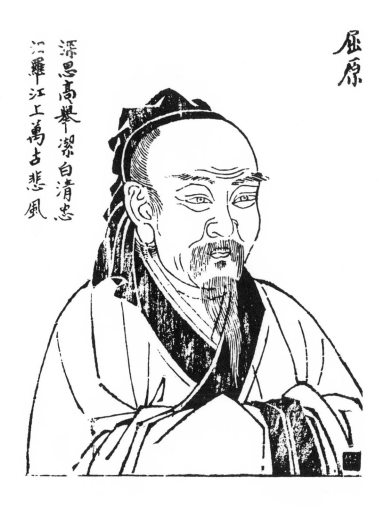

深思高舉潔白清忠
汨羅江上萬古悲風

屈原

Ch'ü Yüan. A Portrait by an Unknown Artist of the Ming Dynasty. From the *Ch'u Tz'u t'u* (Illustrations of the *Ch'u Tz'u*).

anthologies are equally important for their poetic excellence and for their influence on later writers. Together they constituted the two main streams of ancient Chinese poetry. Though the *shih* in the *Shih Ching (Classic of Poetry)* became the principal form of Chinese verse, the *Ch'u Tz'ŭ* evolved as a poetic genre that later inspired the highly important *fu* of the Han dynasty.

Ch'ü Yüan (340?–278 B.C.), the chief poet in the *Songs of Ch'u*, was a member of the ruling house, a statesman and diplomat. In his youth, he had a brilliant official career and was made a court minister and at one time the Ch'u envoy to Ch'i (in Shantung), a great neighboring state. But Ch'ü Yüan's comet-like success incurred the jealousy of his fellow ministers, who slandered and intrigued against him. In consequence Ch'ü Yüan lost the king's favor and was dismissed from office. There were several ups and downs in his career—for after each banishment he was recalled to court, only to be again rebuffed and disgraced. In the meantime, his country was in danger. Failing to heed Ch'ü Yüan's advice, the king of Ch'u foolishly went to a conference with the king of Ch'in (in Shensi), the most powerful military state in that period; he was held there by the Ch'in army and died in captivity. His son, the new king, instead of avenging his father's death, made a humiliating peace with his enemy. This, however, did not deter Ch'in's aggressive designs against Ch'u, and Ch'ü Yüan, who had started his exile as a result of his political failure, lived long enough to see the capital of his state plundered and ruined by the conquering army of Ch'in in 278 B.C. At that time, Ch'ü Yüan was already an old man of over sixty, and the fall of the Ch'u capital was the last blow to his patriotic hope. He does not seem to have long survived this disaster, for the next we hear of him is that he had drowned himself in the river Mi-lo.* Tradition says that his death occurred on the fifth day of the fifth moon; the Dragon Boat Festival commemorates his drowning. As the first known great poet in China, Ch'ü Yüan has been called the father of Chinese poetry and has become, in the opinion of some, a national culture-hero.

A large number of poems in the Ch'u anthology have been attributed to Ch'ü Yüan. His poetic canon consists of twenty-odd pieces, including *Encountering Sorrow, Heaven Questioned, Summoning the Soul,* the *Nine Songs,* and the *Nine Compositions.* The dates of these poems are hard to determine and even the authorship of some of them is in doubt. They are written in a language and style characteristic of the romantic songs of Ch'u and express a kind of sentiment and thought typical of

---

* A tributary that flows into Lake Tung-t'ing in Hunan which was part of the state of Ch'u. Though the locale of Ch'ü Yüan's death has been commonly accepted the date of his death is still a point of debate among scholars, the one given here being the most popular.

the southern poets. Some may have been forged by later writers; if so, they are hardly distinguishable from the genuine ones.

The *Nine Songs* are probably Ch'ü Yüan's earliest poems. They eulogize local deities of Ch'u such as the Great Sovereign of the East, the Lord and Lady of the river Hsiang, and more universal ones like the Lord of Clouds, the Lord of the East (Sun God), the Great and Young Arbiters of Fate, the River God, and the Mountain Spirit. Besides the *Nine* there are two additional songs, one of them a commemoration of the national heroes who have sacrificed themselves on the battlefield, the other an epilogue on ritual offerings. It has been surmised that this group of songs may originally have been sacrificial hymns used by shamans in temple ceremonies and that Ch'ü Yüan, who found them in the course of his travels, may have impressed them with the stamp of his own genius, thereby transforming the crude originals into artistic forms in which the beauty of the sentiments is matched by the beauty of the words.

An important feature of these songs is their dominant note of love for and intimacy with the gods and goddesses whom they praise and worship. They express a kind of romantic yearning for the spiritual and the beautiful. Sometimes the feeling for the divinities is so intensely personal that it transcends the boundary between the worlds of man and deity. "The Mountain Spirit," for instance, brings the human and divine together in what is essentially a poem of love:

> There seems to be a man in the deep mountain,
> Clad in creeping vine and girded with ivy,
> With a charming look and a becoming smile.
> "Do you admire me for my lovely form?"
>
> She rides a red leopard—striped lynxes following behind—
> Her chariot of magnolia arrayed with banners of cassia,
> Her cloak made of orchids and her girdle of azalea,
> Culling sweet flowers for those dear in her heart.
>
> "I live in a bamboo grove, the sky unseen;
> The road hither is steep and dangerous; I arrive alone and late.
> Alone I stand on the mountain top
> While the clouds gather beneath me.
>
> "All gloomy and dark is the day:
> The east wind drifts and god sends down rain.
> Waiting for the divine one, I forget to go home.
> The year is late. Who will now bedeck me?
>
> "I pluck the larkspur on the mountain side,
> The rocks are craggy, and the vines tangled.
> Complaining of the young lord, sadly I forget to go home.
> You, my lord, are thinking of me; but you have no time."

26

The Mountain Spirit. Attributed to Li Kung-lin (b. 1049), a Sung Dynasty Artist. From the *Ch'u Tz'u t'u*.

"The Mountain Spirit". By Hsiao Ch'ih-mu (1596–1673) noted for his *Li Sao t'u* (Illustrations of the *Li Sao*).

The man in the mountain, fragrant with sweet herb,
Drinks from the rocky spring, shaded by pines and firs.
"You, my lord, are thinking of me; but then you hesitate."

The thunder rumbles and the rain darkens;
The gibbons mourn, howling all the night;
The wind whistles and the trees are bare.
"I am thinking of the young lord; I sorrow in vain."

Any rendering of ancient Chinese poetry has to be based upon the translator's own understanding of the particular poem, derived from its numerous commentaries both old and new. These could differ greatly in the interpretation of certain key words and phrases, of the persons referred to and described, and, as in this instance, of the sex of the Mountain Spirit. Much divergence of opinion, which results in different translations, is due to the absence of inflections and the frequent omission of the sentence subject in early Chinese usage, as well as to obscurities in the actual text. The theory that the *Nine Songs* are a product of shamanistic sessions further complicates the issue. It has been asserted that a typical form of these songs consists of two parts: (1) the meeting of the shaman with the spirit; (2) the sorrows and lamentations of the shaman, now forlorn and deserted by the spirit, once the so-called mantic honeymoon is over.[2] It has also been stated that the shaman could be a man if the deity is female or a woman if the deity is male. Following this formula, the Mountain Spirit is either a male deity, the object of love of a female shaman, or vice versa.[3] But whatever its cultural interpretation, this song, like the others in the same group, can be best appreciated as a work of high poetic beauty. Indeed, it would be unusual if such fine poetry had come from the mantic utterances of an untutored religious practitioner. Another theory has been advanced that the *Nine Songs* might have been the work of some later poet of the Ch'u court.[4] In our opinion, unless there should be strong evidence to the contrary, it is pointless to conceive of these songs as being by anybody else but Ch'ü Yüan, with whom they have long been associated.

Another early work, "A Hymn to the Orange," appears in the *Nine Compositions*, a group of unrelated poems written in different periods of the poet's life. It sings of the beauties and virtues of this southern fruit, which are symbolic of the attributes of youth:

Green foliage, white blooms,
How exuberant and lovely!
On overhanging twigs and prickly thorns,
In clusters grows the rotund fruit.
A riot of blended green and yellow

Gleams in a gay composition.
Elegant in color, pure within,
Like someone loaded with virtue—
Flourishing and graceful,
Here is beauty without blemish.

In the next stanza the moral excellences alluded to become more specific in phrases such as "standing alone and steadfast," "unyielding against the tide," "possessing a nature free from selfishness," and "without excess." The virtues of the orange, therefore, are those of a young man or, possibly, of the poet himself.

In *Heaven Questioned* Ch'ü Yüan poses to Heaven one hundred and seventy-two questions on the creation of the world, the nature of light and darkness, the locations of Heaven's nine divisions, the motions of the sun and moon, as well as the stories of early Chinese myth and legend. Though mostly disconnected and obscure in sense and allusion, these questions are original, curious, and thought-provoking, as in the following opening lines:

The beginning of hoary antiquity—
Who was there to tell and transmit it?
Above and below all was shapeless,
What means were used to examine it?

Light and darkness were murky;
Who could have probed them?
Images were formless and profuse;
How could they be recognized?

Bright day and dark night,
What has time to do with it?
Thrice the *yin* and *yang* have blended;*
Which is origin?** Which, mutation?

Heaven's arc is ninefold—
Who planned and measured it?
What function does it serve?
Who first created it?

Whereon is tied the pivot-handle?†
Whereupon is raised Heaven's pole?
What do the eight pillars face?‡
Why is there a gap in the Southeast?

* resulting in the birth of all creation.
** i.e., the origin of species.
†the pivot on which the world rotates.
‡ i.e., the eight pillars that support the world.

> The horizon of the Nine Heavens,
> How far does it reach; where is it attached?
> Caves and coves are numerous;
> Who would know their number?

As a whole *Heaven Questioned* seems to be a collection of cosmological riddles and pseudohistorical queries, the latter forming the bulk of the poem. According to an early commentator, it was originally a series of rhapsodical lines written by Ch'ü Yüan on the walls of the temples and ancestral halls of the nobility, and was later collected and put together by his followers in Ch'u. This idea of "wall poetry" is probably farfetched, but it is quite possible that in the course of his wanderings Ch'ü Yüan did visit a number of temples and halls on which were painted episodes from the myths and legends of the Southern region, and that inspired by them he wrote down his impressions of and reactions to the many strange and fantastic tales found in primitive mythology. Thus, though *Heaven Questioned* contains a number of difficult passages hardly intelligible to the modern reader, leaving him "in infuriating uncertainty as to its real meaning,"[5] it is nevertheless a rich mine of information on the cosmogonic beliefs and legendary history of China, and as such is unique in Chinese poetry.

In *Summoning the Soul*, the poet invokes the lost soul of the king of Ch'u to return.[6] The poem abounds in beautiful passages describing the rich material life of the Ch'u aristocracy as well as its supernatural beliefs. Here are described all sorts of horrible things in the four corners of the world: the soul-sucking giants of the East, the black-toothed, tattooed cannibals of the South, the quicksands of the West, and the icebergs of the North. Contrasted with the horrors of these strange lands are the familiar sights and delights at home. Here are towers and terraces rising beside the hill, palaces with great halls and lofty domes, beautiful chambers with vermilion doors, black marble beams, and ceilings painted with snakes and dragons. Inside are

> Kingfisher feathers on pearly quilts
> Resplendent and blending in color;
> Rush mats spread against the wall;
> And over them gauze curtains,
> With tassels of pure and variegated silk
> Adorned with beautiful gems and jade.

For the nobles' amusement pretty girls with moth-eyebrows and alluring looks dance and sing; there are games like chess and draughts; and most tempting of all, a sumptuous feast with foods of all kinds and descriptions:

Glutinous rice and early wheat,
Boiled together with yellow millet.
Salt, vinegar, and bitter spice,
Made tasty with ginger and honey.
Tendons from fat cows,
Thoroughly cooked and succulent.
Sour as well as bitter,
Well blended is the broth of Wu.
Stewed turtle and roast lamb
Served with syrup from sugarcane;
Goose in vinegar and wild duck with juice;
Swan and crane fried together;
Fresh chicken and large tortoise;—
Their soup is savory but not pungent.
Cakes sugared with honey and malt,
And sweetmeats of all kinds.
Pure mead with honey added
Poured into feathered goblets;
Iced drinks distilled and without dregs
Are cool and refreshing.

While each of the poems mentioned above has its own theme and contribution, Ch'ü Yüan is at his best in a group of intimate personal poems
that afford an insight into his character and mind. They also serve as
records of his life at the time of his disgrace, for it was then that he burst
forth into songs of anguish and protest. All the poems in the *Nine Compositions*, with the exception of the "Hymn to the Orange," are the out-
pourings of an agonized heart beset by doubt, bewilderment, and disappointment. In one of them he laments the capture of the Ch'u capital
by the army of Ch'in, and in another he announces his resolve to seek
death by drowning as a means of escape from further indignity. Viewed
as a whole, the prevailing tone of the *Nine Compositions* is that of sadness, and in them are shown the sufferings of the poet's soul; but this
gloomy atmosphere is considerably lightened by the beauty of imagery
and the nobility of feeling. Even in his great affliction Ch'ü Yüan re-
affirms his faith and integrity:

In the life of all men,
Each has his own destiny.
With a steady heart and a broad mind,
Why should I be afraid?

Deeply afflicted with sorrow,
Forever I sigh and moan:
The world is foul and knows me not,
The heart of man cannot be told.

30

> I know death is inevitable,
> But I have no desire to pity myself.
> Clearly I say to the noble lord:
> I shall follow you as my guide.[7]

The heights in this type of personal poetry are attained by Ch'ü Yüan in his masterpiece, *Encountering Sorrow*, which abounds in imagination, allegory, and historical allusions. One of the longest autobiographical poems in the Chinese language, it begins with a brief account of the poet's ancestry and character, his noble lineage, his illustrious father, his auspicious name, his innate qualities and cultivated talents. Next, it tells the story of his political life: his efforts to guide the king and country, his struggles at court and defeat by the opposite faction, his uprightness and loyalty which make him unfit for the crooked and debased ways of the world. But in spite of all, he continues to aspire to the ancient ways, to show sympathy for the people, and to keep intact the purity of his character. At the same time, he persists in the cultivation of his grace and virtue; they are symbolized by the fragrance and beauty of the flowers he uses as ornament. Firmly he asserts:

> Everyone has his own joys and tastes;
> I alone am fond of cultivating my grace.
> Though dismembered, I would not change.
> How could I impair my heart because of this?

The poet then reports some worldly advice given him by a female friend and contrasts it with his own feeling as he states his cause before a legendary sage-emperor. After thus unburdening his heart, he sets out on an imaginary journey to Heaven:

> I water my horse at the heavenly pool;[8]
> I fasten my rein on the mulberry tree.
> Plucking a sacred sprig* to brush the sun,
> I roam around, leisurely and carefree.
>
> I bid the Moon-charioteer to lead the way,
> The Wind God to run along and follow behind.
> The King-phoenix acts as my herald,
> But Master Thunder tells me he is not ready.
>
> I order the phoenix birds to soar aloft,
> To continue the journey day and night.
> The whirlwinds gather and then scatter,
> Marshaling the clouds and rainbows to greet me.
> In confused masses they merge and disperse;
> In variegated hues they drift above and below.

---

* From *Jo-mu*, a fabulous tree with luminous green leaves and red flowers supposed to have grown on the western extremity of the K'un-lun Mountain, where the sun sets.

31

> I order Heaven's gateman to open the portal,
> But he leans on the door and stares at me.
> The day grows dark; it is nearly spent;
> I tarry there, tying the orchids in a wreath.

The poet next courts the nymphs and legendary beauties of history, but again he is rejected, after which he exclaims:

> The inner chambers are deep and far away;
> The wise king, moreover, has not yet awakened.
> Intense is my emotion, but there is no outlet,
> How could I bear to live like this to the very end?

As a last resort, he seeks the oracles of the Sacred Diviner and the Great Wizard, who both advise him to leave the country and to seek his fortune elsewhere in this wide world. Spurred by their words, and alarmed at the sudden fall of the beautiful flowers from sweetness to filth, he makes a final decision to leave his native land. With a heavy heart he starts his voluntary exile:

> I am about to ascend the splendors of Heaven
> When suddenly I catch a glimpse of my homeland.
> My groom sighs and my horses neigh in grief;
> Tarrying, they gaze back and refuse to proceed.

The poem ends with an envoi:

> All is over now!
> In this country there is no one who knows me;
> Why should I cherish vainly my native city?
> Since there's none worth helping who reigns wisely,
> I shall go where P'êng Hsien makes his home!

According to one commentator, P'eng Hsien was a wise and good minister in the court of the tyrant Chou Hsin, the last king of the Yin dynasty. In protest at the king's iniquities, P'eng Hsien committed suicide by drowning himself in a river. This story, however, is not substantiated by any historical record, and P'eng Hsien could very well have been a recluse, whose withdrawal from the world, instead of drowning, may have given Ch'ü Yüan his frame of reference.

As a representative poet of ancient China, Ch'ü Yüan recreates vividly the mood of his time and country; he also transforms his ideas into splendid words and images through the use of allegory. And just as his artistry gives us a colorful picture of this mundane society, so does his imagination lift us to the realm of the spiritual and aesthetic. He had a great love for the beautiful in all forms, whether it were in flower, ornament, woman, or spirit. Foremost of all, he loved a beautiful ideal: to live righteously and to serve well his country and people. All his romantic yearnings and dreams were centered in this one magnificent vision, but contrary to his expectation, the real world he discovered was full of ugliness, and in it he found himself an outcast. Hence Ch'ü Yüan's tragedy is that of a man of noble nature thrown into a disappointing world, for the sins of which he sought to atone by his death. But death did not put an end to Ch'ü Yüan as a poet; his works such as *Encountering Sorrow*, the *Nine Songs*, and the *Nine Compositions* have ensured for him the highest place in ancient Chinese poetry.

Taken together these poems establish Ch'ü Yüan as a superb artist, capable of sustained imagination and skillful in the use of imagery, thus belying the Western concept of Chinese poetry as limited to short, beautiful, but often sad lyrics, usually connected with parting. The reader may be excited to discover in Ch'ü Yüan's poems a haunting beauty—indigenous and exuberant—rarely found in any literature. The Elizabethan madrigals, although they form a closely related corpus of songs, often written for the lute, and sometimes preoccupied with flowers, are too sophisticated to compare with *Encountering Sorrow* and Ch'ü Yüan's other poems. One would have to look to ancient Hebrew literature, to the *Song of Solomon*, to find anything that could approach these Chinese songs in their use of imagery and symbol and their sensuous descriptions of nature. But even this would be a misleading comparison.

In contrast to the *Classic of Poetry*, the *Songs of Ch'u* strike deeper chords of feeling; they find their response in men who have suffered much. To appreciate this one should read, in addition to Ch'ü Yüan's poems, those of his followers such as Sung Yü whose *Nine Arguments* begins:

> Alas for the breath of autumn!
> Wan and drear! flower and leaf fluttering fall and
>   turn to decay;[9]

Or the opening lines of *Great Summons*, where, in spite of superficial gaiety, there is underlying melancholy:

> Green spring follows the old year and the bright sun shines,
> And the breath of spring stirs, quickening all creation.
> Dark winter's frosts melt away. O Soul, do not flee!
> O Soul, come back! Do not go so far away![10]

The *Songs of Ch'u* had a continuing influence on Chinese poetry, bringing to it a greater poignancy and a wider scope of technical expression, but also, perhaps, a certain enervation as a result of too much languorous sorrow, too much self-pity. In any case, here again it was emotion which created poetry; it was poetry which moved the heart of Ch'ü Yüan's later imitators, several of whom, besides Sung Yü, found their place in this remarkable anthology.

3 : The Development of Chinese Prose

About the time of these activities in Chinese poetry, significant progress was being made in the style and expression, the form and content, of Chinese prose. Among its more important types are historical narratives, philosophical discourses, and imaginative essays. Written in a new language with a comparatively rich and vivid vocabulary, these works are noted for their literary excellence and for their historical and philosophical content. Classical prose, marked by terseness, verve, and directness, was evolved during this period as a standard form of Chinese writing. Although it has become somewhat stereotyped as a result of long usage and constant imitation, its enduring qualities make it a suitable medium of literary expression even to the present time.

The historical tradition of the Confucian classics was continued and further developed in the several commentaries on the *Spring and Autumn,* compiled during the fifth to the third century B.C. From the literary point of view the most remarkable of these is the *Commentary of Tso.* According to tradition, it was written by Tso Ch'iu-ming (or Tso-ch'iu Ming), said to be an immediate follower of Confucius. Tradition also asserts that Tso was a blind historiographer of the state of Lu and the author of another historical work, the *Discourses of the State.* The *Commentary of Tso* is a much enlarged version of the *Spring and Autumn,* whose simple entries are elaborated and commented on, often expanded into long narratives replete with discourses and descriptions. Two examples may be mentioned to illustrate this point. On the entry "The King of Heaven hunted in winter at Ho-yang," the *Commentary of Tso* has the following passage:

> At that assembly, the marquis of Tsin, having summoned the king (of Chou), presented to him the lords of the state, and then made the king conduct a winter hunting expedition. Chung-ni said: "For a vassal to summon the king is not a lesson for posterity." So he wrote: "The King of Heaven hunted in winter at Ho-yang"

to show that this was not a proper place (for such an expedition) and also to illustrate the moral power (of the marquis of Tsin).[1]

In another instance the terse entry in the *Spring and Autumn*, "Autumn, the ninth month, on *i-ch'ou*, Chao Tun of Tsin murdered his lord, I-kao," is expanded in the *Commentary of Tso* into the following long narrative:

> Duke Ling of Tsin did not behave like a lord. He levied heavy taxes to paint the palace walls; from the terrace he would shoot at the passers-by to see how they dodged the pellets. When the chef did not cook the bear's paw well, the duke had him killed and his body dumped into a basket, and then ordered some women to carry it past the court. Chao Tun and Shih Chi saw the hands and having inquired about the matter, were perturbed. They were about to remonstrate with the duke when Shih Chi said, "If we remonstrate together and fail, then no one will succeed us. Please let me go first, and if I fail, you can still follow me." Three times he advanced to the palace but did not attract the duke's attention until he reached the eaves. "I know my fault and am going to correct it," said the duke. Shih Chi bowed his head to the ground and replied, "Who among men is without fault? To err and then to be able to reform is a virtue than which none is greater. The poem says:
>
> Who is without a good beginning?
> But few are able to end well.
>
> Indeed, rare are those who are able to mend their faults. If your lordship is able to end well, then the state will be stable and not your ministers alone will rely on you. The poem says:
>
> The hole in the robe of state—
> Chung Shan Fu alone could mend it.
>
> It means he could mend faults. When your lordship can mend your faults, your robe of state will not be neglected."
>
> Still the duke did not change his conduct. Chao Tun made repeated remonstrances until the duke was so perturbed that he ordered Ch'u Ni to kill him. Ch'u Ni went in the early morning. The door of the bedchamber was wide open. Chao Tun, in full regalia, was ready to attend court, but as it was still too early, he had sat down and dozed off. Ch'u Ni withdrew and said, sighing, "Mindful of the reverence due to a superior, he is indeed a master of the people. To kill the master of the people would be disloyalty; to disobey the lord's command would be unfaithfulness. Since there is no way out, I had better die." He dashed his head on a locust tree and killed himself.

In autumn, in the ninth month, the duke of Tsin feasted Chao Tun with wine and was about to ambush him with armed soldiers. Chao Tun's right-seat driver, T'i-mi Ming, discovered the plot. He rushed up to the hall and said, "It is contrary to propriety for a minister at a feast with his lord to drink beyond three cups." He then supported his master down the steps. The duke set a big and fierce dog on them, but T'i-mi Ming attacked it with his hands and killed it. "However fierce it may be," remarked Chao Tun, "to use a dog instead of man will not do." As they fought their way out, T'i-mi Ming was killed.

Formerly, when Chao Tun had hunted at Mount Shou, he had rested under a shady mulberry tree. There he saw one Ling-ch'ê on the verge of starvation and asked him his trouble. "I have not eaten for three days," the man answered. When food was brought him, he set one half of it aside. When questioned, he said, "I have been studying abroad for three years and do not know if my mother still lives. Now that I am near home, I beg to give half of the food to her." Chao Tun made him finish all his food and then had a basketful of rice and meat placed in a bag and gave it to him. Later the man became the duke's guard. (At this moment) he turned his spear against the duke's retinue and thus saved Chao Tun. When asked why he did it, he replied, "I am the starved man by the shady mulberry." However, when asked about his name and place, he refused to answer, but withdrew and disappeared.

On i-ch'ou, Chao Ch'uan attacked Duke Ling in the peach garden. Chao Tun, who had not yet left the hills (on the border of Tsin), returned. The grand historiographer wrote the words, "Chao Tun murdered his lord," and showed them in the court.

"That isn't true," said Chao Tun.

"You are the chief minister. You fled from the state but did not go beyond its borders; you returned but did not punish the murderer. Who would have murdered the lord if not you?"

"Alas!" said Chao Tun:

The object of my anxiety
Has brought on me this sorrow.

"Does this not apply to me?"

Confucius said: "Tung Hu was a good historian of olden times; his principle for writing was not to conceal. Chao Tun was a good minister of olden times; because of the principle, he had to suffer ignominy. Too bad—he would have been spared if he had crossed the borders."[2]

In many passages like the above, the *Commentary of Tso* recreates in animated prose the men and politics of the feudal period. In its use of the narrative and dialogue, moral comments and poetic quotations, it exemplifies a mastery of the Chinese language rarely found in ancient texts.

Apparently there had occurred between the fifth and the third century B.C. a significant development in Chinese prose. The *Strategies of the Warring States*, another historical work of this time, gives a vivid and colorful picture of the events and personalities in the seven warring states. This was one of the most exciting periods in Chinese history, enlivened by wars and military alliances, political intrigues and philosophical arguments; and the *Strategies of the Warring States*, which recorded these happenings, was indeed a book of lively narratives and eloquent speeches. While the present version may have undergone important revisions in the Han dynasty, its basic materials seem to have been drawn from the original chronicles of the warring states.

In the same centuries, philosophical writings which aim to theorize, to argue, and to convince, developed alongside historical writings. Whereas from the viewpoint of sheer literary style, the *Analects* is a book of brief disconnected sayings, and the *Book of Tao* (a work attributed to Lao-tzu but probably of later authorship) a conglomeration of incoherent prose and doggerel verse, the works of Mo-tzu, Mencius, and Chuang-tzu (all about fifth to fourth century B.C.) are better prose writings that contain extensive, carefully organized, and well-developed discourses. They were followed by Hsün-tzu and Han-Fei-tzu, whose writings marked another development in ancient Chinese prose.

Best known for his doctrines of universal love, anti-aggression, and utilitarianism, Mo-tzu was the first ancient philosopher to make an effective use of polemic prose. Though his writings are sometimes dull and repetitive, they usually present his ideas clearly, emphatically, and precisely. Take, for example, the following passage on the condemnation of aggressive war:

> The murder of one person is called unrighteousness and incurs one death penalty. Following this argument, the murder of ten persons will be ten times as unrighteous and there should be ten death penalties; the murder of a hundred persons will be hundred times as unrighteous and there should be a hundred death penalties. All the gentlemen of the world know that they should condemn these things and brand them as unrighteous. But when it comes to the great unrighteousness of attacking states, they do not know that they should condemn it. On the contrary, they applaud it, calling it righteous; they are really ignorant of its being unrighteous. Hence they have recorded their judgment to bequeath to posterity. If they knew that it is unrighteous, then why should they record their false judgment to bequeath to posterity?[3]

As a logician, Mo-tzu introduced the use of methodological reasoning in Chinese prose, as is shown in the following quotation:

> Some standard of judgment must be established. To expound without regard for the standard is similar to determining the directions of sunrise and sunset on a revolving potter's wheel. By this means the distinction of right and wrong, benefit and harm, cannot be known. Therefore any statement must have three criteria. What are the three criteria? Mo-tzu said: "Its basis, its verifiability, and its applicability." On what is it to be based? On the deeds of the ancient sage-kings. By what is it to be verified? By man's sense of hearing and his sense of sight. How is it to be applied? By adopting it in penal laws and government and by observing its benefits to the country and the people. This is what is meant by the three criteria of every doctrine.[4]

Mencius, whose teaching of the innate goodness of man won him philosophical fame, contributed to prose literature his eloquence, his elegant diction, and his facility of style. To combat the rival teachings prevalent at his time, he was often drawn into long verbal encounters with kings, politicians, and philosophers. A veteran debater, he knew how to take advantage of his opponent's weaknesses and then to attack and overpower him with forceful, irresistible argument, as illustrated in the following conversation between him and a follower of Hsü Hsing (an agriculturist who advocated farming for everyone and who criticized the ruler for not working in the fields):

> "Master Hsü, to be sure," said Mencius, "plants the grain and eats from his own produce."
> "Yes."
> "Master Hsü surely weaves the cloth he wears?"
> "No, Master Hsü wears haircloth."
> "Has Master Hsü a cap?"
> "Yes, he wears one."
> "What kind of cap?"
> "A plain one."
> "Did he weave it himself?"
> "No, he bartered grain for it."
> "Why didn't Master Hsü make it himself?"
> "That would have interfered with his farming."
> "Does Master Hsü use pots and pans for cooking, and iron shares for plowing?"
> "Yes."
> "Did he make them himself?"
> "No. He bartered grain for them."

"Well," said Mencius, "if he did no harm to the potter and smith when he bartered his grain for their wares, why should the farmer be harmed when the potter and smith bartered their wares for his grain? Moreover, why doesn't Master Hsü himself take up pottery and smithery, thereby using those articles made on his own premises? Why all this multifarious dealing with a hundred craftsmen? Why does Master Hsü go to so much trouble?"

"The business of the hundred craftsmen cannot possibly be carried out together with farming."

"Is it then the government of a state which alone can be carried out together with farming? There is the business of the great men; there is also the business of the little men. Moreover, if the work of the hundred craftsmen should be combined in one person, and if one has to use only the things one makes oneself, this will but lead the whole world on the road (to confusion). Hence the saying, 'Some toil with their minds; others toil with their bodies.' Those who toil with their minds govern others, and those who toil with their bodies are governed by others. Those who are governed produce food; those who govern are fed by their fellows. This is a principle universally recognized."[5]

In an argument with Master Kao on the subject of human nature occurs the following colloquy of the two philosophers:

"Human nature," observed Master Kao, "is like whirling water. If a breach is made to the east, it flows to the east; if a breach is made to the west, it flows west. And just as water does not discern between east and west, so man's nature is indifferent to good or bad."

"It is true," said Mencius, "that water will flow indifferently to east and west, but will it flow equally well up and down? Human nature is disposed toward goodness just as water tends to flow downwards. There is no water but flows downwards, and no man but shows his tendency to be good. Now, by striking water hard, you may splash it higher than your forehead, and by damming it, you may make it go uphill. But, is that the nature of water? It is external force that causes it to do so. Likewise, if a man is made to do what is not good, his nature is being similarly forced."[6]

Mencius was always fond of using comparisons, stories, and allegories to illustrate and drive home the point he wanted to make. In an allegory on the deforestation of a once wooded mountain, he compared the despoiling of its beautiful trees to the abuse of man's innate nature.[7] As an example of man's shameless degeneration, he told the story of a person of Ch'i who bragged to his womenfolk of the lavish entertainment given him by the wealthy while in fact he was begging for the leftovers of the sacrificial offering at the cemetery. "In the eyes of a gentleman," Mencius concluded, "the way men seek riches and honors, success and gain, is seldom such that their wives and concubines would not weep together for shame."[8]

Even more than Mencius, Chuang-tzu, another great writer of philosophical prose, was fond of using anecdotes and allegories to expound his mystic Taoist views. His imagination seems to soar with the fabulous roc (*p'eng*) which mounts aloft upon a great wind amidst the floating marsh-mists, the dust-specks, and "the living creatures blowing their breaths among them."[9] It is this poetic quality that makes his writings entertaining as well as thought-provoking. Chuang-tzu was a humorist who poked fun at man for his near-sightedness, his littleness, and his ignorance. In the same allegory, just as the great roc was on its winged flight towards the southern ocean, it was espied by a lake sparrow. Watching the roc's movement, the sparrow laughed and said, "Pray, where may that creature be going? I leap into the air and then settle down again after being up for a few yards. This fluttering of mine among the reeds is as much as any one would like to fly. Now, where can this creature be going?"[10]

In his near-sightedness, man has made much fuss of life and death, not knowing that life is only a dream and that the love of life is after all a delusion. Chuang-tzu wrote:

> Those who dream of carousing, wake up to lamentation and sorrow. Those who dream of lamentation and sorrow wake up to join the hunt. While they dream, they do not know they are dreaming. Some will even interpret the very dream they are dreaming, and only when they awake do they know that it was a dream. By and by comes the great awakening, and then we find out that this life is really a great dream. Fools think they are awake now, and flatter themselves that they know—this one is a prince and that one a shepherd. What narrowness of mind! Confucius and you are both dreams; and I who say you are dreams—I am but a dream myself.[11]

Elaborating on the statement that he himself was a dream, Chuang-tzu told the following story of the butterfly:

> Once upon a time, Chuang Chou dreamt that he was a butterfly, fluttering happily like a butterfly. He was conscious only of his happiness as a butterfly, unaware that he was Chuang Chou. Suddenly he awakened, and there he was, veritably Chuang Chou himself. Now he does not know whether the butterfly is a dream of Chuang Chou or whether Chuang Chou is a dream of the butterfly.[12]

Chuang-tzu's metaphysical thought, often animated by poetry, can be seen in the following passage:

> But suppose there is one who chariots on the normality of the universe, rides on the transformation of the six elements, and thus makes excursion into the infinite, what has he to depend upon? Therefore it is said that the perfect man has no self; the spiritual man has no achievement; and the sage has no name.[13]

or in one of his famous discourses on the soul:

> For whether the soul is locked in sleep or whether in waking hours the body moves, we are striving and struggling with the immediate circumstances. Some are easygoing and leisurely, some are deep and cunning, and some are secretive. Now we are frightened over petty fears, now disheartened and dismayed over some great terror. Now the mind flies forth like an arrow from a crossbow, to be the arbiter of right and wrong. Now it stays behind as if sworn to an oath to hold on to what it has secured. Then, as under autumn and winter's blight, comes gradual decay, and submerged in its own occupations, it keeps on running its course, never to return. Finally, worn out and imprisoned, it is choked up like an old drain, and the failing mind shall not see light again.
>
> Joy and anger, sorrow and happiness, worries and regrets, indecision and fears, come upon us by turns, with everchanging moods, like music from the hollows, or like mushrooms from damp. Day and night they alternate within us, but we cannot tell whence they spring. Alas! Alas! Could we for a moment lay our finger upon their very Cause?
>
> But for these emotions I should not be. Yet but for me, there would be no one to feel them. So far we can go; but we do not know by whose order they come into play. It would seem there was soul; but the clue to its existence is wanting. That it functions is credible enough, though we cannot see its form. Perhaps it has inner reality without outward form.
>
> Take the human body with all its hundred bones, nine external cavities and six internal organs, all complete. Which part of it should I love best? Do you not cherish all equally, or have you a preference? Do these organs serve as servants of some one else? Since servants cannot govern themselves, do they serve as master and servants by turn? Surely there is some soul which controls them all.
>
> But whether or not we ascertain what is the true nature of this soul, it matters but little to the soul itself. For once coming into this material shape, it runs its course until it is exhausted. To be harassed by the wear and tear of life, and to be driven along without the possibility of arresting one's course,—is not this pitiful indeed?

> To labor without ceasing all one's life, and then, without living to enjoy the fruit, worn out with labor, to depart, one knows not whither,—is not this a just cause for grief?[14]

Both Hsün-tzu and Han-Fei-tzu flourished toward the end of the Chou dynasty in the first half of the third century B.C. By that time, Chinese prose was already a well-established medium of expression, and its maturity of style enabled both writers to expound effectively their respective teachings, Hsün-tzu's ritualism and Han-Fei-tzu's legalism. As a whole, their writings are penetrating and apposite, Han-Fei-tzu's essays containing perhaps a more vigorous style and poignant interest than Hsün-tzu's. Their contribution to the development of Chinese prose was not so much in breaking new ground or in discovering new horizons as in attaining new heights in the use of prose as a vehicle of communication.

This statement, however, has to be modified in view of the five *fu* (prose-poems) written by Hsün-tzu on rituals, knowledge, clouds, the silkworm, and admonition. This variety of unrelated topics in the same form shows that Hsün-tzu was actually experimenting with a new form which has been aptly described as a rhyming riddle, as in the following *fu* on the silkworm:

> Is this then a creature with a slender body and a horse-head, often changing forms but never attaining a long life; kind to the young but negligent of the old; born of parents but of neither sex itself? It hibernates in winter and roams in summer; eats mulberry leaves and spits out silk, which first appears disorderly but later becomes regulated. Born in summer, it dislikes heat; loving dampness, it hates the rain. The larva it considers as mother; the moth as father. Three times it lies low; three times it climbs up; and then all is accomplished.
>
> This is indeed the principle of the silkworm.[15]

A unique literary genre of the Chinese, the *fu* stands on the border line between poetry and prose. Strictly neither the one nor the other, it contains elements of both. This is due to the fact that except for the use of rhyme and meter in traditional poetry, there is only a thin line of demarcation between poetry and prose—an observation which holds as true for Chinese poetry as for Western poetry. A work of prose with heightened emotions and beautiful descriptions, it often soars into the realm of the poetic. The *fu*, moreover, is characterized not only by an abundance of parallel euphuistic expressions, in which Chinese writers were fond of indulging, but also by the use of rhymes in its main body. These considerations have led many critics to include the *fu* among the poetic genres.[16]

The *fu* has probably a southern origin in the state of Ch'u, where Hsün-tzu spent a large part of his later life. Some of Sung Yü's works have also been classified as *fu*. But there is a noticeable difference between the *fu* of Sung Yü and those of Hsün-tzu; the former are essentially imaginative and lyric whereas the latter are expository and instructive.

Thus by the third century B.C., the Chinese had already experimented with different types of prose in historical and philosophical writings. When translated, these are as informative as the works of Herodotus and Thucydides, Plato and Aristotle. What is more remarkable, the archaism of the early Confucian classics had almost disappeared by that time and a new prose had been created that is not far removed from the literary Chinese still in use today. Characteristically, this prose is simple and concise. It stresses economy of words to the extent of being laconic; it has a predilection for allusions and quotations; it abounds in antithetical expressions, and in repetitions that often become unwieldy in translation. Chinese is an articulate language. It is at its best in creating an emotional mood and in expressing ideas and arguments in a sonorous and rhetorical style. But little of this early literature, particularly of the belles-lettres type, has been rendered into English, and Western knowledge of Chinese prose of the post-Chou period is limited indeed.

4 : Literature in the Han Dynasty

The Han dynasty rose with renewed glory from the ashes of the militant, despotic Ch'in, which collapsed shortly after its unification of the country. During the reign (140–87 B.C.) of Emperor Wu, the best-known of the Han rulers, the Chinese empire extended from the Yellow River and the Yangtze regions southward to Annam and northward to Mongolia and Korea. In the Northwest, Chinese expeditions to Central Asia led to the opening of a caravan route, whence Chinese silk was sent in large quantities to the Roman Empire. At home, Emperor Wu promoted Confucianism as a state doctrine, enlisting its followers to serve in his administration, while at the same time he flirted with the Taoist idea of longevity and the elixir of life. Thus he gathered at his court a strange medley of Confucian scholars and Taoist practitioners. He also surrounded himself with men of letters, who contributed to the manifold literary achievements of the Han period, among which are Music Bureau poems (*yüeh-fu shih*), five-word poems (*wu-yen shih*), prose-poems (*fu*), and historical prose.

The Music Bureau was established in 120 B.C. by Emperor Wu, himself a lover of music. Its primary function was to provide music and songs for ceremonial occasions at court. These ranged from temple hymns and sacrificial odes to chamber music and songs for feasting and dancing. Mostly eulogistic in nature, they comprise praises of imperial virtue and invocations for blessings from spirits and gods. But most important for posterity is a group of folk songs collected by the musicians of the Bureau. The music of these songs is now lost, but the words have remained as specimens of Han folk poetry, which is comparable to the *Classic of Poetry* in scope and variety.

Like any other poetry, the Music Bureau poems deal with the common themes of life—love and separation, poverty and war. They were written to be sung to the accompaniment of musical instruments such as the flute, bamboo mouth organ (*sheng*), drum, zither, and harpsicord. The short flute and flageolet of foreign origin were also used in some of the hunting and battle songs taken from the nomadic Tartar tribes. These northern tunes introduced a martial note not commonly found in the native Chinese poems.

Altogether about one hundred of these Han folk songs have been preserved. Some are simple verses like the following:

> South of the river one may gather lotus seeds.
> The lotus leaves, how abundant they are!
> The fishes sport among the lotus leaves:
> The fishes sport east of the lotus leaves,
> The fishes sport west of the lotus leaves,
> The fishes sport south of the lotus leaves,
> The fishes sport north of the lotus leaves.

The primitive simplicity of this reminds one of the inscriptions on the Yin divination bones, and its repetitious lines suggest a form of choral singing. Others, though equally artless, are fine compositions in the best folk tradition. The "Song of the Orphan" relates his hard lot in such moving lines:

> My hands are sore,
> My feet without sandals;
> Sadly I tread on the frost
> Amidst thorns and brambles.
> As I pull out the thorns,
> How bitter my heart is!
> My tears fall and fall
> In an endless stream.

The "Eastern Gate" tells how a poor man, forced by poverty and hunger, is about to leave his wife and child to seek his fortunes abroad. His wife tries to detain him, and the following conversation takes place:

> "Other people desire wealth and rank;
> I am content to share my gruel with you.
> Above is the blue expanse of the sky,
> And below, this suckling child."
>
> "Alas! If I do not leave today,
> It will be too late.
> My hair is growing white;
> Longer I cannot stay."

One of the war poems, "Fighting South of the City," contains the following words of a dead soldier, whose corpse is being devoured by the crows:

46

Tell the crows for me:
Welcome, feast yourselves!
Lying unburied in the wilds,
How could my rotted body be spared?

Though most of the Music Bureau poems are written in lines of varying length, some of them have a regular form of five words in each line, with rhymes on the even lines. This is an important development of Chinese poetry and an improvement over the four-word poems in the *Classic of Poetry* in that the addition of an extra word to each line makes it much more flexible and melodious.

Besides these Music Bureau poems, the best known earliest examples of the five-word verse can be found in a group of "Nineteen Ancient Poems." While they differ in content and theme, and were written most probably by different writers in the Han period, they are uniform in the use of the five-word verse as a poetic medium. In the following lines the original form of the Chinese poem is indicated by the words italicized:

Green, green, the *grass* by the *river bank;*
Thick, thick, the *willows in* the *garden.*
Fair, fair, the *lady* in the *upper chamber;*
Graceful, graceful, she *faces* the *window lattice.*
Lovely, lovely, her *toilet* of *rouge* and *powder;*
Slender, slender, she *shows* her *white hands.*
Once she *was* a *girl* of the *singsong house;*
Now she *is* a *wandering man's wife.*
The *wandering man* has *left* and *not returned;*
It is *hard alone* to *keep* an *empty bed.*

It also illustrates the compactness of the Chinese poetic language, which is usually devoid of articles, prepositions, and pronouns. Thus in a Chinese poem each word is significant, meaningful, and often suggestive. The beauty of simplicity and directness is obvious in this and the other poems in the group, most of which have been admirably rendered into English.

A number of other five-word poems of the Han period have been attributed, rather dubiously, to certain historical persons such as a general, a diplomat, a scholar, and an imperial concubine. These poems were very popular and have been repeatedly translated. Of more poignant interest, however, is a long poem entitled "Sorrow and Indignation," written supposedly by Ts'ai Yen,[1] the daughter of a famous scholar in the Later Han period (second century A.D.). At the time of the dissolution of the Han empire, she was captured by the invading Huns (about A.D. 192) and taken from the capital northward to the Tartar land. After having stayed there for twelve years, during which she bore two sons to a Hun chieftain, she was at last ransomed back to China. In the poem are recounted graphically the bitter experiences in her life: the long civil war toward the end of the Han dynasty, the sufferings of the Chinese in the hands of the Hun invaders, and the sorrows of the captured women on their way to the northern wilds. Finally, when the news of her ransom came, she rejoiced and grieved at the same time, for in spite of her joy at returning to China, she couldn't bear the thought of having to leave two sons behind her in an alien land:

> The children came forward to hug my neck
> And asked, "Whither is mother going?
> People say that mother is leaving,
> But when will she come back?
> Mother has been kind and tender:
> How could she be so without pity?
> We are not yet of age,
> Why doesn't she think of us?"

> Seeing them thus, my heart was sundered.
> And it seemed I was suddenly seized by frenzy.
> Wailing, I stroked them with my hands.
> I was about to start and again I tarried.

> There were those of my companions
> Who came to see me off, to say farewell;
> They envied that I alone should return,
> And loudly they cried with heartrending voices.
> The horses stood in bewilderment,
> The carriages failed to roll on,
> The spectators sobbed and sighed,
> And the roads, too, sadly groaned.

In the immediate post-Han period (early third century A.D.) appeared three poets from the imperial family of Ts'ao, which founded the Wei kingdom in northern China after the fall of Han. They were patrons of poetry as well as poets themselves. The most talented among them, Ts'ao Chih (192–232), gave the five-word verse form a new status and dignity. He made poetry a vehicle for the conveyance of personal sentiments, which in his case underwent three stages of change, concerning: an early life of ease and enjoyment as a young prince; a middle period of political disappointment and persecution by his brother, the emperor; and a last period of frustration, fear, and brooding over the brevity and insecurity of life, and of a futile search for immortality through magic. These feelings were expressed with acumen in a group of six farewell poems written to his younger brother, another prince, who had been suffering similar treatment at the hands of the emperor. Forebodings of a long separation and thoughts of mortality plagued him in the last poem of the group:

> Why should I worry about this bitter grief?
> Heaven's decree is indeed dubious!
> In the realm of the Void I sought the immortals,
> But Master Red Pine has long deceived me.
> In a twinkling comes the great change.
> Who could live to a hundred years?
> Parted now, we will never meet again;
> When could we hold hands once more?
> Prince, take good care of your precious self.
> Together, let us enjoy the age of the yellowing hair.
> Restraining my tears, I start the long journey;
> Holding my pen, I bid you farewell forever.[2]

If Ts'ao Chih represented the best of the literary poets of the period, the anonymous author of "The Peacock Flies Southeast" showed equal mastery and facility in the folk use of the five-word verse. One of the longest poems in the Chinese language, it is a remarkable narrative of sustained interest and incomparable pathos. The poem has another title, "An Old Poem Written for Chiao Chung-ch'ing's Wife." This tragedy took place toward the end of the Han period (early third century A.D.): Chiao was a petty clerk in the prefecture of Lu-chiang in modern Anhwei. His happy married life was disrupted by the interference of his mother, who, taking a dislike to the daughter-in-law, forced him to send her back to her parents' house. His pleadings having failed, the couple were finally separated. At the moment of their parting, they swore eternal faith to each other:

> The horse of the prefect clerk was in front,
> The carriage of the young wife behind.
> Rumbling and trampling as they went,
> The two met at the mouth of the broad road.
> He dismounted and entered the carriage;
> Bowing his head, he whispered to her:
> "I swear I will never be separated from you!
> Just return home for a little while.
> I shall go back briefly to the prefecture,
> But will soon come back to get you.
> To Heaven I swear that I shall never fail!"
> The young wife said to the prefect clerk:
> "Thanks for your feeling for me, the humble one.
> Since you have made known this intention,

> I shall expect you to come back soon.
> You should be like a great rock,
> And your handmaiden a rush.
> The rush fiber is as pliable as silk
> While the great rock does not budge and change."

The return of the deserted wife brought much sorrow and dismay to her parents, but no sooner had she settled down than the matchmaker came to negotiate her marriage with the young scion of a noble, official family. Seeing that objections were futile, she bowed to her family's wish and preparations were made for the wedding ceremony. In the meantime, the prefect clerk had heard the news and came to see her on the day before the wedding. Hearing the horse's neigh, she hastened out to meet him.

> The prefect clerk told the new wife:
> "Congratulations for your advancement!
> The great rock, towering and solid,
> Would have lasted for a thousand years.
> The rush, pliable only for a moment,
> Snaps during the time from dawn to evening.
> You will attain honor and success every day,
> While I go alone toward the Yellow Spring."*
> The new wife told the prefect clerk:
> "How could you utter such words?
> In the same way we have been oppressed—
> You were forced and so am I!
> We shall meet at the Yellow Spring;
> Don't break the promise just now spoken!"

Relinquishing each other's hands the two parted and went their separate ways. That same night, the woman, taking off her shoes and lifting her skirt, walked into the clear pond near her green wedding tent, and the prefect clerk hanged himself from the southeastern branch of the court-yard tree. After the tragedy, the two families buried the lovers together at the side of a great mountain. There the pines, cypresses, and *wu-t'ung* trees grew tall and luxuriant until their boughs and leaves touched each other and provided a shade for the mound and a nesting place for the birds of love (*yüan-yang*), which would raise their heads and call to each other every night until the fifth watch.

> The traveler stays his feet to listen;
> The widow gets up to wander listlessly.
> Thankful are the men of later generations
> That they may be forewarned and forget not.

* The Chinese equivalent of Hades.

The date of the poem is debatable, but it could not have been written much later than the tragic incident itself, when its memory was still fresh in the minds of the people. The fact that the poem shows great skill in the handling of the five-word verse form need not argue for a later date because in China usually a new poetic form was first evolved among the people before it was adopted by literary writers. In any case, it is obvious that this important form of ancient Chinese poetry was already toward the end of the Han dynasty well developed as a medium of lyric expression and sustained narrative.

Another important literary form of the period was the *fu* or prose-poem, first introduced, as we have seen, in the early third century b.c. By Han times it had become essentially descriptive in nature. One definition of the Han *fu* is that it "extends" or "spreads out" in detail the objects or topics it treats. Its essence is therefore "ornate elaboration." Structurally the main descriptive part is generally in rhymed verse so that its music and elegance of style may alleviate somewhat the monotony of lengthy description; on the other hand, the introductory and concluding passages, often in the form of question and answer, are in prose. The content ranges from the description of minor objects like fans and flutes, and personal items like the female body and toilet, to the splendor of cities and palaces, the beauty of mountains, rivers, and trees, and sometimes the imaginary wonders of fairyland. Human activities like hunting and feasting also figure largely in prose-poetry, which, besides being descriptive, can also be lyrical, expository, argumentative, and satirical. "The heart of a *fu* writer," it is said, "embraces the universe."

Prose-poetry has an advantage over some other forms in the adaptability of its length. Some prose-poems are short, but even the shortest ones are generally much longer than most other poems. In the course of its development many a prose-poem has run to thousands of words. This flexibility as to length is due to the unrestrained mixture of poetry and prose; even in a poetic line, the number of words can vary on the average of from four to nine, and often the use of particles, as in the songs of Ch'u, makes the sentences more supple and expressive. Also, in the hands of a master, poetic epithets enhance the prose-poem, but in the hands of a lesser writer create an aura of artificiality or improbability, pendantry rather than beauty.

The popularity of prose-poetry in the Han dynasty can be ascribed to a number of factors: the influence of the songs of Ch'u, from which it evolved; the long period of peace and prosperity, which encouraged poetic production; and most important, the promotion of this literary form by the aristocracy. During the reigns of Emperor Wu and later emperors, many writers of prose-poetry gained imperial favor and official position. Moreover, the brilliant material culture of the period, which was crystallized in the luxury and elegance of court life, provided inspiration for many writers, who in turn glorified it in their writings.

The representative writer of Han prose-poetry was Ssu-ma Hsiang-ju (179–117 B.C.), a talented poet and musician. In imitation of the songs of Ch'u, he first established the *fu* form, consisting mainly of parallel or antithetic verse, often rhymed, in which the descriptive element predominates over the lyric. In his famous piece, "Master Figment" (*Tzu-hsü fu*), he created an imaginary conversation between Master Figment and Mr. Nonesuch in the presence of Lord Nonexistence. Hunting is the topic of their conversation, in which Master Figment, an envoy from a neighboring kingdom, belittles the hunting party given in his honor by the prince of the host state and praises instead the grandeur of the chase given by his own prince in a splendid pleasure park (called Cloud-Dream) in his native state, and of the feasting and dancing that followed it. However, he is reproved by Mr. Nonesuch for his discourtesy to the host state and for his bragging about sensual enjoyment to the detriment of princely virtues. In spite of its moralistic ending, this piece is ostensibly a display of the worldly pleasures of the rulers.

In the sequel, "The Shang-lin Park," written especially for Emperor Wu, Lord Nonexistence is given the platform and after a brief introduction indulges himself in a glowing account of the emperor's chase in the imperial park, much more splendid than that of the feudal princes:

> Then, with autumn gone and winter approaching,
> The Son of Heaven went hunting with his troops.
> He rode in a carriage of carved ivory,
> Drawn by six jade-adorned hornless dragons (horses).
> With rainbow-banners trailing
> And cloud-flags wafted by the wind,
> The imperial carriage, covered with tiger-skin, led the procession,
> Followed by the chariots heralding the way and chariots for pleasure.
> Sun Shu held the reins, assisted in driving by Lord Wei.
> The royal retinue marched sideways,
> Cutting in and out of the four armed columns.
> Loudly the drums beat and the bells boomed,
> As the hunters dispersed.
> Horses and chariots rumbled like thunder;
> Heaven resounded and earth quaked.
> Rivers and rivulets served as bourns,
> Mount T'ai as a lookout.
> In every direction, hither and thither,
> They scattered and departed for the chase—

Flitting and flowing along the hills and moors,
Like clouds spreading and rain descending.
Leopards were captured alive,
Wolves tackled with fists;
Bears seized in handgrips,
Antelopes trampled under feet;
Long-tailed pheasants enmeshed,
White tigers ensnared.
Wrapped in mottled skin and riding spirited stallions,
The hunters climbed perilous ridges and descended rugged slopes;
Threaded steep paths and traversed dangerous courses;
Passed ravines and waded through waters.
They smote the dragon-sparrows
And sported with one-horned stags;
Attacked the *hsia-ko* beast,
And speared the *meng-shih* bear;
Grappled with fiery steeds,
And shot wild boars.
The arrows aimed only at the vital organs,
Splitting the neck and sinking into the brain;
The bow was never drawn in vain
As the game fell in response to the twang.

After such ornate description, the prose-poem concludes, as it begins, in a moralizing tone, for the emperor is said to have repented at last of his lavishness in hunting and feasting and to have ordered the restoration of the hunting grounds to the people as farms for cultivation. This seems to be an anticlimax, a moral platitude rather than the indirect criticism and remonstrance some critics have read into it.

The pleasure park, the chase, and the feasting all lend themselves to an ostentatious display of fine words and phrases, arrayed in paired lines. Obviously, there is an effort to search for the uncommon, the recondite, and the pretentious to impress the reader with the author's talent and erudition. Interestingly enough, the Chinese style at that time (second century B.C.) possessed such a rich, inexhaustible vocabulary and such an ornateness of usage that its nearest counterpart in English is to be found in the euphuistic exaggerations and conceits of certain early Elizabethan writers in England some sixteen centuries later. But this over-elaborateness and ultrarefinement could result only in great artificiality. Today this type of high-flown diction is obsolete, the style seems affected, and the content, divested of its trappings, shallow and insubstantial.

A host of prose-poetry writers followed in the wake of Ssu-ma Hsiang-ju, but only a few succeeded in breaking away from the pattern set by him. Among them were two successful writers, Pan Ku, (32–92 A.D.), the his-

53

torian, and Chang Heng (78–139 A.D.), the mathematician and astronomer. The splendor of this type of extensive, elaborate description is fully revealed in accounts of the twin capitals of Han written by the two men, one in emulation of the other.[3] Chang Heng also introduced a new type of prose-poetry, characterized by briefer descriptions, greater simplicity in diction and style, and a personal note. His work "Return to the Field," in which he described the kind of life he proposed to lead, contains quite pronounced Taoist ideas:

> Then comes young spring, in a fine month,
> When the weather is mild and the air clear.
> Plains and swamps are overgrown with verdure
> And the hundred grasses become rank and thick.
> The kingly osprey flaps its wings;
> The orioles wail mournfully—
> Their necks entwined, fluttering,
> They call to each other in tender notes.
> Thus happily I roam and play,
> My feelings to cherish:
> I am like a dragon chanting on the moor
> Or a tiger roaring in the mountain.
> I gaze up and let loose the slender bowstring;
> Looking down, I fish in a long stream.
> The loitering bird, struck by the arrow,
> Drops from the clouds.
> And the shark, hooked for greediness,
> Is suspended in the watery abyss.
> Meanwhile, the radiant sun has slanted its shadow
> And is overtaken by the moon-charioteer.
> Entranced by the supreme joy of rambling,
> I forget all weariness even as the sun sets.
> Moved by the precept handed down by Lao-tzu,
> I wend my way back to the thatched cottage.
> I pluck the five strings with deft fingers;
> I read the books of Chou and K'ung.*
> I flourish my pen and invoke elegant words
> To expound the patterns of the Three Emperors.
> If one but let one's heart roam beyond this realm,
> Why should one know the semblance of honor and disgrace?

By superimposing Taoist ideas over a Confucian background, Chang Heng heralded the metaphysical verse and nature poetry of the later centuries.

* The Duke of Chou and K'ung Ch'iu (Confucius).

Another significant development in Han literature is historical prose, of which the most notable work is the *Historical Records* (*Shih Chi*)[4] of Ssu-ma Ch'ien (145–86 B.C.?). The tutelage under his father, a court historiographer, his access to the imperial libraries, his travels in search of historical materials and relics, his indomitable spirit and resolution to leave behind a literary monument for posterity combine to make Ssu-ma Ch'ien a supreme historian. Almost singlehanded and under difficult circumstances and personal hardships,* he was able to complete a voluminous history of 130 chapters (*chüan*) in half a million words.

The *Historical Records*, compiled around 109–91 B.C., exceeds all previous historical works in scope, length, and breadth of coverage. Not merely a simple chronicle of political events, or a history of a particular period or state, it is a comprehensive general history of ancient China from the earliest prehistoric times to the author's own, covering a period, if we accept the traditional reckoning, of more than 3000 years. Its 130 chapters consist of the principal annals of dynasties and emperors, chronological tables, treatises on the various aspects of Chinese government and institutions, as well as histories of hereditary families and biographies of celebrities. Its merits are seen in the unique organization of the work; in the inclusion of treatises on rites, music, measures, calendar, astrology, sacrifice, rivers and channels, money and food; in the vast, all-inclusive range of the biographies of princes, statesmen, generals, scholars, officials (both good and bad), as well as rebels, assassins, roving braves (*yu-hsia*), humorists, actors, court favorites, and sycophants. There are also historical accounts of the non-Han ethnic groups on the periphery of the Han empire from Korea in the northeast to Szechuan, Kweichow, and Yunnan in the southwest.

In all these instances, the *Historical Records* is a pioneer work in both Chinese history and world history. Many of its features are not found in the works of Herodotus and Plutarch, to whom its author has been compared.[5] Herodotus was less articulate in his prose and followed a much simpler chronological pattern in his historical narrative. Ssu-ma Ch'ien and Plutarch shared a love for biographies, but the Chinese historian excelled over the Greek in literary qualities and in influence. The directness of his narrative, the vividness of his description, and the skillful use of dialogue all contribute to a unique style of Chinese historical prose, of which Ssu-ma Ch'ien was a great master with numerous followers and imitators.

The accuracy of some of his stories has been questioned by critics, and

* Ssu-ma Ch'ien suffered the personal tragedy of imprisonment and castration for having incurred the wrath of Emperor Wu in his defense of a Han general who surrendered to the Huns.

many contradictions in details have been pointed out, but these discrepancies, if not due to later interpolations and changes, are mostly minor in nature and almost unavoidable in a work of such immense scope. It must be remembered that Ssu-ma Ch'ien wrote at a time when historical writing was still in its infancy and opportunities for extensive research were limited. Rather, he was to be credited for his discernment in sifting legends from facts, for his profound learning and diligent research, and for his ability to re-create from the dim past in an animated prose a number of splendid historical scenes, events, and personages. Also to his credit is a certain deviation in his work from the norm and orthodoxy; it shows that Ssu-ma Ch'ien, though an official historian, was independent in his political views and historical judgment.

An example of his successful re-creation of history is given below—a famous episode in the "Principal Annal of Hsiang Yü." It relates the beginning of a long struggle for the empire after the fall of Ch'in between Hsiang Yü, who styled himself king, and Liu Pang, the Lord of P'ei, who later became the First Emperor of Han. At that time, Hsiang Yü, the mighty general, was at the head of a large army of 400,000 soldiers; but with a much smaller force Liu Pang arrived first in the expedition to capture the Ch'in capital, Hsien-yang. He then withdrew his army to Pa-shang but sent troops to guard the strategic Han-ku Pass that led to Hsien-yang. The narrative begins at a crucial moment when Hsiang Yü, enraged at Liu Pang's success and his reported ambition to become king, stormed the pass and was about to attack Liu Pang. The latter went hurriedly to visit Hsiang Yü at his encampment in Hung-men and left unscathed through the help of Fan K'uai, his follower, and the intercession of Hsiang Po, Hsiang Yü's uncle, who favored Liu Pang. The story of their meeting at Hung-men, as told by Ssu-ma Ch'ien, has become so popular that since then numerous versions of it have appeared in folk tales and stage plays:

> The next day, Liu Pang went to visit Hsiang Yü with more than a hundred horsemen. When he reached Hung-men, he said to him: "General, you and I had joined forces to attack Ch'in. You fought north of the Yellow River and I south of it. Unexpectedly, I was able to enter the pass first to defeat Ch'in and to meet you again at this place. Meanwhile, the words of some mean fellow have sown discord between us."
>
> "These were the words of Ts'ao Wu-shuang, your lordship's junior subprefect. Otherwise, such a thought would not have occurred to me," said Hsiang Yü.
>
> The same day, Hsiang Yü asked Liu Pang to stay for a feast. Hsiang Yü and Hsiang Po sat facing east; Fan Tseng sat facing south; Liu Pang sat facing north; Chang Liang waited on them,

facing west. Repeatedly Fan Tseng eyed Hsiang Yü and three times he lifted his jade girdle pendant to signal him for a decision, but Hsiang Yü remained silent without responding. Fan Tseng rose, went out, and summoned Hsiang Chuang, saying to him: "The King is too compassionate by nature. You go in to offer a toast, after which you ask to dance with the sword, thereby smiting Liu Pang in his seat and killing him. Otherwise, you and your clan will all be captives!"

Hsiang Chuang then went in to offer the toast. After toasting, he said: "Your Majesty and His Lordship are drinking. As there is nothing to amuse you in the camp, I ask permission to do a sword dance."

"All right," said Hsiang Yü.

Hsiang Chuang drew his sword and rose to dance; Hsiang Po also drew his sword and rose to dance. With his body he often sheltered Liu Pang so that Hsiang Chuang could not smite him.

At that moment Chang Liang went outside the camp gate to see Fan K'uai.

"How is everything today?" asked Fan K'uai.

"Very bad," said Chang Liang, "Right now, Hsiang Chuang has drawn his sword to dance and his aim is often directed at the Lord of P'ei."

"This is indeed urgent," said Fan K'uai. "I ask permission to go in and share his fate."

Immediately Fan K'uai entered the camp gate, carrying his sword and holding his shield. The guards who crossed spears at the gate were about to halt him and refuse him entrance when Fan K'uai tilted his shield to knock them, and the guards fell on the ground. Fan K'uai entered at once, pushed open the curtain and stood, facing west. He stared angrily at Hsiang Yü, his hair bristled and his eye sockets split apart. Hsiang Yü placed his hand on the sword and knelt up, saying: "What is it you want, visitor?"

"He is Fan K'uai, the Lord of P'ei's carriage guard," said Chang Liang.

"A brave fellow! Give him a gallon of wine," said Hsiang Yü.

Right away he was given a gallon of wine. Fan K'uai knelt down to give thanks and then rose; he stood up as he drank it.

"Give him a shoulder of pork," said Hsiang Yü.

Immediately he was given a shoulder of raw pork. Fan K'uai set the shield on the ground, laid the pork shoulder there, drew his sword to cut it, and then ate it.

"Brave fellow, can you drink again?" asked Hsiang Yü.

Fan K'uai said: "I, your servant, am not afraid of death, why should I refuse a gallon of wine? Well, the King of Ch'in had a heart of tiger and wolf. The number of men he had killed could not be counted and he tortured them as if he were afraid he had not done his duty. So the whole world rebelled against him. King Huai of Ch'u made a covenant with the generals: 'Whoever defeats Ch'in and enters Hsien-yang will become king.' Now, the Lord of P'ei was the first to defeat Ch'in and enter Hsien-yang; however, he dared not touch even a single hair but sealed and closed up all the palaces and houses, and withdrew his army to Pa-shang to await the arrival of Your Majesty. The reason he sent the generals to defend the pass is to prevent the passage of bandits and to guard against emergency. After all this exertion and accomplishment, instead of awarding him with a fief, you have listened to trivial talks and intended to kill this man of merit. Such an act is but a repetition of the course that has overthrown Ch'in. Personally, I venture to advise Your Majesty against it."

Hsiang Yü did not answer but merely said, "Sit down."

Fan K'uai sat beside Chang Liang.

After having sat for a short while, Liu Pang rose to go to the privy and beckoned Fan K'uai to go out with him. After Liu Pang had left, Hsiang Yü sent his military commandant, Ch'en P'ing, to call him back. Liu Pang said, "I left without saying goodbye; what should I do?"

Fan K'uai said: "Great action disregards minute details; great etiquette overlooks trivial niceties. At present, these people are like knife and chopping board and we, fish and meat. Why do we have to say goodbye?"

So they all left.

In contrast with this straightforward, swift-moving prose, Ssu-ma Ch'ien was able to retell stories in a lighter, humorous vein, with more elaborate description but without forgetting that the serious duty of a historian was to draw moral lessons. Innumerable examples show the love of anecdotes and intriguing situations that made Ssu-ma Ch'ien a master storyteller, just as his realistic description and sympathetic understanding enabled him to bring historical figures to life. In some of his biographies, historical objectivity suffers from frequent personal comments, often charged with emotion, but if he did not analyze men and events with the detachment and exactitude of a scientist, his literary abilities saved him from the dry matter-of-factness of the other early historians and helped to make his *Historical Records* a masterpiece from which many later writers drew their inspiration.

5 : Old-Style Poetry Versus Modern-Style

The four hundred years from the end of the Han dynasty to the beginning of the T'ang (third to seventh century A.D.) witnessed severe political, social, and cultural dislocations in China as well as the domination of Northern China by the Huns, the Turks, the Tungus, and the Toba. It was an age of darkness and affliction for the Chinese people. Under such circumstances, the Confucian ideals of political stability, social orderliness, and moral respectability gave place to Taoist yearnings for nature and immortal life, and Buddhist engrossment with the other world.

While Buddhism had its best embodiment in sculpture and painting, Taoist thought pervaded the philosophy and poetry of that time. Taoist romanticism found expression especially in the poets, who also practiced it in their daily lives. Most notable among them were the "Seven Sages of the Bamboo Grove," a group of poet-philosophers who sought refuge from politics in the quietness of nature and the oblivion of wine. Yüan Chi (210–263), their leader, was the author of eighty-two poems, entitled "Singing from My Heart," (*Yung-huai shih*), in which he revealed his sentiments in rhythmic and allegorical verse. The poem which follows is one of his more direct and outspoken works; it is the poet's testimony of his change from Confucianism to Taoism:

> Years ago, when I was fourteen or fifteen,
> My inclination was toward *Poetry* and *History*.
> Though coarsely clad, I cherished in my bosom pearls and jade,
> And aspired to live up to Yen and Min.
> I opened the pavilion windows to gaze on the surrounding wilds;
> I mounted the heights to seek the ones I revered.
> But tombs and mounds have covered the mountain ridge
> And the myriad generations are all contemporaries.
> After a thousand autumns and ten thousand years,
> What will become of a glorious name?
> So I am enlightened by Master Hsien-men
> And mock myself for my past gloom.*

* In this poem, the references are as follows: *Poetry* and *History*, respectively the *Classic of Poetry* and the *Classic of History*. Pearls and jade symbolize beautiful and

59

The vogue for drinking among men of letters was another expression of a romantic trend:

> Brief indeed is a man's life!
> So, let's sing over our wine.[1]

The Seven Sages in their retreat in the Bamboo Grove played music, wrote poetry and drank their wine, thus beginning the Chinese tradition of music and wine as the boon companions of the poets, who found in them consolation, relief, and escape from everyday life. Yüan Chi, for instance, avoided a political marriage into a usurping military family by exhausting the patience of the matchmaker as the latter waited in vain for a sober moment in which to talk business with him. Yüan Chi too is said to have given up a high official position for a meaner post in order to live near an expert brewer. There is also an account of how Liu Ling (about 221–300), another Sage and author of a "Hymn to the Virtue of Wine," outwitted his anti-drinking wife by persuading her to prepare for the gods an offering of meat and wine on the occasion of his renunciation of the alcoholic beverage, and then gulping down all the drink that was intended for the celestial spirits.

By its appeal to the emotions rather than to the intellect, music, too, is able to create a state of happy illusion for the poets in their search for an escape from life. Yüan Chi played the zither and Hsi K'ang (223–262), also a musical virtuoso, was noted for his prose-poem about this instrument (Ch'in Fu). He states that music is representative of the voice of nature, its harmony being in oneness with the great rhythm of the universe. As for the zither, especially in the hands of a master player, it can "move the heart and spirit, and give utterance to the secluded emotions." Hsi K'ang's prose-poem concludes with the following epilogue:

> Serene is the power of the zither,
> Its depth unfathomable;
> Pure in body and lofty of heart,
> Its heights hardly attainable.
> Good instruments and artistic hands
> Can they be found in this world?
> Its many silken strings unite in harmony;
> It surpasses all other arts.
> Those who understand music being few,
> Who would be able to treasure it?
> None but the superior man capable of
> Attaining perfection in the elegant zither.[2]

---

valuable thoughts; Yen Yüan and Min Sun, two Confucian disciples noted for their devotion to learning and their equanimity in the face of poverty; Master Hsien-men, a well-known Taoist immortal and the object of admiration of many a would-be Taoist.

Together with wine and music, nature was another romantic influence of the period and gave rise to the "mountain and stream" school of poetry. While Yüan Chi and the others who lived in the more austere northern regions were keenly aware of the delights of the "Bamboo Grove," nature poetry did not thrive in China until after the fourth century, when the occupation of North China by the barbaric tribes drove the Chinese intellectuals to seek new homes south of the Yangtze. The exquisite charms of the southern scenery left a clear imprint on the life and activities of the poets and artists as they came to know the "embroidered rivers and mountains" of the Yangtze valleys. It was then that landscape painting came to play an important part in Chinese art, and nature poetry in Chinese literature.

The most famous nature poet of the time was Hsieh Ling-yün (385–433), who as the prefect of a province traveled extensively in the regions under his jurisdiction. But obviously, he was more interested in visiting scenic spots than in settling lawsuits. For weeks he would be away from his official seat to explore the mountain ridges, gorges, and caves, where nature's hidden beauty was revealed only to the indefatigable searcher. Hsieh Ling-yün was by no means a silent traveler; once he and his retinue made such a commotion that they were suspected of being bandits. Instead of enjoying mutely his pleasurable moments, he would sing in rhythmic words. Consequently, his poems read like travelogues and their titles are reminiscent of the scenes of his many visits. He also found the charm of nature's changing moods at home in his own garden:

> As early spring expels the lingering wintry winds,
> And the new solar rays alter the ancient gloom,
> Spring grass grows on the banks of the pond
> And garden willows charm the birds into song.
>   ("Mounting the Pavilion over the Pond")

The love of nature and the other poetic tendencies of the post-Han era reached their zenith in the works of T'ao Ch'ien (also known as T'ao Yüan-ming, 365–427), who combined in his poems a passion for music and wine, an outlook on life typical of a Taoist recluse, and a sensibility to the delights of nature, particularly its homely and familiar aspects. This earned for him the title "poet of the garden and field." His writings show how he plowed and weeded in his fields, how he gathered his harvest and ate from his garden produce, and how he enjoyed his own new vintage.[3]

Like Hsieh Ling-yün, T'ao Ch'ien was reared in a well-established gentry family of Confucian tradition, but unlike Hsieh, he found the times inopportune for an official career and gave up several minor posts. His experiences as an official were far from rewarding, if not bitter.

According to a famous anecdote, he was once forced by poverty to take up a district magistracy in order to keep his family alive. But after three months in office, he voluntarily relinquished his official seal when he was summoned before a superior, to whom he had to bow in obeisance. He resigned rather than, as he was reported to have said, "cringe for five pecks of rice," which was the regulation salary of a magistrate. Consequently, his distaste for officialdom, and the dangers of a political career at the time of changing dynasties impelled him to retire to his homestead, where he spent the remaining years of his life in humble circumstances as a gentleman farmer. There is an idyllic tale of how he toiled in the front garden while his wife worked in the back.

T'ao Ch'ien was a poet of varied interests. In a conversation between "Shape, Shadow, and Spirit" (the title of one of his poems), he made an imaginary excursion into the metaphysical realm and came back with the following Taoist admonition:

> Excessive thinking harms life;
> We should go where fate leads,
> And ride on the waves of the Great Flux
> Without joy and without fear.
> If life must end, then let it end;
> There is no need to be full of anxieties.

He wrote repeatedly of his enjoyment of books and the zither. But his great and habitual love was wine:

> All my life I have not given up wine:
> If I stopped drinking, I would feel no pleasure.
> To stop at evening—I would not sleep peacefully;
> To stop at dawn—I would not even rise.[4]

This weakness, however, turned out to be his strength. Wine not only gave him pleasure when he drank alone, but also companionship when he shared his cup with friends and neighbors. It also inspired his poetry. In a preface to a group of twenty poems entitled "Drinking Wine," he wrote:

> Living in retirement, I had few pleasures. Furthermore, the evenings were getting unduly long. So whenever I had some famous wine, I drank every night. Watching my shadow, I would empty my cup alone and soon I was drunk. When drunk, I often dashed off a few verses to amuse myself. Before long the paper and ink made quite a pile but the words were without logical sequence. I merely asked a friend to write them out for me so that we could enjoy them together.

In the same casual way, after having blamed his five sons for their stupidity and the worries they had caused him in his declining years, he wrote:

Such being Heaven's decree,
Let me but fill my cup.

The secret of T'ao Ch'ien's success is his ability to "open his heart" in the poems. They lay bare his personality like an open book, in which is recorded the story of a humble farming poet, who in spite of poverty and trouble "ever wore a sunny smile"; who loved his family and neighbors, his books and music, and above all his cup of wine; who enjoyed the bounties of nature found among the willows and chrysanthemums in the back garden. In the poem "Returning to my Garden and Field," he referred to himself as one who was not suited to his vulgar times and who by nature loved mountains and hills. After having fallen inadvertently into "the dusty net,"—the world with all its snares of wealth and rank—he finally returned to his homestead to preserve his rustic ways. He describes his simple idyllic existence:

Elms and willows shade my garden in the back;
Peach and plum trees stand in a row before the hall.
Dimly, dimly, the hamlet appears at a distance;
Faintly, faintly, smoke rises from the village.
Dogs bark in the deep lane;
Cocks crow atop mulberry bushes.
My house and yard are free from dust and confusion;
Being unoccupied, I have enough leisure to spare.
Long have I been in a cage
And now again I can return to nature.

Out in the country there is little human bustle;
In a poor lane, wheels and harness are rarely seen.
In broad daylight the rustic gate is closed;
Dusty thoughts are kept away from empty rooms.
Often in the wilds, parting the grass,
My neighbors and I visit back and forth;
Meeting each other, we have no random talks,
But only remark how the mulberry and hemp have grown.
The mulberry and hemp have grown day by day,
And every day our fields have extended.
Our constant fear is that frost and sleet will come
To kill the crops as if they were weeds.

I plant beans at the foot of the southern hill;
The weeds are thick and the bean sprouts sparse.
Getting up at dawn, I go out to till and to weed;
Shouldering the hoe, I walk home with the moon.
The path is narrow, the grass and shrubs are tall,
And the evening dew dampens my clothes.
That my clothes are wet I don't mind at all;
I only hope that my wishes are not thwarted.

Happily he attained his wishes and spent the remaining years of his life in a contemplative peace of mind, as is shown in the following verses:

> I built my cottage among the habitations of men,
> And yet there is no clamor of carriages and horses.
> You ask: "Sir, how can this be done?"
> "A heart that is distant creates its own solitude."
> I pluck chrysanthemums under the eastern hedge,
> Then gaze afar towards the southern hills.
> The mountain air is fresh at the dusk of day;
> The flying birds in flocks return.
> In these things there lies a deep meaning;
> I want to tell it, but have forgotten the words.[5]

The wonderful mood created by this poetry expresses the ease and leisure, the serenity and harmony with nature and environment that together constitute the highest bliss of life according to Chinese philosophy. T'ao Ch'ien brings to his readers his simple and yet profound contemplation of life and nature, his warm personal insights, and the spontaneous flashes of his candid heart, which have a great appeal for the Chinese people, and must, because human emotion and thought are universal, endear him to others as well.

Of all the major Chinese poets T'ao Ch'ien is perhaps the easiest one for Western readers to appreciate. He would be a good choice for a first contact with Chinese poetry because his poems are relatively free of literary allusions, and do not demand a knowledge of Chinese history and culture to be appreciated. Anyone who enjoys the warm humanity of Robert Frost's poetry will also enjoy T'ao Ch'ien's. His poems should be read meditatively, ideally out-of-doors on a summer's day, or by the fireside of a winter's night with a cup of warm wine close to hand! Everything he wrote is worth reading, and fortunately a wide selection of his writings has appeared in English translation.[6]

Though highly praised by posterity both in China and abroad, T'ao Ch'ien exerted little influence on the poetry of his time. The main literary tendency of the fifth century was towards an ornate and artificial style. Parallel structure was used by the poets to adorn their verses, and poetic allusions were frequent. To display their erudition, writers vied with each other in searching for unfamiliar, obscure quotations to use in literary contests at court and in gatherings of the literati. There was an equal emphasis on sound and rhythm to create verse harmony. It was then that the theory of matching tones was first evolved and later adopted in poetry. As to content, the poems reflect the extravagant and licentious life of the courtiers. Frivolous and decadent in spirit, they contain descriptions of lovely women in languorous poses, and objects and clothing suggestive of sex, such as hair combs, stockings, and pillows.

The representative poet of the period was Shen Yo (441–513), who lived through three dynasties in the course of his long life. A high official, he was a patron of poets and critics. He was chiefly known for the famous prosodic work, the *Table of the Four Tones*. Well pleased with his discovery of the tonal distinctions, he once remarked that for one thousand years the poets had been writing without knowing the secret of Chinese prosody until he came along to unravel it!

The four tones are (1) *p'ing* or even tone, in which the pitch remains at the same level in the enunciation of a word; (2) *shang* or rising tone, in which the sound of a word rises in its intonation; (3) *ch'ü* or falling tone, in which the sound tapers off; (4) *ju* or "entering" tone, in which the voice is abruptly arrested in pronouncing a word. The monosyllabic nature of the Chinese language does not permit it to have stressed accents; instead, it has these pitched accents to distinguish words of the same sound. This subtle distinction in intonation is hardly discernible to foreigners and even baffles Chinese who do not have a good ear and a proper linguistic training. But the tonal differentiation is extremely important in studying Chinese poetry of the "Modern Style," which owed its rise to Shen Yo's discovery of the tones.

Unlike those of the "Old Style," which make no attempt at tonal arrangement, poems of the "Modern Style," later developed by T'ang dynasty poets, follow a set of tonal patterns. In these patterns, actually only two tones are distinguished; in contradistinction to the *p'ing* tone, the other three, *shang*, *ch'ü*, and *ju*, are grouped together to form the *tse*, that is, the deflected or uneven tone. For instance, in a five-word poem of four lines, a typical tonal arrangement is as follows:

> *tsê-tsê p'ing-p'ing tsê,*
> *p'ing-p'ing tsê-tsê p'ing;*
> *p'ing-p'ing p'ing tsê-tsê,*
> *tsê-tsê tsê p'ing-p'ing.*

An important point to notice here is that there is an antithesis of *p'ing* and *tsê* sounds in each of the two couplets, and that the last words of the second and fourth lines have the same tone, either the *p'ing* tone as found here or the *tsê* tone as in some other patterns. It is here that the rhyme occurs. In a Chinese poem, the scheme is that every even line rhymes, no matter whether the poem be of four, eight or a hundred lines. While each poem has generally one rhyme, it is permissible to use several rhymes in a longer poem.

In addition to tonal pattern and standard rhyme, parallelism is another feature of Chinese poetry. By parallelism is meant that in a couplet, the words in the first line are to match or pair with words of the same position in the second line. The first four lines in Shen Yo's poem on a court beauty can be translated literally as follows to show their parallel structure:

> slackening reins, dismounts carved carriage,
> changing clothes, attends jade bed.
>
> slanting hairpin, reflects autumn waters,*
> opening mirror, compares spring dresses.

For an eight-line poem of the Modern Style, parallelism is required of the second and third couplets. In other poetic types, too, parallel lines are often used as a kind of ornamental device to enhance poetic beauty.

While the courtiers and scholars were busily engaged in producing embellished literary verses, the common people continued the tradition of the early Han period in the creation of simple folk poetry. Generally speaking, the folk poetry of the three hundred years from the third century to the sixth can be divided into the south and the north in accordance with the political division. In the south, the Chinese dynasties had their capital in Nanking, not far from the Wu district around the modern city of Soochow; it was here that the "Songs of Tzu-yeh" were first sung. These short love lyrics have been attributed to a poetess of that name. It is likely, however, that the individual Tzu-yeh never existed; at least, these songs could not have been written by one person. Rather, it is the genius of the locality that has produced this group of exquisite poems, often of a soft plaintive tone, which differ from the love poems in the *Classic of Poetry* in the same way that the southern temperament differs from the northern.

About one hundred and twenty-four of these southern songs have been preserved. One of them, entitled the "Big Tzu-yeh Song," may serve as an introduction to the whole group:

> Of the several hundred songs,
> Tzu-yeh is the most lovely.[7]
> Loftily, it speaks in a clear voice,
> Plain, supple, and spontaneous.

The "clear voice" refers, probably, to the fact that the songs were sung by the women of Wu without any musical accompaniment. In this respect, the folk songs of the south, sometimes called the New Music Bureau poems, are different from the original Music Bureau poems, which were sung to the accompaniment of instrumental music.

The *Tzu-yeh* poems have themes common to folk songs of this type. In them beats the heart of a maiden in love:

---

* That is, beautiful eyes, bright and clear like autumn ripples.

> All night I could not sleep;
> How glittering was the moonlight!
> It seemed that I heard my lover's voice.
> Idly I answered, and "yes" it echoed.

Or the eternal complaint of love's fickleness:

> I remain as the North Star
> For a thousand years without change.
> Your heart is like the white sun;
> It goes east in the morning and west in the evening.

Sometimes she describes naively her maidenly embarrassment:

> Holding my skirt with the belt unfastened,
> My eyebrows unpainted, I walk to the front window.
> The silken dress surges about;
> If it opens a little, I shall chide the spring wind.

At times, she confides with a light heart the enjoyable moments of love and play:

> Taking my pillow, I lie at the north window
> When my love comes to sport with me.
> In playing, he often gets rude.
> Love—how long can it last?

Unlike these southern lyrics, the northern poems are characterized by more direct, unrestrained, and often robust expressions. The love poems, war poems, pastoral poems, and other occasional poems all reflect the bleakness of the northern scenery and the harsh aspects of life after long years of privation and war. Even the love poems have a blunt and artless touch not found in the *Tzu-yeh* poems:

> Sad and joyless in my stomach,
> I'd like to be, my bonny man, your whip:
> In and out, stringed on your arm,
> Skipping; or lying beside your knee.
> ("Plucking Willow Twigs," Song 2)

The war poems display a sense of tragic desolation:

> The men are indeed pitiable creatures:
> Leaving home, they have the sorrows of death—
> Their corpses rot away in the gully;
> Their white bones none collects.
> ("The Songs of Ch'i-yü," Song 4)

67

Or the virile spirit of the hardy northerners:

> A lusty steed for the brave fellow;
> A brave fellow for the lusty steed!
> Only after he has ridden in the yellow dust,
> Could a fellow be adjudged a male or a female.
> ("Plucking Willow Twigs," Song 5)

While weak and effeminate men were looked down upon, brave women achieved a heroic status for their military exploits, as in the "Ballad of Mu-lan." A warrior-maiden disguised as a man, Mu-lan joins the army in her father's place, travels thousands of miles, and fights in a hundred battles before she returns triumphantly twelve years later—her sex undiscovered—to her native village:

> Father and mother, hearing of their daughter's return,
> Go outside the city walls to help and support her by the hand.
> Elder sister, hearing the younger one's return,
> Goes over her rouge make-up in front of the door.
> Little brother, hearing elder sister's return,
> Sharpens the knife, swish-swashing toward the pig and sheep.
> I open the door to my eastern chamber;
> I sit on the bed in my western chamber.
> I slip off my wartime robe,
> And put on my old-time dress.
> Facing the window, I arrange my cloud-like hair;
> Looking into the mirror, I adorn myself with a yellow patch.
> I go out to the door to greet my messmates,
> And they are all stunned with surprise:
> Though they have marched with her for twelve years,
> They have not known that Mu-lan is a girl.
>
> The male rabbit has skipping legs,
> The female rabbit has bleary eyes;
> The two walk side by side on the ground
> And none can tell the male from the female.[8]

6 : Great T'ang Poets

In the T'ang dynasty (618–906), China became the hub of the Eastern world, and all roads from Asia led to Ch'ang-an, its most magnificent metropolis. This was an era of brilliant intellectual and literary activities unsurpassed by any other period in Chinese history. The splendor and the subsequent decline of the T'ang period are reflected in its poetry. T'ang China, like Elizabethan England, was virtually a nation of singing birds. Even through the lapse of more than ten centuries, a large bulk of T'ang poetry, consisting of approximately 50,000 poems by some 2,300 poets, has been preserved to this day.[1]

The writing of poetry, which has attracted the Chinese people since ancient times, became especially popular in the T'ang dynasty. Poets were honored by the public and, in a number of instances, received the patronage of the court. The majority of T'ang poets were officials who had passed the literary examinations, but whose claim to fame was based not so much on their administrative ability as on their poetic achievements. There were also numerous poets among the ranks of emperors and empresses, generals and courtiers, Taoist hermits and Buddhist monks, court ladies and sing-song girls, who together contributed to the greatness of T'ang poetry.

Political stability, economic affluence, imperial patronage, and the high honors accorded poetic talents in public life and state examinations all fostered the growth of poetry in the T'ang era, which attained its full glory during the reign of the Brilliant Emperor (Ming Huang), who was himself a writer of poetry as well as its patron. But it was also during this time that the T'ang empire, having reached the apex of its grandeur, started to decline. The rebellion in 755 of An Lu-shan, a Tartar general, shattered the nation and plunged it into chaos and disturbance from which it never fully recovered. The year 755 was the "great divide" in T'ang politics as in T'ang poetry.

The history of the latter can be divided into four periods: (1) Early T'ang and (2) Flourishing T'ang, representing respectively the freshness and exuberance of its poetry; (3) Mid-T'ang and (4) Late T'ang, during which poetry became mellow and somber before it finally withered away. A host of poets emerged in each of these periods, but only three major figures, Wang Wei, Li Po, and Tu Fu, can be mentioned in this chapter as representative of T'ang poetry at its zenith.

Wang Wei (699–759) exemplifies in his life and works a happy combination of the arts of painting, music, and poetry. His monochrome landscapes are just as famous as his poems. It is said that there are pictures in his poetry, even as there is poetry in his paintings. But for a brief interruption by An Lu-shan's rebellion, Wang Wei had a long, uneventful official career in North China, mostly in Ch'ang-an. He was detained by the rebels at Loyang at the time of their occupation, but was able to clear himself later of a collusion charge with a poem he had written about a feast which An Lu-shan gave at the Pool of Frozen Green in the palace:

> The myriad households are sad at heart and wild smoke arises.
> When will the hundred officials again have audience with Heaven?
> The autumn locust drops its flowers in the empty courtyard;
> From the Pool of Frozen Green is heard the sound of flutes and strings.

These lines were taken as a testimony of his loyalty to the T'ang emperor, symbolized here as "Heaven." The "wild smoke" indicates that it is not chimney smoke from household cooking but the smouldering remains of houses burnt during the rebellion. In his last years, he retired to his country residence at Wang-ch'uan outside of the capital and enjoyed there a leisurely life of reading Buddhist canons and discussing metaphysical ideas with his monk friends. He was devoted to his mother, who was also a Buddhist; remained celibate for thirty years after his wife's death; and became a vegetarian in the later part of his life.

Wang Wei's Buddhist inclinations are clearly expressed in his poems. Writing to one of his Buddhist friends ("Two Poems to the Buddhist Scholar Hu, Written When We Were Both Sick"), he boldly proclaimed in the second poem:

> To cultivate blessings, I worship Buddhist saints,
> Mocking Confucius for his quest for virtue.

In a quatrain from the first poem, he indulged in more speculative philosophizing:

> How could sufferings be relieved through purification?
> To know the Path is to get lost at the ford.
> Indeed, sickness comes from worldly love
> And poverty begins with the pursuit of greed.

As a Buddhist thinker, Wang Wei loved peace and meditation in the manner of Zen Buddhism, whose concept is clearly indicated in the last line of the poem "To Sub-prefect Chang":

In late years I desire only peace;
For worldly affairs my heart has no concern.
I have no long-range plan for my own care;
All I know is to return to the old woods,
Where the pine wind blows on my loosened belt
And the mountain moon shines on the strung zither.
You ask the law of failure and success—
"The fisherman's song enters the river bank deep."

His enjoyment of a leisurely life amidst the beauties of nature is shown in "My Retreat at Mount Chung-nan":

In my mid-age I loved greatly the Path;
In late years I made my home by the Southern Hill:
When the spirit moves, I often wander alone
Among lovely scenes known only to myself.
I ramble where the stream ends,
Then sit and watch the clouds rise.
Occasionally I meet an old man in the woods,
So we talk and laugh without thinking of going home.

Or in "Living Leisurely at Wang-ch'uan, to P'ei Ti, the Budding Genius":

Cold mountains turn verdant blue;
Autumn stream daily flows on.
Leaning on a staff outside the wattled door,
I face the wind and listen to the evening cicada.
At the ford lingers the setting sun;
From the village hamlet rises one lonely wisp.
Again it happens that Chieh Yü has been drunk,*
Singing madly before the Five Willows.**

Like T'ao Ch'ien, Wang Wei is best known for his nature poems. His religious propensities and his love of nature, especially its calm and peaceful aspects, combine in the following poem, "In my Country Residence at Wang-ch'uan after a Long Rain":

Rain being stored in the empty woods, smoke rises slowly.
Boiled herb and cooked rice are sent to the eastern fields.
Over the vast, watery lowlands a white egret flies;
Under the shady summer trees the yellow oriole sings.
Meditating in the mountains, I watch the morning hibiscus;
Fasting under the pines, I pluck dewy sunflower seeds.
After the old rustic has ceased to contend for the seat of honor,
Why should the sea gulls still become suspicious?

* A hermit, called the Madman of Ch'u, (*Analects*, XVIII, 5), here referring to P'ei Ti.
** An allusion to T'ao Ch'ien, who calls himself the Master of the Five Willows; here the poet compares himself to T'ao Ch'ien.

He wrote some fifty poems about beautiful places at Wang-ch'uan, such as the Deer Stockade, the Golddust Spring, the Whitestone Sandbank, the Spicetree Orchard, the Elegant Apricot Lodge, the Lakeview Pavilion, and others. Take, for instance, the poem "Bamboo Lodge":

> I sit alone in the dark bamboo grove,
> Playing the zither and whistling long.
> In this deep wood no one would know—
> Only the bright moon comes to shine.

or the "Deer Stockade":

> Deserted mountains—not a man is seen,
> Only the sound of voices can be heard.
> The sunbeam, entering the deep wood,
> Reflects again on the green moss.

In these poems the beauty of nature is reproduced realistically; its charm is further enlivened by the animated but unobtrusive presence of the human spirit. Written in the same technique but in a different vein are the following lines:

> You, sir, who came from the old village,
> Should know the things that happened there:
> The day you left, in front of my silken window,
> Was the cold plum clothed with blooms?

Wang Wei's descriptive poems excel in pictorial effects. Just as a painter creates his landscape with a few strokes of the brush, so Wang Wei, the poet-painter, produced in his poems poetic pictures with a few choice expressions. The artistry of words is very pronounced in the following couplet that describes the scene he witnessed on his way home to Mount Sung:

> Desolate city-wall overlooks ancient ford;
> Setting sun fills autumn hills.

These ten brief words, here translated literally, evoke vividly an entire landscape complete with time and season, near object and distant view, and most important, a prevailing mood. The poem describes neither the freshness of spring nor the exuberance of summer, but the somberness of autumn, behind which winter cannot be far away. The time is late afternoon, perhaps approaching twilight. The scene in the foreground shows the city wall and the ferry, while in the distance looms a range of hills flooded by the rays of the setting sun. This landscape, however, would not be so impressive if it were not for the prevailing mood of desolation that broods over it. Thus the city wall is dilapidated, the ferry ancient and

The "Bamboo Lodge". From *T'ang-shih hua-p'u* (A Collection of Illustrations of T'ang Poetry).

deserted, the sun setting, and the hills are imbued with autumn hues—through a combination of these key words is created a single, deep, and unified emotion. Yet this feeling of desolation is by no means starkly oppressive; although the near view is dark and dismal, there are colors and even splendor, as we can imagine, in the refulgent afterglow on the distant hills.

Li Po (701–762), a contemporary of Wang Wei, is perhaps the best known of all Chinese poets. A precocious boy, he started to write poetry during his childhood days in Szechuan but did not gain widespread fame until, in his early forties, after years of traveling and visits to the mountains and rivers of Central and North China, he reached Ch'ang-an, then at the height of its prosperity and magnificence. There he was greeted by his fellow poets and soon received the patronage of the Brilliant Emperor. He was made a member of the Han-lin Academy (for scholars with the highest literary attainment) and invited to compose poems for court festivities. He was also a frequent visitor to the city taverns. Once, as told by his younger friend, Tu Fu, he was heavily drunk in a wine-shop when he received an imperial summons:

> A hundred poems Li Po wrote after a cask of wine.
> He was asleep at a tavern in Ch'ang-an
> When the Emperor called; he would not board the imperial barge,
> But said, "Your humble servant is a god of wine."

Li Po's court life, brief but brilliant, has been the subject of many anecdotes. There is, for instance, the story—a fitting sequel to the above poem—of his having been so drunk that he had to be splashed with water to regain soberness, after which he dashed off more than ten songs for his sovereign. Another tells of Li Po's asking the emperor's favorite eunuch to pull off his boots. Because of this insult, it is said, the eunuch slandered him before the emperor. Whatever the reason, after three years in the capital, Li Po left for a prolonged tour of the empire, during which he was entertained as the honored guest of local officials, his fame as a poet having spread far and wide.

At the time of An Lu-shan's rebellion, Li Po was traveling in the Yangtze region. Though he was not personally affected by the war that raged in North China, he became involved in another rebellion, that of the Prince of Yung—one of the Brilliant Emperor's numerous sons—who commanded the T'ang army in East Central China. After the prince's defeat, Li Po was imprisoned and later exiled to the southwest interior for complicity in the uprising. Before he reached his destination an amnesty brought him back to the lower Yangtze, where he died of sickness several years later. Widely circulated is the legend of his romantic death one night as a result of having leaned too far out of the boat in a drunken effort to embrace the moon's reflection in the water.

Romanticism is the keynote of Li Po's life as of his poetry. A rebel against all forms and conventions, he believed in the enjoyment of the good things of life such as poetry and music, love and friendship. Like all T'ang poets, Li Po wrote numerous occasional poems: farewells to his friends, drinking songs, and the like. A constant theme is the parting of friends, as in "To Wang Lun":

> Li Po takes a boat and is about to depart
> When suddenly he hears the sound of footsteps
>   and singing on the shore.
> The water in the Peach Blossom Pool is
>   a thousand feet deep,
> But not as deep as Wang Lun's parting love for me.

Or in "Parting at a Wine-shop in Nanking":

> Willow blossoms, blown by the wind, fill the wine-shop
>   with fragrance.
> A girl of Wu, pressing wine afresh, urges the guests to drink.
> The young men of Nanking come to bid me farewell;
> The traveler and those seeing him off all drain their cups.
> "Please go and ask the river flowing to the east,
> If it can go farther than the parting love of a friend?"

While parting is sweet sorrow, drinking with one's boon companions is a pleasure not to be lightly forborne, particularly as an avenue of escape from the sorrows of life. The following is a translation of the song, "Wine will be Served":

> Do you not see the waters of the Yellow River, coming down
>   from Heaven,
> Rush and roll into the sea, never to return?
> Do you not see how men mourn their white hair at the bright
>   mirror in the great hall—
> What was silken black in the morning has turned to snow
>   by night?
> To be elated in life, one should enjoy oneself to the full
> And never let the golden goblet stand empty toward the moon.
> My Heaven-endowed talents must have their use;
> Throw away a thousand gold coins, and they will all return.
> Roast the sheep, slaughter the ox! Let's take our pleasure,
> And with one long drink, empty three hundred cups!
> Young scholar Tan-ch'iu, Master Ts'en,
> Wine will be served;
> Don't stop drinking!

Let me sing you a song;
Please incline your ears to listen.
Bells, drums, and jade vessels are not to be treasured;
One desires only to be forever drunk, never to be sober again.
The sages of olden times are all still and lonely.
Only the great drinkers have left their names behind.
Prince Ch'en* once gave a feast at the Temple of Peace and Joy;
A cask of wine worth ten thousand cash they drank, indulging
        in mirth and jest.
Why should the host say he has no money?
Go and fetch wine to drink with you.
The five-colored horse,
The thousand-gold fur—
Let's call the boy to take them out and pawn them for good wine,
That drinking together we may dispel the sorrows of myriad years.

When no friends are around, drinking companions can be sought among inanimate objects. His mood becomes more sober and his imagination soars in the poem, "Drinking Alone under the Moon":

With a pot of wine among the flowers,
All alone I drink—no dear ones at my side.
Raising my cup, I invite the bright moon
To make with my shadow a group of three.
But the moon does not know how to drink
And the shadow vainly follows me around.
For a while, with moon and shadow as companions,
I would seek pleasure while it is spring.
I sing and the moon rambles;
I dance and the shadow runs helter-skelter.
While sober, we enjoy ourselves together;
After drinking, we part with each other.
Forever, we'll pledge a non-sentimental journey,
Awaiting each other at the distant Milky Way.

In love and romance Li Po sought refuge from melancholy. During his travels he encountered many beautiful women who lingered in his memory and found a place in his poetry. The lovely lasses of Wu (Soochow) and Yüeh (Chekiang) in the Yangtze region enchanted and enticed him:

The lasses of Wu are mostly dazzling white.
They love to rock the boat for fun.
They sell their glances and fling away the heart of spring,
Plucking flowers to flirt with the wandering man.

* Ts'ao Chih, the poet-prince, see pp. 48–49.

Equally charming are the Tartar girls of the North:

> The Tartar girl with a face like a flower—
> She stands before the stove,* laughing at the spring wind.
> She laughs at the spring wind
> And swishes her silken dress.
> Where would you go and get drunk, if not here with her?

At Ch'ang-an he met and wrote a poem "To a Beautiful Woman on the Road":

> A noble steed with a proud gait tramples the fallen flowers;
> The swinging whip brushes straightway a gaily colored carriage.
> A beautiful woman laughs and pulls up the pearl curtain;
> Pointing to a red pavilion in the distance, she says:
> "There is my humble home."

He also sang of the lamentation of court ladies confined to the forbidden grounds, all alone and unloved as in "Grief at the Jade Stairs":

> White dew grows on the jade stairs;
> In the long night it has wet her silk stockings.
> Now she lowers the crystal screen
> And watches through the beads an autumn moon.

And of the sorrows of women waiting in vain for the return of their husbands. His "Song of Ch'ang-kan" relates the story of a neighbor boy and girl who were married early, the girl at fourteen. In spite of their childhood acquaintance—once the boy riding a bamboo horse had come circling around her and thrown plums at her—the young bride was shy on the nuptial night:

> So bashful that I never smiled;
> I bent my head low toward the dark wall
> And would not turn once to your thousand calls.

When she was sixteen he left her for a long journey up the Yangtze Gorge and had never been heard of since:

> Your lingering footsteps at the front gate
> Were hidden, every one of them, under the green moss.
> The moss was too deep to sweep away,
> And the leaves fell with the first spring wind.
> In the eighth month, the butterflies turned yellow,
> In pairs they flew over the grass in the west garden.
> Moved by this sight, my heart was saddened,
> Lest the bright cheeks would soon become furrowed.

* Where wine is warmed.

76

Another means of escape from the heartbreaks of life is to nourish one's spirit in communion with nature. In accordance with the Taoist philosophy, Li Po considered this life as "a big dream," for which one should not toil with one's body in vain. Awaking from his drunken stupor in the front porch one afternoon, he heard a bird sing among the flowers in the courtyard:

> "Please, what season is it?"
> The spring breeze whispers to the oriole.
> Moved by it, I want to sigh,
> And so by myself I drink.
> Singing aloud, I await the bright moon;
> The song having ended, all my feelings I forget.

While forgetfulness of this existence may be obtained through singing and drinking, it would be preferable to withdraw from this world to lead the life of a hermit:

> Lazily I wave a white feather fan,
> And lie naked in the green forest;
> I hang my cap on a crag,
> My bare head sprinkled by the pine wind.

Or a nature lover:

> All the birds have flown up and gone;
> A lonely cloud floats leisurely by.
> We never tire of looking at each other—
> Only the mountain and I.

However, it is in the bosom of nature itself that the best healing influences are to be found. There one nourishes the wounds of life and cultivates the purity of spirit in ethereal surroundings. In the famous lines, "Conversation in the Mountains," Li Po wrote:

> You ask why I nestle in the green mountains.
> I laugh but answer not—my heart is serene.
> Peach blossoms and flowing waters go without a trace;
> There is another Heaven and Earth beyond the world of man.

Quietude, serenity, and leisurely life in the mountains may have consoled Li Po in his moments of agony, but he was too restless to be able to stay long in any place even with such allurements. He was one of the most travelled among Chinese poets. As we have seen, his footsteps covered a large part of the mountains and rivers of this great land. Like his predecessor, Hsieh Ling-yün, he recorded in his travel poems the enjoyable moments and lovely scenes he had encountered. But instead of describing them directly, he related his impressions of them in majestic, imaginative lines as in the "Song of Lu-shan":

Lu Mountain stands gracefully along the Southern Dipper,
Displaying its cloud-like embroideries like a "Ninefold Screen,"
Its shadows falling on the crystal lake with a dark-blue sheen.
The Golden Gate opens onto two lofty peaks;
From the Silver Stream hang upside down three stone beams,
Overlooking at a distance the cascade at the Censer Peak.
Winding precipices and rocky ledges rise to the blue sky,
Where azure shadows and red clouds reflect the morning sun,
And no flight of birds could reach the distant sky of Wu.
I climb to the top to gain a grand view of Heaven and Earth:
The Great River, vast and boundless, flowing on without return;
Yellow clouds, driven by the wind for thousands of miles;
And white waves, rolling away in nine folds from the snowy peaks.

In the poem, "T'ien-mu Mountains Ascended in a Dream," he blended the grandeur of nature with the fairyland of his creation, thereby producing a mood of delightful surprise and a willing suspension of disbelief:

Halfway up appears the sun in the sea;
In midair is heard the Cock of Heaven.
Among a thousand crags and ten thousand ravines, the road meanders.
Lured by flowers and leaning on a rock, suddenly, I find it is dark.
Bears roar and dragons chant, agitating the mountain spring;
The deep woods quake with fear and the towering ridges tremble.
The clouds turn dark blue with the impregnating rain;
On the placid waters mists rise.
Lightning flashes and thunders rumble;
Hills and peaks crack and crash.
The stone gate in the fairy cave
Splits asunder with a shattering sound:
The blue depths are vast and their bottom is invisible.
The sun and moon shine on the Tower of Gold and Silver;
Clad in rainbow raiments and riding on the wind,
The Lords of the Cloud descend in a train,
With tigers playing the harp and phoenixes drawing the carriages;
The fairies stand in long rows like a field of hemp.
Suddenly my soul is startled and shivers;
Dazed, I wake up in fright and a long sigh I heave.

His power of description reaches its zenith in the lines on Mount Omei in the song, "Hard Road to Shu":

Above is the Tall Signpost where six dragons encircle the sun;
Below, the twisted river with lashing waves and whirling eddies.
Even the winged yellow crane finds it impassable,
So pity the apes and monkeys that grow weary of climbing.
The Green Clay, how it coils and curls,

Making nine turns around the peak in each hundred steps!
Brushing Orion, passing the Well Star, the traveler gazes and gasps;
He beats his breast and sits down to heave a long sigh.
May I ask when you would return from this journey westward?
Perilous paths and precipitous cliffs are hard to climb.
Seen only are the screaming birds in an ancient forest,
The male flying after the female as they circle the trees.
Also heard are the cuckoos that wail at the night moon,
Mournfully in the lonely mountains.
The road to Shu is as hard to scale as the blue sky—
Even to hear of it turns the bright cheek pale.
The interlocked peaks are barely a foot below heaven,
Where withered pines hang, top down, from the ledges precipitous.
Foaming torrents and plunging cataracts outroar one another;
Thundering down myriad ravines, they lash the cliffs and
       roll the rocks.

This turbulent and mighty view of nature is found almost nowhere else in Chinese poetry. Li Po wrote in an original and bold style. Disdaining the restraints and exigencies of prosody, his words seem to flow spontaneously and soar with his spirit as he dashes off his lines with great ease and facility of expression. They are laden with overflowing sentiments (sometimes melancholic, yet often warm and genial), which crave for expression, sympathy, and appreciation, and which readily touch responsive chords in the reader's heart. Li Po has been called a "banished angel," for his poems are unearthly, transcendental, and touched with a divine madness.

In contrast, his younger contemporary, Tu Fu (712–770), excels in craftsmanship and technique. The two are as wide apart in temperament and philosophical outlook as in poetic practice. While Li Po, the Taoist romanticist, sought escape from this world in wine, women, and nature, Tu Fu, the Confucian moralist, was anxious to be useful to society and country, his one ambition in life being to serve his sovereign faithfully. And just as Li Po summarized in his romantic songs the grandeur of the T'ang dynasty, so Tu Fu testified in his realistic and humanitarian poems to the disorders and troubles that befell the dynasty.

Tu Fu came from a poor scholarly family in Honan. Notwithstanding many years of studious preparation, he failed in the literary examinations which he took at Ch'ang-an, but was awarded later some minor official position at court. Trapped there by the An Lu-shan rebellion, he suffered many hardships. Subsequently, he escaped from the rebels and made his way, starving and in rags, to the temporary court of the new monarch, who had succeeded the Brilliant Emperor. After the restoration, he took up his post at the capital as a censor, but was soon relieved of his position for his outspoken defense of a fellow official. Finally he settled down on a minor local job in Ch'eng-tu and spent his remaining years in a thatched cottage, writing poetry and leading a life of peace and contentment. The death of his friend and patron, the military governor, caused him to resume his wanderings in his old age. He died while traveling in Hunan in Central China. A popular anecdote attributes his death to overeating in a feast after having been rescued from a flood.

A good Confucianist, Tu Fu was first and foremost a devoted family man. Especially touching are those poems to his wife and children, from whom he was separated for years on account of poverty and the wars. One of the moving passages in a long poem, "Uttering my Sentiments in Five Hundred Words on My Trip from the Capital to Feng-hsien," describes his returning home from a hazardous journey only to find that his youngest son had died of hunger:

> My old wife stays in a strange land,
> Our ten mouths separated by wind and snow.
> Who would have left them long uncared for?
> So I went home to share their hunger and thirst.
> Entering the door, I heard a loud wail;
> Our youngest boy had died of starvation.
> How could I forbear from sharing this great sorrow?
> Our neighbors too sobbed and sighed.
> Ashamed am I to be a father
> That the lack of food should have caused his death.

The following poem, "Moonlight Night," was written when he was alone in rebellion-torn Ch'ang-an, thinking of his wife at Fu-chou:

> Tonight the moonlight at Fu-chou—
> She will be watching alone from her chamber.
> I pity the little ones, so far away,
> Who have no recollection of Ch'ang-an.
> Fragrant mist wets her cloudy tresses;
> Bright beams chill her jade-white arms.
> When could we lean toward the soft door curtain,
> The moon shining on us, till our tears are dry?

In "Northern Journey," another homeward trip under more perilous circumstances during the war, Tu Fu drew a vivid picture of a family reunion with all its pathos and humor:

> After a year I reached the thatched cottage—
> The clothes on my wife and children had a hundred patches.
> Our sad wailings were echoed by the pines,
> And the grieved spring shared our sobs.

The boy whom I fondled all my life—
The color of his skin whiter than snow—
Seeing his father he cried, his back toward me;
Dirty and greasy were his sockless feet.
My two little girls were in front of the bed,
Their patched dress barely over the knee:
The waves ripped from the sea pattern,
And old embroideries turned zigzag—
The sea god and the purple phoenix
Standing upside down in the short skirt.
The old man was troubled and sick at heart,
He vomited and purged, then slept for several days.
"How could I be without silk in my bag
To save you from shivering in the cold?"

Now, powder and black are unwrapped,
Quilts and bedclothes gradually displayed.
The face of my emaciated wife shines again;
And the doting girls comb their own hair.
Imitating their mother in every manner,
They daub at random the morning toilet;
Then, with powder and rouge all over them,
They draw their eyebrows wide and broad.
To return alive to these children
Is like forgetting one's own thirst and hunger.
When asking for things, they vie to pull my beard,
But who could straightway howl at them in a rage?
Remembering the sorrows suffered in the rebel camp,
I bear willingly all the hubbub and turmoil.
Newly returned, I will just cherish my sentiments;
Why should there be talk about making a living?

Tu Fu also wrote about the daily routines of family life, with its warmth, joy, and peace, and the journeys they took together. In spite of the hardships on the road, he seemed to have enjoyed their trip to the Szechuan mountains:

The servants talk to each other as they penetrate
    the bamboo grove;
The children shout as they enter the clouds.
The hobgoblins are startled when the stones are overturned;
The black apes and chipmunks fall at the arrow shot.
These indeed provide fun and mirth,
To console me at the extremities of my journey.
    ("Three Poems Written on a Trip to the Szechuan
    Mountains from Lang-chou, Accompanied by My Wife
    and Children")

The intimate and uneventful aspects of his home life in Ch'eng-tu are described:

> My old wife draws on the paper a chessboard;
> The children hammer wire to make a fish hook.
> ("River Village")

Also:

> In the morning I take my old wife for a boat ride;
> When the sun shines, I watch the children bathe in a clear stream.
> ("Boat Ride")

While these vignettes of his personal life reveal Tu Fu as a family man, his accounts of the changing times rank him foremost as a social historian. His poems, the best surviving documents from a critical historical period, record faithfully and vividly the deterioration of Chinese society, the extravagance of the high officials, the privation of the masses, conscription for military campaigns, and the disasters and devastations of war, which the poet personally experienced. Even in the supposedly prosperous reign of the Brilliant Emperor, Tu Fu already foresaw the danger signals and the approaching storm in the inequality between the rich and poor, the heavy taxation on the people, and the draft for border warfare, which he indicated in the poem "My Trip from the Capital to Feng-hsien":

> The silk that was bestowed at the vermilion court
> Came originally from some poor shivering women;
> Their husbands were whipped and flogged
> So that it could be levied as a tribute to the imperial city.
>
> .   .   .   .   .
>
> Inside the vermilion gate wine and meat are stinking;
> On the roadside lie the bones of people frozen to death.
>
> .   .   .   .   .
>
> All my life I have been exempt from taxes,
> My name has not been listed in the muster roll.
> If I should feel bitter and grieved at past experiences,
> The commoners indeed would have more reason to be angry.
> Silently I think of those who were unemployed,
> And of the soldiers summoned to guard the frontier.

While the territorial expansion of the T'ang empire and its military conquests in the heyday of the Brilliant Emperor might have embellished the pages of T'ang history, Tu Fu provided a sober reminder to the militarism of his time in the "Song of the War Chariot," here translated in full:

> The chariots rumbling,
> The horses neighing,

Soldiers on the march, each holding at the waist
      a bow and arrow.
Fathers and mothers, wives and children come to
      see them off—
The dust makes invisible the bridge at Hsien-yang.
Tugging their dresses, stamping their feet, they
      block the road and cry,
The sound of their wailing reaching up to the clouds.

A passerby on the roadside asks the man marching,
Who says merely that conscription is pressing.
Some since fifteen have been north guarding the River;
Now at forty they are sent west to till the camp farm.
When they started out, the sheriff wrapped their heads for them;
Upon return, their hair already white, they still have
      to guard the border,
Where, by the army post, blood flows and makes a sea—
The Martial Emperor is still intent on opening up the frontier.
Have you not heard that in two hundred counties east
      of the mountains of the Han empire,
Thorns and brambles grow in thousands of villages?
Even if there are husky women to hold the plow and hoe,
The grain grows wild among dikes and fields in all directions.
Moreover, the soldiers of Ch'in could endure tough battles,
Driven as they were like dogs and fowls.
Though you, the elder, have asked me,
How dare I, a draftee, make a complaint?
For example, in the winter this year,
Unrelieved are the soldiers west of the Pass.
The county officer presses for tax collection,
But where could the tax money come from?
Truly, it is unlucky to bear sons
And far better to have daughters.
Girls can yet be married into the neighborhood,
But boys are buried under the hundred weeds.
Do you not see at the top of the Blue Sea,
The white bones lying there uncollected since olden times?
New ghosts moan and murmur while old ghosts wail,
The sky is gloomy, the rain drenching, and sad the sound
      of sobbing.

Descriptions of the urgency of conscription, coupled with the harshness
of the recruiting officer, constitute a series of three of his famous poems,
one of which is the "Recruiting Officer at Shih-hao":

In the evening I stayed at Shih-hao village,
Where an officer came by night to seize people.

The old man jumped away over the wall;
The old woman went to the door to take a look.
The officer's shouting, how angry it was;
The woman's cry, how mournful and bitter!
Listen to her words as she came forward:
"My three sons on garrison duty at Yeh-ch'eng:
One of them recently sent a letter home
And said that the other two had died in the fighting.
The one living barely manages to survive;
The dead are finished long ago.
There are now no men in the house
Except a grandson sucking at the breast.
Because of him, the mother has not gone,
But she has not a whole skirt to wear, whether at home or
        going out.
Although I am old and feeble in strength,
I plead to go with the officer tonight,
To answer urgently the recruit for Ho-yang;
I can at least prepare the morning meal."
The sound of voices subsided in the depth of night;
Only indistinctly heard were sobbing and moaning.
At dawn I continue my journey
And say farewell to the old man alone.

The conditions in the country were even worse after the rebellion, as the intermittent wars had further devastated the countryside and impoverished the people. Tu Fu's poetic records of the post-rebellion era are unflinchingly realistic. He wrote of the piled-up corpses that stank among the grasses and trees, of the overflowing blood that reddened the streams and plains; of the empty lanes, where the foxes growled at the shrivelled sun, their hair standing up; of the boys and girls being sold everywhere so that by "severing kindness and forgoing love," the parents could pay the farm tax and for draft exemption. These government exactions, which were at the root of the people's woes, are symbolized poignantly in the mermaid's pearl-tears that turn into blood.

A guest came from the South Seas
And presented me a mermaid's pearl.
There were cryptic words on the pearl;
I would have liked to decipher them but could not.
So I kept the pearl in a bag until such time
As it could be used to meet official demand.
Today, when I open the bag to take a look,
        the pearl has changed into blood—
I lament that I have nothing else for tax payment.
        ("A Guest Came from the South Seas")

Tu Fu's own experiences aroused in him a vast and boundless love for the suffering masses. Just as he was indignant toward injustice, so he had great compassion for the wretched and oppressed. He was a humanitarian full of love for his fellow men and often acted as their spokesman even though he himself belonged to the privileged scholar-official class. In these extraordinary times, however, only a thin line divided the masses from the impoverished and distressed scholars. In the poem, "My Thatched Cottage Demolished by the Autumn Gale," he described how he failed to rescue the windblown thatches of his house from the neighboring boys who ran away with them to the bamboo grove, taking advantage of his feeble old age. Then at night, rain came after the wind in the darkened sky:

> For many years, the cloth quilt had been as cold as iron;
> The darling child, who slept badly, now trod and ripped it.
> The roof leaked and no place was dry on the beds,
> As streams of rain poured down like hemp threads without end.
> Ever since those times of woe, I had had little sleep,
> And now, dripping wet during the long night,
> > I yearned for the dawn to come.

But instead of inspiring self-pity, his personal woes merely sparked his sympathy and hope for other poor scholars like himself:

> Would that there were a broad mansion with thousands
> > and thousands of rooms
> To shelter all the poor scholars of the land so that
> > they would show a happy countenance,
> Unshaken by the wind and rain, stable as a mountain!
> Alas! When would this house appear suddenly before my eyes?
> Though my cottage were ruined and I alone froze to death,
> > I would be content.

Lastly, mention must be made of Tu Fu as an artist among poets. To him, one good word of poetry is worth a thousand ounces of gold. He said of himself:

> An odd weakness I have, for I dote on good verse.
> I shall not die in peace until I have found words that
> > will startle the readers.
> > ("A Brief Note about the River When Its Waters Rise
> > Up Like the Sea")

A lover of the exact word, Tu Fu sought and achieved artistic perfection in a strict and difficult poetic form, the regulated verse, of which he was an acknowledged master. In this instance, he was the opposite of Li Po, who delighted in the freedom of the ancient-style poetry and Music Bureau songs. Tu Fu once wrote to Li Po:

When could we, with a goblet of wine,
Again discuss literature carefully together?
    ("Thinking of Li Po in Spring")

Though these lines are not necessarily to be construed as a sly remark on Li Po, they show, nonetheless, Tu Fu's earnest attitude toward literature and poetry. His fine craftsmanship has remained exemplary to this day. While Li Po is the best-known of Chinese poets, Tu Fu is considered the greatest by most critics. This evaluation, however, is weighted by the predilection of the Confucian scholars for Tu Fu's moral integrity as against Li Po's romantic nonconformity, for Tu Fu's artistry as against Li Po's spontaneity. As mentioned before, Li Po's genius is inimitable, whereas Tu Fu's craftsmanship encourages and attracts a large following, for which reason his influence on Chinese poetry is great and lasting. A great controversy has raged over the relative merits of the two poets, but as Han Yü (768–824), a later T'ang poet, has aptly remarked:

> The works of Li and Tu will remain forever,
> Their radiance a hundred feet high!
> How stupid is this brood of children
> Who vainly seek to have them slandered.
> The large ants that try to topple a big tree
> Are indeed ridiculous for their lack of self-knowledge.

Whatever their individual merits, the T'ang poets developed to perfection two new types of Chinese poetry of the Modern Style in contradistinction to the Ancient Style of previous periods. These are the regulated poem (*lü-shih*) and the truncated verse (*chüeh-chü*). The first is an eight-line poem with five or seven words in each line. As its name implies, regulated verse follows the most strict rules of prosody such as a standard rhyming scheme, fixed tonal patterns, and paired or antithetical lines. Symmetry and melody are the goals to be attained in this type of poetry. By truncated verse is meant a truncated version of the regulated verse, that is, a four-line poem with five or seven words in each line. Hence, the shortest Chinese poem is a five-word four-line poem, totaling twenty words. In such a form the artistry obviously depends on the suggestiveness and economy of words. Like the Japanese *haiku*, the *chüeh-chü* is the easiest to write but the most difficult to write well, as virtually every line of it, to borrow the words of an English poet, has to be "loaded with ore."

Thus, by the end of the flourishing T'ang period, all major forms of Chinese poetry known as *shih* had attained the acme of their development, and later poets could only refine these forms and introduce new ideas and phraseology, but none could surpass or match the three great

T'ang poets in the beauty of their verse, the splendor of their imagination and the breadth of their humanity, which have left a lasting impression on generations of Chinese; at the same time the universality of their appeal is by no means lost to Western readers because numerous translations have been made of their representative poems.

7 : Later T'ang Poets

Although T'ang poetry reached the zenith of its glory in the works of Li Po and Tu Fu, it continued to flourish in the second half of the dynasty. An impressive number of poets wrote during this period and the poetic output was larger than ever before. Moreover, the later poets were by no means imitators of the earlier masters; they either branched out in new directions toward realism and social criticism, aestheticism and symbolism, metaphysics and literary criticism, or extended the art of narration. Here again space permits the mention of only a few of the major poets though there were literally dozens of them.

Best known of the mid-T'ang poets was Po Chü-i (772–846), who took a serious view of poetry and used it as a weapon to attack the evils of the time. After having successfully passed the literary examination in his twenty-eighth year, Po Chü-i had a long and distinguished official career as a scholar of the Han-lin Academy, a censor, the governor of several cities (including Soochow and Hangchow), and Secretary of the Board of Punishments—a career only occasionally interrupted by short intervals of retirement and exile. But he was also a devoted poet who left to posterity more than two thousand six hundred poems. From this profuse poetic material, it is possible to reconstruct in detail his private life and to know him personally in many of his inspired and expansive moments. He wrote when he communicated with friends and when he traveled, visiting fine landscapes and historical spots like T'ao Ch'ien's old house and Li Po's grave; he also sang of the seasonal changes, his daily life, his domestic joys and sorrows, such as the birth of a daughter—Golden Bell —in his late middle age and her untimely death. In these poems, his candid and sincere sentiments endear him to his readers. Without reserve or ostentation, he takes them into his confidence and reveals to them his failings—here "Singing Madly Alone in the Mountains":

> Everyone has a weakness—
> My weakness is for poetry.
> My ties to life have all but disappeared;

Only this foible has not left me:
Every time I see a beautiful scene,
Or encounter some dear old friend,
I sing aloud in a rhapsody,
As if I have met the gods face to face.

Even his laziness is made the subject of a jocular song, "Idle and Carefree," and one wonders what kind of official he made, after one has listened to the following:

Not that there are no books on the shelf—
My eyes are too lazy to read them.
There lies a zither in the case,
But my hands are too lazy to pluck it.
My waist is too loose for the belt;
My head too carefree for an official cap.
I indulge in a long afternoon nap,
Having eaten for lunch what there is for food.
One meal satisfies me the whole day;
One slumber lasts peacefully all the night.
Hunger and cold are nothing to worry about;
Moreover, I am neither starved nor shivering.

Since Po Chü-i's time, Chinese poetry has become not only an inspired comment on life, but also a faithful record of the author's everyday feelings and thoughts, and of his contacts with the people surrounding him. Thus a popular form of poetry is the occasional poem, written on any occasion, about any subject, at any time whenever the poet's spirit moves him.

Po Chü-i himself, however, considered as his most important contribution a collection of satirical ballads, in which he attacked the evils of his time such as militarism, officialdom, heavy taxation, extravagance, and popular superstition. Deploring the decadence of poetry into mere "sporting with wind and moon, and toying with flowers and grass," he and his younger friend, Yüan Chen, asserted that poetry should have as its mission the redress of social iniquities and the exposure of human foibles. They reiterated the utilitarian and moral concept of poetry long advocated by the Confucian critics. In a letter to Yüan Chen, also a well known poet, Po Chü-i wrote: "Literary compositions should be written to serve one's generation, and poems and songs to influence public affairs." In this view he was influenced by Tu Fu, whom he praised highly, but he went further than his predecessor in his intense interest in the problem of society. Whereas Tu Fu merely reported with a human touch his observations and experiences, Po Chü-i, it seems, had an explicit aim in composing his satirical poems. As he wrote in his preface to a group of fifty

"New Music Bureau Poems," he chose to make his words straightforward and his narrative close to the facts so that the listener would be moved by these poems and, warned by the serious nature of their content, would not regard them lightly as literary tours de force.

One of these poems, the "Old Man with a Broken Arm," has as its hero a draft dodger who suffers the pains of a self-inflicted broken arm rather than the perils of military service and the certainty of death in frontier wars. Now an old man at eighty-eight, supported by his great-grandson, he relates the circumstances that led to his broken arm. During the T'ien-pao reign (742–755) of the Brilliant Emperor, when he was twenty-four, there was a great levy of men for an expedition against the southern barbarians in Yunnan. Having heard the woeful tales about the journey to Yunnan, where malaria vapors rose from the river Lu and the water seethed as if boiling, he decided to evade conscription by breaking his right arm with a big stone.

> Not that broken bones and wounded sinews failed to hurt,
> I merely chose rejection from draft to get back home.
> This arm has been broken ever since—for sixty years:
> Though one limb is crippled, the wholeness of the body is preserved.
> Even now, on dark wintry nights when there are wind and rain,
> I bear the pain and remain sleepless until early dawn.
> To be in pain and sleepless
> I can never regret,
> But rejoice that my old body still stays alive.
> Otherwise, years ago, at the head of the Lu River,
> The body would have rotted, the soul flown away, and the bones lie
> ungathered,
> And I would have stayed in Yunnan, a homesick ghost,
> Wailing mournfully over the graves of countless soldiers.

"The Old Charcoal-Seller" is a satire against government requisition:

> An old charcoal-seller
> Cuts wood and burns it to make charcoal in the southern hills.
> His face, covered with dust and soot, has the color of smoke,
> His temples are hoary and his ten fingers all black.
> The money from selling charcoal, how does he spend it?
> For the clothes on his body and the food in his mouth.
> Pitiable indeed is he that the coat over his body is so thin,
> Yet he yearns for cold weather so that the price of coal will not drop!
> Last night a foot of snow fell outside the city wall;
> In the morning he drove the charcoal cart over the frozen track.
> The ox was weary, the man hungry, and the sun already high,
> When he rested in the mud outside the gate south of the market.

Who are those two horsemen that prance up so gallantly?
A courier in a yellow livery and a lad in a white shirt.
With a warrant in hand and an imperial decree by word of mouth,
They turn back the cart and shout at the ox to pull it northward:
A cartful of charcoal,
Weighing a thousand catties and more,
Is seized by the court messenger and no complaint can be made.
A half bolt of red gauze and ten feet of damask
Are tied to the head of the ox as payment for the charcoal!

The story of "Heavy Taxation" has been told since ancient times and Tu Fu's poems have numerous references to its dire consequences among the people, but it was Po Chü-i who drew a complete picture of rural communities bankrupt as a result of the burdensome tax, describing succinctly the demands of the greedy officers, the levies exacted all the year round, the payment of even unfinished silk cloth and floss by the villagers, and their wretched living conditions. After this description, the poet continues:

Yesterday, as I went to the yamen to pay my remaining tax,
I peeped in through the gate of the official storehouse:
There silk pieces and fabrics piled up like hills;
Gauze threads and floss like assembling clouds.
These are the so-called "surplus goods"
Presented every month to the great monarch.

"You rob my body of warmth
To curry favor for yourself!"
Once the silk pieces have entered the royal treasury,
They will stay there and turn to dust after long years.

In the poem, "Buying Flowers," Po Chü-i deplored the extravagance of the rich who squandered on flowers money that would buy the bread of life for the poor. Like "Heavy Taxation," the poem was written at the time of the poet's stay in the capital. During the so-called "peony season" in the late spring, red and white flowers were sold in the city market, which was sheltered by awnings above and protected by wattled fences on the sides. Carriages and horses went noisily by, one after the other on a flower-buying spree. By chance there came to the market an old farmer. Seeing these flowers, he bowed his head low and sighed long—a sigh which the city people did not seem to understand:

A cluster of dark colored flowers—
The tax money from ten middle-peasant families.

Superstitions of the people such as belief in the elixir of life, images and idols, fairies and fairyland, are ridiculed in a number of poems. "The

Man Who Dreamed of Immortality" exposes the folly of one who imagined that he would have immortal life after having dreamed of an audience with the Jade Emperor, the chief Taoist deity. Waking up with joy and wonder, he went to live, separated from his family, the life of an immortal-to-be in a rocky cave:

> His morning meal consisted of mica dust,
> At night he sipped the essence of dewy mist.

For thirty years he waited patiently but in vain for the arrival of the heavenly carriage that was to take him to the celestial land. Thus he gradually languished and pined away until one day "his body became one with the soil and manure." At the end of the poem, Po Chü-i moralized:

> Gods and immortals, if indeed they exist,
> Their ways are beyond the strivings of mortal men.
>
> .   .   .   .   .
>
> Alas! The man who dreamed of immortality,
> A single dream spoiled his whole life!

As was to be expected, these poems offended the rich and powerful and caused their author political troubles that led to his demotion and banishment. In those autocratic times the writing of social satire was always a perilous business. While Po Chü-i's poetic sallies against current evils set a new direction in Chinese poetry, few poets dared follow him because of the personal dangers involved.

Po Chü-i's poems, however, were immensely popular with the people. Most important of all, they are simple and easy to understand. His criterion of good poetry, it was said, was that it should be readily understood by an "old country woman." By doing away with scholarly allusions and ornate diction, Po Chü-i appealed to the common readers with his simple language, forthright expression, and popular sentiment. He himself attested to his great contemporary fame in a letter to Yüan Chen: "All the way for three to four thousand *li* from Ch'ang-an to Kiangsi I found my poems publicly written everywhere: in village schools, Buddhist temples, inns, and ships; they were often chanted by scholars, monks, widows, and young girls." They were also copied out and displayed for sale in the marketplace, and given in exchange for wine and tea. An anecdote, told by the poet himself, relates that when a military officer was courting a sing-song girl, she boasted, "I can recite the 'Song of Everlasting Sorrow' by the scholar Po; how could I be the same as the other girls?" So she put up her price.

The "Song of Everlasting Sorrow" is one of Po Chü-i's most popular narrative poems and also the most often translated.[1] It tells the famous story of the Brilliant Emperor and Lady Yang, beginning with her first appearance in the imperial harem, through days of love and pleasure-seeking, to their flight from Ch'ang-an during the An Lu-shan rebellion and the eventual death of Lady Yang by hanging at the soldiers' demand. In the first part of the poem is the following description of her life in the palace:

> On cool spring days she bathed in the Flower-pure Pool,
> Her soft creamy skin laved by the smooth, warm waters.
> When helped up by her waiting maids, so languid and delicate
> was she—
> That was the time she first gained the emperor's favor.
> Her cloudy tresses, her flowery face, her gold headdress
> quivering with every step—
> The spring nights spent warmly inside the hibiscus curtain.
> Spring nights were too short; she did not arise until the
> sun was high.
> Henceforth, the Emperor held no more his morning court.

This forms a strong contrast with the tragic scene of her death at the Ma-wei slope in Shensi on the road to Szechuan:

> Her hair ornaments were scattered on the ground—no one
> picked them up—
> Kingfisher, golden sparrows, and hair clasps of jade.
> The Emperor, powerless to save her, covered his face;
> Then looked back to where the blending tears and blood flowed.
> Yellow dust dispersed widely and the wind blew cold and bleak,
> Where the cloudcapped path spiraled to the Dagger-Tower.
> Only a few passersby wended their way beneath Mount Omei;
> The pennons and flags lost their gleam and the sun grew faint.

After the suppression of the rebellion, when the Brilliant Emperor re-turned to the capital, he was grieved at the familiar sights in the palace without the presence of Lady Yang:

> The hibiscus by the Pool of Primeval Fluid, the willows by
> the Hall of Never-ending Night—
> The hibiscus was like her face and the willows her brows.
> In such presence how could he refrain from tears?

So at his behest a magician was sent to search for her spirit form, whom he found at last on a fairy island:

> Having risen newly from her sleep, with her cloudy coiffure
> half slanted
> And her flowery headdress disarranged, she came down the hall.
> Her fairy sleeves, wafted by the wind, fluttered gracefully,

> As if she were dancing the "Rainbow Skirt and Feather Jacket."
> Her jade face was sad and cold, her tears were falling fast,
> She looked like a sprig of pear blossom, bearing the spring
>   raindrops.

The poem ends with her avowal of eternal love for the emperor:

> Heaven and Earth, long lasting as they are, shall someday fall,
> But this great sorrow will endure, forever without end.

But in spite of this and other popular poems of his (such as "The Song of the Lute"), Po Chü-i is remembered chiefly as the leader of a group of poets who held the belief that in any work of literature there should be a fitting moral and a well defined social purpose.

During the late T'ang period, in reaction to the trend toward greater realism and didacticism, poets turned to the aesthetic and the symbolic as the source of their inspiration. It seems that by this time the country had gone from bad to worse and they so despaired of influencing the course of political events with their writings that they retreated into an ivory tower and were satisfied with expressing their sentiments in an exotic diction replete with abstruse and mystic ideas. While not as highly regarded as those of the flourishing T'ang poets, their poems are significant in their effort to introduce some distinctive new elements into Chinese poetry. Specially noteworthy in this effort were Li Ho and Li Shang-yin, two of the comet-like writers who lived toward the end of the dynasty.

A brilliant young poet, Li Ho (790–816), whose life was cut short in its prime,[2] wrote highly sophisticated poems at an early age, went to participate in the literary examination at Ch'ang-an before he was twenty, and died at twenty-six, his name already well-known in the literary world of the capital. The story goes that every morning as the slender, emaciated youth went out to mount his lean horse ("donkey" in another version), accompanied by a dwarf slave carrying an old embroidered bag, he would throw into the latter scraps of paper on which were written whatever good verses he had composed; these he would complete when he returned home in the evening. Apropos of this habit, his mother remarked prophetically, "This child is not going to desist from writing until he has spat out his heart."

While many T'ang poets continued to write court poems in the tradition of the Six Dynasties, it was Li Ho who gave the genre stimulus and a new look. Like most "harem poems," Li Ho's are adorned with fragrance, colors, and ornaments, but instead of dwelling on the loveliness of the female body with its sensual appeal, Li Ho introduced what might be called a weird and erratic charm into his descriptions. What interests him is apparently not the seductiveness of these harem ladies but sheer aesthetic pleasure derived from their beautiful forms and adornments.

His poems are couched in esoteric, carefully wrought expressions that surprise with their originality.

An example is the "Song of a Beautiful Lady Dressing Her Hair":

> Hsi Shih* reposes in her morning dream; the silk bed-curtain is cold—
> On her fragrant hair, the knot fallen and partly disarrayed.
> The cranking of the windlass tinkling like pieces of ornamental jade
> Startles the hibiscus-one from her fresh and ample sleep.
> A pair of fairy birds opens the mirror to reveal its autumn-
> > watery gleam.
> Her hair loosened, she stands, facing the mirror, on the
> > elephant bed.
> A plait of fragrant silk lies scattered like clouds on the
> > floor;
> The jade comb slips silently into her glossy tresses.
> Her tiny hands coil up the crow-colored hair,
> The jade on the precious pin too slippery to hold it.
> Spring wind, so lustrous, vexes the lovely indolent maiden;
> Her eighteen coils are too many and little strength is left.
> Her hair dressed, the knot perching on one side but not slanting,
> Her cloud-skirt counts the steps like a wild goose walking
> > on the sand.
> Whither is she heading, without speaking and not telling anyone?
> Going down the steps, she picks for herself a sprig of cherry
> > blossoms.

The use of rare, unusual words in singularly designed lines constitutes an important characteristic of Li Ho's poetry. For instance, the word *ni* in the eighth line of the above poem—meaning literally "greasy" and here rendered as "glossy"—beggars the resourcefulness of the translator. Other examples are numerous. In Li Ho's case the following isolated, wonder-inspiring lines can be quoted out of context with little danger of misrepresenting the poet:

> If Heaven has feelings, Heaven too will become aged.

> Fragrance flying, red roaming, spring all over the sky.

> Willow catkins flap at the bed curtain—spring clouds are warm;
> Tortoise shell screens the wind—drunken eyes tied up in a knot.

> Enlivened by wine, he shouted at the moon to make it walk
> > backwards.

> The Heavenly prince blows the reed-organ with its long goose-quill
> > pipes

> To summon the dragon to plow smoke and plant jade grass.

* A famous Chinese beauty of the fifth century B.C.

95

> The stonecutter at Tuan-chou is as crafty as a god,
> He treads the sky and, sharpening his knife, severs the purple
> clouds.

In the creation of these unique verses Li Ho, so to speak, spat out the blood of his heart and thus died a premature death.

Even in this short space of time, Li Ho lived in frustration, gloom, and sickness. Some of his poems show a kind of morbid melancholy, compared with which Li Po's appear almost buoyant. Sensitive and temperamental, Li Ho cherished thoughts that are solitary, eerie, and abysmal. One peculiar trait of his poetry is the frequent use of words such as "blood," "tears," "death," and "ghosts." He takes the reader far away from the noisy crowd to desolate and dismal scenes where ancient graves open between poplars and withering grass, where bronze camels cry at night amidst lonely smoke and weeds, and where ghost lamps glitter in shady chambers, ghost rain sprinkles the empty grass, cuckoos spit out blood in wailing, and ancient owls laugh quaintly from their nests lighted by a greenish-blue fire. It is for this reason that he has been called the ghost-poet in contrast with Li Po, the angel-poet.

This does not mean, of course, that the world of Li Ho is entirely a ghostly one. Some of his poems, like the following taken from a series of thirteen poems called "Southern Garden," while paying the same scrupulous attention to the choice of words, show an unmistakable feeling for the delights of nature:

> Spring water newly risen, the young swallow flies;
> A tiny-tailed yellow bee returns after flapping among the flowers.
> The window enclosing a distant view opens from the study curtain;
> A fish hugs a sweet hook by the stone wharf.

The earliest biography of Li Ho was written by his admirer, Li Shang-yin (812–858), himself a poet noted for his obscurity and mysticism. Li Shang-yin's poetry not only defies comprehension but also because of its abstruse nature admits of a number of interpretations. Modern critics are especially intrigued by the allegory and symbolism in his poems, of which the most famous is "The Embroidered Harp":

> This embroidered harp, for no reason at all, has fifty strings:*
> Each string, each nut, brings back memories of the flowery years.
> Student Chuang was bewitched in his morning dream by the butterfly;
> King Tu entrusted his spring heart to the cuckoo.**

---

* The harp is inlaid with lines like embroidery. A Chinese harp has ordinarily twenty-five strings.

** See above, p. 41, for Chuang Chou's dream of the butterfly. In the original poem, King Tu is "Wang-ti," the courtesy name of Tu Yü, king of Szechuan; the legend says that he was transformed into a cuckoo after his death.

In the dark sea, where the moon was bright, the pearl had tears;*
On the blue field, the sun being warm, smoke grew on the jade.**
These feelings can expect to linger long in the mind,
But at that moment I was indeed desolate.

This poem reflects the ingenious use of striking, colorful words and a deliberate search for unique expressions. Chuang Chou's turning into a butterfly in his dream is a commonplace allusion, but the word "bewitch" casts a spell on what otherwise would have been a flat line. Equally well known is the story of King Tu Yü's transformation into a cuckoo, but here it gains a new significance in the use of the verb "entrusted" and its object, "spring heart." In the fifth and sixth lines, the pearl having tears and the jade producing smoke recall strange romantic tales. The use of symbolism and allusions, however, can be stretched too far and often results in obscurity and differences in interpretation. Thus "The Embroidered Harp" has been variously regarded as a love poem to a rich man's beautiful concubine with the name "Embroidered Harp"; as a poem of self-lamentation over the poet's unrecognized and unused talent; and also, as it is translated here, as a poem mourning the death of the poet's wife. The key to this last interpretation is the term "broken string," traditionally used to indicate the death of one's wife, and the strings in this harp are all broken, each into two halves, for ordinarily a harp has only twenty-five strings. If it is true that the poet's deceased wife was a harp player, as has been asserted, then we have here a clever blending of fact and symbol.

A number of Li Shang-yin's love poems are entitled "Without Title" not because the titles have been lost or are unknown, but because for obvious reasons the poet was unwilling to give them telltale titles. Stories have been circulated of his numerous amours such as that with the concubine of a high official who was also his patron, with a Taoist nun in the convent, and with court ladies with whom he is said to have made assignations in the imperial grounds. But these love poems are so obscure, vague, and whimsical that they are more like poetic riddles that exhaust the ingenuity of the commentators than lyrics that excite the reader's emotions.

Given below are two of these poems, both "Without Title," in which the use of symbols is apparent:

---

* The same allusion as in Tu Fu's poem (quoted above p. 84), that the tears of the mermaids were pearls.
** The blue field, located southeast of Ch'ang-an, is a mountain where jade is produced. According to one story, when a certain scholar went to mourn at the grave of his dead lover by the name of "Jade," she suddenly appeared to him, but vanished like smoke when he tried to embrace her.

97

It is hard to get together, and equally hard to part;
The east wind is strengthless and the hundred flowers fade.
The spring silkworm will weave its last thread until it dies;
The candle will burn to ashes before its tears are dried up.
In the morning mirror, one is grieved by the changing color of
    the cloudy hair;
Singing at night, one feels that the moonlight is cold.
The road is not far from here to the fairy mountain;*
I'd ask the blue bird to busy itself to inquire the way thither.

You vainly promised to come, but you have forsaken me without a
    trace,
As the moon shines obliquely on my chamber at the fifth watch.
No wail can call back the dream of long separation;
The ink still pales on the note hurriedly completed.
Candle light half envelops the gold kingfisher;
Musk incense wafts lightly from the embroidered hibiscus.
Gallant Liu once regretted that the fairy mountain was far away;**
Here I am separated from it by ten thousand peaks.

In contrast to Li Shang-yin's amatory poems are the philosophical poems of Ssu-k'ung T'u (837–908). While the latter does not rank high among the T'ang poets, he has found favor with Western scholars for his metaphysical views, rare in Chinese poetry. After many years of official life Ssu-k'ung T'u retired to the mountains, where he visited and wrote poems with Buddhist monks and Taoist hermits. These associations influenced his attitude toward life and provided a strong undercurrent of philosophical thought in his poems. His "Critique of Poetry," written in twenty-four stanzas in the archaic four-word form, is significant as a specimen of impressionistic or creative criticism by a poet. It expounds, with illustrative verses for each, the many traditional attributes of poetry, such as "Majestic and All-embracing," "Tranquil and Dispassionate," "Slender and Abundant," "Calm and Composed," "Lofty and Ancient," "Graceful and Elegant," "Polished and Refined," and others.

The first stanza of the poem, given here as an example, combines philosophical ideas with poetic imagery in an effort to explain one of the inexplicable terms of criticism, "Majestic and All-embracing":

* The P'eng-lai Mountain, supposedly the abode of the fairies.
** A popular reference by the T'ang poets to Liu Ch'ê, Emperor Wu, of the Han dynasty. In his old age, Emperor Wu, like the First Emperor of Ch'in, sought the elixir of life on the P'eng-lai Mountain east of the empire. Some commentators believe that it refers to the story of Liu Ch'en (also of the Han dynasty) and his companion who met two beautiful girls in Mount T'ien-t'ai, where they stayed for half a year before they returned. This reference, however, does not seem to have much relevance here.

Great expenditure leads to external decay;
Pure substance has inward fulness.
Reverting to emptiness is entering the all-embracing;
Accumulated strength becomes majestic.
Consummated are the myriad things,
The great void cutting across them.
Vast are the dense clouds;
Solitary is the strong wind.
Transcending the phenomena,
One gains the center of the ring.
Nothing is stronger than when it is held fast;
Inexhaustible it becomes when it emerges.

The last of the great T'ang poets was Wei Chuang (836–910), the author of "The Lament of the Lady of Ch'in." The poem was written in 883 shortly after Huang Ch'ao, a bandit general, had devastated the Ch'in or Shensi region, where Ch'ang-an was located. During this rebellion, the capital itself was sacked and its inhabitants were massacred. Two of the often-quoted lines in the poem give a graphic description of the calamity:

The imperial treasury was reduced to ashes;
On the heavenly street, the bones of great officials
    lay trampled.

It is said that when Wei Chuang himself became an official, he regretted the writing of this poem and forbade its perpetuation by his descendants. Thus it was excluded from his poetic works and lost to posterity for more than a thousand years until copies of it were found among the Tun-huang papers now housed in the British Museum in London and the Bibliothèque Nationale in Paris.

The "Lament of the Lady of Ch'in," one of the most remarkable long narrative poems of the T'ang dynasty, compares favorably with and is even longer than the "Song of the Everlasting Sorrow." A tragic story of the war told by an eyewitness, it was written when the country was still seething with turmoil and misery. Therefore, the narration is realistic, direct, and effective. Although lacking the poise and elegance of Po Chü-i's poem, it gains in spontaneity and vividness, and appeals powerfully to the emotions in some of its heartrending scenes.

After an introduction which relates the poet's meeting with the Lady of Ch'in in the desolate quietness of Loyang, the poem continues with a long narration by the Lady of Ch'in of the unhappy incidents which she has witnessed personally. At the time of the fall of Ch'ang-an, the womenfolk were especially the victims of fear and violence:

> The women of the northern neighborhood, flocking together,
> Ran amuck outdoors like a herd of stampeding cattle.

Although her life was spared, she was forced to become the mistress of a rebel:

> Three years had passed since I fell into rebel hands.
> All day long, my heart broken, I lived in sorrow and fear.
> At night I slept amidst spears and swords a thousand-fold;
> In the morning, I had the same dish of sliced human liver.
> No joy I knew when entering the mandarin-duck curtain;
> Little love I had for the treasure hoard, however abundant.
> The men's hair was unkempt, their faces begrimed, their eyebrows
>   shaggy and red—
> Several times I turned my glance at these fellows but could not bear
>   the sight of them:
> Their dresses in disarray, their dialects quaint and different;
> On their faces were tattooed words that boasted of their might.

After further tales of woe and distress, she recounted the story of her flight from the capital. Even the golden god she encountered on the roadside was helpless to shield her; he himself was being starved for the lack of sacrifices and was fleeing to the mountains for shelter. Next, she met a wretched old beggar, formerly a rich peasant, whose plight was attributable more to the government soldiers than to the rebels. The following two lines summarize vividly this grim episode in Chinese history:

> In vain the wilderness allures with its beautiful hues the
>   warrior's ghost;
> Of the water in rivers and streams, one-half is the blood of
>   innocent men.

About twenty years after Huang Ch'ao's rebellion, the T'ang dynasty came to an end (in 906) and was followed by a succession of five short-lived dynasties. Wei Chuang himself went to Szechuan around 900 to become an official under its governor, who set up an independent kingdom in this southwestern region after the fall of T'ang. During his stay there, Wei Chuang became a leader of the famous Szechuan school of *tz'u* poets. Thus, while his youthful masterpiece, "The Lament of the Lady of Ch'in," was a fitting monument to the tragic end of the brilliant T'ang era, his *tz'u* poems made popular a new poetic form that first developed in T'ang and that was to blossom in the next four hundred years from the Five Dynasties to the end of Sung.

8 : The Origin and Flourishing of *Tz'u* Poetry

After Chinese poetry of the *shih* type had reached the height of its attainment in the T'ang dynasty, post-T'ang poets did little beyond continuing its great tradition, branching out into various minor schools. They were limited in extending the domain of poetry, handicapped as they were by the necessity they felt of competing with their great predecessors. Nevertheless many talented poets lived in the refined Sung period (960–1279) that came after the T'ang; in particular they succeeded in bringing to perfection the new type of poetry, the *tz'u*, which as we have seen had made its debut in the T'ang period. Sung poets wrote both *shih* and *tz'u*, but their achievement was significantly in the latter.[1] Before turning to these poets, we should trace briefly the origin and development of the *tz'u* before the Sung period.

Characteristically, *tz'u* has been called a "long and short verse." Unlike *shih*, which has a uniform number of words—four, five or seven—in each line, a *tz'u* poem, generally divided into two stanzas, has lines of varying length from one to eleven-and-more words. There are as many as six hundred *tz'u* forms, each with a definite pattern consisting of a fixed number of words and lines. A stricter form of versification than the *shih*, the *tz'u* is governed by rigid tonal requirements, a prescribed verse pattern, and a rhyming scheme. Originally it was written to music, but unfortunately the scores have been lost and only the patterns and titles of the tunes remain. To write *tz'u*, therefore, is to fill a pattern or tune with appropriate words. While the *tz'u* is thus artificial and rather restricted, it succeeds in bringing out to advantage the musical qualities of the Chinese language through a well-designed tonal and metrical arrangement. Because it admits colloquial words and expressions, it is also more flexible than the *shih*, which became formalized after the T'ang period.

The writing of *tz'u* requires a mastery of the language and an ingenuity and dexterity that come with constant practice. While it is a severe task for the novice, a *tz'u* expert, like a sonnet writer, finds it delightful to "dance in shackles." He derives a sense of satisfaction in his accomplishment and, once he has mastered the technique, can wield it with great ease. But even then, the *tz'u* is limited in scope. Essentially lyrical in nature, it is best suited to expressing sentiments such as love, sorrows, and joys, and reflections on life; only great poets can range freely beyond its established boundaries. The best *tz'u* are lyrical songs in which the beauty of sentiment is combined with the melody of words.

Like other forms of Chinese poetry, the *tz'u* had its origin among the people. The introduction of foreign music from Central Asia and the creation of new melodies by the musicians demanded a poetic form that would be more pliable and adaptable to musical requirements than the *shih.* Thus was evolved in the T'ang period, outside of the regular five-word and seven-word verse, the new *tz'u* form written to a song melody. The great activity of the T'ang musicians and entertainers among the urban population stimulated the composing of *tz'u* songs as early as the eighth century. These were later developed and improved by literary writers. By the end of the T'ang dynasty, the *tz'u* was already a popular poetic form that had engaged the attention of many well known writers.

To some of the T'ang poets like Li Po, Po Chü-i, and Yüan Chen have been attributed a number of early *tz'u* poems, but their authorship is dubious; anyway their output of *tz'u* poetry is insignificant when compared with the vast bulk of their *shih* poetry. It was not until the late T'ang period that two important *tz'u* poets appeared: Wen T'ing-yün (818–870) and Wei Chuang, whose poems are included in a unique anthology entitled *Amidst the Flowers* (940). It is a collection of some five hundred *tz'u* songs by eighteen poets, most of them natives of Szechuan, or Northerners who, like Wei Chuang, had recently made their home there. Their songs are not as mellifluous and flippant as those of the others; taken as a whole, the poets of this school wrote mainly love lyrics that make a sensual appeal with their descriptions of female traits and trappings. They suggest strongly the glamor of metropolitan life either at court or in the entertainment world. The preface to the anthology explains the occasion for these songs:

> Gallant men at the gay feast and lovely ladies before the embroidered curtain: the men send their billets-doux on flowery paper, their words woven into a beautiful brocade; the women raise their tiny jade fingers to beat rhythm on two pieces of fragrant sandalwood. They are not lacking in extremely elegant compositions that depict their graceful and charming manners.

A few years later there emerged in Nanking another group of *tz'u* poets. Nanking was the capital of the Southern T'ang Kingdom (937–975),

one of the ten minor kingdoms that existed at the time of political dis-
unity prior to the unification of the country by the Sung. Decadent though
they were, the officials and rulers of Southern T'ang were great poets and
their court at Nanking was the scene of brilliant poetic activities in the
mid-tenth century. The most famous of the royal poets was Li Yü (937–
978), the last king of Southern T'ang, who surrendered to the Sung and
was taken as a prisoner to the Sung capital at Kaifeng, where he died in
captivity. One story has it that he was poisoned by imperial order upon
the discovery of one of his *tz'u* poems that reveals a poignant nostalgic
feeling for his lost kingdom.

Li Yü's works fall into two periods: an early period of love and joy,
for a time marred by his grief over the untimely death of his beloved
queen; a later period of melancholy and desolation during his years of
captivity in the north. His early songs show a casual and light-hearted
mood as in the following description of the luxury and delights of court
life (in the *tz'u* to the tune of "Washing Sand in the Stream":

> The morning sun has already risen,
> > fully thirty feet high.
> Golden tripods, one after another, are filled
> > with incense-animals.
> The red brocade carpet
> > ruffles with every step.
>
> The lovely one dances tip-toe,
> > her gold hairpin slipping out;
> Nauseated by wine, she often plucks
> > flower buds to smell,
> While from the other palace is heard dimly
> > the music of fifes and drums.

Even more vivid is the love song to the tune of "A Casket of Pearls,"
written to his charming and vivacious queen:

> Evening toilet newly done,
> She applies softly a bit of dark rouge to her lips,
> Revealing slightly her lilac tongue.
> A melody of clear song
> Temporarily induces the cherry lips to part.
>
> Her silken sleeves are stained
> > with the scarlet dregs
> Of fragrant wine, which tints the deep goblet.
> Leaning aslant on the embroidered bed,
> > her charms indescribable,
> She chews until pulpy the red flossy silk
> And laughingly spits it out at her lover.

103

The following *tz'u*, to the tune of "Pounding the Boiled Raw Silk," is probably a song of lamentation over her death:

> The deep court is quiet,
> The small garden empty,
> Intermittently the pounding of the washing
>   on the cold stone
> And intermittenly the wind—
>
> Unbearable in the long night to
>   the sleepless man—
> Their several sounds blending with the moon
>   enter the screened windows.

The *tz'u* songs written in his later period reflect a sad weariness of life, the pangs of remembrance and remorse, and a sense of futility and emptiness. They attain the essence of lyricism in expressing the sentiments of deep solitude, interrupted occasionally by dreams and imaginary visits to the past. Many of these songs are deservedly famous, but only a few can be quoted here:

> Without words, I mount alone the western chamber:
> The moon like a hook,
> The *wu-t'ung* tree solitary,
> A clear autumn locked up in the deep courtyard.
>
> Cut—still unsevered;
> Unraveled—still entangled—
> The sorrows of parting—
> A strange taste that lingers in the heart.
>   ("Crow Cries at Night")
>
> How much grief
> Was there in my dream last night?
> It seemed I was visiting the royal park as
>   in olden times:
> The carriages streaming like rivers,
>   the horses like dragons,
> With the flowers and the moon in the spring breeze.
>   ("Yearning for the Country South of the River")
>
> Spring flowers and autumn moon,
>   when will they come to an end?
> How many things of the past does one recall?
> The east wind visited again my small chamber
>   last night;
> I could not bear to look back to my native land
>   in the clear moonlight.

Carved railings and marble stairs should still be there;
Only these ruddy cheeks have changed.
I'd like to know how much sorrow one could have.
"As much as a stream of spring waters flowing eastward."
("The Beautiful Lady Yü")

It is said to be this reference to his native land, the east wind, and the spring waters flowing eastward that aroused the Sung emperor's suspicion and caused Li Yü's death. Thus were cut short the poetic activities of a tender, sensitive spirit now stained with tears and blood instead of perfumes, rouge, and the dregs of wine. One of Li Yü's contributions lies in his ability to cast his feelings into images that touch the heart directly. He enlarged the scope of *tz'u* poetry as first defined by the poets of the *Amidst the Flowers* group and introduced new materials and techniques that exerted a profound influence on later writers.

The hundreds of *tz'u* songs preserved among the Tun-huang materials represent the efforts of folk poets in contradistinction to those of literary writers and royal versifiers. Contemporaneous with the latter were those anonymous songs which contain colloquial and indigenous phrases smelling of the soil and the marketplace. Most of them reflect the manifold aspects and activities of urban life, describing spontaneously and vividly the trades-people, the artisans, the conscripts, the men on the road, and the women left alone at home. One of these *tz'u* songs, whose charm is derived from a combination of simplicity and conceit, may be quoted here:

Intolerable is that magpie with many bragging words!
What evidence is there for the lucky message it brought me?
After having flown here several times, it was caught alive
And locked up in a golden cage to stop its blabbing.

"I was full of good intention to bring you happy tidings.
Who would have thought that you would imprison
    me in the golden cage?
Would that her soldiering man might come back soon,
So I could be set free to soar into the blue skies!"

These songs by both literary and folk writers paved the way for the flourishing of the *tz'u* poetry in the Sung dynasty, which can be divided into two periods: Northern Sung (960–1126) and Southern Sung (1127–1279). In the first period when the country was comparatively peaceful and prosperous, the Sung Chinese were able to build up, particularly in Kaifeng, a highly sophisticated and cultured society with all the gaiety and refinement of metropolitan life. At that time, *tz'u* poetry, which provided entertainment at official feasts and literary gatherings, reached the pinnacle of its glory. After the fall of North China to the Jurchens, the Sung court and the intelligentsia retreated southward to the Yangtze region and established themselves in Hangchow, which soon became a new center of Chinese political and intellectual life. Some literary activities were noticeable in North China under the Jurchen control, but it was in the South that the great tradition continued. All in all, hundreds of poets wrote during the three hundred years of the Sung dynasty, but space permits a discussion of only six of its representative poets: Liu Yung (990?–1050?), Su Shih (1037–1101), and Chou Pang-yen (1057–1121) of the Northern Sung period; Li Ch'ing-chao (1081–1143), Lu Yu (1125–1210) and Hsin Ch'i-chi (1140–1207) of the Southern Sung.

In the early years of the Sung dynasty, many poets had contributed to *tz'u* poetry, but it was Liu Yung who set a new standard for its form and style. Unsuccessful in the literary examination, Liu Yung held only minor positions in the outlying provinces and spent most of his time in the gay and congenial world of the capital. A profligate, he was addicted to the pleasures of the "singing towers and dancing pavilions," where he moved amidst "a bevy of red sleeves in the upper chamber." Friend and patron of the singing girls, he wrote *tz'u* songs to the new melodies they had learned to sing. He was popular with the common people, and his *tz'u* songs were sung wherever they gathered to draw water from the well.

Like most Chinese poets, Liu Yung is at his best in depicting the sorrows of farewell and separation, particularly the sad plight of the lonely wanderer in an alien land. On these occasions, his attitude becomes serious and his emotions genuine and profound. The following *tz'u* poem to the tune of "The Rain-Soaked Bell" is one of the best and most often quoted parting songs in the Chinese language:

> A cold cicada, sad and desolate,
> Faces the long pavilion at twilight,
> The showers having recently ceased.
> Outside the city gate, drinking in the tent continues
>   without end.*
> I am about to linger awhile,
> When the magnolia boat urges me to start my journey.
> Holding hands, we look into each other's tearful eyes—
> Without words, throats choked—
> As I think of my voyage through a thousand miles
>   of mists and waves,
> Where the evening clouds are somber and the distant skies vast.[2]

---

* Friends bade farewell to the departing traveler by drinking to him in a temporary tent erected outside the city gate.

Lovers have suffered since ancient times the
    sorrows of parting.
How can I bear further my solitude in
    this clear autumn season?
Where shall I be when I wake up from my drink tonight?—
Willow banks, the breeze at dawn, and the waning moon.
During this long year of separation,
All fine moments and lovely scenes will appear to me in vain.
Even if there are a thousand varieties of tender emotion,
To whom could I impart them?

The *tz'u* to the tune of "Eight Sounds at Kan-chou," written to his wife,
expresses exquisitely an unsuspected and genuine aspect of his heart:

I look toward the skies, whence the bleak evening rain has
    sprinkled the river,
Washing and cleansing the autumn day;
Gradually, the frosty wind becomes biting and dismal,
The frontier-pass and the stream cold and deserted,
And the upper chamber aglow with the twilight sun.
Here the red fades away and the green dwindles;
Imperceptibly, all objects and flowers go to rest,
Except the long river flowing ever silently eastward.

I cannot bear to ascend the heights and watch the distant
    view,
Gazing at my native land so remote and indistinct,
My homeward thoughts hard to restrain.
I sigh for the footsteps of the passing years—
Wherefore should I tarry so long and painfully?—
And think of the lovely one looking out from her dressing
    chamber,
Mistaken several times that there were a home-bound boat
    on the horizon.
How would she know that I,
Leaning on the rails of my balcony,
Am thus about to be congealed with grief?

When compared with the *tz'u* songs of his predecessors, Liu Yung's are
much longer, for it was he who first introduced and popularized a kind of
slow moving melody suitable for extended and detailed description. His
presentation of vivid poetic pictures helps to merge sentiment with scenery. Thus in the "Eight Sounds at Kan-chou," the first half is a description of the landscape the poet viewed from an upper storey balcony. But
here in the song, nature itself becomes animated and transformed by the
poet's imagination into a series of memorable scenes such as the sprinkling

of the river by the bleak evening rain, the washing and cleansing of a clear autumn day, and the gradual fading and diminishing of its gorgeous evening colors. The descriptive words in this passage help to build up in the second half a mood evoked by the bleak scenes that surround the poet and culminate in his being "congealed with grief." The use of a slow melody for descriptive purpose in what is essentially a lyric song set a new trend and pattern for *tz'u* poetry.

If Liu Yung was a *tz'u* expert pure and simple, Su Shih might be called an all-round man of letters, for whom the composition of *tz'u* was merely one of his numerous intellectual efforts. Besides being an artist skillful in painting and calligraphy, he attained mastery in many kinds of prose and poetry, his complete works containing some four thousand *shih* and three hundred *tz'u*, as well as scores of *fu* (prose-poems) in addition to numerous essays, letters, and memorials. His political writings are noted for their eloquence and a firm grasp of the problems discussed; his informal essays for their facility of expression and discerning taste; his prose-poems for their imaginative power and descriptive beauty (see pp. 139–140; and his *shih* and *tz'u* poems for their overflowing and inexhaustible emotions like a running stream—"flowing where it should flow and stopping where it cannot help but stop," as he himself has said of his poetic style. He is equally good in all these literary genres, but from the long view of Chinese literature, Su Shih's great contribution seems to lie in *tz'u*, in which he reigned supreme even in this golden age of *tz'u* poetry. Again, some other poets may have excelled in certain aspects of style or technique, but Su Shih distinguished himself by the vastness of his scope, the great variety of his expression, and an over-all poetic excellence derived from a happy combination of technical skill with a fine imagination, genuine emotion, and a superior intellect.

Su Shih, a native of Szechuan, came from an established literary family, whose members, including his father, brother, and sister, were all writers of renown. A precocious child, he passed the literary examination at the age of twenty and afterward had a long, distinguished official career until his death more than forty years later. Like most scholar-officials, his political life was marked by many ups and downs, his troubles caused mainly by the controversy that raged over the reform measures introduced by the prime minister, Wang An-shih (1021-1086). Like other scholars of the period, Su Shih opposed these innovations and suffered slander and demotion during the years when Wang An-shih was in power. He was exiled in his midlife to Huang-chou in Hupeh for five years, and again in his old age to southern Kwangtung, as far as Hainan Island, for seven years. A conservative statesman of great integrity, he was popular with the people, whom he aided and benefited during his many years in office. He helped them to battle with the Yellow River in flood which threatened the city of Hsü-chou; he initiated irrigation projects for the farmers; he dredged the rivers and built the famous Su embankment on the West Lake in Hangchow to replace the one built centuries ago by Po Chü-i. His political and travelling experiences, his contact with and intimate knowledge of the people, as well as his genial disposition and versatile talent undoubtedly combined to enrich his poetry, and provided much of the inspiration for his vast literary production.

Su Shih's writings have a Confucian background, but they contain, too, an admixture of the Taoist concept of life and the Buddhist idea of emancipation; also perceptible is the influence of T'ao Ch'ien. In all these, he typifies a new tendency toward an amalgamation of the three Chinese philosophies—a tendency that started in the late T'ang period and culminated in the Neo-Confucian movement of Su Shih's own time. Above all, he manifests a cheerful and broad outlook on life that transcends the transient emotions conditioned by any one individual's narrow environment and that gives his poetry vigor, warmth, and perspicacity. He accepted and faced bravely the afflictions of this world with a well fortified ideal of life, seeking compensation and consolation for his sufferings in the joys of nature, friendship, and philosophy.

In his *tz'u* poetry, Su Shih broke away from the practice of subjecting words to the exigencies of metrical pattern. He was a true poet who valued more highly the beauty of words and sentiments than a scrupulous and impeccable correctness in versification. His style is vigorous and sprightly, his content broad and all-embracing, and the scope of his movement uncircumscribed by historical or technical limitations. It has been said that whereas Liu Yung's verse, "Willow banks, the breeze at dawn, and the waning moon," could best be sung by a young girl of sweet seventeen or eighteen as she beat rhythm on a "red ivory tablet," Su Shih's line, "The great river flowing ever eastward," should be sung by a tall fellow from west of the frontier, holding in his hand a big iron tablet.

Su Shih's verse referred to above comes from the *tz'u* song, "Meditations on the Red Cliff," written for the music "Remember Me for My Tenderness." It has often been quoted as an example of the unbridled imagination with which he turned a visit to a historical scene into a sentimental journey to the heroic past. The Red Cliff on the Yantzge River in Hupeh was the scene of a famous battle between Ts'ao Ts'ao, leader of the Wei kingdom, and Chou Yü, commander of the allied forces of Wu and Shu Han, in the early years of the third century A.D. It is the subject of both Su Shih's prose-poem and the following *tz'u*, in which the heroic image of Chou Yü is vividly projected against the romantic background of the billowing Yangtze and the precipitous Red Cliff, where Chou Yü inflicted heavy losses on the Wei navy.

> The great river flowing ever eastward,
> Its waves have washed away all the gallants of
>   ancient times.
> West of the old rampart, so people say,
> Lies the Red Cliff of young Chou Yü of the Three Kingdoms.[3]
> Riotous rocks cleave the clouds;
> Roaring billows rend the shores,
> Rolling up a thousand piles of snow.
> The river and mountain look like a picture.
> How many heroes were there at that time?
>
> I think of Chou Yü in those days,
> Newly married to the young Ch'iao girl—*
> His heroic looks, majestic and spirited.
> Holding a feather fan and wearing a silk kerchief,
> Amidst talk and laughter,
> He reduced his strong enemy to flying ashes and
>   smoldering smoke.
> In this spiritual tour of the ancient kingdom,
> I should be laughed at for being so sentimental,
> My hair turning gray in these early years.
> Life is but a dream.
> Let us pour a goblet of wine as a libation to the river moon.

The last line, while seemingly unrelated to the main theme of the song, brings the poet back from his spiritual excursion to the realities of the present visit and the beauties of the rugged landscape that have inspired him in the first stanza.

In songs like this Su Shih brought the *tz'u* poetry of the Sung period to a great height and a new frontier. All sorts of material—lyrical, descriptive, and philosophical in nature—is now admitted as proper for the *tz'u* form and given a personal touch in Su Shih's inimitable style. It ranges from the highly imaginative poem sung to the tune of "Top Song in a River Melody" to a description of city festivity to the tune of "Butterfly Loves the Flowers." The first was written during the mid-autumn moon festival to his younger brother, who like him was a poet and at the same time a political exile in a distant land:

---

* The younger daughter of the Ch'iao family was married to Chou Yü, the older daughter to the ruler of Wu.

念奴嬌 赤壁懷古

大江東去浪淘盡千古風流人物故壘西邊人道是三國（一作當日）周郎赤壁亂石崩雲驚濤裂岸捲起千堆雪江山如畫一時多少豪傑 遙想公瑾當年小喬初嫁了雄姿英發羽扇綸巾談笑間強虜灰飛煙滅故國神遊多情應笑我早生華髮人間如夢一樽還酹江月

"**Meditations on the Red Cliff**". From a 1320
Edition of Su Shih's Poetry.

When will there be another bright moon?
Holding a jug of wine, I ask the blue sky.
In the celestial palace, I wonder,
What time of the year is this night?
I yearn to waft there with the wind,
But fear that in the jasper tower under jade canopies
It would be so cold as to be insufferable.
So I rise to dance and frolic with my shadow.
No place is better than here in this mortal world.

Circling around the red pavilion,
Stooping at the silk-screened door,
The moon shines on those who lie sleepless.
No grievances it should have;
Yet why is it often full at parting time?
Man has sorrows and joys, separation and reunion;
The moon has light and shadow; it waxes and wanes—
This imperfection has been since ancient time.
Would that we could live a long life
And together share the moonlight a thousand miles away!

The *tz'u* to the tune of "Butterfly Loves the Flowers" relates against the background of the lantern festival a tale of two cities, metropolitan Hangchow on the picturesque Ch'ien-t'ang River and the dreary, backward rural Mi-chou in mountainous Shantung, to which the poet had recently moved from Hangchow:

Lantern lights on the Ch'ien-t'ang on the night of
    the fifteenth—
The bright moon shines like frost,
Illuminating the people as in a picture.
Inside the curtain the reed mouth-organ is played
    and musk perfume spreads forth.
Not a speck of dust in the wake of the horses.

In this desolate mountain city I am growing old.
There drums beat and fifes sound
For festal sacrifice at the field and among the mulberry.
Fire chills, lights dim, frost and dew fall—
Darkly, there is a hint of snow as the clouds hang
    heavy over the wilds.

A personal note on his returning home one night after a drinking party marks the following *tz'u* sung to the tune of "The Immortal Looking down into the River":

> Carousing one night on the East Slope, I get drunk again after
>   having sobered.[4]
> When I return home, it seems, around the third watch,
> The house boy has been snoring like thunder;
> To my knocks on the door he gives no answer.
> Leaning on a staff, I listen to the sound of the river.
>
> I often grieve that I am not master of my own body.
> When can one forget all this striving and bustling?
> Night wanes, wind calms down, and the ruffled ripples are
>   smooth.
> In a little boat I shall float away henceforth,
> My lingering life committed to the rivers and seas.

The poem was written during his exile at Huang-chou. When it was circulated the next day, rumors spread that the poet had hung up his official
hat at the riverbank to disappear into the rivers and seas. The magistrate
was so perturbed by the news that he went immediately to the poet's
home to visit him; there he found him happily snoring away like the
house boy.

Deeply touching is the following *tz'u* to the tune of "The River City,"
in which he dreamed he caught a glimpse of his deceased wife, buried
ten years ago in Szechuan:

> For ten years the living and the dead have been far apart,
> Incapable of remembering each other,
> And yet finding it hard to forget.
> Your lonely grave being a thousand miles away,
> There is no place where we can talk of our sorrows in the past.
> But even if we met, you would not know me,
> My face being covered with dust,
> And my temple-hair as white as frost.
>
> Tonight in my lone dream I suddenly return home.
> By the small porch window,
> You are making your toilet.
> Looking at each other, we have no words
> But tears in endless rows.
> I expect, where the heart breaks every year, it would be
> On a bright moonlit night,
> On yonder mound of low pine trees.

The *tz'u* written to the tune of "The Divining Abacus" is an intriguing
lyric that admits of various interpretations:

> A broken moon hangs on a sparsely leafed *wu-t'ung* tree.
> The water-clock has ceased dripping and human noise has
>   newly subsided.

Frequently there is seen a solitary man rambling alone,
Faint and fleeting like the shadow of a lone swan.

Startled, it turns back to look around;
Its grief no one seems to understand.
It flies over all the wintry boughs, but on none it chooses
    to perch.
Silent and forlorn, the sand bar in the river is cold.

As translated here, the song attempts to convey the poet's feelings of lone-liness during his exile in Huang-chou, the lines gaining in subtlety and sublimity with the metaphor of the lone swan for the person of the poet himself.

The examples quoted above show how Su Shih made important con-tributions to *tz'u* poetry. By expanding considerably its domain and creat-ing a new language and style, he broke the barrier between *shih* and *tz'u* and used the latter to express ideas and sentiments that are traditionally considered as suitable only for the former. He wrote *tz'u* poetry on all occasions—to describe scenery, to record daily happenings, to relate his-torical events and personages, to discuss moral and philosophical ideas. By arresting the course of the *tz'u* toward effeminacy and by cleansing it of its stains of rouge and perfume, he gave it greater strength; by dis-pensing with the niceties of technical requirements, he increased its maneuverability. He made *tz'u*, just like *shih* in the hands of the T'ang masters, a fitting medium for the expression of personal emotions and thoughts; he revealed in these *tz'u* songs his perspicacious mind, his win-some personality, his genial outlook on life, and above all, his intellectual resources and poetic inspiration.

While Su Shih paved the way for the separation of *tz'u* poetry from music in later periods, Chou Pang-yen, chief musician of the Imperial Music Bureau, took an opposite direction in his effort to perfect the *tz'u* patterns and melodies. An expert in musicology, he improved and stan-dardized old *tz'u* tunes and created new ones. As a music master, he ob-served strictly the rules of prosody; as a poet, he was skillful in his choice of words to increase verse harmony. But his *tz'u* songs appear meager in thought content and lacking in imagination and creative power. His con-tributions are limited to the technical aspects of *tz'u* poetry, with an em-phasis on elegant diction, elaborate description, and musical effect.

With the loss of music scores and the discontinuance of the practice of *tz'u* singing in the post-Sung period, the musical quality of Chou Pang-yen's songs becomes less obvious and any English rendering can do little justice to their melody. So only two examples will be given here. The song to the tune of "A Young Man's Pleasure-Visit" is quoted as follows be-cause of an interesting story behind it:

Ping-chou knife gleams like water;
Soochow salt is whiter than snow.
Her tiny hand splits a fresh orange.
The embroidered curtain newly warm,
Incense rising from an animal-shaped censer,
They sit face to face, playing the mouth-organ.

Softly she inquires, "Whom else will you visit tonight?
On the city wall, the third watch has sounded.
Horses slip; the frost lies heavy;
It is better not to leave here.
Indeed, few would have ventured out."

These lines are supposed to relate the emperor's visit to the house of a famous courtesan. According to this story, the poet, who was with the courtesan, had to hide himself under her bed when the emperor suddenly arrived. This gave him, however, a vantage point to play the eavesdropper and inspiration for the song.*

The sorrows of parting, as we have seen, a favorite theme of Chinese poetry, find an exquisite expression in the *tz'u* entitled "Early Parting" to the tune of the "Butterfly Loves the Flowers":

A luminous moon startles the crows that fail to perch—
Water will soon cease to drip from the clepsydra—
The windlass revolves and draws from a golden well.
Waking up, her two eyes are clear and bright;
Tears fall on the pillow and chill its red cotton.

They hold hands as the frosty wind wafts the shadows of their
    hair;
His will to depart then falters and strays,
And those sad parting words become barely audible.
Now, on the upper balcony lies aslant the Dipper's handle;
The dew is cold, the man far away, only the cocks answer each
    other.

In analyzing the poem we can see that pre-dawn noises—the crows crying because they have no place to perch, water dripping from the clepsydra, and servants drawing water with a squeaking windlass—finally wake up the lovers who have newly gone to sleep after a long night of talking and crying. Thus their eyes are not drowsy, but clear and bright, though their tears have already become cold on the pillow's red cotton. At the mo-

---

* The story continues that later when the emperor heard the song from the courtesan he was so angry that he ordered the poet's banishment from the capital. On the day of Chou's departure, the emperor went again to the courtesan's house but had to wait there for a long time before she came back. Then she sang to him another *tz'u* song, in which the poet bade farewell to her. This time the emperor relented. He recalled Chou and offered him a position in the Imperial Music Bureau.

ment of parting, the man is seen, after holding hands with his love, leaving the house to brave the inclement weather, lingering with every step from the bed chamber to the courtyard, until finally he is actually on the road, her parting words no longer within earshot. The empty balcony with only the morning stars shining there reveals that the woman has gone inside to cry again, and the feeling of the wanderer on the lonely, wild road can well be imagined. It can be seen that Chou Pang-yen was at his best in depicting tender feelings, delicate situations, and exquisite scenes, all of which have become the hallmarks of *tz'u* poetry in later centuries.

In the intervening period between the Northern and Southern Sung dynasties lived Li Ch'ing-chao, one of the most celebrated Chinese women poets. An atmosphere of cultural refinement surrounded her early years in an opulent scholar-official family in Shantung; and later congenial tastes in art and poetry brought happiness to her married life with a young scholar from a well-matched family. The two would spend delightful times together, studying, examining and fondling rare objets d'art such as bronze vessels, rubbings from stone monuments, old paintings and books that they had collected. This kind of idyllic existence in the coziness of their studio lasted for several years, until it was shattered rudely by the alarums of war in 1127 during the Jurchen invasion of North China. Together with others, the couple fled south to the Yangtze region, leaving behind them the bulk of their priceless collection. The death of her husband two years later was to Li Ch'ing-chao a cruel blow from which she never recovered; it was also the beginning of a long aimless wandering that was to last until the very end of her life.

Of Li Ch'ing-chao's poetic work very little has been preserved for posterity. About fifty-odd pieces are all that are left in her name, but even some of these are of dubious authorship. While it is difficult to study her poetry from these meager remains, the few *tz'u* songs that have survived and been considered as genuinely hers show clearly her gift as a poet. They compare well with the works of her contemporaries, among whom, though a woman, she ranks supreme. She was also a literary critic, displaying a serious attitude toward poetry and an acute judgment of the *tz'u* poets of her time. In her own writings she experimented with difficult rhymes and novel metrical devices. Though subjecting her poems to the most rigid requirements of versification, she attained commanding heights of lyricism.

In her songs Li Ch'ing-chao succeeded in depicting the emotions and vicissitudes of a young woman. Many Chinese poets have attempted to delve into the inner recesses of the female mind in the so-called "palace poems" that form an important part of China's poetic heritage, but they fall short in the presentation of a genuine woman's feeling with all its intimacy, delicacy, and immediacy. In this respect, Li Ch'ing-chao's poems are unmatched. Moreover, they are enriched by the fullness of her emotional experiences, which became crystallized in the last years of her life. Her *tz'u* songs fall into two different moods, the early ones marked by a delicate and sprightly outlook and the later revealing the depth of woe into which she had sunk.

To the first group belongs the song to the tune of "A Sprig of Plum Blossoms," in which is described the tender thought of a young wife after her husband's departure from home:

Fragrance fades away from the red lotus-roots;
The lovely bamboo mat becomes cold in autumn.
Gently loosening his silk robe,
He mounts alone the magnolia boat.
Who would have sent an embroidered letter from
    among the clouds?
When the message comes back from the wild goose,
The moon has filled the western chamber.

Flowers fall and waters flow by themselves.
It is the same kind of yearning—
An idle sorrow in two different places.
This sadness cannot be dispersed or banished:
It has just left the eyebrows
When once again it enters the heart.

The following *tz'u* to the tune of "Drunk under Flower Shadows" conveys her sentiments to her far away husband in his official post:

Thin mists and thick clouds gloom the everlasting day;
Camphor incense fades away from the golden animal.
Once again it is the Double Ninth Festival.
Through the jade pillow and gauze bed curtain,
Coolness begins to penetrate at midnight.

When I hold up the wine-cup by the eastern hedge,
In the twilight a hidden fragrance fills my sleeves.
Do not say that one's soul cannot be rapt!
When the bamboo screen rolls up in the west wind,
I look thinner than the yellow flower.

In the last line, highly praised by critics, by deliberately introducing a whimsical comparison in which a person can be thinner than a flower, thus challenging the realities of life and nature, the poet aimed on the one hand to restrain an overflowing emotion and on the other to leave on the reader's mind a tantalizing impression that although the song is ended, the feeling it expresses lingers on.

In the *tz'u* poems written after her husband's death, the sense of grief is so deeply imbedded in her heart that it no longer appears on the surface but passes into a state of sublimation. At the time she composed the following song to the tune of "Spring in Wu-ling," she was staying with her brother's family at Chin-hua in Chekiang, the Twin Stream being the name of a place there:

> The wind has subsided, the earth is scented with fallen flowers.
> The day being late, I am too tired to comb my hair.
> His things remain, but the man is gone, and life has
>   ceased to be.
> I want to talk but tears begin to flow.
>
> I have heard that spring is still fair at the
>   Twin Stream
> And intend to go there, sailing in a light boat.
> But I am afraid that the skiff at the Twin Stream
> Cannot hold sorrows so heavy.

The *tz'u* poem written to the tune of "Every Sound, Lentemente" is most often quoted for its unique use of seven pairs of monosyllabic words in the first three lines. These create a striking melodious effect in the original when sung slowly according to the music. A part of this effect, however, is lost when rendered into English with its characteristic consonantal endings:

> Seek . . . seek, search . . . search;
> Lone . . . lone, cold . . . cold;
> Sad . . . sad, pain . . . pain, moan . . . moan.
> In a season that is barely warm but still cool
> It is hard to nourish oneself and rest.
> With two or three goblets of weak wine,
> How could one withstand the evening wind so impetuous!
> A wild goose has passed by,
> My heart is wounded,
> But then I recognize it is an old friend.
>
> The ground is covered with yellow flowers,
> All withered and ruined;
> What else is worth plucking at this moment?
> I stay at the window,
> All alone; oh, how dark it gets!
> Rain drizzling on the *wu-t'ung* tree,
> Drop by drop it falls until dusk.
> All this sequence of things—
> How could it be summed up in just one word: Grief?

117

Here at a painfully slow pace, the poetess dwells on the season, the wine, the sound of the wind, the crying of the wild goose, the wilted chrysanthemum flowers, the lone twilight watch, and the rain pattering on the *wu-t'ung* tree; then, after having marshalled all these elements of nature to create a prevailing mood, she quickly and abruptly ends her poem with the one word she has saved until the very last—the word that, like the drawing of the eyeball on a pictured dragon, gives it animation and illumination.

At the time of Li Ch'ing-chao's death, the Sung Chinese, who had taken refuge in the Yangtze region, already despaired of reconquering North China and were content with maintaining a precarious peace with the Jurchens, who had established the Chin dynasty in North China. The tragic death of the patriotic general, Yo Fei (1102–1141), who was himself the author of the famous *tz'u* to the tune of "The River Flooded with Red," tolled the bell for any lingering hope of unifying the country; and the many Southern Sung writers who grew up under such distressing circumstances could only voice in poems their overflowing sentiments. They are represented here by Lu Yu and Hsin Ch'i-chi, who were also two of the most important Southern Sung poets, Lu Yu known mainly for his *shih* poetry and Hsin Ch'i-chi for his *tz'u* poetry.

Lu Yu witnessed during his life and reflected in his writings a critical episode in Chinese history. Although he himself was born in Chekiang, he had cherished ever since his childhood patriotic feelings inculcated by his father, who, together with other scholars, would talk excitedly about the disturbing political situation, sighing and sobbing, their teeth gnashing and their eyes blazing with righteous indignation. When he grew up, Lu Yu learned the Confucian classics as well as the books of military strategy with the hope that he might someday play an important part in national affairs. This hope, however, he was never destined to fulfill. In his middle age he went to Szechuan twice, first as Secretary to the Pacification Commissioner and later as Councilor under Fan Ch'eng-ta (1126–1193), the Military Governor of Szechuan, who was also a poet[5] and a friend of Lu Yu. During his two separate sojourns there Lu Yu participated in military expeditions and was for some time at the front with the army. These frontier days were most exciting and memorable for him. Later he took minor positions in the Yangtze and coastal provinces and showed a great concern and sympathy for the people, recording their sufferings in his poems. In his mid-sixties he retired to his native Chekiang, where he spent the last twenty years of his life in peace and poverty, only occasionally interrupted by brief visits to the court. His often quoted poem to his sons represents the appropriate end of a long poetic career:

> I know well that in death everything becomes empty,
> But mourn that I shall not see the Nine Regions united.
> The day the imperial armies march north to pacify the Middle Plains,
> Do not forget to tell your Sire at the family sacrifice.

Like his great predecessor Su Shih, Lu Yu was a voluminous writer of poetry and prose. His complete poetic works in eighty-five volumes (*chüan*) contain about 10,000 pieces, the bulk being *shih*. His poetry is characterized by a broad humanitarianism, a spontaneous imagination, and a fine appreciation of natural beauty. Above all, he was a worthy successor to Tu Fu as a patriotic poet who instilled into his writings a passionate feeling for his country. Patriotism, then, is the key to Lu Yu's life and works and is the main thread that strings together his divergent poetic elements: his lofty and fervent sentiments, his keen observations of life and nature, and his precise, realistic descriptions.

In his early years Lu Yu came under the influence of the so-called Kiangsi School of poetry,[6] with a tendency to oddity in poetic style and a fastidious search for unusual words, but as his poetic power matured, he soon evolved a style of his own. His descriptions of nature are often animated by a touch of imagination, as in the following lines:

> The sudden drop of a green leaf signals a bird perching;
> The slight movement of blue duckweed reveals the fish swimming.
>
> .   .   .   .
>
> Supporting myself on a staff, I go where the frozen clouds are
>   the thickest
> To inquire whether there is news of the plum blossoms along
>   the stream.

In his patriotic poems, he showed admiration:

> For those brave men with lifelong ambitions for the four quarters,
> To have their corpses wrapped in horse hides is quite the norm.

Sympathized with

> The poor masses, who, complaining to the blue skies,
> Yearn day and night for relief from distress;

and commented bitterly on the army's inaction:

> Stabled horses die of obesity; strings unstrung break on the bow;
> Horns and bugles from the battle speed the falling moon.

Lu Yu displayed in his *tz'u* poems alternating moods of calm and passion, tenderness and gravity, serenity and excitement. The peaceful and

119

leisurely life of a fisherman is depicted in the following *tz'u* to the tune of "Happy Affairs Near at Hand":

> Of late years I love to go east to my native land,
> To wipe away all traces of the market and the court.
> I have chosen a spot encircled by jagged mountains,
> Where I can fish in a deep pool of limpid green.
>
> Selling fish for wine, I become in turn sober and drunk;
> The affairs of my heart I entrust to the flute.
> My home lies beyond a thousand layers of clouds,
> Its whereabouts known only to the sea gull.

In another song to the same tune, he lets his imagination roam in the realm of the immortals:

> Waving my sleeves, I left this world of men
> To fly secretly over steep cliffs and dark precipices.
> I sought and found the red crucible of the ancient immortals,
> Where white clouds lay amassed in heaps.
>
> With a heart like a pool of deep water, calm and unruffled,
> I sat down to count my breathings several thousand times.*
> At midnight I was suddenly startled by an unusual sight:
> The whale's undulations in the full glare of the sun.

Often his poems, like the following *tz'u* sung to the tune of the "Spring Saturated Garden," are inspired by exhilarating emotions and a robust attitude toward life, and are the more remarkable for having been written in his old age:

> A lone crane that flew homeward,
> Passing once again the skies of Liao,
> Found that the people there had changed.**
> This makes me think of the heaped, ruined mounds—
> The dimly distant dreamland—
> Where kings and princes, together with ants and moles,
> Have all turned to dust.
> Oft in my youth I carried wine to the fields and woods,
> Or inquired about flowers in the streets and lanes.†
> In those days I never lightly turned my back on spring.
> The fleeting years have changed me too.
> I sigh that the waist belt has become loose
> And my temple-hair is newly streaked with frost.

* Like a Zen Buddhist.

** A reference to an immortal of the Han period who, transforming himself into a crane, flew back to his native land to have a look. He found that though the city walls were still there, the people had all changed.

† This can be interpreted in an allegorical sense to denote his pleasure trips to the courtesan houses in his early years.

Friends and relatives have dispersed like clouds.
I never expected my body would still be whole at this age.
Luckily, my eyes are clear and my health is good;
The tea is sweet and the rice soft.
I am not alone in being old;
And there are many others who are also poor.
Having escaped all the crises in this life,
And thrown to the winds my lusty ambitions,
I now leisurely pluck water-cress* in a small skiff on the lake.
Why should I complain?
The old fishermen and I get drunk together;
Neighborly are the friends along the stream.

The last of the great Sung poets, Hsin Ch'i-chi can be classified with Liu Yung and Chou Pang-yen as a *tz'u* specialist. Like Lu Yu, he was noted for his patriotic and military activities. Born in Shantung after its occupation by the Jurchens, he was another who cherished throughout his life a burning love for his country. When he was barely twenty, he headed a band of 2,000 peasant guerrillas in a revolution against the Jurchen rulers in his native district. He displayed great bravery invading the Jurchen camp to seize alive a Chinese traitor who had thwarted the uprising and surrendered to the enemy. He then went south, where he was offered a military post by the Sung government. He became successively army general, deputy transportation commissioner, and pacification commissioner in a number of localities in the Yangtze region. When he was commissioner in Hunan, he built barracks and bought horses and provisions for his newly organized cavalry, the Flying Tigers, to strengthen the national defense against the Jurchens. But his efforts incurred the jealousy and suspicion of his enemies at court and two years later he was removed from office. Thus began the intermittent periods of his enforced retirement just at the prime of life, his ambitions unfulfilled and his efforts frustrated. In later years he spent most of his time in his country home but returned occasionally to government service, only to suffer further disappointments, especially, near the end of his career, with the disastrous failure of a northern expedition.

Hsin Ch'i-chi's six hundred *tz'u* songs constitute the single largest production of *tz'u* poetry by any Sung writer. He continued the movement led by Su Shih to liberalize the forms and patterns of *tz'u*, to broaden its scope, and to create a new style, in which to express freely his sentiments and thoughts on current events and daily occurrences. He employed with great skill familiar quotations from literary sources such as the *Analects*,

---

* Originally, *ch'un*, an edible water plant, grown only in certain districts around Soochow and Hangchow; it is especially delicious when served with fish soup.

the Taoist treatises, and the poetic works of Ch'ü Yüan, T'ao Ch'ien, and the T'ang poets; he made a clever use of historical and literary allusions which enhance, rather than burden, his verse. He also introduced colloquial words and expressions whenever he saw fit. By thus enriching the language of the form and giving it a greater freedom of movement, he attained a new height in *tz'u* poetry, which became in his hands so malleable and serviceable that he was able to employ it on all occasions and to weave into it the colorful threads of his life and personality.

The most famous of Hsin Ch'i-chi's *tz'u* songs, noted for its spontaneity and artless simplicity, is the following written to the tune of "The Ugly Slave":

> When young, I knew not the taste of sorrow,
> But loved to mount the high towers;
> I loved to mount the high towers
> To compose a new song, urging myself to talk about sorrow.
>
> Now that I have known all the taste of sorrow,
> I would like to talk about it, but refrain;
> I would like to talk about it, but refrain,
> And say merely: "It is chilly; what a fine autumn!"

His *tz'u* to the tune of the "Green Jade Table" can be compared with Su Shih's on the same theme, the splendor of the lantern festival in Hangchow; Hsin's poem, however, is enlivened by the description of a personal episode in the second stanza:

> At night the east wind blows open the blooms on a thousand trees,
> And it blows down the stars that shower like rain.*
> Noble steeds and carved carriages—the sweet flower scent covers
>   the road;
> The sound of the phoenix flute wafts gently;
> The light of the jade vase revolves;**
> All night the fish and dragons dance.
>
> Decked in moths, snowy willows, and yellow gold threads,†
> She laughs and talks, then disappears like a hidden fragrance.
> Among the crowds I have sought her a thousand times;
> Suddenly as I turn my head around,
> There she is, where the lantern light dimly flickers.

Also comparable to Su Shih's song to the midautumn moon is Hsin Ch'i-chi's written to the tune of "Magnolia Flowers, Lentemente":

---

* Both lines refer to the lanterns at the festival.
** That is, the moon. Some commentators believe it also refers to the lantern.
† Head ornaments worn by the Sung ladies.

Pitiable is the moon tonight—
Whither will it go,
So lonely and so distant?
Is it somewhere in another world of men,
Where it begins to be seen,
Probably toward the east?
Does it go beyond the Heavens,
That immense empty expanse,
With only a vast and strong wind to speed the midautumn?
Who could tie a flying mirror without roots?
Who would keep at home the unmarried goddess of the moon?*

It floats, so they say, under the bottom of the sea,
   but how could this be?
Somehow, one sorrows and is disquieted
To think that the big whale, ten thousand *li* long,
Would butt the moon sidewise and shatter to pieces
Its jade palaces and jasper towers!
The toad, forsooth, could bathe in the waters,
But how could the jade hare learn to sink or float?**
If you say that it emerges completely unharmed,
Why then does the moon gradually become a hook?

The poem was composed during an all night drinking party, in which the observation was made that whereas there were numerous *tz'u* poems on greeting the moon, none had been written on sending it off—a challenge which Hsin Ch'i-chi immediately took up by dashing off on the spur of the moment a series of questions in the manner of Ch'ü Yüan's "Heaven Questioned."

Reminiscent of T'ao Ch'ien's humorous poems on stopping drinking, Hsin Ch'i-chi wrote a song to the tune of "Spring Saturated Garden":

Wine cup, come forward here!
Today the old man is taking an inventory of his body.
Why should one endure thirst for long years,
The throat like a parched pan?
Nowadays, I am fond of sleeping,
My breath speeding like thunder.
You say, "Liu Ling, a sage of all times,
Did not mind being buried if he died while drunk."
If indeed one should die of drink,
I regret that to your good friend,
You are truly lacking in gratitude!

* Heng O (or Ch'ang O) is the goddess of the moon in Chinese mythology.
** Having stolen the elixir of life, Heng O fled to the moon, where she was changed into a toad. There is also the story of a white hare pounding the herb of immortality in the moon.

Likewise, with singing and dancing as go-betweens,
You work up venomous suspicions in this mortal world;
And hatred, whether great or little,
Is born of that which is loved.
All things, either beautiful or ugly,
Cause calamity when overdone.
Here is my covenant with you:
"Don't stay here; get away fast!
I am still strong enough to wreck you, my cup,
   and expose your corpse!"
Bowing twice, the cup replies:
"I'll go anon, if waved away,
But have to come back, when beckoned."

A military hero turned poet, Hsin Ch'i-chi introduced observations on army life into his poetry as illustrated in the following lines:

In the setting sun, the Tartar dust stretches infinitely;
Facing the west wind, the frontier horses grow obese.

.   .   .   .

He has been thinking of those years,
When, amidst golden spears and armored horses,
His inhalations engulfed all the ten thousand miles like a tiger's.*

.   .   .   .

While drunk, I raise the lampwick to look at the dagger,
And my dream goes back to the bugle-blown, interlinked tents:
There for eight hundred miles beneath the standard, roast meat
   was served,
And fifty strings drowned the noise outside the frontier—
That was the time of autumn roll call at the battlefield.

It has been said that his towering imagination and unbridled sentiments are like those of a soaring dragon and leaping tiger, rarely found in *tz'u* poetry. Disdaining the meticulous art of "pruning the green and carving the red," Hsin Ch'i-chi and the other Sung masters showed in their works a confluence of all the poetic currents of their times, particularly the grand and the heroic, thereby establishing a new high standard of *tz'u* poetry, unmatched by post-Sung writers. Although *tz'u* poetry continued to be written in later centuries, little more need be said about it, for the best work was done in the Northern and Southern Sung periods covered in this chapter.

---

* A reference to Liu Yü, a general, who won a number of military triumphs and later usurped the throne to establish the Liu Sung dynasty, one of the Southern Dynasties in the early fifth century.

9 : The Neoclassical Movement in Prose

While the merits of T'ang and Sung poetry are widely known outside of China, there is insufficient recognition in the Western world of the important achievements of Chinese prose during the same period. The reform movement for prose started by the T'ang masters attained its ultimate triumph in the hands of their Sung followers, and the works of these authors have remained models of prose composition in later ages. This continuous tradition of more than a thousand years from the T'ang to the modern period provided a basis for the homogeneity of Chinese culture, for it is in this medium that the Chinese writers expressed themselves. This accumulated body of prose is essentially Confucian in content and form, and its style is derived mainly from the Chou philosophical writings and Han histories. The initiation and promotion of this neoclassical movement by the T'ang-Sung essayists made Chinese prose literature what it was up to the beginning of the present century.

Coming after the political, social, and intellectual chaos of the Six Dynasties, the T'ang was a critical period in the development of Chinese thought. With the rising popularity of Buddhism and Taoism in the pre-T'ang period, Confucianism waned and its hold on the intellectuals became precarious and uncertain. Had it not been for the determined efforts of the T'ang scholars to reinstate Confucianism, one of its two rival teachings could very well have become the dominant philosophical and religious system of the nation, as Buddhism had threatened to be in North China in the fifth and sixth centuries. Due to a sheer coincidence in the family surname—the imperial house of T'ang was established by the Li clan, and Lao-tzu, according to legend, had the same family name—the T'ang rulers tended to look kindly on Taoism. The state examination, moreover, was then not entirely Confucian-oriented as it was in later times. The T'ang poets, as indicated in a previous chapter, had divergent philosophical backgrounds and leanings. It was the basic Confucian education for the young, the adaptability of the Confucian teaching to government and social order, and the tenacious hold of the Confucian

125

scholars on officialdom that combined to keep the T'ang people from straying into other folds. The neoclassical movement in prose, which is partly an endeavor to exalt Confucianism over Taoism and Buddhism, therefore contributed to the continuity and stability of the Confucian influence on the Chinese nation.

This prose movement advocated a return not only to the contents of the Confucian Classics, but also to the classic style of writing as found in these works. Here again, the T'ang was a crucial period in the evolution of Chinese prose, which hitherto had tended toward an ornate and rhetorical style, comparable to the euphuistic writings of Elizabethan England. Prose literature written in this style is known as *p'ien-wen*, or antithetical prose, the word *p'ien* meaning literally a team of paired horses. As a reaction to this artificial composition of the pre-T'ang period emerged the new prose of the T'ang, called *ku-wen*, or ancient style, in reference to the ancient classics as a source of its inspiration. It aims to divest itself of literary embellishments and trappings, and to introduce a simple and vigorous prose as a fitting vehicle for the expression of thought and feeling as well as for serious discussion and argument. While this return to the classic style counteracts the influence of the high-flown style of the Six Dynasties, its stress on the ancient form also precludes the adoption of the vernacular language for formal literary composition.

The T'ang proponent of this epoch-making prose movement was Han Yü (768–824), one of the best known Chinese writers of all ages. His contribution lies in his championing of Confucian thought as well as in the intrinsic excellence of his writings, which became models of literary prose. A poet as well as an essayist, he headed a school of poetry noted for its use of rare words and unusual expressions. But it is as a prose master of the highest calibre, an advocate of Confucianism, and a great statesman that he earned the title, "the prince of literature."

Han Yü had a sad and hard life in his childhood. After the early death of his parents he lived with his elder brother, a minor official, who also died not long afterwards. The orphaned boy was brought up by his brother's widow together with her own son, under very difficult circumstances. He worked hard and devoted himself to the study of the Confucian Classics, which he soon mastered. After having passed the state examination in his early twenties, he started an official career that was to be punctuated by many upsets and disappointments. Once in 819 he endangered himself by addressing a memorial to the throne against the elaborate preparations being made by the state to receive the Buddha's fingerbone, which he called "a filthy object" and which he said should be "handed over to the proper officials for destruction by water and fire to eradicate forever its origin." This so infuriated the emperor that he ordered Han Yü's death, and it was only through the intercession of his friends at court that the death sentence was commuted to demotion to the governorship of a remote district in Kwangtung. Here he made his famous address to the crocodile, denouncing it for its disturbance of "the peace of the river" and threatening a life-and-death fight to evict it and "its accursed brood southward to the broad ocean, far from the presence of the emperor's appointed official." After the death of the reigning monarch, he returned to court and rose during the next reign to the vice-presidency of the Board of Civil Office. He was posthumously honored as the President of the Board of Rites.

Han Yü was a leading thinker and writer of the T'ang dynasty. He advanced the idea that "the function of literature is to convey the *tao*," meaning here the philosophical and moral principle expounded by the Confucians. As shown in his famous essay "On the Origin of *Tao*," what he called *tao* is not the teaching of Lao-tzu or Buddha, but the traditional Confucian doctrine, handed down by the sage kings, Yao and Shun, through the founders of the three ancient dynasties, (Hsia, Shang, Chou) to Confucius and Mencius. Han Yü conceived of literature as a vehicle for the expression and advancement of the *tao* or Confucian orthodoxy. He strove for the spread of Confucian morality and political thought, and the defense of the Confucian faith against the encroachment of heterodox teachings, in particular Buddhism, which he denounced as unproductive, antisocial, and alien. He demanded that literature should help to propagate moral, political, and social ideals, and that to do it effectively, it should revert from the artificial and extravagant style of the pre-T'ang period to the simple, direct, and forceful style of the Classics.

Han Yü's neoclassical movement went beyond a mere restoration of the classical style; it was actually a re-creation on the basis of ancient writings of a practical and logical prose capable of presenting the ideas and stating the arguments effectively. He objected just as much to the slavish imitation of archaic style and the repetition of stale phrases and expressions as he did to literary adornments that obscure meaning and content. Instead, he advocated the use of a new language that was vigorous, well disciplined, and pruned of superfluities. Han Yü was a born propagandist, energetic and fearless. "In the beginning of his campaign," testified a contemporary writer, "the people were startled; in the middle, they ridiculed and opposed him (Han Yü, however, became even more resolute); and in the end, they all united in his support, and the task was accomplished."

A great and influential teacher, Han Yü was for a number of years instructor at the Imperial Academy (literally, Academy of the Nation's Youth) and junior tutor of the crown prince. He had a large following, their support accounting for his widespread influence and the success of his literary campaigns. He had some interesting observations on education itself. In the essay, "A Talk on Instruction," he dwelt on the relationship between instructor and student. He wrote: "It matters not whether the person is noble or mean, old or young; so long as the true doctrine resides in him, he is my teacher." "Therefore," he concluded, "a student is not necessarily less good than his teacher, and a teacher not perforce more sagacious than his student. It is only that there is a difference in the time of learning the true doctrine and in the specialization of one's skill and profession."

An imaginary episode at the Imperial Academy is related in Han Yü's essay, "An Explanatory Note on the Advancement of Learning," which reveals poignantly the many mortifications of his life. The essay starts in a mock-heroic tone:

> Mr. Instructor of the Nation's Youth entered the great academy in the morning and summoning all the students to stand below in the hall, lectured to them: "The scholar becomes proficient in learning through diligence but suffers from indolence. The way of life is attained through deliberate thought but ruined by casual negligence. . . . You students should worry that you are not proficient in your learning but not that the officials are unenlightened; you should worry that your way of life is unaccomplished but not that the officials are unfair."

Before he was able to finish, one of the pupils interrupted him. Laughing aloud, the student said that this speech was not borne out by the example of the teacher himself, who had devoted his life to learning, distinguished himself in literary writings, and cultivated diligently his character, and who yet had lived a frustrated and impoverished life:

> The winter is warm and yet your children wail for being cold; the year is plentiful and yet your wife sobs for hunger. Your head is as bald as an infant's and your teeth have wide gaps. What merit has your life if you die in the end? You do not seem to worry about all this and instead, you attempt to teach us to do the same.

In the last part, Han Yü tried to defend his position, but rather feebly and half-heartedly. His only consolation was that even Mencius and Hsün-tzu, the two great followers of Confucius, suffered a fate similar to his.

This essay may be interpreted differently, but it seems to be in the main a humorous and dispassionate exposition, through the mouths of the instructor and the student, of the author's own mental conflict and his stoic acceptance of the failures and frustrations of his career. While Han Yü generally impresses the reader as a serious scholar and a writer of formal polemic essays, he had nevertheless a light side to his nature and at times would blend earnest thought with dry humor, not peculiarly his but typically Chinese, as in his playful address to the crocodile. He was also a master of satire, which is often pungent but never crude. In "Bidding Farewell to Li Yüan upon His Return to the P'an Valley," after having compared the men of nobility with the hermit, he bent his satirical barb on a third type of person, the lowly sycophant,

> he who attends at the gate of the high official's residence and who walks along the road of profit and influence. He is about to put his foot forward when he stumbles; about to open his mouth when he stutters. He lives in filth without a sense of shame and dies by execution after having fallen into the net of crime and punishment. Should he be lucky enough to escape such a fate, he would not desist in his lowly action until his death in old age. Do you consider this kind of person virtuous or degenerate?

Perhaps his best piece of satire is the following allegorical essay, "Miscellaneous Sayings, Number Four," which alludes to Po-lo, a famous connoisseur of noble steeds, as weeping over one that was straining to draw a salt wagon:

> In this world Po-lo appeared first before there were fleet horses capable of a thousand *li* a day. Thousand-*li* horses are common enough, but Po-lo is not. For this reason, although there have been noble steeds, they merely suffer at the hands of the lackeys and die in the stable together with the hackneys without being recognized as thousand-*li* steeds. A steed capable of a thousand *li* sometimes consumes a peck of rice for one meal. Its feeder, however, does not know that it eats because of its capability for a thousand *li*. This kind of horse, even though it has the ability, is not fed sufficient food; therefore, its strength is deficient and its beauty not outwardly shown. Thus it fails even to match an ordinary horse and how could it be expected to be capable of a thousand *li*?
> One whips it in the wrong way and feeds it insufficiently so that it cannot show forth its utmost ability. Failing to understand the meaning of its neighs but holding a whip before it, one says: "There are no noble steeds under the heavens." Alas! Are there really no noble steeds or is it that they are not known?

The multi-faceted aspect of Han Yü's prose is also shown in his essay, "In Memoriam, for the Twelfth Young Gentleman," that is, the twelfth male member of the clan generation, who was no other than his elder brother's son. Although long separated from each other since Han Yü had left home in search of an official career, the two had been able to maintain a close relationship and exchange frequent messages; then suddenly the news of his nephew's death broke upon Han Yü. He seemed to be inconsolable for the loss of the young man, whose parents had so befriended him in his orphanhood. Thus he exclaimed in this sacrificial address:

> Alas! It is true! My elder brother's abundant virtue notwithstanding, his offspring has died young. And you, a man of pure intelligence fit for engaging in the affairs of the family, do not live to receive its favors. Unfathomable indeed is the decree of Heaven and inscrutable are the workings of the gods; incomprehensible is the so-called eternal principle and unknowable the span of a man's life.

The essay concludes with a deeply moving emotional outburst:

> O, you, blue heavens, why do you bring me to such extremities? Henceforth, I have no desire to live in this mortal world. I will seek a few hundred acres of farmlands on the banks of the I and Ying to while away my declining years, teaching my boy and your boy, if haply they may grow, and our daughters until they are married. And that is all! Alas! All words will end but the emotions last forever! Do you know or do you not know? Alas! I am woebegone! I beg you to partake of this sacrifice.

The same mournful feeling pervades the memorial essay and grave inscription Han Yü wrote for his friend, Liu Tsung-yüan (773–819), another great T'ang writer. The two conceived a warm friendship and shared equal fame as poets and prose writers. They were, however, quite different in temperament and philosophic ideas. Liu Tsung-yüan was a man of retired and modest nature, less given to self-praise and publicity. The scope of his thought is broader and more liberal than that of his friend, who seems to have had a one-track mind. Liu Tsung-yüan, in fact, did not share Han Yü's strong prejudice against Buddhism and Taoism. Although he was also a good Confucian, he was tolerant of other philosophical systems and their believers, recognizing their merits as well as their weaknesses. The broadness of his mind, the temperance of his nature, and his noble endurance of the hardships of life have endeared him to many readers.

Liu Tsung-yüan passed through the usual stages in the career of a T'ang writer: success in the state examination, official preferment at court, and involvement in government politics. After the failure of his faction, he was exiled to posts in remote regions, first as sub-prefect of Yung-chou in Hunan and later as governor of Liu-chou in Kwangsi, where he died in office at the age of forty-six. While these last years constituted a sad chapter in his life, they nevertheless contributed to the enrichment of his experience and the heightening of his literary achievements. Just as the poverty and misery of the backward southern regions provided him with food for thought and literary composition, so the unspoiled natural beauty of these places inspired him in many of his landscape essays. He is also known for his short biographical sketches and allegorical fables of a satirical nature. As a whole his prose works, including those on history and philosophy, are lucid in presentation, penetrating in observation, and lively in description. The fine workmanship and compact structure of his essays distinguish them from the other prose writings of his time.

Liu Tsung-yüan was noted for some of his animal fables, each of which has a clear-cut moral and a biting satire directed against human foibles and rapacity, as in the following piece, "The Rats of a Family in Yung-chou":

> A certain person in Yung-chou was extremely superstitious about the days that are tabooed. Since the year of his birth fell on *tzu** and the symbolic animal governing *tzu* is the rat, he loved rats. He did not rear cats and dogs and forbade his house boys to hit the rats. His granary and kitchen were wide open to their intrusion, no matter what havoc they caused. Hence the rats spread the news to one another and all came to his house where they fed themselves without fear of danger. No utensil in the room was left unbroken and no dress in the clothes-horse was whole, while the food and drink were mostly the leftovers of the rats. In daytime, they roamed in crowds with men; at night they pilfered and gnawed, fought and rioted. Their noises were of countless varieties and no sleep was possible. Nevertheless, he was not disgusted.
>
> A few years later, the man moved to some other place. When another came to live in his house, the rats behaved as in the past. The newcomer said, "These are the abominable animals of the *yin* species. Their looting and rioting are particularly excessive, but why is it that things have come to such a pass?" He then borrowed five or six cats, closed all the doors and, removing the roof tiles, poured water into the rat holes. He also hired boys to catch them. The slaughtered rats piled up in a mound and when their bodies were thrown away into the wilds, their stench lingered for several months. Alas! They had considered that to be well fed and to live without the fear of danger was something that would last forever!

In Liu Tsung-yüan's short biographies appear a great variety of people, particularly artisans, villagers, and other commoners of the town and market. Some of them are distinguished by their professional attainment, such as the master carpenter who does not know how to fix the limping foot of his bed but who directs and orders around the other workmen with the skill and authority of a born leader; others by the intuitive knowledge of natural law such as the gardener, Camel-back Kuo, whose trees, whether

---

* *Tzu* is the first of the twelve terrestrial branches.

planted or transplanted, always thrive and yield abundant fruit. When asked about his secret, he replies that he is merely following the natural bent of the trees, unlike the other gardeners who are either too fond of or too anxious about their plants, watching them at dawn and stroking them in the evening. Having already walked away, they yet turn round to look back.

> Some even scratch the tree barks with their fingernails to ascertain whether they are dead or alive, or shake the tree trunks to examine the firmness or looseness of their planting. Thus they interfere every day with the natural bent of the plant so that love becomes a bane, and anxiety turns into enmity. Therefore they do not do as well as I—not that I have any special ability.

The essay ends with the Camel-back extending his discourse on tree-planting into a philosophical discussion of government reminiscent of Taoism. On the other hand, "The Snake-Catcher" is an illustration of the Confucian statement that "tyrannical government is fiercer than a tiger." Here the satire is extremely bitter, inspired no doubt by the author's own sentiments on the subject and perhaps by his personal experience in Yung-chou. The wilds there yielded a breed of snake with a black body and white stripes. Though highly venomous, it was greatly valued for its healing properties—when caught and dried, its flesh was used to cure leprosy, rheumatism, and cancer, to remove sloughing flesh, and to kill the "three vermin."* For this reason it was in great demand by the imperial court as a tribute, for which tax exemption was allowed. The family of the snake-catcher had been engaged in this employment for three generations. Although both his father and grandfather had died of snake poison, the man had kept to the family profession for the past twelve years, and when offered a different kind of occupation burst into tears, saying:

> So you would take pity on me and keep me alive! Nonetheless, the misfortunes of this service are not as great as those of restoring my tax payment. If I had not continued in this employ, I would have suffered long ago. Our family has lived here, altogether sixty years now. During this time, the livelihood of our neighbors has become more difficult every day. They have exhausted the yield of the land and used up the resources of the house. Wailing and crying, they moved away; thirsty and hungry, they wore themselves out and fell prostrate on the road. Struck by wind and rain, they endured cold and heat; inhaling deadly poison, they died constantly in confused heaps. Of those families who were here in my grand-

---

* Creeping insects that are parasitic on three parts of the human body, viz. head, belly, and feet.

father's time, there remains at present not more than one in every ten; of those in my father's time, not more than two or three; and of those here with me during the last twelve years, not more than four or five. They are either dead or gone elsewhere, but I alone survive because of snake-catching.

When the fierce officers descend on our village, they cry and yell in the east and west; they hustle and bustle to the south and north. Agitated and frightened, even the chickens and dogs have no peace. As for myself, I rise attentively to look into the jar, and finding that my snakes are still there, I feel relaxed and lie down to sleep again. Carefully I feed them and offer them to the government when the time comes. Then I retire to eat with relish the produce of this land, awaiting the completion of the allotted span of my life.

Thus, only twice a year have I courted death while at other times, I enjoy my life peacefully. How would this compare with the lot of my neighbors who suffer every day! And even though I sooner or later am to die here, my death will come much more slowly than that of my neighbors. How dare I complain!

While Liu Tsung-yüan lacked Han Yü's eloquence and fervor, he surpassed his friend in his ability to describe the beauties of nature. His best works are the landscape essays written in the last years of his life at Yung-chou and Liu-chou. Based upon his keen, on-the-spot observations, his descriptions of the mountains and rivers in these essays are alive with the vivid images of poetry and the clear colors of painting. Recording the building of a thatched hut on the sunny side of Ma-t'ui Mountain in Kwangsi—"with the white clouds as a fence and the blue mountain range as a screen to show my frugality"—he wrote as follows:

This mountain rises precipitously amidst a vast azure expanse, rushing straight up to the clouds for a distance of tens and hundreds of *li*. Its tail coils around desolate and distant nooks while at its head the water pours into an immense stream. The other mountains come to it for an audience like stars encircling it and bowing in obeisance. Its fantastic verdant range spreads like an embroidered silk of variegated colors and shapes.

When he was in Yung-chou, he discovered a beautiful and secluded spot which he frequented. West of it was a little hill with strange rock formations:

By the stone dam stands a hillock overgrown with bamboo. There, innumerable are the rocks that either thrust up in anger or prostrate themselves like cripples, but all protrude with a load of earth as if to compete against each other in their oddly fantastic shapes. Those descending from lofty positions in massed layers are like oxen and horses drinking in the stream, while others rushing up and butting forward in horned formations are like bears clambering among the mountains.

Further west, Liu Tsung-yüan found a small stone-bottomed pool, which he described in a short essay as beautiful as a gem:

> Walking westward about one hundred and twenty paces from the knoll, I heard from across a cluster of bamboos the sound of flowing water like tinkling girdle pendants. I rejoiced at heart. Cutting down the bamboos to make a path, I saw below a small pool, whose waters were unusually clear and cool, with one huge rock for its bottom. Near the bank the stream emerged from its stony bed, shaped variously like a shoal, an islet, a grotto, or a cliff. Verdant trees screened and wavered; green creepers trailed and entwined; upward and downward they canopied and brushed. In the pool were hundreds of fish, all suspended in the stream. The sunbeams fell like lucent water; the fishes cast their shadows on the rocks, dozing and motionless, then abruptly disappeared, darting far away. Their coming and going were sudden and swift as if they were frolicking with the roaming visitor.
>
> Looking away southwestward from the pool, I found the stream crooked like the Dipper and winding like a snake, sometimes clearly in view and sometimes hidden away, the contour of its shoreline zigzag like a dog's teeth, and its point of origin untraceable.
>
> I sat down by the pool, encircled on all sides by bamboo trees, alone and desolate, without any human track in sight. Still and sad, deep and secluded, the place numbed the soul and chilled the bones. Finding it too purified to be good for a prolonged stay, I recorded the scene and then went away.

By introducing into these descriptions a personal note of sorrow and solitude, he also gave the inanimate objects of nature an emotional context, personifying them and rendering them meaningful. For instance, while in Yung-chou he built his home on a stream which he called the Muddled Stream, because he himself was so muddleheaded as to incur the emperor's displeasure and to be thus exiled to this place. Above the Muddled Stream rose the Muddled Hill, not far from which were located a Muddled Spring, a Muddled Ditch and a Muddled Pond. In the center of the pond was a Muddled Islet, on which stood the Muddled Hall to the east and the Muddled Arbor to the south. His "Preface to the Poems on the Muddled Stream" concludes as follows:

> Although the stream profits not this world, it reflects clearly the innumerable species. It sparkles and penetrates; it tinkles like bells and stones. It makes the muddleheaded one laugh with joy, full of longing and admiration, and so enraptures him that he can hardly leave.

> Even though I am unfit for this mundane world, I often console myself with literary writings with which to cleanse a multitude of affairs and in which to captivate the hundred postures without any taboo. I sing of the Muddled Stream in muddled verses that are both incomprehensible and unoffending, abstruse and so intended. They will transcend the primeval atmosphere of nature and blend with the inaudible and the unseen. No one will know me there, secluded and alone. So I compose these eight muddled poems and have them carved on the rocks of the stream.

With such fine specimens of verbal landscape painting, often animated by poignant but unruffled emotions, Liu Tsung-yüan succeeded in establishing for the first time in Chinese literary history a new and important genre of literary prose, the landscape essay, of which he was both inventor and acknowledged master.

In the Sung dynasty, after a brief period of reversion to the euphuistic style with emphasis on artistry and erudition, the works of Han Yü and Liu Tsung-yüan were established as the patterns of Chinese prose to be followed by all later writers. As a whole, the Sung dynasty witnessed the rising popularity and ultimate triumph of neoclassic prose. All Sung prose masters were outstanding in the world of politics as in the world of letters. They contributed to the development of Chinese prose with their political and economic treatises, historical writings, and philosophical colloquies.

The most important Sung author responsible for the propagation and success of the neoclassical movement was Ou-yang Hsiu (1007–1072), an admirer of and worthy successor to Han Yü. Like Han Yü, Ou-yang Hsiu struggled for an education in his childhood, his father having died before he was four and left the family in great poverty. He received his education from his mother, who taught him writing first. He was so poor that he could not afford pen and paper, but had to write with a reed stem on the earth. With diligence and perseverance, he managed eventually to distinguish himself in academic and political circles. Except for a few years of banishment to provincial posts, he had a successful official career and attained eminent positions at court, once rising to the premiership. The great authority he wielded as the supervisor of state examinations attracted to his doors many men of literary talents. Under his patronage and tutelage, several Sung writers rose to fame and eminence. His sphere of influence widened when his protégés, like Su Shih, had their own groups of friends and disciples. As an arbiter of the literary taste of his time, Ou-yang Hsiu was instrumental in bringing to a successful conclusion the task that Han Yü had started so energetically.

Like most of his contemporaries, Ou-yang Hsiu was an indefatigable and voluminous writer, well versed in both poetry and prose, and orthodox in his literary criticism. He believed that literature should have a serious purpose and bear the author's distinctive individual traits. After having enumerated the many sages of the Confucian school, he wrote: "They are all different in character, each attaining true faith in his own manner." He asserted that those who were superior in the true faith, that is, the Confucian orthodoxy, would have little difficulty in gaining literary excellence. On the other hand, he opposed the use of high-flown words without substance. "I personally deplore those whose writing is so ornate and whose language so flowery that they are not much different from the luxuriant plants waving in the wind and the sweet voices of birds and beasts that pass through the ears."

Substantial in content, broad in scope, and of permanent value, Ou-yang Hsiu's own writings consist of essays of all kinds: narratives, biographical sketches, prefaces, memorials, epistles, and epitaphs. He was also a co-author of the *New History of the T'ang Dynasty* and the compiler of the *History of the Five Dynasties*, the dynasties which preceded the Sung. The following, "An Essay on the Biographies of Court Entertainers" in his *History of the Five Dynasties*, is quoted in full as an example of his formal historical writing:

> Alas for the law of prosperity and decline! Although regarded as Heaven's decree, is it not truly the handiwork of men? This is known from the way in which Emperor Chuang gained the empire and then lost it.* It has been said that his father, the Prince of Tsin, on his deathbed handed his son three arrows, saying, "Liang is our enemy; the Prince of Yen was set up by us and the Khitans have sworn brotherhood with us—yet they have both deserted us to follow Liang. That I could not avenge this wrong before death is my great regret. Now, take these three arrows and forget not your father's wish!"
>
> Emperor Chuang received the arrows and stored them in the ancestral temple. Later, whenever he started a war, he would send his attendants to inform the temple with the sacrifice of a sheep. He would ask for one of the arrows, place it in an embroidered quiver, and carry it to the forefront of the battle. Upon returning from victory, he would put it back. At one time he bound with a silver cord the father and son of the Yen princely family; at another time he enclosed in a box the heads of the Liang monarch and his ministers. On both occasions, he entered the Grand Temple and returned the arrows to his deceased father, informing him of the successes. How splendid was his spirit, which indeed could be called exalted!

* Emperor Chuang of the Late T'ang dynasty overthrew the Liang dynasty, the first of the Five Dynasties, but later lost his empire through neglect and, it was said, dalliance with actors and musicians.

But after the enemies had been overthrown and the empire established, suddenly one night the outcries of a commoner were echoed and answered by rebels on every side. This time Emperor Chuang was forced to flee eastward in haste, his soldiers dispersed even before they had sighted the enemy—this time the sovereign and his ministers, gazing at each other with no place to turn to, could only swear to Heaven, cut their hair, and weep until the tears drenched the lapels of their clothes—what a fall it was! Is it true that the empire is difficult to gain but easy to lose? Or is it that the causes of success and failure are all traceable to human actions?

The *Classic of History* says, "Haughtiness invites disaster; humility receives benefit." That proper anxiety and diligence can restore a nation while dissipation and ease can bring ruin is a law of nature. Therefore when he flourished, not all the heroes of the empire could contend with him, but when he declined, only a few scores of actors and entertainers could harry him until he perished, a laughingstock of all the world, his empire destroyed. Indeed, woes and calamities are often caused by some indifferent, trivial occurrences, and the intelligent and brave are often wrecked by those they indulge. Not alone are the actors to be blamed in this respect!

The last sentence, according to Chinese critics, is an artistic and ingenious way of ending the essay. It is suggestive and significant in that it has the effect of arousing a lingering feeling and a ruminating mood. Thus the subtle beauty of the original is somewhat marred in the following translation: "Truly misfortunes ofttimes spring from trivial and unexpected causes; and wisdom and courage are often marred by foibles other than a passion for theatrical display."[1]

Ou-yang Hsiu made a very interesting comment on the relationship between poverty and poetry in the first paragraph of his "Preface to the Poetic Collection of Mei Sheng-yü":[2]

I have heard that poets rarely become successful in life but are commonly indigent. Could that be true? Generally speaking, the poems that have been transmitted to posterity are the compositions of certain hard-pressed men of antiquity. Scholars who cherish great thoughts but fail to apply them in life are often fond of visiting mountain peaks and river banks. Whenever they see insects and fish, grass and plants, wind and clouds, birds and beasts, they investigate the rare and curious aspects of the many objects and species. Within them there is also a latent accumulation of depressed thoughts and resentful feelings. These sentiments, when allegorized in a satire or a lament to express, as it were, the sorrows of outcast officials and widowed women or to depict some almost unutterable human emotions, become the more refined the poorer the poet gets. Thus it is not poetry that causes poverty, but poverty that leads to artistic excellence.

Ou-yang Hsiu's genial personality is shown in the essay, "The Old Drunkard's Arbor." It contains a vivid description of the idyllic beauties of nature; of the happy, peaceful existence of the common people—burden carriers, wayfarers, old people hobbling along, and children carried in arms or dragged along by hand; and of the conviviality of the feasts and games presided over by the old drunken governor, in whose honor the arbor was named.

> Soon, when the setting sun lies on the mountains and the shadows of men become disorderly, he returns home, followed by his guests. In the shady darkness of the woods are raised the voices of birds and beasts, above and below; that is their rejoicing after the human visitors have gone. The birds and beasts, however, know only the joys of the hills and woods, not the joys of men; the people know that they rejoice with the governor by following him in his excursion, but they do not know that the governor rejoices in their rejoicing. When drunk, he shares his joy with others, and when sober, he narrates it in a literary composition. Such is the governor: Ou-yang Hsiu of Lu-ling.

In the hands of Ou-yang Hsiu, the *fu*, previously described as a prose-poem, becomes more prose than poetry. Although there are still paired sentences and rhyming quatrains in his *fu* compositions, they have fewer elaborate descriptive passages and less piling up of ornate epithets and obscure allusions. His *fu*, "The Autumn Sound," is one of the finest specimens of this genre. It combines a beautiful description of autumn with philosophical disquisitions on the workings of nature, interposed with the author's own moral sentiments. Toward the end of the *fu*, he becomes so overcharged with emotion that he bursts forth into rhythmic utterances typical of the *fu*. The following translated extract aims to reproduce the sentiment and style, not the rhyming scheme, of the original:

> Alas! Grass and plants are inanimate and in due time they fade and wilt. Man is a sentient animal, the divinest of all living things. A hundred cares agitate his heart and ten thousand affairs exhaust his body. What perturbs him internally will perforce wreck his spirit-essence. Moreover, he ruminates on what his strength cannot attain and grieves over what his intelligence is incapable of comprehending. No wonder the thriving and the ruddy-colored becomes as withered as a stick, and the glossy and black is streaked with grey. How could man, who possesses not the qualities of metal and stone, ever hope to compete for prosperity with the grass and plants? Having thus realized what the killer is, why should there be any cause for grievance against the autumn wind?

This type of *fu* was further enriched by Su Shih, whose poetic writings have been discussed in an earlier chapter. A prolific writer like Ou-yang Hsiu, his chief contribution is the *fu*, which he brought closer to the realm of prose. His compositions are lucid and fluent with a poetic flavor and a sensitive appreciation of the cadence of words. In them are expressed his enjoyment of the finer things of life and nature, his philosophical ideas and tenets. His all-embracing philosophy transcends the narrow limits of any particular school, for like the Neo-Confucianist Chu Hsi, Su Shih had distinct Taoist and Buddhist inclinations. He associated with the devotees of both faiths and his mind was open to all ideas that came his way. In the "Tower of Transcendence" he advocated the idea of "roaming beyond the nature of things," doing which one cannot but be happy wherever one goes. On the other hand, those who "roam inside the nature of things" can only court sorrows and disasters, for "human desires are endless, but the things that can satisfy them are limited." Then he continued in a philosophical vein reminiscent of Chuang-tzu's writings:

> Not that there is greatness or smallness in the things themselves. When viewed from within, there is nothing that is not tall and immense. He who towers above me from such a commanding height and with such massiveness always dazes and confuses me, turning everything upside down, as if I were watching a fight through a knothole; and how could I know where victory or defeat lies? Hence, beauty and ugliness grow rampant everywhere, and sorrows and joys are born. What a tragedy!

A moralizing tendency, characteristic of most Chinese essayists, is found in "A Tower across the Void," which expounds the theme of the inscrutability of mundane affairs, particularly the rise and fall, the fulness and decay of all things; and in "The Arbor of Flying Cranes," which exalts the joys and advantages of a carefree hermit life:

> Alas! A south-facing monarch cannot even fondle something as pure and leisurely in its flight as a crane, for the love of this bird will cost him his kingdom; whereas a scholar who withdraws to the mountains and forests will not be harmed even by something as corrupt and dissipating as wine. Indeed what harm is there in the crane? From this, one may observe that the pleasures the two derive from life are so different that they cannot be mentioned in the same breath.

Perhaps the best example of Su Shih's philosophical flight and moral excursion, happily illuminated by poetic imagination, is the *fu* "The Red Cliff." It relates a boat trip Su Shih took one moonlit night on the Yangtze, where the Red Cliff stood. In a conversation with his companion Su Shih is reported to have remarked as follows:

Friend, how much do you know about the water and the moon?
Though flowing away like this, the water is always here; though
alternately waxing and waning like that, the moon has neither
diminished nor grown. That is, from the viewpoint of whatever is
changeable, even Heaven and Earth last no more than the twinkling
of an eye; but from the viewpoint of whatever is unchangeable,
then the objects and I are all eternal. So what is there to yearn for?
Moreover, every object between Heaven and Earth has its own
master. If the thing does not belong to me, not even a single par-
ticle can I take. Only the clear wind over the waters and the bright
moon amongst the mountains—one makes music when caught in
the ears and the other becomes color when encountered by the eyes
—only these two may be taken without restraint and used without
depleting their supply. They are the inexhaustible hidden wealth of
the Creator and the joys you and I share together.

Hearing this, "The guest was pleased and laughed with rapture as the cups
were rinsed and refilled with wine. After having consumed all the meat
and fruit, amid a litter of cups and plates, we lay down in the boat jumbled
against each other, not knowing that there was already whiteness in the
eastern skies."

Such a work shows clearly that the *fu*, first compiled by Ssu-ma
Hsiang-ju and other Han writers as an elaborate descriptive prose-poem,
has undergone important changes during the Sung dynasty and, aside
from the occasional use of the rhyme (which cannot be reproduced in
translation), has become almost indistinguishable from any ordinary
prose. Thus the T'ang-Sung essayists not only established a new prose
form, divested of all the trappings and artificialities of the antithetical
style, but also brought what was originally a cross breed between poetry
and prose into the enlarged domain of prose. These changes were brought
to fulfillment in the works of Ou-yang Hsiu, Su Shih, and other Sung
writers, many of them also first-rate poets; together with the T'ang
masters they enriched Chinese prose with many of their own substantial
contributions. In the meantime, the growth of colloquial literature was
so phenomenal in the Sung and post-Sung periods that it deserves special
attention in the following chapters.

10 : Literary and Colloquial Tales

The six hundred years of the T'ang-Sung period (from the seventh century to the thirteenth), which may properly be called the Chinese Renaissance, stood midway between the ancient and the modern in the long literary progress of the Chinese people. After a temporary lapse into inactivity and mediocrity during the middle ages (third to sixth centuries) Chinese literature flourished once again with increasing exuberance and vigor. While Chinese neoclassical literature reached a new zenith of greatness, Chinese colloquial literature made its formal debut about the same time, thus paving the way for its later development, which will be the main subject of the remaining portion of this book. The germs of both fiction and drama had, of course, long been existent in pre-T'ang times, but it was in the T'ang and Sung periods that they emerged from their embryo stage.

Fables, anecdotes, and legends abound in the philosophical and historical writings of the Chou and Han dynasties, the Chinese being no exception to the apparently universal human love of stories. A great deal of narrative writing unconnected with philosophy and history also appeared. By the first century A.D., there were in existence some 1,380 stories in fifteen collections.[1] Mostly in the form of sayings and notes, legends and myths, these were originally street talk and roadside gossip collected and put into writing by minor court officials. They were regarded as the works of the *hsiao-shuo chia* (literally "minor-talk writers")—hence the Chinese term *hsiao-shuo* for fiction. But while *hsiao-shuo* may have described appropriately these Han or pre-Han stories, the use of the term by later scholars for any kind of fiction, including a full-length novel, is rather misleading.

The earliest Chinese stories extant were written during the Six Dynasties from the fourth to sixth centuries A.D., the authenticity of those claiming an earlier date being dubious. The topics range widely from the myth of creation, legendary rulers and heroes, strange tales of mountains and seas, travelogues, wit and humor, fairy and ghost tales, to conversational pieces about ancient and contemporary celebrities. The popularity of supernatural tales is due probably to the influence of the Buddhist and Taoist religions. One of these early tales, "The Young Student of Yang-hsien" by Wu Chün (469–520), the author of a collection of strange and humorous stories, shows clearly traces of Buddhist origin. It is a curious tale of "lovers within a lover"—also a flagrant example of faithless love. First, a young student, traveling in a goose cage kept by a scholar-official, spat out from his mouth a beautiful woman with whom he feasted. Then as he fell asleep from drink, the woman spat out a handsome youth to dally with. Later, when she went to join the student, the youth in turn spat out a female companion with whom he jested and drank. Finally, as the young student was about to wake up, the other three all disappeared, one swallowed up by another, until only the student was left to say farewell to the scholar-official, who witnessed and recorded the story.

Crude and incidental in nature, meager in plot interest and characterization, these anecdotes are not comparable in literary quality with later stories. It was not until the T'ang dynasty that Chinese fiction made an important stride in its development. While continuing the storytelling tradition, T'ang writers introduced the new *ch'uan-ch'i*, or tales of the marvellous, written in the literary style. Among the influences that contributed to the rise of this form are the neoclassical movement in prose, which provides a suitable medium for narration; the practice of the candidates in state examinations presenting specimens of their writings, including literary tales, as a form of introduction to the examiner and other influential officials; and the prosperous, brilliant metropolitan life with all its gaieties and tragedies, from which much of the T'ang fictional material was drawn. The literary tales flourished during the hundred years from mid-eighth to mid-ninth century, toward the end of which also appeared a number of story collections by individual writers. *Ch'uan-ch'i*, the term for this literary genre, is actually the title of one of these collections.

T'ang story writers seem to have been mostly men of letters who congregated in Ch'ang-an in quest of opportunities for political advancement and literary fame. Some attained high official positions while others distinguished themselves in literary circles. As artists, they aimed to create interesting and moving tales in a simple, effective prose devoid of poetic flourishes and interpolations. While supernatural elements still abound in these stories, there is an obvious tendency to introduce realistic human material to reflect life in metropolitan society. Vividly depicted are the numerous activities of the T'ang city dwellers such as merchants, artisans, courtesans, vagabonds, and beggars. Like most other types of Chinese literature, these tales teach a moral lesson, often in the form of satire, or of admonition expressed in no uncertain terms at the end of the story.

T'ang literary tales deal mainly with three subjects: (1) the supernatural, (2) love, and (3) chivalry. Their boundaries, however, are not at all well defined. Love, for instance, may be of a supernatural kind between man and spirit or ghost; and a chivalric swordsman may play an important role in bringing lovers together. A supernatural tale may relate dreams that reproduce or repudiate real life. Moreover, none of the writers specialized in any story type. Thus this classification is rather arbitrary and intended only for expediency in discussion. As the authors are generally unfamiliar, their names are usually not mentioned here.

The earliest tale, "The Ancient Mirror," written in the first years of the T'ang dynasty, may be regarded as a summation of the supernatural stories of the Six Dynasties. With an ancient mirror as the central focus, the author has brought together a series of strange episodes of the fox, snake, tortoise, monkey, cock, and rat, all of which have assumed human forms but are exposed and reduced to their original shape by the magic mirror. Also woven into the story are descriptions of the mirror's radiance, its signs and emanations, and its healing properties. But although unity is gained by the use of the mirror as a source of the wonders that have been wrought, the tale is merely a parade of incidents without motive or plot.

"The White Monkey," though bordering on the supernatural, is the first Chinese short story with a genuine human interest, a sustained narrative, and some fine description. The story relates the kidnaping and recovery of a general's beautiful wife in the mountainous regions of the southwest hinterland. Her captor was a powerful white monkey, whom "even a hundred men could not subdue." The discovery of a rain-drenched embroidered shoe amongst a dense growth of vines and bushes led the general to the monkey's mountain den. Here, in a rock-hewn hall, his wife lay sick "on a stone couch covered with thick cushions and piled-up mattings." In this place were many other women captives, with whom the husband plotted the death of the white monkey. It was agreed that the general and his men would first bring to the mountain fine wine and fat dogs as well as many catties of hemp strings. While they remained out of sight, the women would feast the white monkey with wine and meat and then bind him tightly on the couch after he had become drunk. The plot proved successful. When the general rushed in with his soldiers at the women's call, he saw "a huge white monkey bound to the bed by his four paws. The creature recoiled at the sight of the men and struggled to free himself, his eyes flashing like lightning. They vied with each other to strike him with their weapons, but the blows fell as on iron and stone. It was only when they stabbed at his belly below the navel that the blades sank into the body and blood gushed out in streams." The general's wife,

143

however, was already pregnant by her captor and the child born of this strange wedlock grew up to be one of the famous writers of his time.

As both the general and his son were prominent figures and the son was known to be apelike in appearance, it has been suggested that this anonymous story may have been the work of an enemy attacking the general's family. Others saw in it a resemblance to the Indian epic, *Ramayana*, in the monkey's role as the kidnaper of beautiful women. Whatever its origin or intention, this story of the early T'ang dynasty heralds the beginning of a new type of short story far more advanced in technique than all those that had appeared before.

While "The White Monkey" is a fine example of an animal tale, the "Governor of the Southern Tributary State," in spite of its supernatural framework, is primarily a moral satire. The author has clearly stated his position at the end of the story: "Believing it to be quite genuine, I have compiled this tale for those who are curious. Although it deals with strange supernatural things and unorthodox affairs, it is intended mainly as an admonition to the ambitious. Let future readers not regard this tale lightly as a mere series of coincidences, and let them beware of taking pride in worldly fame and rank." The story ends with the following quatrain:

> Noblest is his official position and rank,
> Overwhelming is his power in the capital,
> And yet, in the eyes of the wise men,
> He is not much different from the dwellers in an ant heap.

Power and pomp are the substance of a dream by a disappointed scholar and military man, the protagonist of the tale. One day, as he lay in a drunken stupor, he was taken by two purple-clad messengers down a hole under a big ash tree in the courtyard to the Kingdom of Ashendon. There he was given in marriage to the king's beautiful daughter and made the governor of Nan-k'o, the Southern Tributary State (literally, "the Southern Bough"). "The officials of the state, monks and priests, elders, musicians, sedan-carriers, guardsmen, and carriage drivers with bells clanging, all came out to greet him. People thronged and bustled about. Bells and drums made a loud din for miles around. A splendid array of turrets and pavilions, temples and monasteries, enveloped in a festive atmosphere, came into view as he entered the great city gate, above which were inscribed in big gold letters: 'The Southern Tributary State.'" He remained there for twenty years as governor and was so well liked by the people that monuments were erected to extol his virtue and temples built for sacrifice to his living spirit. Fame and success crowned his public life while five sons and two daughters blessed him at home. But at the zenith of his career, troubles and sorrows started to creep in. He was afflicted by the defeat of his army by that of a neighboring kingdom, the death of his wife, and the false accusations of a court enemy, which led to the king's animosity toward him. Deprived of attendants, isolated from friends, and confined to his house, he sank into a deep grief until one day he was sent back to the mortal world, accompanied by the same purple-clad messengers, taking the same road, but in a shabby carriage without the paraphernalia of his former journey. When he reached home, he saw his other self lying in the eastern verandah of the hall; suddenly frightened, he woke up from his dream.

Later, when he told it to his friends, they made a search of the hollow under the ash tree, where after much digging and cleaning, they found a big hole, "clear and well lighted and large enough to hold a couch. Above it were mounds of earth shaped like city walls, towers, and palaces, in which gathered swarms of ants. On one ant hill was a small tower, reddish in color, where lived two huge ants, three inches long with white wings and red heads. They were flanked on both sides by scores of big ants so that the others dared not approach them. These huge ants were the king and queen, and this was the capital of Ashendon." To its south lay another ant hill with smaller towers, which he identified as his Southern Tributary State. That same night there was a fierce storm and in the morning when he looked again at the holes, the ants had all gone. The popularity of this T'ang story has made the "dream of Nan-k'o" a euphemistic term for the fickleness and emptiness of materialistic life.

There are two distinct types of T'ang love stories: those between men and women, and those between men and animal spirits or ghosts. In the weird world of the T'ang stories, men had strange marital relations with female ghosts, fox ladies, and the dragon king's daughter. In all these, however, supernatural events have inevitably a human moral implication. Faithful love induces the disembodied soul of a sick girl to join her lover for five years and to give birth to two sons before the soul is reunited with the body, which suddenly becomes hale. The unusual beauty and incredible virtue of a vixen spirit help to make the life of a poor fellow happy and successful, even though he has to lose her in the end when she is set upon by hounds. "Alas! How wonderful that a supernatural being should have feelings like those of men," comments the author. "In her ability to protect her virtue in the face of violence and to remain faithful to her husband until death she is matched by few women nowadays!" In another tale, the daughter of a dragon king appears in a human form to marry a young scholar and to repay him for the favor of having delivered a letter to her father and thus freed her from the persecutions of her former dragon husband. Afterwards, the two live together not only forever happily, but

145

also as immortals. "Among the five categories of living creatures," so runs the moral of the story, "the best ones always possess spiritual powers . . . . Man, a hairless naked animal, has transmitted his virtues to the scaly creatures."*

Other tales have as their themes the comedies and tragedies of human love in the multicolored T'ang society. The tragic stories, which outnumber the rest, relate the romantic love of a high official's concubine for a young student, a love that causes her to be flogged to death at the hands of her master; the unhappy fate of a courtesan forced into concubinage by a general who has at home a jealous and shrewish wife; the pathetic end of a former princess abandoned by a young poet who professes to love her. All these stories have as their chief characters the concubine and the courtesan, examples of unfortunate, downtrodden womanhood in Chinese society.

In literature, however, the courtesan or sing-song girl appears in a different light from the ordinary run of prostitutes in that she sells her talents and intelligence as well as her bodily charms. In real life the product of an affluent and refined society, she entertains her patrons by singing, dancing, and playing music; well read and versed in poetry, she is the fitting companion of fledgling scholars and poets.

In the T'ang dynasty, Ch'ang-an was particularly the haunt of such aspiring young men from the provinces, who found life in the metropolis fascinating, dazzling, but lonely, and who therefore sought the company of these beautiful and gifted girls. Thus emerged a wealth of material on the courtesans in all types of Chinese literature, including the literary tales.

One of the best T'ang tales, remarkable for its narrative interest, vivid character portrayal, and rich descriptive details, is "The Story of Li Wa" by Po Hsing-chien (d. 826), younger brother of the poet Po Chü-i. The aim of the narrative is stated in an introductory paragraph:

> Li Wa, the Lady of Chien-kuo, was once a courtesan in Ch'ang-an, but as her conduct was admirable, unmatched, and worthy of praise, I, Po Hsing-chien, a supervisory censor, have undertaken to record and transmit her story.

The hero of the story was a young student from a noble and wealthy family. Like all other such youths, he was sent by his father to the capital for the state examination with ample money, fine clothes, attendants, a carriage and horses. One day, while driving around the city, he saw "a girl of exquisite and bewitching beauty such as the world had never seen

---

* The ancient Chinese divided all living creatures into five categories: (1) feathered (birds); (2) furred (beasts); (3) shelled (tortoise); (4) scaly (fish); and (5) hairless (man). The dragon is the chief of the scaly creatures.

before," leaning on a maidservant by the door of her house. Unable to tear himself away from her, he dropped his whip and waited for his servant to pick it up as he kept ogling the girl. She returned his glances with a look of responsive appeal, but he went away without daring to exchange a word with her. From his friend, an old-timer in Ch'ang-an, he learned that she was a well-born courtesan, who was favored by men of wealth and rank, and could hardly be moved without a million cash. This, however, did not deter the student from his love quest. The next day, he went to make a call at her house, pretending that he was looking for a place to rent. After having been received by an old, grey-haired woman with a bent back, he was taken inside to a guest hall.

> The old woman said, "I have a daughter who is young and tender. She has very few accomplishments, but she always enjoys the company of visitors. I would like to present her."
>
> Thereupon she called her daughter to come out. The girl had sparkling eyes and white wrists. She moved with such a charming grace that the student immediately rose up in confusion, not daring to raise his eyes to look at her. After having exchanged greetings and made a few remarks about the weather, he saw that her charms were indeed such as he had never seen before. He sat down again. Tea was made and wine served, the utensils all spotlessly clean.
>
> After a long while, it grew dark and the curfew drums resounded in all directions. When the old woman asked him how far out he lived, the student lied by saying, "several *li* beyond the Yen-p'ing gate," with the hope that he would be asked to stay because of the distance.
>
> "The drum has sounded," said the old woman, "you had better go right away or you will violate the curfew."
>
> "I have enjoyed so much the pleasure of your company," replied the student, "that I have not realized how late it has become. The road is long and far out, and I have no relatives in the city. What am I to do?"
>
> "If you don't consider our house too shabby," said the girl, "and since you have shown an inclination to live here, what harm is there if you stay overnight?"
>
> Several times the student glanced at the old woman. Finally, she said, "Good, that's fine." He then summoned his house boy to bring in two bolts of silk, which he offered for the expense of an evening meal.
>
> The girl laughed and stopped him, saying, "That's not the proper way between guest and host. Tonight, you must allow us, poor as we are, to offer you what crude fare we have. You can wait to treat us some other time." He persisted in his offering, but she refused to yield.

147

Presently they went inside to sit in the western hall. The drapes, screens, and couches dazzled the eyes with their brightness, and the toilet boxes, quilts, and pillows were most magnificent. Then candles were lighted and dinner was served, the food rich and delicious. After the dishes had been removed, the old woman withdrew. The student and the girl then began to talk intimately, laughing and jesting, and indulging in all sorts of pleasantries.

"When I passed by your house the other day," the student said, "you happened to be standing at the door. Afterwards, the thought of you remained in my heart all the time. Even when I ate or slept, I could not give you up."

"My heart was similarly affected," the girl answered.

"I came here today," he went on, "not simply to look for a lodging but with the hope that you would grant me the wishes of a lifetime. I wonder how lucky I may be."

He had not finished his words when the old woman returned and asked what they were talking about. When they told her, she laughed and said, "Between men and women a great desire exists. When love prevails, not even parents can forbid it. But my daughter is of humble birth—how could she be worthy of sharing your mat and pillow?"

Thereupon the student went down the hall steps, bowed low, and thanked her, "Please accept me as a slave." So the old woman regarded him as her son-in-law. They did not part until they had drunk heartily.

The next morning, the student moved all his baggage to the Li house and made his home there.

Henceforth, the young man withdrew from his friends and relatives, and spent all his time in the company of pleasure girls and entertainers until he had exhausted his money and sold everything he had. Then the two women abandoned him through a ruse, leaving him homeless, penniless, and seriously ill. He was picked up by his former landlord who, thinking that he was dying, took him to a funeral home. The people there had pity on him and fed him until he was able to get up and earn a living for himself. While there he learned to sing the funeral chants and became the best mourner in town. One day, as he chanted in competition with another funeral house—"his voice rising so clear and shrill that the echoes shook the trees in the forest"—he was recognized by his nurse's husband who had come to the performance with his father. The latter was in the capital for an annual conference with other provincial dignitaries. When informed of the mourner's identity, he was so enraged that he had his son brought to him and had him flogged severely until he fainted. The father then left him for dead. The young man, however, regained consciousness and was saved by his fellow mourners.

For more than a month, he could hardly lift up his hands and feet, and the sores left by the thrashing festered and stank so badly that his friends found him revolting and one night had him cast off on the roadside. The passersby all took pity on him and many threw him scraps of food so that he was able to fill his stomach. Three months later, he managed to walk around on a staff. Clad in a cloth coat that was patched in a hundred places and as tattered as a quail's tail, and holding a broken alms bowl, he tramped the neighborhood streets and engaged in begging as a profession. From autumn through winter, he spent his nights among dunghills and in caves and his days making a round of the marketplace.

It was at this point that the Li girl finally redeemed herself by coming nobly to the student's rescue. One day, it happened that driven by hunger, he went out to beg in a snowstorm and unknowingly passing the girl's house, cried aloud for alms. Upon recognizing his voice, the girl came out and was so deeply moved by his sad plight that, in spite of her mother's objection, she took him in, lived with him, and nursed him with tender care until he was well again. Then equipping him with a complete wardrobe out of her own savings and buying him all the necessary books to read, she urged and encouraged him to study diligently day and night, keeping him company all the time. After several years of intensive preparation, the student distinguished himself in the examinations and was awarded high official positions. The story ends—all is well that ends well—with reconciliation between father and son, and marriage between the student and the courtesan. Now a devoted wife and good mother, she bore him four sons who all grew up to be officials, and she herself was ennobled as the Lady of Chien-kuo, thus earning the admiration and praise of all who had heard the story.

Considering the fact that it was written as early as 795, this tale of the sing-song girl, based on an oral tradition, is probably one of the world's finest specimens of early prose fiction. With a realistic love story as the main theme, it is remarkable for its high literary quality in a complicated, well sustained, and deeply moving narrative, its faithful depiction of urban society, and its dramatic enactment of the changing situations of life.

In the chivalric tales brave swordsmen and swordswomen of supreme skill, who are loyal to their masters, daring in their deeds, and noted for their feats, play the heroes' roles. Many of them possess the supernatural ability to fly in the air and ride on the clouds, to wield magic weapons, and to transform themselves into various shapes. In their chivalry, here defined in terms of qualities such as valor, righteousness, and dexterity in arms, they are the forerunners by several centuries of the medieval knights

149

in Europe. The Chinese swordsmen, however, are ordinary folk of humble origin without the nobility of birth and bearing that are the badges of a European knight.

As a whole, these chivalric tales are not as well written as the others. Their plots are less convincing and their style is somewhat euphuistic. In "The K'un-lun Slave,"—these slaves were of Malay origin brought to China from the South Seas—the hero is an old family servant who effected his young master's union with the pretty maid of a court minister. Possessing miraculous power and strength, he carried the young man into the official's well-guarded compound to a rendezvous with the maid; then, with the youth and the girl on his back, he vaulted over ten or more high walls in the same way he had entered. Later, when he was besieged by armed soldiers sent to capture him, he flew away over the walls like a winged eagle as arrows converged on him like rain.

The "man with a curly beard" is the hero of the story that bears his name. There are also several other important characters such as Li Shih-min, the future emperor of the T'ang dynasty; Li Ching, who later became his minister; and "the girl with a red whisk," who ran away from a high official's house to be married to Li Ching. The plot runs thus: toward the end of the Sui dynasty, many brave and ambitious men were awaiting opportunities to rise as future rulers of the country, and among them was the man with a curly beard. He had amassed a great fortune for this purpose, but upon seeing Li Shih-min he immediately recognized him as the heaven-ordained, true sovereign, against whom there could be no competition. So he gave all his property to Li Ching with which to help Li Shih-min to conquer the empire, while he himself went overseas to establish an island kingdom. Though of historical interest, the story is loose in structure and conventional in characterization. Nevertheless, some chivalric tales of the T'ang period have continued in popularity in later centuries and have become the prototypes of full-length novels.

A literary curiosity, which belongs to none of the above categories, is "A Visit to the Fairy Lodge"[2] by Chang Tsu, who flourished between the seventh and eighth centuries. His writings, more highly prized abroad than in China, were purchased with gold and gems by Korean and Japanese envoys to the T'ang empire. This story creates a literary genre by itself, for it has the curious combination of an ornate, antithetical style with crude colloquial language, the latter used extensively in the dialogue and in riddle-like poems, with which the narrative is generously larded. Told in the first person, the story relates how the author, on an official mission to the remote Northwest, encountered in a fairy lodge two beautiful women with whom he drank, played musical instruments, danced, jested, and flirted in double entendre verses. After having thus enjoyed himself, he stayed overnight with one of the women, and the passage that describes their amorous scene, though cast in a euphuistic prose, is so strikingly frank that its like has never been seen in any previous Chinese writing now preserved. However, the influence of this work on Chinese literature is negligible, for it was long lost in China and was circulated only in Japan, where it was highly regarded by Japanese writers.

Another interesting aspect of the "Visit to the Fairy Lodge" is its use of alternate prose and poetry, which closely resembles in form the fictional material found in Tun-huang. Although any relationship is hard to trace, there being little apparent connection between the two, it is noteworthy that this unique way of storytelling has remained one of the important influences in Chinese literature. The similarity of the Tun-huang tales to the French *chantefable*, such as the thirteenth century romance *Aucassin et Nicolette*, has also been noted. The possibility of an indirect Chinese influence on the French through Turkish or Arab intermediaries has been suggested,[3] but no conclusive evidence of it has been found so far.

Popular recitation of Buddhist stories by the monk preachers developed very early in the T'ang period, at the latest by the end of the seventh century. Poems written in the seven-word form were introduced for singing by the reciter, perhaps with accompaniment by instrument. Illustrative pictures may have been shown at the recitation to arouse greater audience interest. In Ch'ang-an, a number of Buddhist monks attracted a large following with their popular lectures. When the Japanese monk Ennin visited the city, he went to some of these recitations and recorded in his diary for the year 841 the names of several Buddhist reciters, among whom the most famous was Wen-hsü.[4] He was noted for his melodious and deeply moving voice in chanting the sutras as well as in reciting non-canonical Buddhist tales. Once he was accused by a contemporary writer of telling vulgar and lewd stories: "Ignorant men and dissolute women were fond of hearing his tales. The listeners packed and suffocated the monastery compounds." Popular recitations were also held in Taoist monasteries and in public places outside the religious establishments. There is little doubt that this kind of story recitation was not the monopoly of Buddhist monasteries and that it had spread and gained great popularity among the people.

While the Tun-huang manuscripts are predominantly Buddhist in content, the eighty-odd literary pieces known as *pien-wen* also include a number of secular ballads and tales about emperors, ministers, generals, scholars, and commoners. Among these is the story of Lady Meng Chiang in quest of her husband's remains beneath the Great Wall:

After she had finished crying, her heart and soul were lost in grief. She was greatly anguished by the thought that her husband should have thus fallen and died. Take pity on her chaste heart that is even now both resentful and sorrowful! The skulls are countless—not just one person has died. The bones are strewn all over the place; what evidence is there for identification? Biting her fingers to draw blood, she sprinkled it on the Great Wall to show her loyal heart, hoping thereby to pick out her husband's bones.

Meng Chiang wailed, saying, "What am I to do?
Here among the yellow sands his precious remains lie dispersed.
People say there are signposts on the grave mounds,
But tell me, which is his among these heaps of skulls?
Alas! Alas! It is hard to make the right choice.
Looking at them makes my heart sad at once.
One by one, I'll pick them up to look at closely,
And biting my finger to draw blood, I'll try an experiment:
If these bones are my husband's, blood will sink into them;
If they are not his, then bones and blood will stay apart.
If I should find his remains, I'll return them home.
I pray that I don't have to discard them here!"
Loudly she wailed, her voice choking in the throat
And tears flowing down unceasingly from her eyes.
"Should the yellow skies thwart these tender feelings,
This humble maid would die together with him at the Great Wall."

This passage has little literary merit but it illustrates the crude efforts of the folk artists at storytelling, as well as the alternate use of prose and poetry in these tales.

Of the Buddhist stories, the longest is a popularization of the Vimala-kirti Sutra, which would undoubtedly assume epic proportions in its complete form; the several fragments that are preserved run into almost a hundred thousand words. Other interesting pieces are "The Crushing Defeat of Mara" and "The Subjugation of the Evil Spirit." The first relates the defeat of Mara's hosts by the Buddha and the failure of Mara's three daughters to tempt him; the second tells of the magic contests between a disciple of Buddha and a heterodox Buddhist monk. But the most fascinating and certainly the most popular of the Buddhist tales is "Great Mu-lien Rescuing his Mother from the Hades."[5] After the death of his parents, Mu-lien became a Buddhist monk and soon attained Arhatship. Later when he met his father in Heaven, he was told that his mother had been thrown into Hell for her sins. So he started a long quest for her in the numerous cells of the underworld. Finally he reached the Avici Hell, where his mother was confined.

Mu-lien pressed forward and reached Hell, but while he was still more than a hundred paces away, he was sucked in by the flames and almost fell down flat.

The Avici Hell has steep iron ramparts, their massive structure linked to the clouds. Swords and lances stand like forests; knives and spears pile up in heaps. The dagger-tree is a thousand fathoms tall, interspersed with prickly thorns and pointed needles; the knife-mountain, eighty thousand feet high, spreads out like a confused mass of interlinked precipices. A fierce fire, swift and dense, leaps over the skies, trailing behind it roaring clouds; the dagger wheel, with clusters of blades, flashes past like bright stars, illuminating the dust specks. Iron snakes spurt flames, their scales stretching out in all directions; bronze dogs inhale [sic] smoke, barking ferociously on three sides. Furze thorns, falling all over from the air, prick men's breasts; sharp pointed awls, flying sidewise in the sky, pierce women's backs. Iron rakes poke into the eyes, red blood flowing west; bronze prongs stab the waist, white plasma spurting east. As the knife-mountain penetrates into the charcoal furnace, the skulls are cracked, bones and flesh smashed into a pulp, sinews and skins broken, hands and gall bladders cracked. Mashed flesh splits and spatters outside the four doors; curdled blood overflows beside the prison furnace. The sound of wailing wafts toward a vast and lofty sky. Thunderbolts roll and rumble upwards; clouds and smoke, dispersing, spread downwards. Iron bells clang excitedly and without order; arrow-feathered ghosts mutter and skulk away; bronze-beaked birds shrill and yell. The prison guards, several ten thousands of them, are all ox-headed and horse-faced. Even if your heart were like iron and stone, you would have lost your soul and shivered in your gall.

Crude and cumbersome in expression, this passage is at best an immature piece of antithetical prose, but the horrors of hell as invoked by its author must have impressed those "ignorant men and dissolute women" who gathered around to listen.

In whatever forms these Buddhist stories are written, whether in verse, prose-poetry (*fu*), or straight prose, their style is quite different from the polished style of the literary tales. The marks of folk artists are visible here, and their lack of literary attainment is compensated by the native wit and unbridled imagination of the popular storytellers. To these popularizers the important thing was not so much to receive the praise of the literary critic as to hear the applause of a folk audience that demanded effective verbal communication, story suspense and excitement, listening pleasure derived from songs and music, and a language that, however artificial, was earthy and colloquial enough to be readily understood.

The T'ang religious and secular tales provided the missing link between the popular storytelling tradition in ancient times, of which there is only a meager record, and a similar one very much in evidence in the Sung period. These tales seem to have paved the way for the vast scope of Sung fiction and the immense popularity of its practitioners, who must have been the veritable heirs of the "cassocks and bowls" of their T'ang predecessors. One evidence of the continuation of this storytelling tradition from T'ang to Sung is the similarity in form and style between the T'ang popularizations (*pien-wen*) and the Sung story scripts (*hua-pen*) that have survived. In style both are marked by an alternate use of prose and poetry, the only difference being that there is in the Sung tales a larger representation of the colloquial language which is more mature and better written, due probably to its long use through the centuries. Moreover, as a result of the influence of the T'ang-Sung neoclassic prose, antithetical construction was no longer popular with the Sung storytellers. In its place appeared a sort of new vernacular prose, expressive and well articulated, which happily has become the chief medium of Chinese fiction in all later ages.

During the Sung dynasty, the Chinese short story came of age. Storytelling became a regular profession and each professional storyteller specialized in one of the four major categories, namely, (1) realistic stories of love, supernatural stories of female ghosts, and numerous others, the telling of which was introduced and accompanied by music played on a silver-lettered flute (*yin-tzu-erh*); (2) stories of murder and law suits, sword fights, contests with cudgels, and larger battles; (3) religious tales, mostly Buddhist; (4) historical recitations.[6] Most popular were the storytellers of the first two groups. In a certain period in Southern Sung, there were in Hangchow as many as fifty-two such storytellers as against twenty-three who specialized in historical fiction and seventeen in Buddhist tales. These men became so professionalized that they were organized into "guilds," one of which was known as the "Society for Eloquence." Large booths were erected for the storytellers alongside those for the dramatic actors and others in the amusement centers of the city.[7]

The extant Sung-Yüan short stories number forty and more. They form what may be called the beginning of a bourgeois literature, the realistic stories reflecting the social activities of the Sung people, the historical and supernatural stories their imaginative and creative power. Whereas T'ang literary tales are mostly the works of the scholar-officials, and T'ang Buddhist tales those of the monk preachers, the Sung colloquial tales represent the creative efforts of the middle-class writers. After many generations of oral tradition, they now brought the technique of storytelling to a new height.

Several early story collections preserved from the past are of Sung-Yüan origin. The most important is the *Capital Version of Popular Stories*, of which eight stories and a fragment have survived. These include (1) a semihistorical tale of the lewd dissipations of a Jurchen ruler; (2) another, of the "Stubborn Minister," Wang An-shih, whose reform measures proved to be unpopular among the people; (3) a supernatural tale of some ghosts who upset the humdrum life of a poor schoolteacher; (4) a tragicomedy about the marriage, separation, and eventual happy reunion of a rebel leader with an official's daughter he has captured; (5) the account of a monk-poet, falsely accused of adultery but later cleared of the charges just as he passes into the Buddhist Nirvana; (6) the story of an honest clerk who refuses the solicitations of his employer's young wife both when she is alive and after she has become a ghost; (7) a tale of murder and law suit involving a number of innocent people, caused by fifteen strings of cash, punishment being meted rather belatedly to the culprit; and (8) the elopement of a prince's maid servant with a jade carver, which ultimately causes their destruction. The last three, entitled respectively "Chang, the Honest Clerk," "Fifteen Strings of Cash," and "The Jade Bodhisattva," are among the best of the group, but space permits a discussion and summary of only one, the "Jade Bodhisattva":

The story opens with a long introduction presenting a series of poems on the spring season,[8] which serves as a prelude to an account of a great Sung prince's pleasure ride in Hangchow. On the way the prince saw the young daughter of a poor artisan, and later took her into his palace as a bondmaid with the name, Hsiu-hsiu. One day when the prince's palace caught fire, Hsiu-hsiu fled with some gold and pearls in her keeping and ran into Ts'ui Ning, a young jade carver, also of the prince's household.

> "Mr. Ts'ui," she said, "I was slow in coming out. As the other maids in the palace had all run off, each in her own direction, I was alone and deserted. Now, there is no way out but for you to take me somewhere for shelter."
>
> Presently, Ts'ui Ning and Hsiu-hsiu left the palace gate and walked along the river bank until they came to the Lime Bridge. Hsiu-hsiu said, "Mr. Ts'ui, my feet hurt and I can't walk any farther."
>
> "Just a few more steps," Ts'ui Ning said, pointing ahead, "and right there is my house. You can come in to rest your feet. That will be all right."
>
> Just after they had got to his house and sat down, Hsiu-hsiu said, "I am hungry. Could you go out to buy me something to eat, Mr. Ts'ui? After all this fright, a few cups of wine will do me a lot of good."

Presently, Ts'ui Ning brought home some wine and after two or three cups, it was just as the poet said:

Three cups of "bamboo leaves" having penetrated the heart,
Two peach blossoms appear on the cheeks.

It cannot be gainsaid that "spring is the best doctor for the flowers, and wine is the lovers' good go-between."

"You may still recall," Hsiu-hsiu said, "the night in which the prince was enjoying the moon on the terrace and promised me to you in marriage, and how you bowed gratefully to thank him. Do you remember it or not?" Folding his hands respectfully, Ts'ui Ning could only answer in the affirmative. Hsiu-hsiu continued, "On that day all the people applauded for you and said, 'What a nice couple!' How could you have forgotten it?" Again Ts'ui Ning could only reply in agreement.

"Instead of waiting like this, why don't we become man and wife tonight? What do you think?"

"I don't dare," Ts'ui Ning said.

"You know, if you refuse," said Hsiu-hsiu, "I will shout for help and you will be ruined. Anyway, how is it that you have got me here in your house? I am going to tell them at the palace tomorrow."

"Please don't, young lady," said Ts'ui Ning. "It is all right with me if you want to be my wife. But, upon one condition: we can't stay here any longer. The only way is for us to take advantage of the fire and the confusion to slip away immediately tonight."

"Since I'll be your wife," said Hsiu-hsiu, "do as you please."

That same night they ran away with all their money and belongings to a city in far away Hunan, where Ts'ui Ning resumed his trade as a jade carver.

A year later, a sergeant of the prince's palace happened to come to that city on business and found Ts'ui Ning and Hsiu-hsiu together in their new quarters. When he went back and reported it to the prince, the latter had the couple arrested and brought to the capital. During his campaign against the Tartars, the prince had wielded two swords, one called "Little Green" and the other "Big Green." Countless Tartars had fallen under them. Now they were sheathed and hung on the wall of the palace hall. When the couple was taken to the palace, the prince ascended the hall and upon seeing the pair, "how fuming with anger he was! Taking down with his left hand the 'Little Green' from a peg in the wall, he unsheathed it with his right hand. Sword in hand, he stared with his Tartar-killing eyes and gritted his teeth with a crackling noise." But upon his wife's persuasion he refrained from killing them. Instead, he sent Ts'ui Ning to the prefect's yamen and kept Hsiu-hsiu at the rear garden of the palace. Ts'ui Ning was found guilty, flogged and sentenced to exile. As he was about to leave the city gate, suddenly a sedan chair caught up with him and the woman who dismounted was no other than his wife, Hsiu-hsiu. They went together to the place of exile and he started there once again his business.

It chanced that one day when the emperor was looking at a jade Bodhisattva presented to him by the prince, one of the bells came off. Upon learning that Ts'ui Ning was the original carver, the emperor pardoned him and had him summoned to the court to fix it. So Ts'ui Ning returned to the capital, repaired the bell, and opened a new workshop not far from where the old one had stood. It was not long, however, before the same sergeant walked by the store. Just as he was talking to Ts'ui Ning, he espied a woman behind the counter. He was so frightened at the sight of her that he left in a great hurry and went straightway to report to the prince what he had seen:

> "Just now as I was walking along the Clear Lake River, I went to Ts'ui Ning's jade-carving shop. There I saw a woman behind the counter, and she was no other than the maid Hsiu-hsiu."
>
> The prince said impetuously, "Nonsense! I had her beaten to death and buried in the back garden. All this you witnessed yourself. How could she be still alive? Are you trying to make fun of me?"

The sergeant insisted that what he said was true and promised to fetch Hsiu-hsiu back to the prince. "Go and get the woman here," said the prince. "If she is really alive, fetch her and I'll cut her head off with my own sword; but if she is not there, then you have to test the sword in her place."

The sergeant went immediately to Ts'ui Ning's house and putting Hsiu-hsiu in a sedan chair, had her carried back to the palace. The prince was already waiting in the hall when he entered.

> The sergeant, bowing low, said, "I have brought here the maid Hsiu-hsiu."
>
> "Fetch her in," said the prince.
>
> The sergeant went out and called, "Young lady, the prince wants you to come in." But when he lifted the sedan curtain to take a look, he felt as if a bucket of water had been poured over him, his mouth wide agape without being able to close, for inside the sedan Hsiu-hsiu was nowhere to be found.

In the end, the sergeant's life was spared but he was heavily flogged; on the other hand Ts'ui Ning was dragged away by his wife's ghost and followed her to the nether world.

From the above excerpt, it can be seen that in the hands of the Sung professionals, the crude supernatural tale of the Six Dynasties has become, in the course of its evolution, a realistic presentation with a swift-moving and ingenious plot, many surprises and much suspense, some lifelike characterization, and a clever use of dialogue written in simple, expressive, colloquial language. Although it has not attained the fine craftsmanship and the subtle psychological probings of the modern short story, it is nevertheless an exceedingly well told tale with all the important elements that a good narrative should have. There still lingers, to be sure, a vestige of the supernatural in the form of a ghost, a dream, or divine revelation, but as a whole most of the stories develop naturally, and the Sung society they present is depicted faithfully and vividly. As the work of folk artists, they lack the literary polish of the accomplished scholars but this shortcoming is partially remedied in some of the later versions. In the meantime the same influences that produced these stories were also at work in the creation of the long novel, which in a sense is merely a series of stories linked together in a loose plot. Therefore, a knowledge of these stories is essential for an understanding of the first Chinese novels that were to appear later. But we must now turn to an entirely new subject, the rise of the drama in the Sung-Yüan period.

11 : Early Theatrical Entertainments and Activities

The theatrical activities of the Chinese people went back to the very beginning of their history. Popular mediumistic séances, dancing at temple sacrifices, palace entertainments, and court buffoonery by dwarfs and clowns were current in ancient times. The jesters, in particular, were a time-honored appendage of the feudal court and some of their names have been preserved. One of them mimicked so well the manners and gestures of a dead state minister that when he appeared in the latter's official dress and hat, everyone at court thought that the minister had come back alive.

Another form of theatrical entertainment, acrobatics, was brought over to China from the Western Regions (Central Asia) in the last years of the second century B.C. When first introduced, the acrobatics consisted of boxing, wrestling, and fencing, but soon came to include such feats of strength and skill as tumbling, somersaulting, ropewalking, poleclimbing, tripodlifting, swordswallowing, firespitting, and many others, to form the so-called Hundred Entertainments. Sometimes the players disguised themselves as leopards and bears, tigers and dragons, fairies and nymphs, and sang amidst floating clouds and drifting snowflakes.[1] The introduction of stories which they acted out further increased their popularity in later centuries.

Singing and dancing cast in the framework of a story were apparently the chief attractions of two types of plays: "The Big Face" (also known as the False Face or Mask), and "The Swinging Wife," both evolved during the sixth and seventh centuries. The first originated from the story of Prince Lan Ling of the Northern Ch'i dynasty. To cover his beautiful feminine face, the warrior-prince wore to the battle a horrible mask that frightened his enemies. This remarkable feat soon gave rise to a military play, "Prince Lan Ling," in which the actor danced and sang in the prince's purple robe and awe-inspiring mask as he fought under the city

159

wall at the head of his troops, shouting his commands at them and brandishing his weapons against the enemy.

"The Swinging Wife" dramatizes the story of an unhappy woman who used to complain to her neighbors of the beatings she received from her drunken husband. To imitate her, the actor would swing his body to and fro as he sighed and sobbed, and then burst into songs of grief with the listeners joining in the refrain:

> Walking and swaying,
> Walking and swaying,
> Oh, rueful is the wife!

Often, another actor would play the red-faced drunkard and engage the wife in a quarrel and fist fight. In some later plays, a debt-collector from a pawn shop would enter the scene to abuse the couple in a low comedy that was rather irrelevant to the original story. As a whole the play seems to be developed with a great deal of singing and dancing, and some action and dialogue.

Alongside the two dramatic types mentioned above, a new type, "The Military Counselor," appeared in the T'ang dynasty. The counselor of the title owed his dramatic being—a kind of infamous immortality—to the peculiar punishment he got for graft. Arrested for having appropriated for his own use several hundred bolts of silk from the public treasury, he was ordered by the emperor to act as an entertainer at state banquets. There, dressed in his stolen silk, he was publicly humiliated and made the butt of raillery by the court fool in the presence of the guests. Some singing and dancing may have been included, but these were merely incidental as "The Military Counselor" was primarily a spoken drama with a plot and dialogue. In its later development, a different story was introduced in the form of a comedy, a farce, or a political satire. Thus "The Military Counselor" became also a dramatic type, and its hero a stock comic character on the stage.

In the meantime, singing and dancing played an important part in court entertainments given by the emperors. In the T'ang capital at Ch'ang-an, besides the famous Pear Garden, where the actors were trained, there were other centers for the instruction of young people in the choral and choreographic arts. In one of these establishments, according to a contemporary description, as many as one thousand trainees drew salaries from the government, and every day at dawn, when the fledgling musicians practiced, the building reverberated with the sound of drums and flutes. Girls from ordinary families, chosen for their beauty and talent, were taken into the palace and housed in a separate compound, named "Designed for Spring," where they learned to dance, sing, and play musical instruments such as the lute and flute. With this elaborate training of entertainers of all kinds, the magnificence of court entertainments at the T'ang period can well be imagined.

Similarly, in the Sung period many emperors found pleasure in drama, music, and pageantry. Elaborate court banquets were given in spring and autumn and on other festive occasions such as the emperor's birthday anniversary. In addition to wine and feasting, theatricals occupied an important part in these entertainments. The program included singing, dancing, instrumental music, and acrobatics, as well as a new theatrical show called the "Variety Play" (tsa-chü).[2]

In the gay and spacious world of the Sung people, the drama was by no means a monopoly of the ruling class. The common man too had his share of fun provided him by professional entertainers such as musicians, singers, dancers, storytellers, actors, jugglers, and acrobats. While the most talented entertainers were recruited and trained at the Imperial Training Center (chiao-fang) for services at court or in the yamen, the lesser ones offered their theatrical wares for the amusement of the masses.

The professional actors would organize themselves into small companies of five to seven each. They were often members of one family so that men and women could band together without creating too much of a scandal. Many were known by nicknames such as Ch'en, the Orange Peel; Hou, the Big Head; the Powdered Head; Dimples; the Swallow Head; the Gold Fish; the Silver Fish and so on. The life of a Sung actor was a busy and strenuous one. To earn his living, he would not only give performances in the city theaters but would also tour the countryside, where his presence often attracted crowds in village squares and teahouses. While in the city, he might be required to render his service in the yamen to entertain the feasting dignitaries. Promptness was demanded of him, and he had to give up his own public performances in order to be present at these urgent official calls, failing which he would be subjected to forty strokes of the bamboo.

It is quite possible that some of the talented actors in the Imperial Training Center, the head actors especially, wrote their own plays. But most of the scripts seem to have been furnished by members of the "Book Guilds" (shu-hui) that had sprung up during the Southern Sung period at its capital, Hangchow. In fact, all sorts of entertainment groups mushroomed at that time. There were societies of young amateurs from rich and noble families doing plays, dancing, and music. There were groups of girl singers; there was also an organization of professional football[3] players called the Round Club. But most important were the organizations of professional writers, who supplied the public with scripts for plays, stories, and songs—no doubt for a fee. The names of some of these

161

"Book Guilds" are still known as are some of the plays they contributed.

The Sung drama was performed either in a regular playhouse or on a temporary stage set up for a special festivity. One of these occasions was the Lantern Festival on the fifteenth day of the first month. In addition to the colorful pageants and fireworks, dramatic performance was an important feature of the celebration. In a temporary theatrical area set up in a busy section of the city, a great variety of shows was given. Sometimes the number of spectators was so overwhelming that an entire area had to be fenced in with briars and branches to keep the surging crowds from elbowing their way to where the musicians and actors performed on the stage (called open terrace or music booth).

The actors also performed in regular playhouses situated in amusement areas known as "tile districts."[4] In Kaifeng, the Northern Sung capital, the theatrical center was located in the southeastern corner of the city in an area covered by the Sang Family Tile, the Middle Tile, and the Inner Tile, where stood fifty or more theaters. Some of them like the Lotus Playhouse, the Peony Playhouse, the Raksha Playhouse, and the Elephant Playhouse were huge structures that could each accommodate several thousand spectators. In Hangchow as many as seventeen "tile districts" with innumerable theaters were devoted to entertainments of all kinds.

To picture a typical playhouse in the thirteenth century or earlier, let us imagine a rustic fellow from the countryside making his first grand tour of the theater. It would begin with his landing at the tile district in front of a fenced gate, on which were posted colorful playbills, and above which were hoisted flags, streamers, and canopies of all descriptions to announce the opening of the theater. Then, entering the gate and paying the entrance fee of two hundred coins, he would climb a planked slope and, as he picked his way up, would see in front of him a large crowd-packed balcony (divine tower) in the shape of a bell tower. It would be flanked on both sides by the galleries (waist sheds) also filled with long rows of spectators. Dazzled by these sights, he would look down into the open pit, and there again would be a vast sea of people shouldering each other in endless waves. He would then thread his way to another part of the theater opposite the balcony, to a spot happily quiet and empty, not knowing that this was the stage itself. Worn out by the journey, he would sink to rest himself on one of the seats reserved for the musicians in the performance, but would be immediately shoved away by a theater attendant. After this bewildering trip, our country cousin would finally settle down in the balcony and soon begin to enjoy himself tremendously, scarcely able to hold his sides from laughing at the scenes of buffoonery on the stage.[5]

A great variety of entertainments was offered in the Sung tile districts.

Among these, puppet shows and shadow plays were immensely popular. The origin of the marionettes has been traced to the Han dynasty. Formerly used in connection with funeral rites, the puppets first appeared in feasts and festivities towards the end of the dynasty. In the third century, wooden marionettes, playing fifes and drums, and moving around on wheels controlled by a mechanical device, were used in court theatricals. Later during the Sui dynasty (early seventh century), these shows were further elaborated. In one of them, figures of female musicians, about two feet in height, dressed in embroidered silks and ornamented with gold, floated in wooden boats along the winding river of the imperial city, while playing as an orchestra on stone chimes, bells, and stringed instruments. Often, stories were enacted by these marionettes impersonating historical figures in episodes such as Fu Hsi (a legendary emperor) receiving the eight trigrams from the back of a sacred tortoise.

In the T'ang period, puppet shows became immensely popular in countryside, capital and town. Music generally accompanied singing and dancing during the performance, and cymbals are known to have been used. Life itself is a common theme of these shows, in which old men are the main characters, as the following poem testifies:

> Carved from wood and pulled by strings,
> It acts the part of an old man.
> With wrinkled face and white hair,
> How life-like it looks!
> In a brief moment the play is over,
> And the rest is silence.
> So even a puppet-play lasts no more
> Than the dream of life itself.[6]

But it was in the Sung period that the puppet play attained the height of its development. There was not only a great variety of stories acted by the puppets but also a great variety of "actors," namely, wooden stick puppets, silk-thread puppets, water puppets, and puppets in-the-flesh. The nature of the first two, which survive to this day, can be deduced from their names. The water puppets have been described above, although most likely the Sung marionettes were controlled by hand, and not by the mechanical devices used in the earlier period. The most interesting of the types is the flesh puppet show, in which children were held up by the puppet-master to enact the characters in the story. Thus we encounter the paradox of finding children used as puppets though puppets originally were designed to represent human beings.

Like other theatrical entertainments, the puppet show was performed at court, in the tile districts, on temporary stages erected for festival occasions, and for the birthdays of the numerous temple deities. In the regular theaters, puppet plays were presented daily to thronged houses, and spectators often went there at dawn to catch the first show.

At Hangchow, in the Lane of the Su Family alone, there were twenty-four houses where puppets were made and sold. Many represented female figures clothed in gorgeous dresses and wearing flower hats adorned with imitation pearls and jade. These slender-waisted wooden beauties must have looked life-like in their dainty postures. Likewise, the art of wood carving must have reached perfection in the hands of the unknown artists who turned out these lovely puppets by the dozen to meet the demands of a thriving theatrical profession.

Unlike the puppet play, which had a long history of development from the third century on, the shadow play, an innovation of the Sung entertainers, did not become popular until the eleventh century. Earlier, in the T'ang and the Five Dynasties, Buddhist monks had illustrated their popular evening lectures with reflections of the Buddha's image on a screen. In the Sung period, figures of all kinds were cut out from white and colored papers; finally, when the shadow play became a regular theatrical performance, the actors were made from brilliantly painted sheepskin (used for its durability). The figures were attached to strings pulled by the shadow player, and great skill was shown in the way these strings were manipulated. By projecting the parchment heroes and villains on the screen, the shadow player was able to make the historical tales into a "movie." The most popular was the romance of the Three Kingdoms. Thus sang a later poet:

> A new shadow-play theater has opened in the South Tile,
> In its brilliant light is re-enacted the rise and fall of
> empires.

The shadow plays matched the puppets in popularity among the people, but so far as contemporary records show, they were never performed during state banquets. This form was probably considered less important as entertainment, and while actors, singers, dancers, and marionettes performed in the musical booth in the city center during the Lantern Festival, the shadow players were relegated to street corners where children gathered. But this does not mean that the shadow plays were banished from the regular theater or that their puppeteers were neglected as artists; on the contrary, the names of as many as twenty-two shadow play workers have been recorded in the writings of the Sung period. There were different kinds of shadow plays, but the most interesting was that in which men performed as shadows. And just as children had been made into puppets, so men now cast their shadows to act in a type of play (known as "the big shadow") comparable to the modern movie.

In the development of Chinese drama, the influence of the puppet show and the shadow play must have been significant. It has even been suggested that the regular drama originated from these two, especially from the puppet-in-the-flesh and the big shadow. Though this theory does not seem sufficiently plausible for serious consideration, it is apparent that the dramatists of the Sung dynasty must have found inspiration in the stories and techniques made popular by these folk entertainers who had successfully conjured up shadows and puppets to perform in some of the great acts of the Chinese drama.

In the meantime, regular plays were being given in both North and South China. The Sung Variety Play, which had its beginning in Kaifeng, continued to develop in the North under the rule of the Chin (Jurchen) conquerors; it also migrated with the Chinese people southward to Hang-chow, where it flourished anew. Unfortunately, none of the Sung Variety Plays is extant. Only a long list survives of some two hundred and eighty titles performed at court; nonetheless, these mere titles tell an eloquent story of Sung dramatic activities. First of all, we can deduce that these plays must have been short since we know that from two to four Variety Plays were included on the packed programs of court banquets, where singing, dancing and acrobatics also took place. Second, the titles themselves indicate that even in these early days poetry must have played an important part in dramatic composition. While all kinds of poetic forms known at that time seem to have been employed by the Sung playwrights, the Big Song,* used in one hundred and three of these plays, was undoubtedly the most popular. Furthermore, the plays were quite varied in subject and broad in scope: some were historical, supernatural, literary, or didactic; others dramatized contemporary, realistic stories; while not a few were satirical or farcical. Obviously they deserve the name by which they are known—*tsa-chü* or the Variety Plays.

So far as we are able to reconstruct it, a Sung Variety Play consisted of three parts: a prelude, the main play in one or two scenes, and a musical epilogue. The prelude was usually low comedy. The play proper consisted most probably of a poetic episode with much singing and dancing. We are not sure, however, how well developed the plot was, what relation it bore to the songs, and whether there was spoken dialogue at all (though presumably there would have been).

* The Big Song (*ta-ch'ü*), first introduced in the T'ang dynasty, is an elaborate form of poetry containing a group or sequence of ten or more songs preceded by a prologue and ending with an epilogue. The songs all deal with the same theme and together give a sustained story.

Probably a later development of the Variety Play, the *yüan-pen* or Professional Script was a type of drama known to have flourished in North China during the Jurchen occupation (twelfth century). A vast collection of dramatic literature must have existed at that time, there being 690 known titles of these Chin Professional Scripts, but they too have failed to escape the ravages of time. The Professional Scripts and the Variety Plays could have been practically the same in substance, as is shown in the similarity of many titles, but since none of this material has been preserved, comparison is impossible.[7] The *yüan-pen*, erroneously considered by some scholars to be a dramatic script from a courtesan house, is actually a script used by the professionals, that is, by the theatrical profession in general, including both the courtesans and the regular actors.[8] Far from being a new type of drama developed in the pleasure quarters, the *yüan-pen* was an heir to the early theatrical traditions of the Sung period and a first cousin of the Variety Play.

Side by side with the Variety Play, there emerged in the district around Hangchow the Southern Drama (*nan-hsi*), which is the most important type of drama we have discussed so far. Like all other dramatic types, it was the creation of folk writers whose names have long been forgotten. But unlike the Variety Play, which became a part of court entertainment, the Southern Drama remained a living form among the people, even after it attained popularity in Hangchow.

With the Southern Drama we have for the first time in Chinese literary history a regular drama in the modern sense. Whereas our information is rather vague about the nature of the Variety Play and the Professional Script, we have a good knowledge of the Southern Drama, of which several songs and three complete plays written in the Sung and Yüan periods have been preserved. These works show that the dramatists had already taken long strides toward evolving a new type of play, the poetic drama.

In form and structure, the Southern Drama is undoubtedly a great improvement over all the other theatrical compositions of the Sung dynasty. It is a full-fledged play that tells a long sustained story in songs (*ch'ü*) and dialogue. While the dialogue advances the dramatic action, the songs, arranged in sequences, express in vivid words the heightened sentiments of the characters. True to their origin, most of the songs in the Southern Drama are written in a simple colloquial language and are therefore more expressive than the artificial and embellished poems of the literary writers. In some instances, when the playwright is at his best, his verses rank high for their naturalness and spontaneity of feeling as well as for their melodies, which were derived from popular tunes sung in street corners and marketplaces.

Three complete Southern plays of the Sung and Yüan period have been preserved through a curious combination of circumstances. Originally, they formed Volume 13991 of the *Grand Library of Emperor Yung Lo* (reigned 1403–1424) of the Ming dynasty. Owing to its unmanageable size, this vast collection was never published, and the few hand-written copies that had been made of this immense work were later scattered and destroyed. The last complete copy preserved in the Imperial College in Peking suffered from the burning and looting by soldiers at the time of the Boxer Uprising in 1900. Along with the bulk of the *Grand Library*, the three plays disappeared, and no one knew that they were still in existence until they were discovered in 1920 by a Chinese scholar in a curio shop in London. This story is interesting enough in itself, but what makes it worth recording is the fact that it exemplifies the way in which literally hundreds of old Chinese plays have been fortuitously recovered in the last three or four decades.

These three particular plays were written by professional playwrights of the Book Guilds in Hangchow. They deal with popular folk stories: adultery and murder in a humble butcher's family; the struggles and aspirations of a poor student who finally succeeds in earning the coveted degree of Doctor of Letters, but who proves to be a faithless and ungrateful lover; the romantic life of a mandarin's son who has joined a wandering troupe of actors. The language of these plays is colloquial; they contain a number of slang expressions that are hardly intelligible. But their simplicity and local color have an appeal lacking in the literary plays of the later period.

Among the three, *Chang Hsieh, the Doctor of Letters*, stands out as being the longest and also the most important. The play has two parts: a poetic prelude which serves as a summary of the play, and the main story told by dialogue and songs. This unusual structure is very illuminating for it gives a concrete idea not only of how some early Chinese plays were written, but also of how closely related they were to the Sung Variety Play, which, as mentioned before, also contained a prelude and a main play. To be noted too is the technical improvement which the Southern Drama shows over the Variety Play. In the former a sort of unity is achieved through combining the prelude with the main plot to form a complete play, the first part serving as an introduction to the second; these are not just two separate unrelated parts as in a Variety Play. Therefore a study of *Chang Hsieh, the Doctor of Letters* gives us a better understanding of the Sung Variety Play, of which our knowledge is slight.

Both internal and external evidence shows that *Chang Hsieh, the Doctor of Letters* must have been the earliest of the three recovered plays.

In the opinion of competent critics, it should be placed in the early thirteenth century as an example of the first extant play in the Chinese language. The dates of the two other plays, *Little Sun, the Butcher* and *An Official's Son* are harder to assign. Perhaps they were written in the intervening period between the Sung and Yüan dynasties when a great dramatic movement had already started in North China, a movement that was to produce the greatest as well as the richest dramatic literature ever known in China, and by dint of its brilliant production, to relegate to neglect and oblivion the humbler efforts of the Sung dramatists.

12 : Yüan Drama

That the flowering of Chinese drama occurred in the Yüan period (1234–1368), while China was ruled by Mongol conquerors, is a curious fact.[1] Originally a nomadic people ignorant of the amenities of civilized life, the Mongols contributed little to Chinese culture, and in retrospect the Mongol period was a dark age—its glory and wealth, marveled over by Marco Polo in his *Travels*, were a mere flicker of the splendor that had flamed in the Sung dynasty.[2] But indirectly the Mongols were responsible for the growth of the drama. Their early emperors before Kublai Khan had a deep distrust of the Confucian scholars, who remained unreconciled to the new and alien government. The abolition of the literary examination (not restored until 1314) in the first half of the Yüan dynasty was a telling blow to the aspirations of almost four generations of scholars. This misfortune to classical scholarship, however, proved a blessing to popular literature. The Confucian monopoly of learning had been challenged and its hold on arts and letters broken. The writing of the drama, hitherto considered a literary occupation limited to the Book Guilds and the acting profession, hence unworthy of the efforts of scholars, was now pursued with enthusiasm by a new group of writers who needed to earn a living or make a name. In these attempts they were encouraged by the Mongol rulers and officials, who could appreciate at least drama, music, and singing. They had also the support of the vast Chinese theater audience in such metropolitan centers as Peking and Hangchow. With the creative genius of the Chinese writers diverted to playwriting and liberated from the Confucian tradition, the drama flourished in the Yüan period.

From the point of view of continuity, there was nothing accidental in the spectacular rise of the Yüan drama. It was the natural offspring of the T'ang and Sung drama, whose repertoire already included well-integrated plays that presented complete and sustained stories. In the first half of the thirteenth century, there was a parallel development of the drama in the North and South. About the time *Chang Hsieh, the Doctor of Letters* was written in Hangchow, a new type of Northern

Drama called *tsa chü* also emerged in Peking, capital of the Yüan dynasty. The Yüan *tsa chü*, however, as has been pointed out,[3] was entirely different in form from the Sung *tsa chü* (Variety Play). As written by its founders Kuan Han-ch'ing, Wang Shih-fu and others, it was already a full fledged poetic drama destined to play a leading role in the history of drama in China.

Unique in form and structure, the Yüan play is well-knit, with four acts or song sequences. It may also include a *hsieh-tzu* or "wedge" in the form of a prologue or interlude. The "wedge," whether placed before the first act or between acts, is an integral part of the drama. It differs from a regular act in that it is shorter and contains fewer songs, which may or may not be sung by the protagonist of the play. Indeed, another requirement of the Yüan drama is that all the sung parts in the four acts, except the "wedge," should be assigned to the protagonist, whether male or female. This gives a sort of unity to the play. There is also the rule that all the songs in each sequence or act should be in the same tonality or key in the musical scale although different acts always have different tonalities. The tunes or airs of these songs are typical of the North, especially of Peking.

The Yüan drama is more flexible in structure than the Greek, its only unity being that of action. Like Greek drama, with a small number of actors and no sub-plot, it gains in intensity because of the unified dramatic movement. On the other hand, there is no rule that calls for the observation of the unities of time and place. The dramatic action in a play usually covers a number of months, if not years, and only in rare cases is it confined to one locality. In place of the Greek choral ode, the Chinese introduced a large number of songs or *ch'ü* between parts of the dialogue; these songs sparkle like gems in a piece of finely wrought dramatic mosaic. In Chinese usage, Yüan *ch'ü* (songs) is the preferred term for this drama.

Like his Greek counterpart, a Chinese dramatist is perforce a poet. A play is judged not so much by its plot and prose dialogue, though these are important, as by its poetry, which is what matters most. Many Yüan plays have little action and very few incidents. The dialogue is conventional and rarely tends to characterization. In most cases, humor is crude and incidental. In view of these limitations, a new criterion must be devised for the Yüan drama—essentially, the criterion of imaginative poetry, in which it excels. In fact, many Yüan playwrights were also the great poets of their age, equally adept in the composition of dramatic and nondramatic songs.

A certain similarity exists between the dramatic conventions and activities of Yüan China and those of Elizabethan England.[4] Chinese drama had long flourished in the popular theaters before it was taken over by men of letters. So did early English drama before the appearance of the University Wits. And just as these Tudor writers, originally trained to be preachers and lawyers, turned to the theater because it was more congenial and lucrative, so did the Yüan writers after the literary examination had been suspended and the doors of official preferment closed to them. With little to employ themselves, they ventured into the dramatic world and by dint of their superior training and talent managed to replace the actor-playwrights as masters of a new theatrical art.

Most of the known Yüan dramatists, about one hundred in number, lived insignificant and uneventful lives as district judges, magistrates, clerks, and school superintendents, while others withdrew altogether from public service. Their biographies are fragmentary, if they exist at all. Compared with some of the T'ang and Sung poets who attained eminence in both political and literary history, Yüan playwrights are certainly the least known writers of China. Glory and success were denied them in their own times, and until recently posterity has done little justice to the marvelous works they produced.

In spite of this neglect, the number of Yüan plays is astonishingly great—an eloquent witness to the immense creative activities of the age. Even after a lapse of six centuries, there are preserved to this day the titles of some six to seven hundred plays, of which about one-fourth survive.[5] This vast bulk can be divided into the following categories of plays: (1) love and intrigue; (2) religious and supernatural; (3) historical and pseudohistorical; (4) domestic and social; (5) murder and lawsuit; (6) bandit-hero.

Of the drama of romantic love, the best known is Wang Shih-fu's *Romance of the Western Chamber*, an unusually long play of twenty acts, a pentalogy, each part containing four acts. According to a traditional account, which however has not been generally accepted, the first four parts were written by Wang Shih-fu and the fifth and last part by Kuan Han-ch'ing. Both are well-known dramatists of the early Yüan period (thirteenth century). Wang Shih-fu, a native of Peking, was the author of fourteen plays, of which three are still extant. Kuan Han-ch'ing, who has been regarded as the greatest of the Yüan dramatists, was a professional playwright and the leader of a theatrical circle in Peking. His dramatic output was immense, and eighteen out of his sixty-seven known plays have survived.

Like English dramatists of the Elizabethan age, the Yüan playwrights made little attempt to invent the plots of their plays but borrowed heavily from previous stories, poems, and plays that were common literary property. The question of plagiarism never came up in those days and the Yüan dramatists felt free to use whatever sources they had. The story of the *Western Chamber*, which deals with a love affair between Student Chang and the girl, Ying Ying, had its earliest beginning in a romantic literary tale by the T'ang poet, Yüan Chen. Popular with poets and storytellers,[6] it had undergone several important changes and improvements in the course of its development before it culminated in the dramatic masterpiece of Wang Shih-fu.

The chief source of Wang's *Western Chamber* was a Medley of the same name written by Tung Chieh-yüan,* a professional versifier in the reign of Emperor Chang (1190–1208) of the Chin dynasty. The only complete Medley in existence, Tung's *Western Chamber*, which may be called an epic of love,** is also one of the longest Chinese poetic compositions. In his work, Tung Chieh-yüan considerably expanded the original story of Ying Ying. Besides adding many new situations and episodes to enrich his narrative and a number of turns and surprises to keep his audience in suspense, he also introduced a daring change in the last part of the narrative. Instead of Yüan Chen's rather pathetic ending— the desertion of Ying Ying by Student Chang—Tung Chieh-yüan brought the romance to a happy conclusion, in which the lovers were finally united. This is also the ending of Wang Shih-fu's *Western Chamber*. In fact, a careful study of the two works shows clearly that Wang's drama is essentially a replica of Tung's Medley, and that in many details he follows his predecessor rather closely. The great length of Tung's Medley explains also the unusually large number of song sequences in Wang's play.

These borrowings, however, do not detract from Wang Shih-fu's contributions to the *Western Chamber*. Taken as a whole, it is a masterpiece of dramatic construction, characterization, and poetry. Like other Chinese dramas, the story unfolds in a leisurely and natural way without the tension and violence that characterize some Western plays of a similar nature. The delicate romantic atmosphere is laden with lovers' sighs and tears, the tingling notes of the zither, the fragrance of incense, the moonlight breeze, flowery shadows, and above all, the yearnings, the expectancy, and the ecstasy of the fulfillment of love. There are intense moments such as the siege of the temple by a rebelling general, who clamors to have Ying Ying as his wife; Ying Ying's threat to end her life; and the dramatic entrance of Student Chang with a clap of his hands and an

* Chien-yüan is not a personal name, but an honorary title given to a scholar.
** This poem may also be compared to the medieval romances of the minstrels and troubadours in Europe at about the same time. Mainly intended for recitation, the Medley has a unique structure of alternate recitative and sung parts, the latter constituting the main bulk of the poem, being chanted to the accompaniment of stringed instruments.

offer to drive away the unruly soldiers. There is also a great deal of humor. This is shown, for instance, in the sacrificial scene at the Buddhist hall, where Ying Ying, who has come to offer incense to the spirit of her departed father, creates such a stir among the monks and novices that they all neglect their duties: the superior seated high above, staring at Ying Ying with a falsely benign face; the head monk striking at the bald pate of a novice, taking it for a music stone; one greatly agitated acolyte forgetting to light the candles and another to burn the incense, with the result that the candles are extinguished and the incense smoke ceases— all because of Ying Ying's bewitching beauty.

Taken together, Ying Ying and Student Chang represent an ideal pair of Chinese lovers, the beautiful maiden and the talented student, to be celebrated henceforth for many centuries in Chinese plays and novels. Student Chang is afflicted with an incurable love sickness and a penchant for writing poetic billets-doux. Although unwittingly creating such havoc among her admirers, Ying Ying is a quiet and modest girl, tender in her love, dignified in her bearing, and when occasion requires, resourceful in her action. Even more fascinating than Ying Ying is the inimitable Hung Niang, Ying Ying's maid and companion. An inveterate matchmaker, Hung Niang is the liveliest as well as the most unforgettable character in the play. She is as adept in repartee and raillery as in the stratagems of love. She knows how to tell innocent lies, how to prevaricate, to tease, to persuade, to convince, to console, and to defy. When forced by Madame Ts'ui (Ying Ying's mother) to reveal Ying Ying's escapade, she even dares to defend her mistress, blaming everything on Madame Ts'ui for her failure to unite the lovers legally. In support of her argument she quotes the good old proverb, "When a girl is grown up, it is unwise to keep her long at home." Her words prove so sensible and her reasoning so convincing that finally Madame Ts'ui consents to solemnize the marriage of the lovers.

Wang Shih-fu excels not only in plot construction and characterization, but also in poetic imagination. Choosing at random any passage in the *Western Chamber*, one finds lines that are romantic, humorous, or tender, but always of the highest quality. Wang Shih-fu's poetry strikes many keys. Take for instance Student Chang's description of the Yellow River with its nine bends of wind-swept billows:

> Its snowy waves rise to the great void
> Like autumn clouds rolling in the far horizon.
> The floating bridges of plaited bamboo span the river
> Like black dragons crouching on the waters.
> East and west it overflows the Nine Regions;

South and north it strings together the hundred streams.
How can one tell
Whether fast or slow is the home-bound skiff?
It is like a strong arrow sped from the bow. (Part One, Act I, Song 3)

In striking contrast to these majestic lines is the following exquisite
passage which tells of Student Chang's first glimpse of Ying Ying:

Her voice is like the oriole's call across the flowers,
And every step of hers arouses one's love.
Her dancing waist, how soft and supple!
A thousand graces and ten thousand charms she has,
Like a drooping willow before the evening breeze.

.   .   .   .

How lightly she treads on the soft fragrant path of fallen petals,
Leaving a faint imprint of her steps which perfume the dust!
Apart from that love in the corner of her eyes,
Her gait alone reveals the stirrings of her heart.
Slowly and lingering,
She draws near the wicket gate,
And has barely moved a step further
When she turns round with a look
That has me enraptured and enthralled!
The angel has now returned to her heavenly abode,
Leaving behind her the willows hidden in mist,
And the sparrows chirping in vain. (Part One, Act I, Songs 9-10)

Even more delicately beautiful is the scene in which Ying Ying, accompanied by Hung Niang, is praying in the garden as Student Chang peeps
in from behind a corner of the wall.

The night is deep; the clouds of incense float in the empty courtyard;
The curtains lie still and the gentle eastern breeze has subsided.
Her worship ended, she leans sideways against the winding balustrade;
Two or three times she sighs long and deep.
A brilliant full moon hangs aloft like a mirror;
Not a trace of light cloud or mist is visible,
Save the incense smoke and the maiden's soft breath
That have enshrouded her and made her seem obscure and blurred.
                              (Part One, Act III, Song 5)

Also deservedly famous is the farewell song in which Ying Ying lays bare a
girl's heart in all its tenderness and affection:

My red sleeves are dripping wet with tears of love;
They are more drenched than your blue gown is soaked.
The oriole flies to the east and the sparrow to the west.

崔鶯鶯燒夜香

Ying Ying Burning Incense at Night. From a Ming Dynasty Illustration of the *Romance of the Western Chamber*.

But ere you go, I would ask first the date of your return.
Although you who now stand before my eyes will be a thousand
    miles away,
I will, at least, empty for you a cup of wine.
But even before I drink, my mind is already intoxicated:
My eyes shed tears of blood,
And my heart is ashen cold.

After you have reached the capital,
Be careful of the change of climate;
And when you are on the way,
Be moderate in your food and drink.
Guard well your precious self at every season:
Retire early in lonely villages in times of rain and dew;
Stay late abed in the country inns when there is wind and frost.
While riding your horse in the autumn wind,
With no one to look after you,
You must take good care of your health.
                    (Part Four, Act III, Songs 13-14)

As Student Chang disappears gradually into the distant mountains, she
continues her song and then mounts her carriage:

Surrounded on all sides by the mountains,
His lonely whip he raises in the setting sun.
All the sorrows of this world have filled my breast—
Oh, how can a carriage of this size ever bear this burden of mine?
                    (Part Four, Act III, Song 19)

Another type of Yüan drama, the religious and supernatural, is likewise
romantic in theme and content. In the supernatural plays are introduced
stories of love between human beings and spirits such as flower fairies
and the dragon's daughter. They also present magic duels and superhuman adventures. But the most interesting plays are those dealing with
the conversion of the hero—a young scholar, a poet, a butcher, or a sing-
song girl—to Taoism or Buddhism. These plays of romantic escapism
afford occasions for exquisite lyrics on the beauties of nature and the
happiness of a leisurely, retired life. One of their best writers was Ma
Chih-yüan, a native of Peking and for some time a minor official in
Kiangsu and Chekiang. Although he had a scholarly career, he seems to
have been closely connected with the theater. His well-known play, the
Dream of the Yellow Millet, was the result of his collaboration with two
actor-playwrights.

The Dream of the Yellow Millet deals with the story of Lü Tung-pin's
conversion to Taoism by Chung-li Ch'üan, head of the Eight Taoist
Immortals. When the play opens, Lü, a Confucian scholar on his way to

the capital to take the imperial examination, has stopped to have a meal at Dame Wang's inn on the Han-tan Road. There he is greeted by Chung-li Ch'üan who tries to persuade him to follow the path of Tao. Deaf to Chung-li's advice, Lü soon falls asleep while waiting for his meal of millet. In his sleep, he suddenly finds himself promoted to a generalship in the army, rolling in wealth and fame and enjoying the blessings of a happy family life. But soon he runs into a host of troubles: he is accused of having accepted bribes from a rebel general, is divorced by his unfaithful wife, and exiled with his two young sons. They are almost frozen to death as they travel in the wilds amid whipping winds and snow. Finally, they are pursued by a fierce husky fellow, who throws the children into a deep ravine and threatens to kill Lü with a knife. He wakes up to find that all this was but a dream! In the meantime, in a corner of the inn, Dame Wang is about to put another bundle of straw on the fire to make the yellow millet well cooked. After having gone through in his dream all the troubles of his life, Lü becomes suddenly enlightened and joins the company of the Taoist Immortals.

In this play, as in the others, Ma Chih-yüan's hero is a pessimist, disillusioned with wealth, rank, and family ties; he is also deeply chagrined at the ephemerality and futility of life. In accordance with Taoist philosophy, he denounces what he considers to be the four archevils of life, namely: excessive drinking, sex, wealth, and temper. All these are to be shunned as injurious to the body and harmful to the cultivation of long life. In the case of drinking, however, a distinction is made between intoxication, the cause of many ills and troubles, and temperate drinking, which one may enjoy in the company of green mountains and bright moonbeams. Fame and glory are to be shunned also, for to seek fame is as dangerous as to balance oneself precariously on a hundred-foot pole while there is below a confusion of deafening sounds that are enough to drive one crazy. Why don't we, asks the dramatist, walk securely on good solid ground?

Ma Chih-yüan's plays are not noted for their plot or characterization. His contributions to drama are his philosophical mood, his outlook on life, and above all his lyricism. He was more at home with nature, poetry, and imagination than with the harsh realities of life, which he brushed aside with the haughty disdain of a Taoist Immortal. At times he introduced an undertone of pessimism in his transcendental utterances, comparing himself to "a broken-hearted man on the edge of the world." In this he expressed the prevailing mood of the Chinese intellectuals at the time of the Mongol rule when the country was ridden by war, confusion, and tyranny. To these people, as to Ma Chih-yüan, the future was one vast expanse of fading autumn reaching even to the distant horizon. So it is not surprising that haunted by memory and despair, Ma Chih-yüan should have yearned for the blessings of Taoist immortality in the great world beyond.

Among the historical plays may be mentioned *Rain on the Wu-t'ung Tree* and *The Orphan of Chao*. Po P'o (1226–1285), author of the first play, was the only Yüan dramatist who had the distinction of coming from a great literary and official family. *Rain on the Wu-t'ung Tree*, perhaps his best work, is a dramatization of the romance between Lady Yang and the Brilliant Emperor of T'ang, made famous by Po Chü-i's "Song of Everlasting Sorrow." As the story itself was well-known, Po P'o's primary concern was to portray the sentiment of love in all its facets: its tenderness and faith resulting in an oath of eternal love sworn by the imperial lovers on the night of the seventh day of the seventh moon; its exquisite charm, shown in the dance of the Rainbow Skirt performed by Lady Yang below the Pavilion of Fragrance; its troubles and sorrows when the lovers were forced to take the long arduous trip to Szechuan at the time of An Lu-shan's rebellion; its tragedy climaxed by the hanging of Lady Yang at the demand of the imperial guards; and finally, the everlasting grief experienced by the Brilliant Emperor as he returned to his palace to find it cold and barren without his lady-love. The highest point in the poetry occurs when the emperor, all alone in the depth of an autumnal night, becomes an unwilling listener to the raindrops on the *wu-t'ung* tree:

> Sometimes intense like myriad pearls falling on a jade plate,
> Sometimes loud like songs and music mingled noisily at a banquet,
> Sometimes resonant like a waterfall from a cold spring at the head
>   of the blue ridge,
> Sometimes fierce like the beating of war-drums below an embroidered
>   flag.
> Alas! How the rain vexes one to death!
> How it vexes one to death,
> With its variety of sounds that stun the ear with their hubbub!
>   (Act IV, Song 18)

Well-known to Western readers, the *Orphan of Chao* was written by Chi Chün-hsiang in the second half of the thirteenth century. It differs structurally from the other Yüan plays in that it has five acts instead of four. But what makes it outstanding is the theme of sacrifice and loyalty exemplified in the deeds of Ch'eng Ying, a subordinate of the great ministerial family of Chao, which was about to be exterminated by a powerful general at the head of the government. Ch'eng Ying sacrificed his own son as well as two friends to rescue the orphan son of Chao so that he could live to avenge the family's wrongs by killing his enemy. Throughout the play there are suspense, urgency, and tragedy. But the reader's agonizing experience of these is considerably relieved by the assertion of poetic justice in the end, and the glorification of man's noble instincts in moments of crisis. These traits must have appealed to Voltaire, whose adaptation of the Chinese play has made it popular with students of European literature.[7]

The repertoire of the Yüan theater also abounds in domestic and social plays. Their outstanding features are realistic descriptions, humorous incidents, an involved plot, and an abundant use of dialogue. As an integral part of Chinese society, the family receives special attention from the dramatists; the virtues of hospitality, friendship, and fraternal love are highly praised. The play *An Heir in His Old Age* written by Wu Han-ch'en, a late thirteenth century writer, tells the story of a goodhearted old couple who because of their good deeds are happily rewarded in the end with an heir born to the old man by a concubine. A bourgeois comedy par excellence, it illustrates the typical Chinese idea that one of the blessings of life is to have an heir in old age. The news of the existence of the male child bursts suddenly upon the old couple as it does upon the audience —a clever use of dramatic surprise that brings the play effectively to its happy conclusion.

The most famous domestic tragedy in the Yüan period is *The Wrongs of Maid Tou* by Kuan Han-ch'ing.[8] The story begins with the scholar Tou selling his only daughter, age seven, to Dame Ts'ai, a usurer, for a few ounces of silver with which to travel to the capital for the imperial examination. This is a prelude to the main story, which takes place thirteen years later when Maid Tou is already a young woman of much experience. During this long interval she has been married to Dame Ts'ai's son, mourned her husband's death, and is now a young widow of twenty. Like a typical Chinese woman, she has become resigned to her lot and has lived dutifully in her mother-in-law's house until its tranquillity is shattered by the intrusion of two suitors: the Elder Chang, courting Dame Ts'ai; and his son Chang the Ass, seeking the hand of Maid Tou. The two men, having once saved Dame Ts'ai from being strangled by a wicked quack doctor, now force their way into the old woman's house to demand compensation for their previous good deed. Dame Ts'ai seems to be willing to remarry, but Maid Tou, still faithful to her husband's memory, refuses. To accomplish his desire, Chang the Ass plans to get rid of Dame Ts'ai so that he may have his will with the young woman when she is left alone. One day, while Maid Tou is preparing for Dame Ts'ai a bowl of mutton tripe soup, Chang the Ass slips into it some poison he has got from the quack doctor. But instead of poisoning the intended victim, it kills the Elder Chang, who drinks it by mistake. Chang the Ass then falsely accuses Maid Tou of having poisoned his father. The case is brought to court, and a corrupt and stupid magistrate has Maid Tou put to the rack and flogged to force a confession. The magistrate also threatens to beat Dame Ts'ai. At this point, Maid Tou's resistance melts, for as a dutiful daughter-in-law she cannot bear to see the old woman suffer. So she makes a false confession and is sentenced to death. On the day of her execution in midsummer, she makes three extraordinary wishes to Heaven to prove her innocence: that it will snow at the hour of her execution; that her blood will gush up to color the white silk pennant hanging aloft on the execution ground; and that there will be three years of drought. Strangely enough, all these wishes come true in due course, for Heaven is moved by the gross injustice done to Maid Tou and sends down calamity as a warning to the people. The drought brings to the district a great dignitary who is no other than Maid Tou's father, now a high official on a tour of inspection. At night when official Tou is reviewing the documents of Maid Tou's trial, her ghost appears before him in the flickering candle light and asks for redress. In the end, the case is re-opened, Maid Tou cleared posthumously of her guilt, and the villain duly punished.

The local story of the murder and trial on which the play was based had a wide circulation among the people of that time, but Kuan Han-ch'ing gave it immortality. Maid Tou's character stands out humanely, pathetically, and yet majestically in the midst of adversity. Her innocence, her sufferings, her courage, and her great virtue move not only Heaven and Earth, but also the human heart. The strength of her character lies in her chastity, widowhood, and filial love. These are all age-old virtues that have gained currency among the Chinese, and their value has never been doubted or questioned. In whatever light one views her, Maid Tou is certainly the epitome of all that is good and great in womanhood according to conventional Chinese standards; what is more, she gains one's admiration by her more universal trait of supreme moral courage in the face of threats and tortures. Though young and tender, she was fearless in her fight against all forms of oppression. Indomitable and unbending, she kept up her spirit to the last, exclaiming as she made her way to the execution ground:

> For no reason at all, I've sinned against the law,
> And unexpectedly brought myself to punishment.
> "Injustice!" I cry, and my wail startles Heaven and Earth.
> In a twinkling my drifting soul will depart for Yen-lo's palace.*
> Why shouldn't I blame both Heaven and Earth for my plight?

* Yen-lo or Yama, the King of Hades.

The sun hangs aloft in the morning and the moon at night.
Spirits and ghosts control the powers of life and death.
Heaven and Earth should be able to distinguish the pure from the
foul;
Why did they bungle in the case of Bandit Chih and Yen Yüan?*

The virtuous suffered from poverty and an untimely death
While the wicked enjoyed a long life of wealth and nobility.
Even Heaven and Earth have come to fear the strong and bully
the weak,
And they too are pushing the boat where the current leads.
Oh Earth, how unworthy! No distinction you make between good
and bad;
And Heaven, vain is your name! You have mistaken for wise the
stupid!
Alas! How my tears course down in two endless streams!

(Act 3, Songs 1–2)

Pure and virtuous, Maid Tou is free from any "tragic flaw" in her character or action; her tragedy is not one of her making but the direct result of human persecution. In this respect Chinese tragedy is different from the Western tragedy of fate or character. It is essentially a social tragedy in which the good and innocent are pitted against the pernicious forces of society and crushed relentlessly by them. The whole is a life-and-death struggle between good and evil; tragedy results when evil prevails. In a Chinese play, pathos is gained not so much from the stature of the hero-figure, who might be just a simple helpless woman like Maid Tou, but from the ultimate defeat of the hero in a desperate but despairing battle against the oppressors. That is why poetic justice is such an indispensable part of Chinese tragedy. A moral lesson must be taught and upheld. Otherwise, life would not be worth living if helpless, innocent people fell victim to the villains, and wickedness ran rampant through society without being punished or checked.

The murder and lawsuit plays, of which *The Wrongs of Maid Tou* is a forerunner, were popular in the Yüan period. Most of them have a complicated plot with many incidents and much dialogue. In some of them knotty cases of law are solved with great skill by clever judges endowed with keen insight, careful reasoning, and resourcefulness. One such example is the *Story of the Lime Pen* by Li Ch'ien-fu (or Li Hsing-tao), an obscure writer. Here through sheer ingenuity Lord Pao, a famous judge, settled a difficult suit between a wife and a concubine, one accusing the

---

* This contrast between the worldly success of a notorious brigand (a contemporary of Confucius) and the misfortunes of a virtuous scholar (a disciple of Confucius) is a common literary allusion in Chinese poetry and prose.

"The Wrongs of Maid Tou". From the *Yüan-ch'ü hsüan* (Selections from the Yüan Drama), 1616.

other of murdering their husband, and each claiming as her own child a young heir of the family. When the case was finally tried by Judge Pao, he ordered an enclosure to be marked out with lime in the presence of the court and the boy to be placed in it. He further ordered the two contestants to pull at the boy, one on each side of him, and announced that she who succeeded in pulling the child out of the enclosure would win the case. Twice the women pulled, and twice the boy was dragged out by the wife. But now Judge Pao retracted his words and decided in favor of the concubine as the real mother, who, so the Judge reasoned, would rather lose the case than hurt the boy by pulling him too hard. Her tenderness to the boy proved that she was the rightful claimant; and so to her the boy as well as the family property should go. Thus decreed Judge Pao after the other woman and her adulterer-accomplice had confessed their guilt. The solution, of course, is crude from the legal point of view, but it must have made a great appeal to the audience of the time, as well as to Western translators and adapters.[9] As a stage make-believe, the play is remarkable for its psychological understanding based upon blood relationship which has formed such an important part of Chinese family life.

But not all judges are like Lord Pao. In the same play, for instance, there is the local magistrate, a typically stupid and negligent official, who cruelly beat the real mother to force a confession. This made her burst forth into a song of protest:

> You officials, so harsh and cruel-hearted,
> Have too much oppressed us, the common people:
> Callously and falsely you have made me confess my crime
>   on that piece of paper.
> Here I cry to Heaven for redress,
> But Heaven is too far above me!
> Oh, how I yearn for an upright judge!
> Oh, how could this ruined body of mine ever hope
> To bear the tortures in this prison of death? (Act 2, Song 12)

This happened of course before the arrival of Lord Pao on the scene. But what makes the song interesting is the universality of its complaint, which is not only that of one helpless woman, but of all the innocents against official corruption and oppression.

If one group of writers saw the people's salvation in the righteous upholders of justice like Judge Pao, still another group found active support and more radical relief from, paradoxically enough, the righteous trespassers against the law. These were the outlaws who lived by the marshes (Shui-hu) on Mount Liang in Shantung province and who revolted against the government in the early twelfth century. They have been popularized and idealized by later storytellers as bandit-heroes who exercised

virtue and justice in the name of Heaven by helping the poor and oppressed, and by robbing the rich and wicked. Since there was only one
Judge Pao in this world of official corruption, it is obvious that he could
not be everywhere to right the wrongs; so the Yüan dramatists had to
seek the aid of the bandit-heroes in their literary combat against the evils
and tyrannies of the time.

In these Yüan plays, the main outline of the *Shui-hu* legend[10] has been
fairly well drawn with its one hundred and eight bandit-heroes, thirty-six
of whom are great chieftains, and seventy-two, lesser ones. Their acknowledged leader was Sung Chiang; his chief counsellor and second-in-com-
mand, the scholar Wu Yung. The most popular hero in the plays, however, is Li K'uei, the Black Whirlwind. Even though their slogan is:

> In high winds we dare set the heavens aflame;
> On dark moonless nights we lift the sword to kill,

all are represented as good, honest and brave fellows, who are more heroes
than bandits, ready to repay any kindness and to risk their lives for the
sake of friends and benefactors. On the other hand, the law enforcers
like magistrates and yamen clerks are represented as corrupt and in many
cases, downright wicked. Thus the world has gone topsy-turvy as it must
have been in the days of the Yüan dramatists with officials becoming the
black sheep, and bandits, champions of the people.

Fairly representative of the bandit-hero drama is *The Black Whirlwind*,
by Kao Wen-hsiu, a young talented dramatist of the thirteenth century.
It tells the story of a young official's elopement with a yamen clerk's wife,
of the husband's search for them, which eventually landed him in jail,
and of his rescue by Black Whirlwind, who exercised the people's justice
by killing the two adulterers. Having committed the murder, Black Whirlwind wrote his own name on the wall with a piece of cloth dipped in blood
as he sang happily and nonchalantly:

> They have provoked me, Black Whirlwind,
> And the fire of my temper has erupted;
> I care not what others would say,
> Whether to kill them is justice or not.
>
> (Act IV, in dialogue after Song 4)

Then with the adulterers' heads, one on each end of a pole, he made his
way back to Mount Liang, where he was greeted by Sung Chiang and
feasted joyfully in their mountain lair.

The Black Whirlwind and other *Shui-hu* plays of the Yüan Period[11]
leave little doubt where the writers' sympathies lay. They help to dispel
the notion that the flourishing of the Yüan drama was due to the patron-

age of the Mongol emperors, for it is hardly conceivable that monarchs and court ministers would relish these plays of brigandage. As a matter of fact, things must have become very bad that dramatists should have sung paeans to the outlaws, who alone seem to have maintained justice. This glorification of banditry, therefore, gives a clue to the social significance of the Yüan drama. Besides being dramatizations of the stories of murder and revenge beloved of folk theatergoers, these bandit-hero plays also represent a small voice of protest by the common man against the political decadence and social injustice of the age.

Taken as a whole, the Yüan drama is a realistic one that gives us a clear perspective of the vast panorama of Chinese life. It is life in all its multicolored aspects as the Yüan people lived and saw it. To be sure, some of the plays are legendary and historical while others are fantastic and romantic. But whatever they are, they reflect the time and society in which the dramatists found themselves. Even historical deeds and settings were transposed to the present by these semischolarly writers, to whom anachronism was no more a fault than plagiarism. Thus, by transcending time and space, the Yüan playwrights peopled the stage with all types and classes of character from the highest to the meanest, the majority being of the urban middle class. The Yüan society, of course, may not have been as bad as that presented in these plays; nevertheless, the latter give eloquent testimony to baseness in human nature and evils in society, a candid if somewhat magnified picture, which the dramatists projected as a warning to all.

Far from giving up hopes of improvement and reform, the Yüan writers were meticulously careful to prove the thesis that justice, whether poetic or legal, does finally prevail. A deep ethical tone pervades all the plays as the dramatists pass their judgment on the characters and their actions, and reward or punish them accordingly. In fact, these dramatists were great advocates of both social and domestic virtues, notably those of filial and fraternal love, friendship, honesty, loyalty, righteousness, and devotion to work and duty. In spite of the terrible things that happen, innocence is always vindicated and wickedness punished. For this reason, few tragedies are found in the entire Yüan repertoire, and even in these few the poignancy of tragic feeling is somewhat lessened by the ultimate punishment of the villain. On the other hand, most Yüan plays are comedies and tragi-comedies which end happily in the marriage of the lovers, family reunion after long years of separation, repentance of wayward sons, reconciliation of alienated brothers, restoration of family fortune, official promotion, literary success, and a thousand and one good things that make life after all worth living.

To conclude, it may be asserted that never before in China was there such a wealth of socio-literary material as in the Yüan drama, which depicts comprehensively and faithfully the varied activities of the Chinese people and the hundred compartments of Chinese life. The Yüan society, in many respects sadly out of joint, is reproduced most vividly in all its kaleidoscopic forms illuminated by the creative genius of the playwrights. It is their social outlook, coupled with their theatrical talent and poetic imagination, that makes the Yüan drama unique. Drawing much of their sustenance and inspiration from the people, the dramatists presented for the first time the common man as the main theme of literature.

13 : *San Ch'ü*, a New Poetic Melody

While the dramatists were creating a new vigorous literature of their own, other Yüan writers were satisfied with following the beaten path of conventional literature. The latter group consisted mostly of scholars and officials who figured prominently in the literary and dynastic histories of the period. They were highly regarded by their fellow scholars as torchbearers of the great tradition, and collections of their poems and essays have been preserved as a part of China's literary heritage. But they lacked the creativeness and accomplishment of their great forebears and played only a minor part in the development of Chinese literature.

One important contribution of the Yüan period, however, was a new type of poetry known as *san ch'ü* or lyric songs. The *ch'ü* emerged as a variation of the *tz'u*: when the *tz'u* had lost its spontaneity and ceased to be creative, the *ch'ü* arose to take its place. In the Yüan period, the lyric song, like the dramatic song, was essentially a product of North China, whence came all the great *ch'ü* poets.

There is one important distinction between lyric and dramatic songs. Though similar in form, they differ in purpose and representation. Whereas the dramatic songs are woven together in a sequence to utter the sentiments of a certain character in a play, the lyric songs are written mainly to express the poet's own feelings and observations. Moreover, though the lyric songs can also be combined to form a sequence, they are completely devoid of the prose dialogue that is interspersed between the dramatic songs. When a play was presented on the stage, songs were sung by the actors to the accompaniment of musical instruments. On the other hand, the lyric songs, whether single or in a sequence, were purely vocal and intended mainly for chanting.

An important rule governing the writing of the lyric songs, as of the dramatic songs, stipulates that there should be one rhyme throughout the song sequence. Another rule specifies that though the songs in each sequence can be different in form and tune, as they usually are, they should belong to the same tonality in the musical system. At the same time, there is a certain order or pattern in the arrangement of the songs. All these technical considerations make the writing of a song sequence extremely intricate and exacting so that only an expert can handle it with ease and adroitness.

In spite of its limitation, the *san ch'ü* has two advantages over the other forms of poetry, including the *tz'u*. First, the *ch'ü* pattern is flexible enough to allow the introduction of several extra words, especially the particles (*hsü-tzu*). Secondly, the *ch'ü* is a poetic medium in which the use of colloquial expressions is suitable. This employment of the spoken language, a significant development, tends to instill into the poetry a new vigor and freedom. In the Yüan period, the *ch'ü* was still fresh and sprightly, in the prime of its youth. Unadulterated by pedantic quotations, allusions, and other artificialities that impede the movement of poetry, the *ch'ü* attained much natural spontaneity.

This new poetic form was immensely popular among all groups of writers, irrespective of class or profession. Practically everyone in the Yüan period, whether a great official or a humble scholar, experimented with the *ch'ü*. And the writing of it was limited to no one school of poets. Many well-known traditional poets also left some specimens of the *ch'ü*, but few succeeded in capitalizing on the advantages of the new melody.

More important contributions were made by playwrights like Kuan Han-ch'ing and Ma Chih-yüan. The song being an integral part of the drama, it is natural that great dramatists should also be great song writers. In this case, they used their dramatic talents either to delineate the sorrows and joys of some fictitious characters or to express in the songs their own sentiments and aspirations. Although little is known of the facts of their outward lives, much about their personalities and inner lives can be gleaned from the spontaneous utterance of these songs.

Among the *san ch'ü* poets, Kuan Han-ch'ing was noted for his delicate love songs. True to his dramatic instinct, he was able to imagine and conjure up tender situations:

> All quiet outside the green silk window—
> Kneeling in front of the couch, he wants to make love to me.
> "Ah, you heartless fellow!" I scold him and turn myself away.
> Though my words sound disdainful,
> I am in fact only half refusing, half yielding.
> ("Love"—to the tune of "Just One Half")

The story of love is told in a similar delightful vein in his song sequences, where the psychology of coy maidens and love-sick women is carefully analyzed and vividly portrayed. In one of these, entitled "Lamentations in the Boudoir" to the tune of "Green Skirt Waist," a lonely wife mourns her wrinkled brows and thinning wrists, her dusty mirror and idle needle-work. Naturally in such a despondent mood, she cannot help thinking of her husband far away, but the more she broods, the more her fervid imagination leads her astray until she asks:

> Where and with whom is he holding hands—
> A cozy chamber, a silver wine pot, and drink and song in excess?
> Oh, could he have forgotten his oath,
> And remembers he not the time we weeded together,
>   bending very low?

The most celebrated of the *san ch'ü* writers, Ma Chih-yüan was noted for his spacious imagination and serene contemplation. He was a disillusioned scholar who wanted to retire from this world to keep company with Taoist hermits and immortals. His plays[1] bear ample evidence of this aspect of his thought, but it is in his lyric songs that are reflected clearly his personality, his taste, and his inclinations. Here one gains a glimpse of the serenity, depth, and sincerity of a poetic spirit in all its changing moods. Sometimes, Ma Chih-yüan sings complainingly of the earthbound limitations of man, in contrast to the roc's happy excursions into space. More often, he is satisfied with his lot and calls himself an indolent fellow without great ability, whose only concern is how to repay "the debt of poetry he owes the pleasant wind and bright moon." At other times, he tries to drown his sorrows in wine and friendship:

> The goblet is deep
> Like an old friend's heart.
> In this meeting, do not refrain from drinking.
> You may sing while I slowly pour out the wine.
> Let Ch'ü Yüan die, if he so desires, of purity!
> Drunk or sober—what difference does it make?
>   (—to the tune of "Pluck, Not Break")

His best way of escape, however, is to withdraw into the bosom of nature, where he can be oblivious to the ills of this world. Thus he stands on the top of a cliff, taking off his hat and loosening his hair as the setting sun puts the pine shadows into confusion, and the ocean wind blows asunder the colored clouds. Or he may spend a long leisurely summer day in the west village, listening to the songs of a new cicada and the mumblings of busy bees as he drowses off on the green pillow of nature, his dreams fluttering away with the butterfly. Often, he likes to fancy himself a fisherman at a river bend or a woodcutter carrying home the mountain moon on a pole. He insists, however, that the woodcutter lay down his axe and the fisherman put aside his boat to enjoy completely a life of inaction and security. But even the fisherman runs risks comparable to those of an official career:

> Green straw cape or purple silk gown—
> Which should I put on?
> But they are both undesirable,
> For even a fisherman lives in the wind and storm.
> Better it would be to find a pleasant spot
> To sit down leisurely and care-free.
>
> (—"Country Pleasures" to the tune of
> "Clear-River Prelude")

If Ma Chih-yüan's short lyric sparkles like a gem, his song sequence is a necklace attractive for the luster of the individual pearls and their combined beauty. Even the titles of the lyrics are poetic: "The Wind Sees the Guests off on the Long River," "Rain Halts the Traveler in His Lonely Inn," "Scooping Water, She Holds the Moon in Her Hands," "Her Dress Full of Fragrance from Playing with Flowers."

The sequence "Borrowing a Horse" shows still another aspect of Ma Chih-yüan's talent—namely, his pathos and humor. Here is depicted what appears to be a miserly man who has newly acquired a horse and is reluctant to lend it to a friend for a day's ride. He would prefer not to part with the horse at all and is worried that it might get hurt in careless hands. So repeatedly he bids his friend take good care of the horse: when dismounting, fasten it to a cool spot in the shade; when riding, choose a smooth road and avoid running over bricks and stones or sinking in the mud. Feed it tender grass when it is hungry, and give it water when it is thirsty. But then remember well the saying, "Don't make it trot when it is well fed; don't gallop when it has drunk." Moreover, never let the whip whiz by its eye or lash against its hair until it hurts. Thus the song goes on until the very end when the "miser" turns out to be a true lover of the horse with an infinite tenderness for the animal.

The most famous of Ma Chih-yüan's song sequences is one entitled "Autumn Thoughts," to the tune of "Sailing at Night." As an illustration of the form and structure of a song sequence, the poem is reproduced here in full:

AUTUMN THOUGHTS

1.

A hundred years are no more than the dream of a butterfly.
Looking back, how one sighs for the things of the past!
Yesterday spring came;

This morning the flowers wither.
Let us hasten with the forfeit cup
Before the night is spent and the lamp goes out.

2.

The palaces of Ch'in and the halls of Han
Have all become wild pastures for the herd;
Otherwise, the fisherman and woodsman would have nothing to
    talk about.
Rows of deserted graves, heaps of broken monuments—
No longer discernible therein are the dragons and snakes.

3.

Here are fox tracks and rabbit holes;
How many heroes have been laid therein!
The tripod, resting on its legs, has broken at the waist.*
Which period was it? Wei or Tsin?

4.

Heaven has made you rich,
But why do you indulge in luxury?
Good days and pleasant nights do not last long.
You, slaves of wealth, how your hearts are like iron
To have vainly squandered the wind-and-moon in an embroidered
    hall!

5.

Before one's very eye, the red sun will again slant westward
As fast as a carriage going down a slope.
Caring not that snowy hair has increased in the mirror,
I'll go to bed, parting with slippers and shoes.
Do not laugh at the foolish dove for failing to build its nest;
Taking life easy, I have all this time feigned stupidity.

6.

Gain and fame I have discarded;
Right and wrong forgotten.
Red dust will no longer entice me outside the gate,
Green trees give a pleasant shelter at the corner of the house,
And blue mountains are good enough to fill a gap in the wall;
Moreover, I have a thatched hut with a bamboo fence.

7.

When the chirping of insects has ceased,
Only then will sleep be peaceful and sound;

---

* An allusion to the division of the Chinese empire into three kingdoms in the
third century A.D. Wei, one of the kingdoms, was overthrown, together with the other
two, by Tsin.

As soon as the cock crows
There will be no end to the multiplicity of affairs.
This striving for fame and gain,
When will it ever come to a halt?
See, how in throngs the ants form their soldiers,
How, disorderly, the bees suck honey,
How noisily the flies fight for blood!
The Green Country Hall of Lord P'ei,
The White Lotus Club of Magistrate T'ao—
What does one love at autumn-tide?
To pluck yellow flowers covered with dew;
To open purple crabs heavy with frost;
To burn red leaves for warming wine.
Just think of the limited cups in a man's life
And the few "mountain days" that one can enjoy!
If people should ask you, my naughty page boy,—
Even though Po-hai has come to visit me—
Just say, "The master has been drunk."*

Another group of poets wrote songs that are realistic, colloquial, and sometimes vulgar. They were almost as revolutionary in breaking away from the decencies of life as from the decencies of poetry. Thus they sang of all sorts of amusing and unconventional subjects—the malaria fever, a man's bald pate, a long-haired puppy "as small as a pig," an amorous fat couple like a pair of "elephantine mandarin ducks," and an elderly woman who got slapped in the bathhouse—subjects which are taboo in traditional Chinese poetry. Contrasted with these "vulgar" topics are the "sweet and pretty" ones that deal with feminine toilet and ornamentation. There are songs about women's red finger-nails and black beauty spots; others dwell on the different styles of women's hair ornaments such as the "flower basket," a hairknot filled with flowers, and the "flower tube," featuring a long jade hairpin, its hollowed inside filled with water or honeysoaked cotton so that flowers placed in it could last for days without withering.

One of the Yüan writers noted for this type of boudoir poem was Ch'iao Chi (1280–1345), a dramatist who enjoyed great contemporary fame. Nearly two hundred of his lyric songs and ten of his song sequences have survived. Ch'iao Chi is credited with the famous dictum that a *san*

---

* The references in this stanza are as follows: P'ei Tu (died 838), a great official, built this retreat in his later years to enjoy a life of literary repose with the poet Po Chü-i and others. T'ao Ch'ien occasionally visited the White Lotus Club which had been founded by a famous monk, Hui Yüan. The mountain day falls on the "double ninth," the ninth day of the ninth month. Po-hai is the literary name of K'ung Jung (died 208), one of the seven literary geniuses who lived at the end of the Han dynasty. He was governor of Po-hai in Shantung. In the original, the words, here translated as "the master," are Tung-li (or "eastern fence"), Ma Chih-yüan's pen-name.

ch'ü should have the head of a phoenix, the belly of a pig, the tail of a leopard. By this he meant that the opening of a song should be striking and beautiful at first glance, its middle full of content and substance, and its end resonant with lingering music. Like other dramatic poets, he showed considerable skill in the use of colloquialisms. In particular, he was able to refine and mold colloquial expressions until they fitted beautifully into the lyric song, thus imparting to it a liveliness and facility of expression otherwise unattainable in the highly stylized literary language. Far from being crude, his poems are extremely refreshing, and are representative of the new melodies in the making.

Ch'iao Chi delighted in dwelling on women's fancy hair styles that allure the "butterflies of the dream"; on tiny curved slippers, each embroidered with a phoenix holding flowers in its mouth. He devoted several songs to a maiden's dimple, "The lovely den where all the fragrance makes a riot of spring and where a thousand pieces of gold can easily be spent." Ch'iao Chi did not, of course, confine his songs to such subjects. On the contrary, he was a gifted and versatile poet whose imagination flowed freely in all directions: he wrote about himself, his friends, and fellow poets; he rhapsodized on the beautiful scenes he enjoyed in his travels; he told of many colorful incidents in his life (such as the snatching away by a powerful official of his sing-song girl on a pleasure boat trip). A number of his songs are autobiographical and give a clear picture of the poet himself, his likes and dislikes. Especially interesting in this connection is the song "On Myself" to the tune of "Heavenly-Fragrance Prelude":

> By the Dipper and the Herd* I fasten my mountain raft;
> With jars of wine and gourds of poetry,
> I retire to the clouds and mists.
> Tired I am of traveling on the road,
> Of the false flowery manners of the world,
> And of a life that is casual and indifferent.
> When my bowels thirst for drink,
> I pick up in the willow shade slices of clouds
>   to cut the melons;
> When the songs are sweet,
> I sweep from the plumtree tops snowflakes to boil tea.
> What do I care about the myriad things of this world?
> Though I have no land in my name,
> It is not as bad as having no home.

Another poet often mentioned together with Ch'iao Chi is Chang K'o-chiu (1265?–1345?), the most voluminous *san ch'ü* writer of his time, with more than seven hundred songs to his credit. Later critics have called

---

* Two stars, representing the weaver girl and the cowherd.

Chang and Ch'iao the Li Po and Tu Fu of the Yüan period. This comparison is inappropriate in that there is little resemblance between the T'ang and the Yüan poets, but it serves to show the high regard the critics have for Chang and Ch'iao. While other Yüan poets wrote in different literary forms, including the drama, Chang K'o-chiu devoted his long life entirely to the *san ch'ü*.

In poetic style and diction, Chang K'o-chiu was a synthesist. Neither elegant like the scholar-poets, nor vulgar like the antitraditional poets, Chang K'o-chiu struck the golden mean both in his choice of subjects and in his use of the language. It has been said of his songs that they read equally well whether in plain style or adorned. This applies to his poems on the West Lake in Hangchow, about which he wrote with great affection. He sang of its twelve painted balustrades, its six bridges like a rainbow screen, and its ten miles of fragrant winds and wine houses; he told of a trip to seek the plum flowers on the Orphan Hill, of a spring morning walk on its tree-shaded banks, and of boating in the sun after snow. He was particularly sensitive to the changing moods of the lake and when away from its beauties, he asked anxiously in the song "Thinking of the West Lake" to the tune of "Falling Plum-flower Wind":

> Who is now master of the embroidered clouds over
>   the West Lake?
> Gently I beat time on the balustrade
> As mists and trees loom on the far horizon.

Chang K'o-chiu, the master of the colorful clouds over the West Lake, was also a master of the colorful nuances of poetry. Likewise, he was a conjurer of the beautiful illusions of poetry, equally at home with every type of verse, sometimes tender and subtle, sometimes serene and majestic, at all times delightfully picturesque:

> The lovely mountain in front of my gate the clouds
>   have possessed;
> No one has come to visit the whole day.
> The pine wind roars over the undulating green;
> Oak leaves kindle in the cinnabar crucible.
> The master lies asleep and drunk
> As spring time grows old by itself.
>   —"Spring Sleep in my Mountain Lodge" to the tune
>   of "Clear-River Prelude."

The *san ch'ü*, as we have seen, is mainly lyrical. It expresses the poet's tender passions and pleasant humor; his love of flowers and trees, mountains and streams; his reactions to the changing moods of the seasons; his delight in beauty, poetry, and wine; his reflections on wealth, fame, and power; his daily contacts with his fellow men and the society in which he finds himself. Only rarely did a *san ch'ü* writer overstep these limits and venture into the province of the essay to discuss social and political ideas. However, a notable exception to the lyrical bent is a group of two song sequences entitled "Presented to Kao, the Inspector General" to the tune of "Proper and Good" by Liu Chih, an official who died in poverty.

These two remarkable song sequences make use of the *ch'ü* form as a vehicle for social protest. Addressed to the same person and dealing with the same subject, they are in fact only two parts of a long poem, the first vividly picturing the famine-stricken multitudes of the period, and the second vigorously exposing official corruption and mismanagement. In precise, realistic, and unforgettable words, the poet describes the miserable condition of the people:

> Dust has gathered on the cooking pot;
> Hungry are the old and weak.
> When rice is like pearls,
> Famine strikes the young and strong alike.
> There is even no place to pawn gold and silver;
> So all lie feebly with empty stomachs in the setting sun.
> Elm barks have been peeled
> And wild herbs gathered for food:
> "Ageless yellow" tasting better than bear's paws;
> Turtle-foot roots taking the place of dry cereal;
> Bitter "goose-belly" cooked with its roots;*
> Reed shoots and rush stems chewed together with leaves.
> Only the trunks of the camphor and the willow are left intact.

> .   .   .   .   .   .

> When plague strikes,
> The sick are buried alive without coffin.
> Houses and lands are sold cheap,
> And so are the children of one's blood,
> Never to meet again.
> Oh, the pangs of parting!
> What a sad scene it is to see
> The unwanted suckling babies thrown away
> And drowned in the Great River!
> Alas! Where could one get some leftover food in the
>   kitchen, and wine in a cup?
> Watching these infants in the river and the mothers on
>   the shore,
> How could I not be choked with sobs and groans?

---

* Some of these unidentifiable plants' names are here translated literally. Bear's paws are a Chinese delicacy.

Liu Chih contrasted this picture of the suffering people with that of the arrogant *nouveaux riches*, who feasted and caroused day and night and whose women had

> On their shoes pearls the size of a cock's head,
> And in the hair gold combs as big as charcoal lumps.

The poet could hardly hold down his anger towards the unscrupulous revenue officers and yamen clerks who fed on the people to get rich. But even then, he was more concerned with facts than with feelings, and he delineated carefully in great detail the tricks and chicaneries with which the officials robbed the government of its revenue and the people of their livelihood. Taken as a whole, the poem is an important historical document of the economic and political system of the period; it also strikes a unique note in a new melody that was to linger on until the Ming and Ch'ing periods.

14 : The Novel as Folk Epic

Chinese fiction developed in the Yüan-Ming period as an outgrowth of the folk art of storytelling. In the hands of the storytellers, historical materials and literary fragments were expanded into complete stories and adorned with rich details and vivid descriptions. This oral tradition was further refined and enriched by the Yüan dramatists in their plays. Thus were evolved in the course of time two immensely popular story cycles which provided the subject matter respectively for two of the earliest major Chinese novels: The *Romance of the Three Kingdoms* (*San-kuo chih*) and the *Tale of the Marshes* (*Shui-hu chuan*).

In the past, Chinese scholars generally professed, at least in public, a lofty disdain for popular fiction. Because of this attitude, although the novel had delighted and influenced many generations of readers, it was not as highly regarded as were poetry and history. So not until modern times, as a result of the influence of the West, has prose fiction come to assume a new status as serious literature. This long neglect, therefore, has made the modern attempt to reconstruct the authorship of the novels and to trace their evolution, as we shall attempt to do below, a difficult and challenging task.

The *Romance of the Three Kingdoms* covers approximately a century of Chinese history from the last years of the Han dynasty (184) to the reunification of China by the first emperor of Tsin (280). This was one of the most eventful ages in China's long history. The country was torn apart by political intrigues and military strife; as a result there emerged three kingdoms: (1) Wei, in the Yellow River plains in North China; (2) Wu, in the lower Yangtze valley in the central east; and (3) Shu Han, in the upper Yangtze valley in the southwest. Culture and the arts suffered, and life was difficult in these troublous times. But this age of military exploits and heroic feats was most fascinating to the storytellers and their audiences.

There were numerous early references to the story of the Three Kingdoms, but the earliest extant printed version of the story, *The Three King-*

doms, A Popular Tale (San-kuo chih p'ing-hua) did not appear until 1321–1323 during the Yüan dynasty. Presumably, it was one of the script books used by the storytellers. Similar ones must have existed in the Sung period, but it is doubtful whether any of them ever went into print.

The main narrative of the *p'ing-hua* version, which is much shorter in length, is practically the same as that of the later novel. The only important episode not found in the novel is a trial scene in Hades, in which the first Han Emperor was accused and found guilty of killing his three generals. To punish him and his posterity, the judge ordered the reincarnation of the generals to overthrow and divide the Han empire into three kingdoms. The judge himself, actually a scholar in this life, also was reborn as a general, who in turn founded the Tsin dynasty to succeed the Three Kingdoms. With the judgment in Hades as a prelude the main tale relates the rebellion of the peasant masses, court intrigues, the usurpation of power by eunuchs and generals, and the rise of contending military groups that plagued the Han dynasty in its last years. Then after a series of shifting political and military fortunes the narration ends with the establishment of the Three Kingdoms and their ultimate conquest by the Tsin.

In the early decades of the fourteenth century, the story of the Three Kingdoms had apparently already achieved definite form and content. While following the main historical pattern and development, it also incorporated many stories of literary and folk origin. In conformity with the growing tendency among the writers of the Sung-Yüan time, it upheld the orthodoxy of the Shu Han Kingdom, founded by Liu Pei, as the legal successor to the Han dynasty, and debased the Wei Kingdom, founded by Ts'ao Ts'ao, as a usurping dynasty. Ever since that time, Liu Pei and his group of warriors have been heroes in popular imagination, and Ts'ao Ts'ao a villain—testimonial to the lasting influence of the Three Kingdoms stories.

In a number of instances, the *p'ing-hua* version, which undoubtedly represented the result of several generations of folk storytelling, bears the marks of work done by a popular writer with a limited education. This is shown in its crude, unpolished literary style, the errors in historical and geographical names, and the distortion of historical facts. But in spite of these drawbacks, it serves as an important link in the evolution of the Three Kingdoms cycle, from the original dynastic history written at the end of the third century to the later novel, which appeared in the Yüan-Ming period.

Another source of the novel is the dramatic literature of the Yüan period. The dramatization of these stories began as early as the Sung, when the heroes of the Three Kingdoms first appeared in the shadow plays. Although these early works have been lost, there are preserved today at least twenty Yüan-Ming plays that deal with the Three Kingdoms stories. Some of them, however, may have been written contemporaneously with or even after the novel itself. In any case, the similarity between these dramatic stories and their counterparts in fiction shows that by this time there must have existed a body of commonly accepted and widely circulated tales of the Three Kingdoms from which writers, whether storytellers or dramatists, drew their material. The main contribution of the novel therefore lies in the molding of these stories into their final shape, from which only slight variations occurred in later times.

Very scanty information remains about Lo Kuan-chung, the reputed author of the novel. It is known that he lived around 1330–1400 during the Yüan-Ming period. A native of T'ai-yüan in Shansi, he seemed to have led a wandering life during the last years of the Yüan dynasty and, like several of the northern writers, may have finally settled down at Hangchow—a fact which accounts for his being referred to as a "native" of that city. A voluminous writer, Lo Kuan-chung has under his name a number of historical novels, but most of these are now lost, and the few that survive have been so greatly revised by later writers that it is difficult to tell how much of Lo's original work has been retained. Even the *Romance of the Three Kingdoms*, as we shall see later, has undergone some significant changes. Lo Kuan-chung was also the author of several plays, one of which, the *Wind-Cloud Meeting of the Dragon and Tigers*, is still extant. This is a historical play that relates the crowning of the first emperor of Sung (dragon) by his generals (tigers) and his conquest of the country with their help. The play has little merit except to show Lo Kuan-chung's life-long concern with history.

The earliest extant edition of the *Romance of the Three Kingdoms*, with a preface dated 1494, was published around 1522, more than a hundred years after Lo Kuan-chung's death. Handwritten copies of the novel must have long been in circulation, but no earlier printed version seems to have existed. This is understandable: any adventurous book trader would have thought twice before embarking on such a big enterprise as the publication of this voluminous novel, while wealthy scholar-officials who could afford the printing expenses would not have cared to publish something which could bring them neither credit nor recognition. So it did not achieve book form until the middle of the Ming dynasty when there was greater prosperity among the people, especially in the Soochow-Hangchow area, when printing became cheaper and more widely available, and when changing literary taste in favor of popular literature encouraged the search for new material for the book market and subsequently the publication of novels, story collections, and plays.

197

At least twenty editions of the *Romance of the Three Kingdoms* are known to have been published in the second half of the Ming dynasty (from 1522 to 1644). The last important edition appeared in the early years of the Ch'ing dynasty about the middle of the seventeenth century. This was the work of Mao Tsung-kang, a literary writer in Soochow. Following in the footsteps of Chin Sheng-t'an (see p.203), the most famous editor of his time, Mao Tsung-kang contributed to his version of the novel new critical comments as well as numerous stylistic improvements aimed at greater clarity and refinement of the language. His editing, however, goes beyond mere stylistic changes, for he also made significant revisions of the content with the aim of bringing the novel closer to history. Therefore, by virtue of its greater readability and adherence to facts, Mao's work, under the imprint "The First Book of Genius," has superseded all previous editions and remains to this day the most popular version of the novel.

The *Romance of the Three Kingdoms* fuses historical reality with artistic truth. It is an imaginative re-creation of formal history enriched by folk tradition. As a novel that is seven-tenths history and three-tenths fiction, it presents on a grand canvas a succession of heroic figures; often illuminated by romantic imagination, it depicts vividly and prominently the political and military events of a historical period. The loose ends of history are attached neatly to the main thread of the novel, which runs through the struggles and fluctuating fortunes of the several contenders for the throne and their numerous supporters. Thus, with all the historical events incorporated into a unifying theme their causes and effects appear clear and logical in the course of the narrative.

Another unifying factor is the author's attitude toward history, which is also the traditional folk attitude crystallized through centuries of storytelling. The novel therefore is not a static account of a remote bygone era, but a lively reconstruction of a familiar, well-beloved past, throbbing with the passions of the people and animated by their imagination and ideals. It exalts certain historical figures to an heroic status while it condemns others by presenting them in the worst possible light.

Although these historical personages and their actions are colored by the author's own predilections, they are nevertheless living characters, that is, they are artistically real. In his characterization, Lo Kuan-chung used to the fullest extent both authentic historical material and the embellishments of the storytellers. With a few epithets and descriptive phrases, he was able to draw a portrait of their outstanding positive traits. To achieve the desired effect, he even resorted to intensifications and exaggerations, though not to an extent that makes his characters unconvincing. He was more successful in creating clear-cut static types than all-round personalities. This is quite natural since his aim is not to make a study of a handful of historical personages but to present in a continuous procession all those people who once trod the stage of history.

Among the character types, Ts'ao Ts'ao becomes the personification of evil, much distorted and debased from his true role in history. Here in the novel, he is villainy itself in his selfishness, hypocrisy, treachery, and ruthlessness. His philosophy of life is summarized in the following saying: "I would rather that I act ungratefully to all the people in the world than that they act ungratefully to me." On one occasion he slaughtered in cold blood all members of his host's family for fear of their murdering him, not knowing that they were merely sharpening a knife to kill a pig to banquet him.

By rejecting Ts'ao Ts'ao of the Wei Kingdom, the novel supports and extols the Shu Han leadership, which consists of three sworn brothers, Liu Pei, Chang Fei, and Kuan Yü. As the legal contender for the Han throne against Ts'ao Ts'ao's usurpation, Liu Pei, though somewhat commonplace and uninspiring, is pictured as a kindhearted and generous leader, who loves the people and country, and who knows how to make his subordinates work faithfully for him. The best-beloved of all the heroes is Kuan Yü, in whom are embodied the virtues of loyalty and righteousness. He is described as a man of great prowess and gigantic stature with a long beard, phoenix eyes, a face as ruddy as ripe dates, and a voice as deep as a bell. His prowess is well matched by his great heart and his immense courage. Nevertheless, even the great Kuan Yü is not without fault and his wilful stubbornness spells his own doom. Chang Fei, the youngest of the sworn brothers, is noted for his supreme bravery as well as for his impetuous temper. While the rude and robust nature of his heroism makes him the darling of the folk audience in the storyteller's version, he assumes a less important role in the novel, which features the marvelous feats of the scholarly Chu-ko Liang, Lo Kuan-chung's concept of what a great scholar and a superior man of letters could accomplish in these chaotic times.

An embodiment of wisdom and intellect, Chu-ko Liang is at once a great scholar, a capable statesman, a shrewd diplomat, and a resourceful military strategist. Immediately upon his arrival on the political scene, after Liu Pei has visited him three times at his thatched cottage to invite him to come out, he takes over the generalship of every political and military campaign, and proves to be farseeing in his predictions, ingenious in his stratagems, and steady and decisive in his leadership. His supernatural accomplishments, however, seem to be overdrawn, with the result that he appears as a semidivinity endowed with magic powers that are a source of delight to an unsophisticated audience but scarcely convincing to the serious reader.

In both characterization and narration, the author displays a keen sense of the dramatic. Following are three episodes of personal bravery, all different in nature but similar in their dramatic appeal. The first episode (Chapter Forty-two) illustrates the bravery of a warrior-hero. When Liu Pei's small band of followers was defeated by Ts'ao Ts'ao's army, Chang Fei was able to halt the onrush of enemy pursuers with a thunderous roar. He looked an image of awesome majesty as he stood on the Long Plank Bridge, his tiger's whiskers bristling downwards, his round eyes glaring fiercely, and his hand grasping his famous weapon, a long serpentine spear. His majestic voice so unnerved the enemy that one of Ts'ao Ts'ao's generals fell, dead, from his horse and the panic-stricken soldiers receded like an ebbing tide, their horses trampling on one another, the spears and shields falling on the roadside in countless numbers.

In another episode (Chapter Twenty-three) is revealed the bravery of a great scholar. Mi Heng, proud and fearless, had incurred Ts'ao Ts'ao's displeasure by his blunt words. He was publicly humiliated and forced to serve as a drummer during a feast in the palace. Mi Heng went there in his old worn clothes, and when asked to change into something more presentable he immediately stripped off his clothes and stood naked in the presence of the guests. As they covered their faces in shame, Mi Heng calmly put on his drawers without changing color. When scolded by Ts'ao Ts'ao for having behaved so rudely in public, he answered: "To flout the emperor and insult one's superior is rudeness indeed. I only bare my natural body, given me by my parents, to show my purity." Then he launched into an eloquent denunciation of the usurper, heedless of the consequences that would befall him.

Still another kind of bravery is displayed by Kuan Yü as he endured without flinching an operation performed on him by Hua T'o, a famous surgeon (Chapter Seventy-five). The latter made with a scalpel wide and deep gashes on Kuan Yü's infected arm, and as he scraped away the poison from the bones, the knife making a hissing sound and the blood over-flowing the basin under the arm, Kuan Yü ate and drank, then played a game of chess without showing the least sign of pain.

Some of the best stories in the novel tell of Chu-ko Liang's genius for strategy. The episode of Chu-ko Liang's "borrowing" arrows from Ts'ao Ts'ao (Chapter Forty-six) is a prelude to the famous Battle of the Red Cliff, which was fought on the Yangtze River between the forces of Wei and those of the allied Wu and Shu Han. Chu-ko Liang, when asked by the commander-in-chief of the allied forces to make 100,000 arrows for the battle, promised to get the job done in three days, failing which he was willing to accept a severe military penalty. But instead of issuing orders to make the arrows, he asked a friend to furnish him twenty ships, each to be manned by a crew of thirty soldiers and a thousand bundles of straw. For two days he did nothing; then on the night of the third day, when there was a thick fog, he launched his ships and sent them toward the north shore of the Yangtze, where Ts'ao Ts'ao's fleet was anchored. As they advanced, Chu-ko Liang ordered the soldiers to shout and beat drums. He himself sat calmly in one of the ships, enjoying his drink. Meanwhile on the other side, Ts'ao Ts'ao, frightened by the din of the approaching ships amidst fog and darkness and suspecting a surprise attack by Chu-ko Liang, kept his fleet moored, and ordered the archers to shoot as fast and thick as they could. The arrows fell downstream like rain on the straw bundles of Chu-ko Liang's ships. When the latter returned at daybreak, they brought with them more than 100,000 arrows!

Chu-ko Liang's fame as a strategist was so great that, as told in another story (Chapter Ninety-five), he was able to repulse an advancing Wei army by using the ruse of an undefended city. After one of his generals had suffered a heavy loss by disobeying his orders, Chu-ko Liang was left with a small force of 2,500 soldiers to face the huge Wei army about to attack him. Instead of retreating, which would be disastrous and too late anyway, Chu-ko Liang ordered his soldiers to stay inside the city wall with all the banners unfurled and the gates thrown wide open. Then putting on his silk head-wrapper and his robe of state trimmed with crane's down, he sat serenely on the ramparts with a page on his left bearing a precious sword, and another on his right holding a yak's tail. His face all smiles, he lighted the incense in the burner and played on the zither as if unaware of the imminent enemy attack. The Wei general was informed by the scouts of Chu-ko Liang's action; riding up to see for himself he found the report to be all too true. Thus led to suspect an ambush, he withdrew his army.

In matters of plot construction, narration, and characterization, Lo Kuan-chung's novel is far superior to the earlier storyteller's version. It is also more faithful to history through the elimination of absurd, exaggerated stories and the addition of authenticated historical material. In all these aspects, the *Romance of the Three Kingdoms* establishes for succeeding generations the pattern of the Chinese historical novel. This differs greatly from its counterpart in the West. Whereas the latter concentrates on the depiction of a single historical figure, like Ivanhoe or Henry Esmond, to whom all the other characters are subordinate, the Chinese novel presents the exciting tales of a single historical epoch with its multiple heroes and villains, its rapid succession of breathtaking events. Although it fails to provide complete character studies, it succeeds in giving a continuous picture of history unfolding from year to year. While this strict adherence to chronological sequence may impede creative imagination and artistic development, it fulfills, nevertheless, the important function of popularizing historical knowledge among the common people, who otherwise may never have the opportunity to learn about Chinese history.

To the common reader, though not necessarily to the literary critic, this kind of novel has an immense appeal. The popularity of Lo Kuan-chung's novel was so great that many of its episodes were made into stage plays, like the "Stratagem of the Empty City," and became well-known to all common folk including their women and children. It is said that during the peasant rebellion at the end of the Ming dynasty, the novel was used by the rebel leader as a guidebook for military strategy, and that the sworn brotherhood of the three Shu Han heroes in the Peach Garden—a vow of faithful comradeship that ends only with death—was emulated by members of the secret societies that mushroomed in the Ch'ing dynasty. In another instance, Kuan Yü, beloved of the people and rulers alike, was ennobled as the "Great Emperor" and offered sacrifices in temples dedicated to him. The tremendous influence of the novel on the Chinese folk speaks eloquently of its importance and merit.

Just as the *Romance of the Three Kingdoms* is a re-creation of an exciting early historical epoch, the second major Chinese novel, the *Tale of the Marshes* depicts a lively but abnormal medieval society during the chaotic times of the early twelfth century. It relates the story of 108 bandit-heroes who had their lair by the marshes, a hide-out near Mount Liang in modern Shantung. Towards the end of the Northern Sung dynasty, this strategic area, a maze of swamps and streamlets, islets and harbors, totaling some 800 square *li*, was the stronghold of several bands of rebellious peasants, fishermen, and desperadoes who rose against the government because of heavy taxation and official oppression. One such group was led by Sung Chiang, whose name appears in the histories of the Sung period. According to these accounts, Sung Chiang, who occupied Mount Liang around 1120, later surrendered to the government and participated in the campaign against Fang La, another bandit leader. The references to Sung Chiang in formal history, however, are very sketchy and little is known of him and his group.

The folk storytellers, on the other hand, had been active in building up and expanding the legends of the Mount Liang bandit-heroes. The stories of their exploits may already have been widely known among the people in the last years of the Northern Sung dynasty, but it was in the Southern Sung that the storytellers began to spin the yarns of these brave outlaws.

About the same time artists sought to portray their likenesses in pictures, which unfortunately have been lost. As mentioned previously, Yüan dramatists further enriched the legends in a number of plays. Out of this vast reservoir of material emerged the novel, the *Tale of the Marshes.*

The evolution of this novel is much more complicated than that of the *Romance of the Three Kingdoms*. Even its authorship is uncertain. It has been attributed variously to Lo Kuan-chung and Shih Nai-an. In Ming editions of the novel as well as in early literary references, either Shih or Lo was named as the author and, in many cases, both names appeared together, one as the compiler and the other as the editor. More recently, it has been surmised that the elusive Shih Nai-an—his life remains practically unknown despite modern efforts to identify him[1]—might have been an early master storyteller who first put together the legend of the *Marshes* (hence was in a sense its originator) and that the versatile Lo Kuan-chung, who was known as a polished literary writer, might have written the first version of the novel.

There was a long, intricate process in the development of the written novel from its original form, presumably from before Lo Kuan-chung's death around 1400 to the publication of the popular seventy-chapter edition of 1641. An important fact to be observed is that there was no literary mention of the printed novel until 1540, in which year appeared the first known edition in 100 chapters. Therefore it may be assumed that the novel was circulated in manuscript for almost a century and a half before its first publication. On the other hand, in the next 100 years between 1540 and 1640 there was a sudden burst of publishing activity which accounted for at least ten important editions of the novel. Some of these differ significantly in content, style, and length. This was also a period of editorial refinement, during which many scholars and publishers contributed, for better or worse, to the shaping of the novel into its present form.

Among these, a 120-chapter edition published in 1614 is the longest and the most complete. It was to be superseded, however, twenty-seven years later by Chin Sheng-t'an's seventy-chapter edition. A critic of singular but discerning taste, Chin Sheng-t'an (d. 1661) was noted for his views on popular literature, which he respected so highly that he even ranked the *Tale of the Marshes* as the fifth book of genius next only to the works of Chuang-tzu, Ch'ü Yüan, Ssu-ma Ch'ien, and Tu Fu. His changes in the novel go beyond the merely editorial. He not only tampered with the text, but also cut off the 120-chapter novel at the waist, retaining only its first seventy chapters. Moreover, he fabricated a preface which he attributed to Shih Nai-an, to whom he also attributed the authorship of the novel. Though critics differ in their estimate of Chin Sheng-t'an's role as an editor and commentator,[2] it is his truncated version of the work that has

203

remained for three hundred years the only widely circulated edition; and it is from this version that translations were made into the English language.[3]

Because of its widely differing versions, a study of this novel becomes complicated. The plot itself (in the complete narrative) has two parts: the first dealing with Sung Chiang's uprising at Mount Liang, and the second with his surrender to the government and his campaigns against four major rebels, one of whom was Fang La. As we have noted, only the first part of the novel appears in Chin Sheng-t'an's version, which ends abruptly with a dream by one of the bandit leaders that all of them were finally captured and executed en masse by the government. While the complete narrative, with its endless array of battles and tournaments, may have aroused greater interest in its own time, from the modern point of view the shorter version has the advantage of a more integrated plot. On the other hand, the implied condemnation of the bandit leaders in the dream not only lacks historical evidence but runs counter to the prevailing concept and sentiments of the novel: in Chin Sheng-t'an's edition the unity of action is gained, it seems, through misrepresentation or rather distortion of the original intent of the folk storytellers and the novelist.

To critics schooled in the Western tradition, the *Tale of the Marshes*, whichever edition one uses, appears episodic and loose in structure. In this long rambling narrative, the only thread that binds together the unrelated episodes is the brotherhood of the bandit-heroes and their common defiance of government authority. The Chinese novel may be compared to the European picaresque novel, with the difference that it contains the adventures not of just one rogue-hero, but of 108 of them. This fictional type is a natural product of the oral tradition of the professional raconteurs, who aimed to attract their audience with a continuous series of exciting events and lively characters in as many storytelling sessions as possible.

If historical continuity is a main factor in the plot construction of the *Three Kingdoms*, social realism is a key to the artistic success of the *Marshes*. Reflecting the life and struggles of the people at different social levels, the latter aims to depict the multitudinous events and personalities of a restive society. By putting together the various episodes, each rich and variegated in detail, into a finished work the novel attains a sort of unity in the breadth of its scope and the grandeur of its concept. The merit of the *Marshes* therefore lies in its ability to present in every shade and color a group picture of many unforgettable characters and the manifold phases of society at a time of national emergency.

The 108 bandit-heroes, of whom thirty-six are major figures, have different backgrounds, different personal traits and appearances, different experiences and contacts; they share, however, a common lot in life as the victims of official persecution that forces them to tread together the path to Mount Liang. The groups from which they come represent a large segment of society: minor officials and village squires, men of letters, yamen clerks and constables, captains and guards, peasants and fishermen, traders and artisans, innkeepers and tavern owners, monks and priests, slaves and vagabonds. In times of peace and order, most of them would have led commonplace and uneventful lives, but the times are abnormal and so is the life they lead. Instead of engaging in peaceful pursuits, they become outlaws who fight and kill; rob and burn; resist arrest, break jails, and rise in insurrection. On the whole, however, they prey only on the wicked and tyrannical, the avaricious and debauched, but lend a helping hand to the poor and distressed. Themselves victims of persecution, they range themselves on the side of the people as champions of the oppressed in their struggles against government officials, military henchmen, and local despots.

The most intriguing and controversial of these Mount Liang heroes is Sung Chiang. A born leader, he knows how to make friends with the other "good fellows of the rivers and lakes"; he helps those who are in need, dispensing his favors like "opportune rain" at a time of drought; he is hospitable and generous, spending gold like dirt. All these qualities, as well as his political insight, military leadership, and organizing ability, combine to make him an ideal arch-rebel. But there is an apparent contradiction in his attitude toward banditry, for although he has had many unhappy encounters with the law and government as a bandit chieftain, he still cherishes a feeling of loyalty to the throne. Even as a bandit, he yearns for a chance to redeem himself with meritorious service to the government so that he may, as he has promised repeatedly, exert himself to his utmost for the emperor. Thus he desires and eventually receives amnesty. In the complete novel, he and his group fight bravely for the government against other rebels and distinguish themselves in many campaigns. The irony, of course, is that his good intentions and faithful service notwithstanding, he finally meets death at the hands of the court ministers, who have him poisoned in the emperor's name.

The characterization of Sung Chiang is complicated by Chin Sheng-t'an's efforts to belittle and slander him. In Chin's opinion, Sung Chiang is a hypocrite; his misgivings, suspicions, and contradictions mark him clearly as a villain in disguise. This view of Sung Chiang's character, however, is inconsistent with his role as a beloved leader; it also beclouds his image as a hero.

Like Sung Chiang, the other major heroes are vividly portrayed and have great popular appeal notwithstanding the shocking deeds they sometimes perpetrate. Perhaps the most popular of the Mount Liang heroes are Li K'uei, Lu Chih-shen, Wu Sung, and Lin Ch'ung. All four are noted for their prowess and feats of strength; they are faithful to the sworn brotherhood, daring and determined in action and, with the exception of Lin Ch'ung, impetuous and violent in temper. But aside from these common characteristics, each has marked individual traits. A simple illiterate villager, Li K'uei is straightforward, honest, and foolhardy, his naiveté bordering on stupidity. His virtues are love for his mother, sincerity to friends, and loyalty to leadership even though he strongly objects to Sung Chiang's obsequious respect for authority; in turn he is scolded and punished for his rude manners and rash action. Lu Chih-shen, formerly a minor army officer, has more worldly experiences than his comrade from the country. Brave and upright by nature, he resents injustice and often comes gallantly to the rescue of the innocent and distressed, heedless of his own safety. His fondness for meat and wine makes a mockery of his vows of abstinence as a monk, drink being his besetting sin and the cause of all his troubles. From the lower strata of society comes Wu Sung, who, because of his bravery as a tiger-killer, is made a head constable in the magistrate's yamen. But he soon loses his job and is exiled as a criminal when he takes the law into his own hands by killing his adulterous sister-in-law and her depraved paramour, who have caused his brother's death. However, instead of acting impulsively like the others he carries out his revenge in a series of carefully planned and fast-moving actions. While these three have a fierce and unruly spirit, Lin Ch'ung is of the good-natured and even-tempered type who minds his own business and is content with his lot in life. He would have remained a trusted military official given to carrying out his superior's orders had it not been for persecution by those in power. But once his sense of rightness is wronged and his ire aroused, he too can act boldly and mercilessly.

All these men have nicknames by which they are popularly known. Sung Chiang is called the Opportune Rain for his generosity. The nicknames for Lin Ch'ung (the Leopard Head) and Li K'uei (the Black Whirlwind) suggest respectively their appearance and temperament, while those for Lu Chih-shen (the Tattooed Monk) and Wu Sung (the Itinerant) refer to their initiation in the Buddhist order. Other heroes have nicknames derived from their physical appearance, such as the Blue Faced Beast, the Red-Headed Devil, the Nine-Striped Dragon, the Dwarf Tiger, and the Beautifully Bearded Lord; or from their disposition, such as the Thunderous Fire, the Iron-faced Yamen Clerk, and the Profligate; from their professional skill, such as the Divine Abacus and the Golden Spear Expert; from the weapons they use, such as the Featherless Arrow, the Big Knife, and the Double Whip.

206

Sung Chiang. Bandit-Hero in the *Tale of the Marshes*. Printed on Wine-Cards made by Ch'en Lao-lien, a Late Ming Dynasty Artist.

Li K'uei. Bandit-Hero in the *Tale of the Marshes*.

This motley group of bandit-heroes have haunted readers for centuries with their daring and startling deeds, some of which are vividly presented through the use of comparison or contrast. There are, for instance, two separate stories of tiger-killing by Wu Sung and Li K'uei. In both episodes, the heroes display courage and prowess, but the circumstances and manners of the fight, each appropriate for the occasion, are different even to the minutest detail.

In the first story, Wu Sung, fortified with wine against fear and heedless of danger, went on a journey alone at night in spite of warnings that the region was haunted by a tiger. He had barely climbed up the mountain ridge and was about to rest on a green rock when suddenly he espied a fierce tiger with upturned eyes and a white forehead:

> Seeing it thus, Wu Sung cried "Ah-ya!," then rolled down from the green rock. Cudgel in hand, he slipped away alongside the rock. The big beast was both hungry and thirsty. Barely touching the ground with its paws, it sprang upward with its whole body and then swooped down from midair. Wu Sung was so startled that the wine he had drunk turned into cold sweat. In a moment Wu Sung saw the tiger was about to pounce on him and he quickly dodged behind the beast's back. It was most difficult for the beast to find anyone from that position, so planting its front paws on the ground and raising its legs at the waist, it lifted itself up. Wu Sung again dodged and slid to one side. When the tiger saw that it had failed this time, it gave out a big roar like a thunderbolt from the mid sky, shaking the mountain ridge. Then it made a scissors-cut, its iron cudgel-like tail standing upside down, but Wu Sung again slipped aside. Ordinarily, the big beast seized its prey either with one swoop, one lift, or one scissors-cut. Failing to grab him by these three means, it lost half of its spirited temper. After a second failure with a scissors-cut, it roared once more and moved around in another circle. When Wu Sung saw the beast turn back, he lifted his cudgel with both hands and brought it down from midair with one swift and mighty blow. There was a loud sound and a tree fell, its twigs and leaves streaming down all over his face. Opening his eyes, he gazed fixedly. In his excitement, he had missed the big beast but struck instead an old withered tree. The cudgel had broken in two, and one half of it he now held in his hand.
>
> Its temper now thoroughly aroused, the big beast bellowed and again turned round with a forward thrust. Wu Sung made another leap, retreating ten steps. The creature had barely managed to place its forepaws in front of Wu Sung when, throwing away his broken cudgel, he clutched the tiger's mottled neck with a cracking sound and pushing it down, held it tightly. The animal attempted to struggle, but Wu Sung grabbed it with all his might and never re-

laxed his grip for a moment. With his foot he kicked the beast over its face and eyes. The tiger started roaring again and dug up with its paws two heaps of yellow mud beneath its body, forming an earthen pit. Wu Sung pressed the beast's mouth straight down the yellow mud pit. It became helpless and impotent. With his left hand grasping tightly the beast's mottled neck, Wu Sung freed his right hand and lifting up his fist—the size of an iron hammer—kept pommeling it with all his strength. After it had been struck fifty to seventy times, fresh blood began to gush out from its eyes, mouth, nose, and ears. Wu Sung, using all his superhuman strength and inborn prowess, in a short while pounded the tiger into a heap as it lay there like an embroidered cloth bag.   (Chapter 23)[4]

Unlike Wu Sung who courted danger bravely and deliberately, Li K'uei fought with a family of tigers as the result of a gruesome, unfortunate incident, which occurred on his way back to Mount Liang with his old, blind mother. After having carried her all the way up to a mountain top, he left her on a big green rock to fetch water for her to quench her thirst. But she was nowhere to be found when he came back; instead there was a pool of blood.

Following the traces of blood in his search, he soon reached the mouth of a big cave and saw there two tiger cubs licking a human leg.[5] Li K'uei reasoned with himself: "I went back home from Mount Liang expressly to fetch my old mother. With endless toil and hardship I carried her on my back to this place,—and then to have her devoured by you! These accursed beasts are dragging a human leg—whose could it be if not my mother's?"

Fire erupted from his bosom and his red-yellow whiskers stood erect. Lifting up the big knife in his hand, he rushed forward to thrust at the two cubs. Terrified by the blows, one of the young beasts crawled forward, flashing its teeth and flourishing its paws. Li K'uei raised his hand and at once stabbed it to death. The other crawled straightway into the cave but Li K'uei pursued and killed it also.

Having crept into the tiger's cave, Li K'uei hid himself inside. As he looked out, he saw a mother tiger come charging to the den with flashing teeth and menacing paws. Li K'uei cried: "So you are that accursed beast that ate my mother!" He laid down the big knife and pulled out from beside his leg a waist knife. After the big tigress had got to the mouth of the cave, it first made with its tail a scissors-cut inside the den and then crouched down upon its haunches. Seeing clearly from inside the cave, Li K'uei pointed his knife toward the bottom of the beast's tail and thrust desperately with all his strength at its anus. The force was so great that the very handle of the knife went straight through the beast's belly. The tigress gave forth a roar and with the knife inside its body jumped from the mouth of the cave to the other side of the stream. Then Li K'uei took his big knife and pursued it out of the cave. The tigress, in great pain, rushed straightway down the mountain precipice.

Li K'uei was about to hasten after her when he saw a gust of wind roll up from the trees beside him, and all the withered leaves and twigs fall down like rain. It has been said since ancient times that "clouds come with the dragon and winds with the tiger." From where the gust of wind rose beneath the bright light of the stars and moon, suddenly a slant-eyed, white-browed tiger leaped out with a great roar. The big beast pounced fiercely at Li K'uei. Li K'uei, however, was neither flustered nor excited. Taking advantage of the force of the tiger's attack, he lifted his knife and struck straight below the tiger's chin. The tiger no longer charged or pounced. First, it had to nurse the wound and moreover its windpipe was broken. It had not retreated five or seven steps before uttering a sound as loud as though one half of the mountain had crumbled. In the next moment, the big beast lay dead below the cliff.   (Chapter 43)[6]

These tiger-killing stories are merely interludes in the main plot, which deals with a tremendous life-and-death struggle between various antagonistic groups and individuals. It has a supreme human interest and social significance beyond the display of physical prowess in man's fight with fierce animals. Throughout the novel, dramas of real life are enacted with breathtaking intensity. Numerous incidents—battles and jousts; fistfightings and drinking bouts; jailbreaking and riot at the execution ground; kidnaping, robbing, and bloodthirsty murders; wholesale slaughter and the burning down of entire villages and towns—have made the *Tale of the Marshes* the most lurid and savage of all Chinese novels.[7]

Such violence, however, is not unrelieved by flashes of fun and humor. One of these, for instance, relates the attempt of a woman tavernkeeper to drug Wu Sung with wine and to kill him for his luggage. He was on his way into exile with two guards for having committed the murders mentioned above. They stopped in a tavern at a crossroad and were served wine and meat by a huge, fierce-looking woman bartender, whose nickname was "Mother Yaksha." Her appearance and manner aroused Wu Sung's suspicion; therefore, instead of drinking the wine as the two guards had done, he poured it away while the woman was looking elsewhere. He then pretended to have felt its potency and dropped down on the floor like the other two. But he was so heavy that the men whom the woman had ordered to take him away could hardly move him. This spurred the woman into action herself. After taking off her green gauze blouse and red silk skirt, she went to pull Wu Sung up. "Taking advantage of the situation, Wu Sung held the woman tight. With both hands, he drew her closer to him, clutching her at the bosom. Next, he pinched her lower body between his legs and pressed her down beneath him as she yelled like a pig being slaughtered."[8] Fortunately for her, the woman's husband entered just in time to beg for forgiveness; he immediately knelt down to kowtow when told of Wu Sung's name.

Lu Chih-shen, another bandit-hero, also had adventures which provide many delightful scenes in the novel. Probably the most hilarious is his drunken beating of a bandit chieftain who was about to marry by force the daughter of an old village squire. After having told the old man to hide the girl elsewhere, Lu Chih-shen entered the bridal chamber as her replacement on the nuptial night. When the bandit chieftain pushed open the door of the room, it was so dark inside that he had to grope his way to the bed. He pulled apart the curtain and was fumbling around with his hand when he touched Lu Chih-shen's belly.

> Taking advantage of the situation, Lu Chih-shen grabbed him by the horn-like tufts of his turban and pressed him down beside the bed. The bandit chieftain was about to struggle when Lu Chih-shen, closing his right hand in a fist, punched him on the ears and neck. "You wife-snatcher!" he cursed. The bandit cried, "Why do you beat your husband?" Lu Chih-shen exclaimed, "So that you would know your wife better!" He dragged him by the bedside and showered him with such blows and kicks that the bandit cried out for help. . . . With lighted candles and lanterns, the old squire hurried into the room at the head of a band of the chieftain's followers. Taking a good look from under the lamp light, the crowd saw a big fat monk, all naked, without a shred of clothing, riding on the sprawling body of the bandit chieftain in front of the bed and beating him soundly.   (Chapter 5)[9]

Even the coarse and ferocious bandit Li K'uei had his moments of pleasantry when he attempted to administer justice in the guise of a county magistrate. One day, when he was wandering about in the town after being separated from his comrades-in-arms, he came to the magistrate's yamen and finding it empty, walked in. (The magistrate had slipped away by the back door upon hearing Li K'uei's name.) He found there the magistrate's official regalia, consisting of a robe, a hat, and shoes. Putting them on, Li K'uei went outside to the great hall of the yamen, sat on the magistrate's chair, and summoned all the constables and clerks to attend on him in a mock trial. Two jailkeepers came forward, one disguised as a plaintiff and the other as a defendant.

> The two knelt down in front of the hall. One complained, "Your lordship, please take pity on me for this man has beaten me." The other said, "He has abused me and so I beat him." Li K'uei asked,

"Who is the one beaten?" The plaintiff said, "It's me." Then Li K'uei asked, "Who is the one who beat him?" The defendant said, "He first abused me and so I beat him up." Li K'uei said, "The one who beat the other is a brave fellow. Let him be released first. As for this good-for-nothing, why did he let himself be beaten? Have him placed in a cangue in front of the yamen for everyone to look at." Li K'uei then stood up, tucking in the lower part of the green robe and placing by his waist the official locust tablet. He took out his big axe and, without taking off the robe and the shoes, he strode away in big steps after he had seen for himself the plaintiff placed in the cangue in front of the yamen gate. The crowd who gathered outside—how could they refrain from laughing aloud?

As Li K'uei walked back and forth before the yamen, he heard suddenly the sound of children reading aloud in a school. He opened the bamboo curtain and stepped in. The teacher was so scared at the sight of Li K'uei that he jumped out of the window and ran away. The pupils cried, shouted, ran, and hid themselves. Laughing aloud, Li K'uei came out the door and happened to run into Mu Hung. The latter exclaimed, "All of us were terribly worried about you and here you are off on a mad excursion. Hurry up to the mountain!"

(Chapter 74)

After he had got there, Li K'uei swaggered up the bandits' main hall and, holding aloft the official locust tablet in his hand, bowed to Sung Chiang. He had not bowed twice before he tripped over the green official robe which he had just let down, and flopped on the ground amidst the laughter of everyone present.

These stories are told in articulate, vigorous language, its effectiveness well proven through a long process of oral tradition. The *Romance of the Three Kingdoms* is written in a simple literary style, while the prose dialogue in the Yüan drama is generally crude and stereotyped. Only some of the Sung-Yüan short stories can be compared with the *Tale of the Marshes* in their skillful use of the colloquial, but the *Marshes* is the first sustained prose fiction that adopts the living language of the people as the medium of narration. It has set an example for all later novels and its influence is lasting and immense.

Any discussion of the theme of this novel is bound to be controversial. Apparently, the primary aim of the novelist, like that of the storyteller, is the telling of a good story—political considerations, if any, being secondary. But one can read into it plenty of political implications whether they were originally intended or not. For one thing, there is little doubt where the author's sympathy lies. The bandit leaders are definitely the heroes of the novel and their uprising can only be attributed to government oppression and tyranny. In a topsy-turvy world, as we have pointed

out in our discussion of the Yüan drama, the outlaws are the adminis-
trators of justice, and their deeds, in contrast with the selfishness and
treachery of the officials, exemplify loyalty and brotherhood. Hence their
hall is the Hall of Loyalty and Righteousness and their duty is to exercise
virtue in the name of Heaven. Though perhaps far from its author's
original intention, the *Tale of the Marshes* may be regarded as a revolutionary novel that epitomizes human suffering and degradation at the
hands of the ruling class. It reveals the rebellious spirit and desperate
actions of an otherwise peaceful and law-abiding people. Such a story
could occur in China only at a time of social disintegration, and such a
work could appear only toward the end of the Mongol dynasty when the
Chinese longed for deliverers—even for bandit-heroes—to free them from
the yoke of decadent foreign rulers.

These political considerations aside, the novel is itself a magnificent
literary document that presents on a vast scale the complex, multicolored
aspects of Chinese society. Like the *Romance of the Three Kingdoms*, it
is a composite work of fictional art. The two novels are similar in that they
represent the combined efforts of a number of storytellers, script writers,
dramatists, novelists, and scholarly editors, all of whom have contributed
to their composition and improvement through a long, continuous process
of evolution. Before they were put together as full-length novels, they
had developed through an oral and written tradition of many centuries,
followed by a century of orientation in the drama; after they had been
written down and printed, another long period of editing and revision
passed before they assumed their present shape. Imitations and continua-
tions followed. Thus, generations of Chinese literary artists have stamped
their genius on the two novels, from the day their stories first enchanted
small groups of listeners, to the present time when the same tales continue
to fascinate all kinds of readers, including many Westerners through
translations. They are no longer regarded as *"hsiao-shuo"* or the gossip of
the storymongers, but as great works of literature.

In fact, both novels are greater than those created by individual artists.
The works not of just a Lo Kuan-chung or a Shih Nai-an, they are the
prose epics of the Chinese people, comparable in scope and grandeur to
the Greek and Indian epics. In them culminate the literary achievements
of generations who have instilled into them their life experiences, their
social knowledge, and their creative talents, thereby making these novels
truly the literary monuments of a great people.

15 : Story Books, Old and New

An important milestone that marks the course of Chinese fiction was erected in the last century (c. 1540–1640) of the Ming dynasty. During this period, fiction began to be accepted by a larger group of scholars as an established form of literature. As a result, commentaries, revisions, and new editions of full-length novels appeared in profusion; extensive collections of original Sung-Yüan colloquial stories as well as later imitations by Ming authors were published. It was also the most productive period of creative storywriting by individual authors, some of whose names are still known. The colloquial short story, in particular, reached the peak of its development with the publication of numerous collections in the first decades of the seventeenth century.

A major factor in the growth of Ming colloquial literature was the new social environment of the period. The Yangtze cities of Hangchow, Soochow, and Nanking emerged as important literary centers in the wake of their early development in the Sung-Yüan period. Many of the authors who came to live in these cities were engaged in writing the type of colloquial stories first introduced by the storytellers. Gradually, these cities also became the centers of a flourishing book trade in competition with the Fukien publishers, who seem hitherto to have monopolized the printing of popular literature. Commerce and handicraft industry, supported by agriculture in rural districts, brought wealth and prosperity to this region and spurred the rise of a populous urban middle class who had plenty of leisure and opportunities for relaxation and light reading. Consequently, a demand arose for a kind of literature which, while manifestly instructive, provided entertaining and exciting stories as its main fare. It was to meet this demand that the short story collections were published toward the end of the Ming dynasty.

The first thing that strikes a reader of these Ming stories and novels is their frankness regarding the sexual relationship, the treatment of which in a number of cases is obviously pornographic in nature. At no time in China, either before or since, has literature been colored by such candid and sensuous descriptions, compared with which even the erotic passages in the "Visit to the Fairy Lodge" seem pale and mild. This erotica catered to the taste of new readers among the urban citizenry in the midst of their material prosperity, while the lack of effective official supervision left unchecked the circulation of licentious publications, which the book trade must have found lucrative. Though the writers were, of course, mainly responsible for the moral decadence of their works, it would seem that they merely depicted faithfully life and society as they found them, these realistic scenes and situations being the facts of life and not fanciful adventures. Moreover, their professed aim was always moralistic: the episodes were included to underscore the sins of the villains and the justice of their eventual, well-deserved punishment!

Like the "Visit to the Fairy Lodge," a large part of this Ming fictional material was taken to Japan and preserved there in private collections, Buddhist temples, and imperial libraries. In China itself, because of a vigorous government censorship imposed later, in the Ch'ing or Manchu dynasty, upon seditious and licentious literature, such Ming works were banned and sank rapidly into oblivion. The conservative and puritanical attitude of the Ch'ing scholar-officials further caused the suppression of all forms of colloquial writing, the nonpornographic as well as the pornographic, thus resulting in an irreparable loss to popular literature. It is only in recent years that a number of the earlier Ming story collections have been unearthed in China or reintroduced from Japan, thus providing scholars with firsthand material for the study of Chinese fiction.

As suggested before, a predominant characteristic of these stories is their realism. They give a vivid picture of Chinese society in the Ming period, its commercial and economic background, its social structure and family system, as well as the other manifold activities, relationships, conflicts, and struggles of individuals. As a whole, these stories are much more interesting and informative than the pseudohistorical and supernatural tales which occupy a less prominent position in the Ming story repertoire. Of course, not all the stories in these collections were first compiled in the Ming period, and a number have been identified as the works of Sung-Yüan times. But there is little doubt that a majority of the stories reflect the taste of middle class readers and follow a technique of storywriting that, having originated in the Sung or even earlier periods, was perfected by the Ming writers. A comparison between the original Sung-Yüan works and the Ming imitations shows that the latter have achieved important progress in a more effective and extensive use of the spoken language, a deeper probing into the minds of significant characters, a greater realism in the depiction of social and family life, and a more complicated plot construction with elaborate details and breathtaking situations.

Two most important authors who contributed to the development of the Ming short story are Feng Meng-lung (1574–1646), a pioneer story collector and editor, and Ling Meng-ch'u (1580–1644), the most voluminous Chinese storywriter. Both lived in the last part of the Ming dynasty and their careers were cut short by the ultimate overthrow of the dynasty, which cost them their lives. Feng and Ling were also alike in that they were men of letters who missed high official positions because of their failure in the state examination. Ling Meng-ch'u was at one time the magistrate of Shanghai, but Shanghai in those days, like Shou-ning in Fukien, where Feng Meng-lung was magistrate (1634–38), was only a small outlying town. With a similar interest in colloquial literature, both wrote plays as well as short stories. As was customary, all their writings were issued under various pseudonyms, and it is only through the careful investigation of modern scholars that Feng and Ling have been identified as the authors and editors of their respective works.

Feng Meng-lung was closely associated with the book trade in Soochow, where his great story collection, *Stories, Old and New*, was published in three successive volumes. These are entitled separately *Instructive Words to Enlighten the World* (1620?),[1] *Popular Words to Admonish the World* (1624), and *Lasting Words to Awaken the World* (1627), each volume containing forty stories; and known together as the *San-yen*, literally "Three Words," from the last character (*yen* or "words") in each of the three titles.

In 1628 appeared Ling Meng-ch'u's story collection, *Striking the Table in Amazement at the Wonders*, followed four years later by a second series with the same name, the two together known as the *Erh-p'o*, literally "Two Strikes." Ling's two volumes, also consisting of forty pieces each,[2] were obviously inspired by Feng's example, but there is one important difference. Whereas Feng Meng-lung's collection includes a mixture of original Sung-Yüan stories, Ming imitations, and probably some of Feng's own creations, most of the stories in Ling Meng-ch'u's collection were written by Ling himself. Altogether, these approximately two hundred stories from the "Three Words" and "Two Strikes" constitute the bulk of the Chinese colloquial short story produced during the five hundred years from the Southern Sung to the end of Ming, with a large number of them compiled in the early seventeenth century.

One of the hobbies of the Ming writers was the editing or rather the restyling of earlier plays, novels, and stories. In his story collection Feng Meng-lung's hand is clearly visible. Besides giving new titles to the earlier tales and incorporating certain stylistic changes, he sometimes made drastic revisions by rearranging the sequence of events, adding new material and episodes, and remolding the plot of the story. This can be seen by comparing some Sung-Yüan stories that have been preserved in an earlier version with those in Feng's collection. Usually, however, Feng's editorial changes seem to be minor. Considering the fact that his collection includes tales both old and new, lightly or heavily edited, original Sung-Yüan stories and later Ming imitations, one is pleasantly surprised by their general uniformity in style, technique, and form. This is due probably to three important factors: (1) the influence of the storytelling tradition; (2) the use of realistic narrative technique; (3) the prevalence in these stories of an urban middle class attitude toward life.

That Feng Meng-lung himself was not unaware of the great appeal of popular literature is shown in the Preface to the first volume of the *Stories, Old and New*:

> As a whole, T'ang writers chose their words to appeal to the culti-
> vated mind, whereas Sung writers used colloquial expressions to
> accord with the rustic ear. In this world, the literary minds are few,
> but the rustic ears are many. Therefore, the short story relies more
> on the popularizer than on the stylist. Just ask the storyteller to de-
> scribe a scene on the spot, and it will gladden and startle, sadden
> and cause you to lament; it will prompt you to draw the sword; at
> other times to bow deeply in reverence, to break someone's neck, or
> to contribute money. The timid will be made brave; the lewd chaste;
> the niggardly liberal; and the stupid and dull, perspiring with shame.
> Even though you would recite every day the *Classic of Filial Piety*
> and the *Analects*, you would never be moved as swiftly and pro-
> foundly as by these storytellers. Alas! Could such results be achieved
> by anything but popular colloquial writing?[3]

The author of this Preface signs himself the "Master of the Green Sky Lodge," who may have been either Feng Meng-lung himself or a literary friend, but whoever he was, his view must have represented that of Feng and his circle. That he should have mentioned the colloquial short story in the same breath as the much revered Confucian books was certainly a bold stroke in a literary world of Confucian domination. The championship of popular literature—short story as well as novel, play, and folk poetry—by Feng Meng-lung was a significant literary event in the first decades of the seventeenth century, but unfortunately had a short-lived influence, which came to an abrupt end with the fall of the Ming dynasty.

The 120 stories in Feng Meng-lung's collection cover practically every phase of Chinese life. Their range includes: quasi-historical tales of kings and generals, faithful friends and filial sons; romantic yarns of strange lands and peoples; supernatural stories of marvels and prodigies, spirits and ghosts, Buddhist monks and Taoist immortals; realistic stories of scandals in monastic establishments; daring exploits of brigands and thieves; murders, lawsuits, and court trials; domestic tragedies and bloody revenges; social comedies and family reunions. In all these, the accent is always on a realistic presentation of life. Even in the historico-romantic and supernatural tales, the characters, whether of the ancient or imaginary world, are often described as living beings of the present. Notable by their absence here are the stories of tender romantic love between young scholars and beautiful maidens such as are celebrated in the so-called "beauty and genius" novels of the period. The supremacy of realism in technique and style can be attributed to the fact that in making this collection Feng Meng-lung kept in mind the tastes and demands of the rapidly growing urban population, for whose reading pleasure these stories were compiled.

Of the various types enumerated above, the most interesting and popular one is exemplified in a group of realistic stories that have for their background the flourishing Yangtze cities. The plots of these stories seem to have been taken mainly from contemporary Ming sources current among the people. They reveal a great maturity in the art of fiction writing; though lacking the freshness and simplicity of the Sung-Yüan story scripts, they compensate by the richness of their details, the clever handling of the plot with all its surprises and crises, and a greater articulation and mellowness of language. Chinese critics today are likely to extol the merits of the Sung-Yüan folk stories to the detriment of their later imitations by literary writers. Exceptions, however, should be made of some of the better written Ming stories in Feng Meng-lung's collection. These can be compared favorably with the short stories written in any period in China, as well as with Western writings of the same period.

The most remarkable thing about Chinese story writers is the ease and dexterity with which they relate the tales of the average people as they tread the stage of life. True to the concepts of bourgeois morality, these characters can be divided into two clear-cut types: the good and the bad, with the latter intriguing and plotting incessantly against the former. Tragedy results when the virtuous and innocent fall victim to the machinations of the wicked and evil forces of society; on the other hand, in spite of some near-tragic situations, everything ends well and happily with the triumph of the good and the punishment of the bad in accordance with folk justice. By placing the characters in two sharply contrasted extremes of black and white, the writers succeed in bringing to a focus the characters' personalities. Though without the blessings of modern psychoanalysis, which succeeds chiefly in creating some oddly assorted groups of eccentric individuals in contemporary fiction, the characters in the Ming stories are not stereotypes, but are like men and women of flesh and blood, whose individual traits are clearly depicted, and develop with the changing situations in life. They are so lifelike that they can be easily recognized as real and familiar types in traditional Chinese society. It is this intimate touch in characterization that has perpetuated some of these stories in the memories of Chinese readers during the last three centuries.

There is little doubt that the authors' sympathies are mostly with the weak and oppressed in society, particularly with those of the female sex. Chief among the latter are the innocent, lovely, but helpless maidens of rich official families; the hard pressed but steadfast and courageous women of humble origin; and the much maligned and injured sing-song girls in the houses of ill-fame. In most cases, the theme of the story centers around love and marriage, with money as a motivating force of the action. The following three stories, which have all been translated into English, can be taken as examples.

In the "Hundred-Year Long Sorrows of Wang Chiao-luan,"[4] one of the few tales of poetic love in Feng Meng-lung's collection, the story begins in the best tradition of all love romances with an exchange of poetic billets-doux between Wang Chiao-luan, an eighteen-year-old daughter of a military commander, and Chou T'ing-chang, the son of an education commissioner. The unfolding and growth of young love was followed by its fulfillment in the girl's chamber, the two swearing eternal faith, but without the formality of the marriage vow. Then came separation when the student returned home on account of his father's sickness. Once he was there, the family took over his matrimonial affairs, and the young scholar was wedded to a beautiful girl of a wealthy family in the same town. "The couple's affection was like fish in water, he having forgotten even the kind of person Wang Chiao-luan was. He knew only the newly bedecked girl of the present moment without caring for the worn looks of his former lover." To Wang's repeated inquiries and anxious poetic messages, Chou turned a deaf ear, and slowly the girl pined away. Finally, a messenger dispatched by her brought back the news of Chou's marriage, thus confirming her worst fears. Brokenhearted, Wang Chiao-luan hanged herself after having sent to her former lover thirty-two poems on ending life and a long ballad entitled "Everlasting Sorrow." In retribution, Chou T'ing-chang also came to a bad end. For his desertion of Wang Chiao-luan and for breaking his troth, he was brought to the mandarin's yamen and there beaten to death by official order—the Chinese storyteller's way of administering justice—as a warning to all faithless lovers.

Based on a very hackneyed theme, the story lacks originality in plot and characterization. It has little to recommend itself except for the poetry with which it is interspersed, but even that is mostly conventional and derivative. It is obvious that the story is the hack work of some unimaginative writer, far removed from the main currents of popular Chinese fiction, which by that time had advanced much beyond the realm of early romanticism. In contrast, "Sung Chin-lang's Reunion through a Tattered Felt Hat"[5] is a typical example of the bourgeois tale written in the colloquial language of the common people. Even though this is an imitation folk story, its popular nature is apparent in the plain and unadorned dialogue, the humble origins of its characters, and the stark, matter-of-fact description of the way of the world, which turns a cold shoulder to poverty and sickness, while admiring unashamedly wealth and prosperity. A tinge of Buddhism spreads over this popular story of the reunion of a once poor, luckless youth—at last grown rich—with his faithful wife.

The son of a pious, good-natured country squire in his late middle age, Sung Chin-lang was born as the reincarnation of a dead Buddhist monk, to whose burial the kindly elder Sung had made a generous contribution. After the early death of his parents, the family fortune declined and the boy suffered deprivation. While traveling in the service of a magistrate, he was dismissed from his master's retinue because of the slander of fellow servants, and forced to lead a life of begging and near-starvation in an alien land. By accident, he met a friend of his father's, Liu, a boatman engaged in transporting goods for merchants from one port to another. The boy was taken into the Liu family boat, where he helped to keep the records and accounts, and so won the confidence of old Liu and his wife that they married him to their only daughter, I-ch'un. But his luck did not last long, for soon he fell ill with consumption and, instead of helping his parents-in-law, became a burden to them. The practical old couple were so dismayed and disgusted with him that they abandoned him while he was cutting faggots ashore in a lonely mountainous region. About to die of hunger and sickness, he was saved by an old Buddhist monk—evidently, the apparition of the same monk befriended by his father—who taught him to recite the *Diamond Sutra*, thereby curing him of his disease. "Because of this incident," says the storyteller, "Sung Chin-lang's luck turned from bad to good, and with the departure of calamities, fortune returned."

Fortune came through his discovery in this desolate region of a treasure hoard, consisting of eight big boxes of gold, jade, and other precious gems, hidden in a dilapidated temple by bandits who were away on one of their forays. Why the treasures were thus left unguarded, except by an array of swords and spears stuck in the ground, is left unexplained in the story. Anyway, the precious hoard fell readily into the hand of Sung Chin-lang, who had them carried away into a merchant ship which happened to pass by. Immediately, Sung Chin-lang became one of the wealthiest men in Nanking, where he made his residence. In the meantime, there was a great deal of commotion on the Liu family boat with I-ch'un, unconsoled in her mourning for her supposedly dead husband, clamoring to follow him by drowning in the river. The denouement came when Sung Chin-lang, in disguise as a wealthy merchant from out-of-town, went to seek his wife and found her still faithful and devoted to his memory. The battered old felt hat which I-ch'un had sewn up for him when he was first taken to the boat served as a memento to link the past with the present. With the sorrows and grudges of the past all forgiven and forgotten in a moving scene of reconciliation, they celebrated their reunion with wine and feasting and then returned to Nanking, where a happy life awaited them. The story ends with the young couple further united in their Buddhist devotion as they recited together the *Diamond Sutra* which they would continue to do until their death in old age.

Perhaps the best written and certainly the most poignant of the three tales in Feng's collection is the tragic one entitled "Tu Shih-niang Angrily Sinks into the River Her Hundred-Jewel Box."[6] In style and method of presentation, it is a clever imitation of the art of the colloquial storyteller. Instead of a complicated plot with many ups and downs, it is a well-told, lively, and tightly knit tale of a courtesan's love for a young student, his fickleness and ingratitude, and her death by drowning. Tu Shih-niang, the heroine, was a beautiful and talented girl, on whom many young men of rich and noble families in the gay metropolis had lavished their attentions. Surfeited with gaiety and dissipation, she yearned for a quiet life of domestic love and warmth, which she hoped to realize in the company of the student, Li Chia, the son of a high provincial official. After having squandered in the "houses of flowers and willows" all the funds provided by his father for his studies, the young man was in hard straits, but his depressed condition only strengthened the girl's resolve to be united with him. Partly with her own savings and partly with the money raised by a friend of Li's, she ransomed herself from the courtesan's establishment, taking with her only a jewel box. After their reunion, the couple traveled southward with the intention of seeking a temporary lodging in one of the Yangtze cities so that Li Chia could return home to placate his father before presenting his bride.

On their way, while waiting to cross the Yangtze, Li Chia struck up an acquaintance with Sun Fu, a young salt merchant whose boat was moored next to his own. After a glimpse of Li's beautiful wife, Sun coveted her for himself. He cunningly advised Li to surrender the woman to him and offered to pay for her one thousand ounces of silver, with which Li could go to his father for reconcilement. The doltish student was easily duped and returned to discuss the deal with his wife. Abruptly and rudely awakened from her dream of a happy married life with her lover, whose despicable nature now bared itself like an open book, she calmly accepted her fate and made a desperate move. Having bedecked and dressed herself in her best, she appeared on board the ship early the next morning; there, in the presence of all, including Li Chia, Sun Fu, and many onlookers ashore, she opened the jewel box she had been carrying with her and, to the astonishment of everyone present, threw into the river all its drawerfuls of precious jewels—gold and jade ornaments, night-gleaming pearls, emeralds, cat's-eyes, and many other gems, the like of which had never been seen before. Then, the story continues:

> Stricken with remorse, Li Chia held Tu Shih-niang in his arms and wept aloud. Sun Fu also came to persuade and plead with her. Shih-niang, however, pushed Li Chia aside and turning to Sun Fu, scolded him:
>
> "Li and I have suffered many hardships and with no easy success have attained this relationship. And now you come along with your lewd intentions and slanderous lies to break up other people's marriage and sever their affection. You are my enemy! If I should have knowledge after death, I would certainly accuse you before the gods. How dare you still covet the joys of the pillow and mat* with me?"
>
> Next, she said to Li Chia: "During these many years of dust and breeze,** I have privately amassed enough savings to support myself for the rest of my life. Ever since I met you, we have sworn by mountain and sea an oath of fidelity unto our old age. Previously, before leaving the capital, I pretended to have received this box as a gift from my sisters in the profession. Actually, the hundreds of jewels it contained were worth ten thousand ounces of silver, with which I planned to fit you out splendidly for your trip home to visit your parents so that they might feel better disposed to me and accept me as your helpmate. If I could thus entrust myself to you, I would have no regret in life or death. Who would have thought that your faith is shallow and confounded by plausible arguments? You cast me off midway in the journey, setting at naught my true love. Today, in front of all present, I have opened my box for everyone to see and to show you that the paltry sum of a thousand ounces is by no means a difficult thing to obtain. There is jade in my chest but I regret you have no pearls in your eyes. Ill-starred is my luck that just after I have escaped from the toils and woes of the dust and breeze, I should have met with desertion at your hands! All you here who have eyes and ears can together bear witness that I have not been ungrateful to the young gentleman, but it is he who has proved untrue to me."
>
> Everyone in the crowd gathered there was moved to tears; they all cursed and spat upon the young lord Li for his ingratitude and disloyalty. He was both ashamed and bitter, remorseful and tearful; he was about to beg Shih-niang's forgiveness, when, clasping the

* A euphemism for love-making.
** A euphemism for prostitution.

jewel box in her arms, she leapt suddenly into the bosom of the river. The crowd at once yelled for help and tried to drag her out of the water. But she had already vanished without a trace as the clouds lowered over the river and the billows rolled over each other. Pitiable indeed was this famed courtesan, as pretty as flower or jade, to be thus suddenly buried in the bellies of the river fish.

Her three souls returned dimly to the watery main;
And her seven spirits entered forlorn the road to the Shades.

This glorification of the courtesan's role is nothing new in Chinese literature. Many such admirable women, noted for their gifts and virtues, have appeared in T'ang literary tales and Yüan drama, but very few works can compare with this story in its graphic presentation of a tense tragic situation and its skillful use of dialogue befitting the character and status of the speakers. Take, for instance, the vulgar and garrulous speeches of Mother Tu, the procuress. After young Li Chia had been reduced to poverty, Mother Tu began to complain of his visits that no longer brought profit to the house. She was even willing to let Shih-niang go to him for three hundred ounces of silver.

> "If it were to anyone else," said Mother Tu, "I'd ask a thousand ounces. It's a pity that this poor wretch can't pay as much, so I merely want from him three hundred ounces to buy for myself another powdered face to take your place. But upon one condition: it must be paid up within three days. As the right hand delivers the money, so will the left hand the person. But if no money is forthcoming after three days, then this old woman, not caring whether three times seven makes twenty-one or whether he is a young lord or not, will myself give him a sound beating with my cane and evict him from this house. Don't blame me at that time!"

At Shih-niang's pleading, Mother Tu finally agreed to extend the time limit to ten days.

> Shih-niang said, "If he can't find the money in ten days, I bet he'll have no face to show up again. What I'm afraid of is that when he has these three hundred ounces, you might regret and go back on your word." Thereupon Mother Tu said, "I'm fifty-one now and moreover I've been observing religiously my fast ten days every month. How would I dare tell lies? If you don't trust me, I'll make a pledge with you by clapping our hands together. If I should go back on my word, may I be changed into a sow, a dog!"

The crude language of the procuress contrasts sharply with the polite expressions of Sun Fu, who disguised his hideous scheme in refined language. While advising Li Chia of his next move, Sun Fu offered him help in a long speech:

You, elder brother, have been adrift in this world for more than a year. Now your stern father cherishes anger toward you, and the womenfolk are alienated from you in their hearts. Putting myself in your position, I would have indeed little time to sleep and eat with ease. Nonetheless, your worthy father is angry with you because you have been infatuated with the flowers and doted on the willows, and have squandered gold like dirt. Having thus forsaken your family and dissipated its fortune, you are bound to become a wastrel unfit to continue the family heritage. Therefore, by returning home empty-handed, you would merely incur your father's wrath. On the other hand, if you could bring yourself to sever your affection for the sleeping mat and act opportunely, I would willingly offer you a present of a thousand ounces of silver. With this money you could go back to your father and tell him that you were actually engaged in teaching in the capital and had never wasted even one cent. Your father would certainly believe you. Henceforth, harmony would reign in the family and no idle talk would be heard. In the twinkling of an eye you would turn calamity into blessing. Elder brother, please think thrice. It is not that I covet the beauty of the lovely one, but that I want to oblige you with just a fraction of my loyalty.

These ingratiating words so pleased the spineless young student that he exclaimed, "After having listened to your great instruction, I am suddenly enlightened in my stupidity." Most versatile of the conversationalists, however, is Tu Shih-niang. She holds her own just as well in her conversations with the student as with the procuress. As quoted above, her words in the address to Sun Fu and Li Chia are not only expressive and well chosen but also vigorous, appealing, and deeply moving.

In this story, the characters of the courtesan and the student are well depicted; they develop as the drama unfolds itself. Li Chia first appears as an ideal lover with his handsome features, amiable nature, and seeming devotion. However, the weakness of his character, at first only intimated, gradually reveals itself. He is afraid to face the reprimands of his stern father; he falls an easy prey to Sun Fu's trap; finally, conscience-stricken, he weeps bitterly and remorsefully, but can only look on helplessly as Tu Shih-niang tosses the jewels and herself into the river. A man without backbone, the lot that awaits him after her death is to brood all day in sorrow and shame until he becomes hopelessly insane. In strong contrast, the courtesan proves to be a woman of unswerving faith and great courage. In addition to looking lovely, she is honest, intelligent, resourceful; most important, although in the profession from a tender age, she still retains a faithful heart. The salient features of her character, some of them unsuspected at first, gradually reveal themselves through her words and deeds. When told by Li Chia of his intention to sell her for a thousand ounces

223

of silver with which to sweeten his encounter with his father, she merely gives a cold laugh and remarks icily, "He who has mapped out such a strategy for you must be a great fellow indeed. You will recover your thousand ounces and I, by going to another man, will no longer encumber you like a piece of baggage. What starts with love now ends in propriety. It is indeed a fine plan that suits us both!" To make sure that she has not misconstrued Li Chia's true intention, she steals a glance at him the next morning, and when she finds him looking pleased realizes that all is lost. She then acts resolutely and swiftly. The dramatic denouement completes the picture of a tragic but lovable personality that has won the sympathy and admiration of all readers. It has been surmised that such a masterpiece of storytelling could have come from no lesser writer than Feng Meng-lung himself.

The immediate popularity of Feng Meng-lung's three-volume collection seemingly stimulated the creative efforts of Ling Meng-ch'u. In a preface to *Striking the Table in Amazement at the Wonders, First Series,* Ling stated that, prompted by the "speedy circulation" of Feng Meng-lung's books, a publisher had approached him to produce some other rare and ancient manuscripts for the book mart, not knowing that Feng had already exhausted most of the old scripts and that "the few leftovers were like broken weeds in a ditch unfit for display." So, instead of searching for old tales, Ling took upon himself the task of creating new ones from his own pen. "Accordingly," he continued, "I have taken those miscellaneous and scattered pieces of the past and present that could refresh one's views and understandings, and contribute to one's conversations and jests; and have expanded and elaborated them in a number of chapters (*chüan*)."[7] As this first experiment proved successful, he was asked to repeat it in a second series, thus publishing in the course of some four years, from 1628 to 1632, a total of about eighty stories. A comparison between the original sources and Ling's own compositions reveals the resourcefulness and fecundity of his genius.

Ling Meng-ch'u made clear in his own words that wonder and amazement are the keynote of his story collection. "In the fall of the year *ting-mao* (1627)," he wrote, "my affairs became skin-deep and hair-thin and have since deviated from their proper course. So when I was wandering around in Nanking, I picked up for fun from among the hearsay of the past and present a few unusual plots worthy of narration to elaborate into colloquial stories, thereby to vent my spleen. It was not that I thought they would go a long way—I merely toyed with them to amuse myself. However, colleagues who came to visit me would ask for them and after having read each piece, would invariably strike the table in acclaim, 'How wonderful it is!' "[8]

Just as T'ang writers aimed to transmit in the literary language wondrous events and marvellous tales, so Ling Meng-ch'u used the colloquial language in stories that aim to arouse surprise and amazement. His writings, however, are much more down-to-earth than the Sung-Yüan folk stories, not to say the T'ang romantic tales. Unfortunately, for this reason the scope of his writings is rather limited. Devoid of romance and idealism, and presenting human nature in the raw, they smack of the vulgarity of the marketplace. Whether deliberately or incidentally, his stories show a mentality and attitude that are not far removed from those of the professional storytellers. While most of the traits described below can also be seen in Feng Meng-lung and other Ming writers, they are especially prominent in Ling's works.

Himself a poor frustrated scholar, Ling Meng-ch'u related with some gusto the wonderful fortunes that befell those students who eventually achieved literary success and high official position and who, often enough, secured a beautiful wife into the bargain. But even in these ideal situations, the narrative is always matter-of-fact, no effort being made to dramatize the love romance or give it glamor. Storekeepers and tradesmen, together with their families, form an important segment of the city population in Ling Meng-ch'u's stories, while pawnshop owners are frequently mentioned as examples of the covetous rich. Monks and nuns, mostly unscrupulous and some wicked and lecherous, add color and zest to the narration. Other social outcasts such as beggars and thieves, prostitutes and procuresses, complete this picture of the Chinese society of the early seventeenth century.

The world of Ling Meng-ch'u is a pragmatic, common sense, and materialistic one in which wealth, family property, and mundane success are the primary considerations of a man's life. The conflicts that center around them result further in intrigues, murders, and court trials. Entertaining and exciting these stories are, but they also contain elements that are improbable and unsavory. The judges who are brought into the story to settle the lawsuits are merely dei ex machina and as such stereotyped. The dispensing of court justice is somewhat crude; in particular, the penalties imposed on the guilty appear extremely harsh and grotesque, and in some cases inhuman. The convicted criminals are often beaten to death in front of the court, while confession is obtained through flogging, torture, and other means of corporal punishment. The sordidness of this world is accentuated by the fact that romantic love is absent and illicit and adulterous affairs abound. Pornography, as discussed before, is taken for granted and many passages describing sexual behavior are found in Ling Meng-ch'u's stories as in other Ming writings.

Beyond this world of the busy, bustling, and striving city bourgeoisie lies another sphere—the unseen, unfathomable, but equally compelling domain of the spirits and ghosts, with whom some of Ling's stories are peopled. He believes explicitly in retribution. Sometimes, according to Ling, the good deeds done or the crimes committed may find their immediate rewards or punishments in this life. The idea is put succinctly in the following verse:

> The deep, azure sky cannot be deceived;
> Known already are the intentions before action starts.
> Virtue and evil will have their recompense in the end;
> The question is only whether it will come now or hereafter.[9]

To illustrate this concept with concrete examples is one of the professed aims of Ling Meng-ch'u's writings. He advises the avoidance of sins and the accumulation of merits in the Buddhist fashion. Although he seldom engages in religious speculations and has no love for the bonzes and nuns, he is nevertheless obsessed by this aspect of popular Buddhism to the point of superstition—a fact which indicates that he shares the views and beliefs of the common people, whom he describes so vividly and intimately in these stories.

From the literary point of view, Ling Meng-ch'u's besetting sin as a writer is his propensity to didacticism. This is probably due to the desire of a literary man to justify his spending so much time and effort in the writing of popular literature. Whereas Feng Meng-lung is aware of the artistic merits of the colloquial story, Ling Meng-ch'u seems to be concerned mainly with its moralizing and propaganda value. But here again, Ling's didactic approach is by no means an innovation; Feng expresses the same view in his use of such key words as "enlighten," "admonish," and "awaken" for the titles of his three storybooks. Both Ling and Feng take the orthodox Confucian attitude in their admonitions and remonstrances with the readers. The Confucian virtues of love and righteousness, loyalty and sincerity, are stressed. Conjugal faith, fraternal love, and filial piety are held up as the cornerstones of human relationship and examples of moral endeavors to be cultivated and emulated, whereas the opposites of such virtues are denounced as moral depravity to be greatly shunned. In these instances, the concept of retribution or punishment comes in handily to support and strengthen the Confucian ideals. To the practical-minded bourgeois, the motto that "virtue will reap its own rewards" will become meaningful only when the rewards are measured in terms of material wealth, social amenities, and political eminence, besides the attainment of long life and the building up of a prolific and prosperous family.

Besides the *Three Words* and *Two Strikes*, many other story collections were published toward the end of the Ming dynasty. Their contents, however, are meager and inferior. As imitative writings, they cannot compare in quality and merit with the great collections of Feng and Ling, in whose hands the Chinese colloquial story attained the height of its development. Still others are merely reproductions and selections, chief among which is the *Marvellous Tales, New and Old*, a book consisting of twenty-nine stories from Feng Meng-lung and eleven from Ling Meng-ch'u. The compiler of this anthology, apparently one of their group, is known only by his pen name, "The Old Man Hugging the Jar." The fact that his name has not been identified may be due to his comparative insignificance in the world of letters, Feng and Ling both being authors of renown with several plays and novels to their credit. But the anonymous editor is certainly discerning and competent in his job, as his selection represents practically the best of the two hundred stories in Feng and Ling. In fact, the popularity of the *Marvellous Tales, New and Old*, was such that it soon overshadowed all the other story collections, including the originals. These latter were relegated to oblivion—Ling Meng-ch'u's works, their moralistic platitudes notwithstanding, suffered from the censorship of the Manchu officials—from which they have been rescued only in recent years. On the other hand, the "Old Man" has hugged, not a jar, but a touchstone, a well tested and much treasured work that is to remain one of the best known and most influential storybooks of all times.[10]

16 : Great Novels by Obscure Writers

Contemporaneous with the short story, the Chinese novel flourished from the middle of the Ming dynasty to the end of the Ch'ing (sixteenth to early twentieth century). Many writers devoted their time and energy to the writing of fiction and their output was impressive, particularly in the late Ch'ing period. This effort was noteworthy because, in spite of the recognition of the novel as an established literary genre, it was still considered a minor art form compared with poetry and nonfictional prose. For this reason, as we have seen earlier, the authors preferred to remain anonymous and used only their pseudonyms; of the known novelists, almost all lived obscure lives unrecorded in dynastic history. The most recognition they achieved was minor official positions and local fame among small groups of friends. An undertone of frustration and bitterness seems to have prevailed in their writings. It is no coincidence that realistic descriptions and satirical expositions of contemporary life have characterized Chinese fiction since the Ming period.

Among the bulk of Chinese fiction written in the last several centuries, four novels stand out as the most important, if not also the greatest. These are *Journey to the West (Hsi-yu chi)*, *Gold Vase Plum (Chin P'ing Mei)*, *Dream of the Red Chamber (Hung-lou meng)*, and *Informal History of the Literati (Ju-lin wai-shih)*; the first being a supernatural novel, the second and third realistic novels of society and family, and the last a satirical novel. In the meantime, the historical romance continued to be popular; in the novel of adventure, brave chivalrous swordsmen, counterparts of medieval knights in Western literature, replaced the bandit-leaders as heroes;* "the novel of beauty and genius," a typical

---

* Endowed with great physical prowess and supreme swordsmanship, the Chinese heroes, like their European counterparts, perform feats of strength and fight in jousts and battles. No religious motive or emotional yearning, however, inspires their deeds. Love, whether sacred or profane, is unknown to them. On the other hand, their efforts are directed at aiding the great officials in the suppression of crime and the apprehension of evildoers, who may be outlaws, wicked officials, or rebellious princes. By combating the sinister forces of society, they render it a great service, for which they are loved by the people.

Chinese love romance, had its vogue not only in China but in Europe as well.* All these types have enriched Chinese fiction and each has its own outstanding examples, but our discussion, brief and only introductory, has to be confined to the four major works mentioned above.

The supernatural novel, represented by the *Journey to the West* (known to English readers as *Monkey***), is as much the product of folk tradition as of the author's creative imagination. It contains a world of fantastic invention, in which gods and demons loom large and vie for supremacy. The supernatural beings are of many varieties: a hierarchy of celestial deities under the Jade Emperor of the Taoist cult; a shadowy world of ghosts and spirits presided over by the King of Hades; a host of local divinities, dragon kings, monsters and goblins. There is also an array of Buddhist saints and arhats headed by Sakyamuni (Buddha) in the Holy Mountains of the West. Most popular among them is the Bodhisattva, Kuan-yin, sometimes called the Goddess of Mercy. The Buddhist idea of retribution and the Taoist search for gold and the elixir of life have further nourished popular belief, to which Confucianism contributed the cult of heroes and ancestors. This polytheistic pantheon has provided Chinese novelists with ample material for supernatural tales.

The evolution of the *Journey to the West* is as complicated and fascinating as that of the *Three Kingdoms* and the *Marshes*. Like them, it has passed through a series of oral and written stages before attaining its present form. Its most important author, but not its sole creator, was Wu Ch'eng-en (1500?–1582), a scholar-official in the Yangtze region. Before the publication of Wu's novel in 1592, there existed a number of earlier works on the same subject: a poetic novelette, a six-part drama, and a crude colloquial story. Other versions have appeared since 1592, including two adaptations, one in a four-part book entitled *The Four Journeys*.[1]

The *Journey to the West* is divided into three parts: (1) an early history

* As specimens of Chinese fiction first introduced to Europe in the early eighteenth century, they are historically important for Western readers of Chinese literature. Translations such as *The Pleasing History* (later retranslated as *The Fortunate Union* and *Breeze in the Moonlight*) and *Two Fair Cousins* first appeared in English and French, and were immediately acclaimed by critics as examples of Chinese refinement and literary achievement. The popularity of these novels was due perhaps to their medium length, from eighteen to forty chapters, which can be easily handled in translation, as well as to their novelty and exotic appeal. It should also be remembered that before that time Europe itself was still under the influence of the elegant courtly society of Bourbon France and that at one time critical opinion in England had been swayed by the works of John Lyly. Like Lyly's *Euphues*, these Chinese novels are characterized by a stereotyped plot, artificial characters, and stale poetry. It is therefore unfortunate that the West should have gained its first impression of Chinese literature from these minor writings.

** Quotations from *Monkey* (translated by Arthur Waley) by Wu Ch'eng-en, by permission of the John Day Company, Inc., publisher.

of the Monkey Spirit; (2) a pseudo-historical account of Tripitaka's family and life before his trip to fetch the sutras in the Western Heaven; (3) the main story, consisting of eighty-one dangers and calamities encountered by Tripitaka and his three animal spirit disciples—Monkey, Pigsy, and Sandy (a fish spirit). In the first part are related the birth of Monkey from a magic rock, his coronation as the monkey king, and his attainment of magic powers. The latter include the ability to turn a somersault of 108,000 *li*; the mastery of seventy-two kinds of transformation; the use of a mighty iron cudgel which can be changed into a small needle to be placed behind the ear; and the trick of turning his hair, when pulled out, into thousands of little monkeys. Armed with these abilities, Monkey extended his sway over earth and sea; but he also coveted an official position in Heaven. Among the riots which he subsequently caused in that celestial sphere, the theft of the immortal peaches in the garden of the Heavenly Queen and the wreck of Lao-tzu's Crucible of the Eight Trigrams are especially well told. In the latter story, Monkey, who had been smelted in the crucible after his capture by the Heavenly Host, was thought to have been burned to death in the fiery flames, but actually he suffered only from smoky red eyes; finally he made good his escape, as described in the following passage:

> Time certainly passed fast and it was already the end of the forty-nine day period when Lao-tzu's alchemic process was consummated.
> One day he came to open the crucible to take out the elixir of life. Monkey was covering his eyes with both hands, rubbing them and shedding tears, when he heard a noise atop the crucible. Suddenly he opened wide his eyes and saw a light. Without waiting any longer, he jumped out with one leap. As he rushed outside, he gave the crucible of the eight trigrams such a kick that it fell with a crashing sound. Greatly flustered, Lao-tzu's servants, who had been watching the fire under the crucible, all came out, as did the other celestial guards and attendants, to drag Monkey back, but he tripped up every one of them like an epileptic white-browed tiger or a mad one-horned dragon. When Lao-tzu himself rushed forward to grab him, Monkey gave him such a push that he fell head over heels. After making good his escape, Monkey took out from behind his ear the magic cudgel, which, when swung against the wind, grew into the size of a bowl in its diameter. Thus armed once more and striking out indiscriminately here and there, he caused again a great uproar in the celestial palace. The Nine Planets were so frightened that they locked themselves in and the Four Heavenly Kings fled without a trace.   (Chapter 7)[2]

The mighty Monkey was finally subdued by the Buddha, who had him sealed inside the Mountain of the Five Elements until such time as he would be set free by Tripitaka in his journey westward.

In addition to the pseudo-historical tale of Tripitaka's life, the second part contains the supernatural stories of the execution of the dragon king for disobeying Heaven's command and of the T'ang Emperor's trip to the underworld, where he had to bribe his way out from the clutches of hungry ghosts. This led to the celebration of the great Mass for the Dead, the choice of Tripitaka as its officiator, and his mission to fetch Buddhist scriptures at the emperor's command. History tells us, however, that instead of being regally equipped for the trip, Tripitaka to make the pilgrimage[3] actually had to brave the persecutions of an imperial ban against travelling abroad.

The bulk of the novel,[4] to which the first two parts are mere introductions, deals with the numerous calamities Tripitaka had to suffer on his westward journey at the hands of monsters, ghosts, and demons, who all clamored to eat him alive. But through the efforts of his animal-spirit escorts, especially Monkey, and with the aid of Buddhist and Taoist gods, who now ranged themselves on Monkey's side, Tripitaka succeeded in overcoming the dangers and reached the Western Heaven, where he later became a Buddhist saint together with his three disciples.

The adventures of the Buddhist pilgrims are related in a way that is not only hair-raising, but also immensely witty and amusing. Pigsy, noted for his stupidity, gluttony, and lecherous desires, became the butt of Monkey's raillery. The latter had a native instinct for mischief and pleasantry, and poked fun at all and sundry, his master not excepted. Thus the novel contains many jocular and exciting stories that fire the imagination of young and old alike. As an illustration is told briefly here the episode of a series of Buddhist-Taoist contests in the Kingdom of Cart Slow, situated along the route of the Chinese pilgrims.

This kingdom was dominated by three animal spirits in human shape who styled themselves Taoist immortals. With the king's connivance, they set out to persecute Buddhist monks and made them do the meanest labor under the supervision of Taoist taskmasters. It happened that at the time of Tripitaka's arrival there was a great drought in the land. So instead of maltreating the Buddhist pilgrims as urged by the pseudo-Taoist immortals, the king ordered a rainmaking contest between the Buddhists and Taoists, promising better treatment for the Buddhists in the kingdom and passports for the visiting monks, if they won. One of the Taoist Immortals was given the honor of starting. Sword in hand, his hair loosened, he mounted a high altar erected in the palace compound for the contest. As he recited his spells, he burned Taoist images, texts, and yellow papers; he also banged his tablet on the altar to summon the spirits. At his repeated bidding came the Old Woman of the Wind, hugging her bag; her boy holding tight the rope at the mouth of the bag; Cloud Boy and Mist Lad; Thunder God and Mother of Lightning. They were all about to perform their tasks when they were stopped by Monkey, and no rain fell. Then came the turn of the Buddhists. Armed with neither sword nor tablet, Tripitaka went up the altar to pray and recite the sutras. At this moment, Monkey displayed his mighty cudgel, pointing it toward the sky. Immediately, the Old Woman of the Wind brought out her bag, the boy loosened the rope at its mouth, and with a great roar the wind rushed out. Bricks hurtled; sand and stones flew; dark clouds covered the city and the palace.

> Presently Monkey pointed again, and deafening peals of thunder shook the earth. It was as though a hundred thousand chariots were rolling by. The inhabitants of the town were frightened out of their wits and one and all began burning incense and saying their prayers. "Now Thunder God," screamed Monkey, "do your work! Strike down all greedy and corrupt officials, all disobedient and surly sons, as a warning to the people!" The din grew louder than ever. Then Monkey pointed again, and such a rain fell that it seemed as if the whole Yellow River had suddenly fallen out of the sky. This rain fell from early morning till noon. The town was already one vast swamp when the king sent a message saying, "That's enough rain. If there is much more it will ruin the crops and we shall be worse off than ever." (Chapter 45)[5]

This was followed by other contests: an endurance test in meditation; a guessing game; and the last, a competition in head-cutting, belly-ripping, and bathing in boiling oil, in which the three Taoist Immortals ultimately met their deaths. The victorious Buddhists were given a great feast and a royal escort out of the kingdom.

The novel, strangely enough, has been variously interpreted by early Chinese commentators as an allegorical treatise on the three schools of Chinese religion and philosophy. The main story, as we have seen, is essentially Buddhist in nature and orientation, but to regard it as an exposition of the new laws of Buddhism is just as absurd as to interpret it as an elucidation of the Taoist formula for refining the golden pill of immortality, or as an allegory of the Neo-Confucian principle of self-cultivation through the illumination of the heart and the revelation of human nature.

Also farfetched is the more recent view of the novel as representing a socio-political struggle, in which, it is said, the oppressive agents of the ruling class are pitted against the righteous forces of the people represented by Monkey. He is seen as the personification of folk ideals and strength in an autocratic society. His rampages in Heaven and Hell are represented as the bold struggles of the oppressed against despotism; his fight with monsters and demons—"claws and teeth of the ruling class"—

as heroic combats against the evil forces of society; his conquest of the impassable mountains and rivers as man's efforts in surmounting the barriers of nature. "The victory of Monkey," the recent critics conclude, "is also the victory of the people."[6]

Perhaps, if any extra significance is to be read into this novel, it can be regarded as a good-natured satire on human foibles and bureaucratic stupidities, and as an allegory of the pilgrim's progress toward Buddhist salvation. To project the satire into the Heavenly realm, which is described as a vast bureaucracy, is not so much to attack the hierarchy of gods as to poke fun, on a higher level, at the follies of the earthly government. The parody of government red tape is shown in the use of a letter of introduction by the T'ang Emperor to gain favorable treatment during his visit to Hades; in his borrowing money on a promissory note; and in his bribery of the hungry ghosts mentioned previously. Even Buddha's disciples demanded gifts when they were sent to accompany Tripitaka to fetch the sacred books from the "Treasury." They said to Tripitaka:

> Having come here from China you have no doubt brought a few gifts for us. If you will kindly hand them over, you shall have your scriptures at once. (Chapter 98)[7]

At first Tripitaka refused and would have brought back to China blank scriptures—even though they are the true ones, according to the author —if he had not detected the fraud in time. Finally, he had to part with his golden alms bowl as a "commission" to Buddha's disciples before they gave him the written scrolls he wanted.

Two aspects of the human spirit are represented in the novel, one by Tripitaka, the other by Monkey. The former is man as he really is. Neither heroic nor superhuman, he falls an easy prey to fierce monsters as well as to his own demon of fear and misgiving. In spite of all his learning and virtue, he cowers before physical dangers. He is frightened by the attack of robbers, spirits, and goblins; his tears fall like rain when the river dragon swallows his horse. But he emerges heroic in the end because he is strong in his devotion. On the other hand, Monkey may be regarded as a symbol of man's restless ambition. As the omnipotent immortal that every man secretly desires to be, he fulfills his wildest dreams. But he misuses his power and defies the gods; thus he gets burned by playing with fire. It is only when he is able to channel his power in a right direction and use it for a right cause that Monkey, like Tripitaka, gains salvation—the one by curbing his ambition, the other his self-doubts.

Interesting as these interpretations are, the novel must be read and appreciated as a work of literature per se. Here, its merits are obvious. The vastness of its fantasy, the rich variety of its supernatural stories and characters, and the inexhaustible fund of its wit and humor combine to make the *Journey to the West* one of the most delightful books in world literature. Moreover, as a novel of religious allegory or a satirical romance, its adventures are more thrilling, more entertaining, and more colorful than its Western counterparts, *The Pilgrim's Progress* and *Don Quixote*, to which it has been sometimes compared.

The most important type of Chinese fiction, however, is the social and domestic novel, in which contemporary life and manners are depicted faithfully, intimately, and almost microscopically in a special Chinese brand of realism. What distinguishes the latter from Western realism is the role of the indispensable narrator. True to the Chinese storytelling tradition, the narrator is present everywhere, for he not only sees, hears, and reports on every detail in the story, but in a sly and insinuating manner he also takes the reader into his confidence and imbues him with his own feelings and attitudes; whenever appropriate he makes his own comments and asides. The art of Chinese fiction lies in the author's ability to tell his tale in such a seemingly artless and effortless way that the reader, while enjoying the story, is so taken in by the storyteller that he becomes happily oblivious of the unlikelihood of the latter's ubiquitous presence.

Such a master novelist is the anonymous author of the *Gold Vase Plum*, rendered respectively in two different English versions as *The Golden Lotus*[8] and *The Adventurous History of Hsi-men and His Six Wives*.[9] The novel was first mentioned toward the last years of the sixteenth century, its earliest extant version containing a preface dated 1617. The author is known by his pen name, Hsiao-hsiao sheng (A Laughing-laughing Scholar) of Lan-ling, or I-hsien in Shantung, in whose dialect the novel is written. This evidence of its authorship by an unknown writer from Shantung, probably a professional storyteller, belies the claim that the novel was written by some famous literary figure of the time.[10] In later editions, some of the local dialect peculiarities have been eliminated or changed into more common expressions.

The first realistic social novel, antedating by at least two centuries its French counterparts, the *Gold Vase Plum* depicts the dark aspects of a Chinese society riddled with filth and corruption, iniquity and rascality. Although the action of the novel took place toward the end of the Sung dynasty (early twelfth century), the society it reflects was undoubtedly that of the author's own time. The chief male character, Hsi-men Ch'ing, the owner of an apothecary shop, was a rake and bully, who through swindling and imposture rose to wealth and local power. In his household were six wives, among whom the two most important were Golden Lotus and the Lady of the Vase, as well as numerous maidservants including

Spring Plum (Golden Lotus' maid). Their names combine to give the novel its title. An archetype of the seducer of women, Hsi-men Ch'ing was a remote cousin of Lothario and Don Juan. He differed from them, however, in that he was a worldly fellow shorn of romantic glamor; the women fell victims to him not because of the gay seductiveness of his person but because of his money and power. Carnal desire, instead of romantic love, guided his encounters with innumerable prostitutes and the adulterous wives of his friends and subordinates.

This one hundred chapter novel may aptly be called the crime and punishment of the Hsi-men family. Here is an interesting case of a Chinese story in which poetic justice descended rather tardily on the evil-doer, whose penalty in this life was no more than cuckoldry. Otherwise, Hsi-men Ch'ing lived a happy wicked life, enjoying his debaucheries to his heart's content. It was only after his death from overindulgence that retribution in a more violent form came to the other members of his family. Most of them, sinners themselves, met their deserved ends in the chaos and disaster that followed the Jurchen invasion of North China in the twelfth century. The lonely survivals were his principal wife, the only decent woman in the novel, and her son, who became a Buddhist monk to do penance for his father's sins.

A powerful and merciless exposure of a decadent society, the book would have been a well-accepted masterpiece if it were not for its unabashed, flagrant pornography. The author, it seems, delighted in salacious descriptions of perverted sex, and no amount of whitewash can cover up the filth of the novel before whose glaring immorality Western works of similar nature, some well-known modern novels not excepted, pale into insignificance. It has been suggested that a major editorial operation could transform it into something more wholesome, but once its foul cankerous tissues were removed, it would no longer be its true self—a naked representation of the corroding body social.

Viewed aside from the moral issue, the *Gold Vase Plum* is one of the greatest novels ever written in the Chinese language. It gives a unique picture of the ways of the world, whose winds blow alternately hot and cold; it depicts vividly and skillfully such scenes of society as are found in the comedies of Ben Jonson, of whom the Chinese author was a contemporary. The characters, everyman in his humor, whose words and actions are reproduced clearly and minutely to the meanest detail, appear before us not as alien ghosts of a remote past but as evil genii that haunt the conscience of the modern man. The novel is a perspicuous presentation of human foibles and failings, too many to be enumerated. It suffices to quote here the following passage, which cleverly blends sarcasm, humor, and pathos as illustrative of the artless art of Chinese realism:

235

Ch'ang Shih-chieh thanked Hsi-men Ch'ing and took his leave, placing the packet of silver inside his sleeve. He went back home in a cheerful mood, but just as he was about to go in, his wife came out of the door to accost him, shouting noisily:

"You good-for-nothing! You, bare stick as lean as a leafless *wu-t'ung* tree! You have gone away for a whole day and left your wife to starve at home, and yet you come back so jolly pleased with yourself. Aren't you ashamed? Here we are without a roof of our own and have to bear other people's bad breath, blown into your wife's ears! Do you think she relishes it all?"

Ch'ang did not open his mouth. He waited until his wife had scolded herself out before he gently fumbled from his sleeve the packet of silver and placed it on the table. Then he took off the wrapping and gazing at the silver pieces, he addressed them thus:

"Oh, you, my square-holed elder brothers! As I set my eyes on you, so glittering, tinkling, and pricelessly precious, how my body tingles all over! What a pity I couldn't gulp you down with a mouthful of water! If you had come earlier, I would not have suffered from the ill breath of this lewd woman."

The wife saw clearly before her a heap of some twelve or thirteen ounces of silver in the packet. She was so overjoyed that she pushed forward closer to her husband and tried to grab it from him.

Ch'ang said, "All your life you have had nothing but abuse for me, your husband, but the minute you see this silver, you want to be near me. Tomorrow I'm going to buy some new clothes with this silver, dress myself up, and spend my days elsewhere all by myself. I'm not going to fool around with you any longer."

The woman asked, all smiles on her face, "My elder brother, where indeed did you get these silver pieces?"

Ch'ang made no reply.

"My elder brother," the woman persisted, "how can you really be angry with me? I merely want you to get ahead in life. Now that we have this silver, I'd like to talk to you about how we could buy a house to settle down. Isn't that splendid? But instead, you are making such a show! As your wife, I haven't done anything wrong. You are angry with me, but that isn't fair."

Ch'ang still would not open his mouth. So the woman just blabbed on, but when he continued to ignore her, she felt remorseful and could not help shedding a few tears. When he saw this, Ch'ang said, "You, woman, neither farm nor weave, but you are pretty good at abusing your husband."

Hearing this, the wife let down her tears in a stream. The two both shut their mouths tight and as there was no one to make peace between them, they sat there sullenly. Ch'ang thought to himself: "Life is hard for this woman. After all the hardships she has had, how could I blame her for complaining? Today I have all this silver with me. If I disregard her, people will say that I have no affection, and if his lordship Hsi-men should get wind of it, he'd blame me."

So he smiled and told his wife, "I of course want to have you. Who's blaming you? Only, you had so nagged me that I had to walk out of the house. But I am not angry with you and I'll tell you plainly about this silver. This morning as I couldn't stay in the house any longer, I went to Second Elder Brother Ying to invite him to have three cups with me in the wineshop. Then we went together to wait on his lordship at his residence. Luckily, he was at home and had not gone out feasting. Thanks to Second Brother Ying, I don't know with how much wagging of his tongue, he finally got for me these silver pieces. I was further promised that as soon as I have found a house I'd be given more silver to make a purchase. These twelve ounces are just for my current expenses." (Chapter 57)[11]

A century and a half after the publication of the *Gold Vase Plum* appeared the most famous of the Chinese novels, the *Dream of the Red Chamber*, over the tragic fate of whose young hero and heroine countless generations of Chinese readers have shed tears of sympathy and compassion. This evidence of the novel's moving power speaks well for its artistic excellence. Few works, whether Oriental or Occidental, are its peers in the vastness of its length, the vividness of its narration, the subtlety of its character portrayal, and the skillful use of the colloquial language. It represents the highest development of Chinese fiction and with it the transition of the novel from collective to individual authorship is completed.

The author of the *Dream of the Red Chamber* has been identified as Ts'ao Chan (1724?–1764),[12] better known as Ts'ao Hsüeh-ch'in. He was the scion of a wealthy official family, which in his early youth became impoverished because of political reverses. Now generally considered as autobiographical,* the novel is epitomized by a verse in the opening chapter:

> Here are pages full of absurd words—
> A handful of hot and bitter tears.
> They all say the author is crazy,
> But who would know his true intent? (Chapter 1)[13]

* Before this autobiographical interpretation of the novel was affirmed by Hu Shih and other scholars, previous interpretations can be summarized as follows: (1) the life and love of a Manchu emperor for a famous courtesan; (2) the love story of a Manchu poet and his talented concubine; (3) a political satire and a veiled attack on the Manchu dynasty. In a modified form the last interpretation has been revised in recent years by the critics on the Mainland who maintain that the novel is anti-feudal in its outlook. It attacks especially the traditional aspects of Chinese morality, political and legal institutions, the marriage system, and the examinaton system.

The affluence of the Ts'ao family during Hsüeh-ch'in's childhood in Nanking must have contrasted poignantly with the poverty of his last days in the western suburb of Peking, where he wrote the novel and where he died. His friends and contemporaries testified to his family's having to eat gruel for lack of money, to his "daily gazing at the Western Hills to feed himself on the evening clouds," and to his dying of sickness without a doctor's care. Ts'ao Hsüeh-ch'in apparently did not finish the novel at the time of his death but left the last part of the manuscript in an imperfect state. Only eighty chapters of the novel were copied and circulated during the author's lifetime[14] and almost thirty years elapsed between his death and the publication of the complete 120-chapter novel in 1791. Based upon a preface and an introduction written for a revised 1792 edition, as well as upon other scattered references, critics have attributed the authorship of the last forty chapters to Kao E, an unsuccessful scholar. This view, however, has been challenged in recent years because of the discovery of new evidence.[15]

In the *Dream of the Red Chamber* is drawn a vast panorama of Chinese family life, represented by the great house of Chia with its two main branches, their numerous offshoots, and a proliferation of kinsmen, as well as a large retinue of dependents and domestics. Compared with the Chias, the Forsytes of Galsworthy's trilogy seem a rather simple family group. Most graphically described in the Chinese novel are the life and activities of some thirty main characters flanked by four hundred or more minor ones who flit in and out of the novel in their secondary roles. This immense body of material, presented in a realistic manner, provides one of the best documents for a study of the extended Chinese family: its structure, organization, and ideals such as clan solidarity and honor, respect for old age, parental authority, filial obedience, sex relationship, the position of women, the role of the concubines, maidservants, and other domestics.

From this vast array of male and female characters emerge three principal figures: Chia Pao-yü and his two girl cousins, Lin Tai-yü (Black Jade) and Hsüeh Pao-ch'ai (Precious Clasp), upon whose triangular love pivots the story of the novel. This love affair, however, should not be regarded as the main plot in the Western sense of the word but rather as the chief episode in a novel of innumerable episodes relating the fall and decline of the Chia family in Peking.

Pao-yü, a talented but spoiled child, was the heir of one of the two great branches of the Chia clan. As such he was doted on by his paternal grandmother, the Matriarch, who protected him from the occasional discipline administered by his severe Confucian father. His offenses, however, were no more serious than truancy in the company of his many sisters and girl cousins, among whom the most lovely were Black Jade and Precious

Chia Pao-yü. By Kai Ch'i, a Ch'ing Dynasty Artist. From the
Hung-lou meng t'u-yung (Illustrations, Accompanied by Poems,
of the *Dream of the Red Chamber*), 1879.

Clasp. Equally fair and gifted, they represent two prototypes of female beauty in the Chinese concept: the former, with a slender, willow-waisted body in danger of being wafted away by the wind, is poetically inclined, highly susceptible, jealous, and given to crying; the latter is more normal and healthy, with a happy disposition and a shapely form somewhat on the plump side. In the company of such charming girls, with whom he versified, flirted, and fell in love, no wonder Pao-yü threw overboard the Confucian classics and read instead the *Romance of the Western Chamber.*

The building of the Garden of Grand View on the Chia family estate marked the climax of the happy, carefree days of the young set, each of them housed in one of the scenic cottages in the garden. Their idyllic existence, however, was not unmarred by jealousy, suspicion, and puerile quarrels which led to many a tearful scene. This is especially true of the relationship between Pao-yü and Black Jade, a pair of sensitive and sentimental young lovers. In one of the episodes the lovers' quarrel was caused by Black Jade's being denied entrance one evening to Pao-yü's cottage, the Peony Court. She was particularly hurt because she overheard inside the laughing voices of Pao-yü and Precious Clasp. Recalling her own orphaned life in a relative's house, she felt deeply grieved and cried bitterly. The next day, brushing aside Pao-yü when he paid her a visit, she went to a corner of the garden where previously she and Pao-yü had buried the fallen peach blossom. There she wept and sang:

> I am here to bury you when you fall;
> I wonder when will come the day of my death?
> People laugh at me for burying the flowers,
> But who would bury me when I pass away?
> Look, spring is waning and flowers have been falling,
> That is the time when fair maidens too wither and die.
> One morning spring departs and youth grows old—
> Flowers fallen, the maiden dead, one unaware of the other.
>
> (Chapter 27)[16]

Her singing was overheard by Pao-yü, who had taken the same path to the "flower mound." Deeply touched by her sentiments, he lay down on the hillside and broke out into sobbing.

> While sadly lamenting her fate, Black Jade heard suddenly the sound of mourning from the top of the slope. She thought to herself: "People say I am crazy. How could there be another as crazy as myself?" She lifted her head to take a look and caught sight of Pao-yü. "Humph!" she said spitefully, "It's that hard-hearted and short-lived one! . . ." There she stopped short and covered her mouth with her hand. She then heaved a long sigh and walked away.

After having moaned awhile and then seen that Black Jade had gone away to avoid him, Pao-yü felt listless. He shook off the earth from his clothes, got up, and took the same way down the hill to go back to the Peony Court. By chance he saw Black Jade in front of him and immediately he hastened toward her and said: "Please stop for a minute. I know you won't look at me, but I'll just say one sentence and then leave you alone."

Turning around, Black Jade saw it was Pao-yü. She was about to disregard him when she heard him say "just one sentence"; so she replied: "Well, go ahead!"

Pao-yü laughed, saying: "Would you still listen to me if I said two sentences?"

Hearing this, Black Jade turned away. Pao-yü sighed behind her and said: "If we had known this we shouldn't have behaved as we did in the past."

When Black Jade heard these words she could not help stopping and turning around. "What happened in the past," she inquired, "and what has happened now?"

"Well! When you first came to our house," Pao-yü said, "who else but me would play with you so that we had fun together? Whatever I loved I gave you if you so desired; whatever I liked to eat, when I heard that you too liked it, I would put away neatly to keep for you when you came back. We ate at the same table and rested on the same couch. Things which the maids failed to think about and prepare for you, for fear you would be displeased, I would do in the maids' place. Cousins who have grown up together since childhood, I thought, would always be nice to each other, no matter whether they had been intimate or not; only then they would draw closer together than the rest. Who would have thought that after you have grown up and matured, you would not even deign to take a look at me—for three days paying no attention to me and for four days refusing to see me? On the other hand, you take to your bosom such remote relatives as Sister Precious Clasp and Sister Phoenix. I have no young brother or sister of my own. The two I have, you know of course, are not by the same mother as mine. I am an only child like you and I supposed your heart would be like mine. Who would have thought that I have gnawed my heart in vain and there is no one to whom I could utter my grievances?" As he spoke these words, he unconsciously fell into crying.

At that moment Black Jade, who had been listening to him and seen with her own eyes how things were, could not but feel afflicted, and she too shed tears, lowering her head without speaking one word.

Surveying the situation, Pao-yü continued, "I know I have been wrong. But even if that were not so, I would never dare do anything bad to you—moreover, if I have been wrong once or twice, you could either instruct me, warn me, or scold and beat me, and I would not feel so disheartened. But you simply ignore me completely and leave me bewildered and spiritless, not knowing what to do! If I should die, I'd be a wronged ghost and no Buddhist monks or Taoist priests of the highest order would be able to say penance enough for me to help me gain reincarnation. You would have to explain all the cause and effect before I could be reborn again!"

Hearing these words, Black Jade forgot right away the episode of the night before, banishing it beyond the clouds of the ninth heavens.   (Chapter 28)[17]

It was at this point that Black Jade learned that the door had been closed in her face by some indolent and garrulous maid without the young master's knowledge, and peace was made between the pair of young lovers.*

This kind of idyllic life in the Garden of Grand View was occasionally disturbed by outside events and visitors, thus providing excitement and fun for its inmates. One such visitor was Liu Lao-lao (Old Dame Liu), a poor relative from the country. Dazed by the glittering wealth of the Chia family and incited by the mischief-loving Phoenix (Pao-yü's cousin's wife) and Mandarin Duck (Matriarch's maidservant), she committed one blunder after another during her visit, leaving behind her memories of hilarious episodes. The purpose of the visit was to present to the Chia family such fresh country produce as dates, melons, and vegetables in exchange for, hopefully, some substantial gift from her rich relatives. This country cousin was lucky enough to have the honor of being presented to the Matriarch. Upon entering the room, though dazzled by the many flowerlike, jewel-bedecked young women present, she was able to guess that the old lady who was reclining on a divan with a beautiful silk-dressed maid massaging her legs must be the Matriarch. The latter took a fancy to the visitor for her country manners and big stories, and invited her the next day to a feast at the Garden of Grand View. Tagging along in the Matriarch's retinue of lovely granddaughters and maidservants, Old Dame Liu took a grand tour of the garden. At dinner time she was given a seat at a side table next to the Matriarch's.

As soon as Old Dame Liu was seated, she picked up the chopsticks which were uncannily heavy and hard to manage. It was because Phoenix and Mandarin Duck had previously plotted to give her a pair of old-fashioned, angular-shaped ivory chopsticks gilded with gold. Looking at them, Old Dame Liu remarked: "These fork-like things are even heavier than our iron prongs. How can one hold

---

* Pao-yü was thirteen in that year; Black Jade, twelve; and Precious Clasp, fifteen. Pao-yü had been only seven or eight and Black Jade probably six, when she came to live with the Chia family. See Chou Ju-ch'ang, *Hung-lou meng hsin-cheng* (*New Evidences Concerning the "Dream of the Red Chamber"*), (Shanghai, 1953), pp. 173–4; 183–4.

them up?" Everyone laughed. By this time a woman servant had brought in a tiny food box and, as she stood there, another maid came forward to lift the lid. Inside were two bowls of food. Li Huan (Pao-yü's elder brother's widow) took one bowl and placed it on the Matriarch's table as Phoenix picked up a bowl of pigeon eggs to place it on Old Dame Liu's table.

Just as the Matriarch had finished saying, "Please eat," Old Dame Liu rose from her seat and said aloud:

> Old Liu, Old Liu, her appetite as big as a cow!
> She eats like an old sow without lifting her head.

Having said her piece, with her cheeks puffed out she looked straight ahead without uttering another word. At first, all those present were astonished, but upon a moment's reflection, all burst out laughing at the same time. Unable to restrain herself, River Cloud (Matriarch's grandniece) spluttered out a mouthful of tea; Black Jade was choked with laughter and leaning on the table, could only cry and groan, "Ai-ya!" Pao-yü rolled down into the Matriarch's lap; joyously she hugged him and cried out, "Oh, my heart! my liver!" Madame Wang (Pao-yü's mother) also laughed, then pointed her finger at Phoenix, but could not utter one word. Aunt Hsüeh (Precious Clasp's mother), unable to control herself, spurted out her mouthful of tea on the skirt of Quest Spring (she and the other "Spring" girls were all Pao-yü's cousins and sisters), whose teacup fell on the body of Greeting Spring. Compassion Spring left her seat and pulling the wet nurse to her, asked her to rub her belly. None among the servants did not twist her waist or bend her back as they giggled. Some slipped out to have a good laugh while squatting down and others, having stopped laughing by now, came forward to change the dresses for the girls. Only Phoenix and Mandarin Duck controlled themselves and kept urging Old Dame Liu to eat.

Old Dame Liu lifted up the chopsticks but they were hardly manageable. Looking at the bowl in front of her, she remarked: "Well, well, even your hens are smarter than ours! They lay such tiny delicate eggs, very dainty indeed. Let me try one!" All the people had just stopped laughing but they burst out again upon hearing these words. The Matriarch laughed so much that tears dropped down; she just couldn't stop them and Amber (Matriarch's maidservant) had to pound her back to relieve her. The Matriarch said: "This must have been the work of that sly, impish Phoenix. Don't listen to her."

Old Dame Liu was still exclaiming about how tiny and dainty the eggs were when Phoenix said jocularly to her: "They cost an ounce of silver apiece. You had better hurry up and taste one before they get cold." Old Dame Liu then stretched out her chopsticks to seize the eggs with both ends, but how could she pick them up? After having chased them all over the bowl, she finally captured one with no little effort and was about to crane her neck to eat it when lo! it slipped off and fell on the floor. She was going to pick it up herself when a woman servant got it and took it out. Old Dame Liu sighed: "An ounce of silver! How it disappears without even making a noise!" (Chapter 40)[18]

In the course of the narrative, as Pao-yü grew up he was faced with two important events in his life: marriage and participation in the literary examination, both of which he resisted as long as he could. Gradually, conflict grew between him and his family, mainly because of his failure in serious studies and his morbid love for the fragile, ailing Black Jade, who had been pining away with consumption. His mind became deranged. The climax came when, hoodwinked by his family, he was led into marrying Precious Clasp, believing her to be Black Jade, as the real Black Jade was breathing her last in her deserted cottage. Her death was followed by a number of other catastrophes: more deaths in the family, Pao-yü's disappearance following his success in the examination, and the general breakdown of the once great and noble Chia clan. The tragedy was only slightly relieved in the end by the news of the restoration of the family fortune and of Precious Clasp's bearing a son by Pao-yü to continue the family line.

The last glimpse the readers have of Pao-yü is illusory but illustrative of the religious import of the novel. Chia Cheng, his father, was on his way home from Nanking, where he had buried the Matriarch in her family cemetery, when the following episode occurred:

> One day he arrived at the P'i-ling post station, with the weather turning cold and snow falling. The boat was moored at a secluded nook on the river. Chia Cheng had sent his servants ashore to present to friends his visiting cards, explaining that he had to decline with thanks their invitation—he would not consider troubling them as he was so soon to set sail. Only a page was left on the boat to attend him. He then set himself to composing a letter home, which he intended to dispatch with a servant by the faster land route. He laid down his pen when he came to Pao-yü's disappearance. As he looked up, suddenly he saw on the bow of his boat someone dimly silhouetted in the bright snow. The person was baldheaded and barefooted, his body wrapped in a flaming red cape of monkey-hair wool. He was kneeling down and kowtowing to Chia Cheng, who, however, failed to recognize him. Chia Chen hurried out of the cabin but before he could get hold of the man to find out who he was, the latter had kowtowed four times and stood up to greet him. Chia Cheng was about to bow back when he looked up and found himself face to face with Pao-yü! Chia Cheng was startled and asked hastily: "Is it you Pao-yü?" The man did not speak; he seemed both happy and sorrowful at the same time. "If you are Pao-yü,"

> Chia Cheng asked again, "how is it that you are dressed like that?"
>
> Before Pao-yü was able to answer, there appeared on the prow two other persons: a Buddhist monk and a Taoist priest. They closed in on Pao-yü, one on each side of him, and said: "Your worldly duties have now been completed! Why don't you hurry away?" While speaking, the three went up the river bank as if wafted by the wind, and walked away. Heedless of the slippery ground, Chia Cheng rushed after them, but the three men were far ahead of him and he couldn't catch up with them.   (Chapter 120)[19]

Ts'ao Hsüeh-ch'in's achievements in the novel are phenomenal but not beyond understanding. He accomplished what others had aspired to do, that is, to present faithfully, realistically, and graphically the picture of a typical upper-class Chinese family. His task was made much easier because the fictitious Chia[20] family was the Ts'ao family itself, in which Hsüeh-ch'in was brought up. As he had enjoyed the wealth and pomp of its heyday, so he witnessed bitterly its decline and ruin. It was caused not so much by the hostility of outward forces, although they had been building up against the family, as by its inner tension and corrosion, signs of which Ts'ao Hsüeh-ch'in must himself have detected during his younger days. It may even be possible to stretch the comparison further by identifying Pao-yü's character with the author's and to view Pao-yü's youthful escapades and penchants as those of Ts'ao Hsüeh-ch'in—such as his antitraditionalism and detestation of official life—though here a line must be drawn between what Goethe, Ts'ao's younger German contemporary, has called *Dichtung und Wahrheit*. It should be remembered that the *Dream of the Red Chamber* is after all a fiction and that to read into it too much of Ts'ao's life and thought or to exaggerate this autobiographical aspect of the novel would be to deny the artistic freedom and imagination of the author.

As indicated before, the *Dream of the Red Chamber* climaxes a long, realistic tradition in Chinese storytelling. It is not only a silhouette of life, but seems very close to life itself. All sorts of things happen in the novel; a motley group of characters pass in and out of it as occurs in this life; in it are ranged many kinds of emotions from the joys of love to the pangs of death—emotions that are sometimes intense and heightened, sometimes distracting and wayward. This point is made clear by the author himself in what is tantamount to a manifesto of realism in fiction. After having criticized the conventional novels of the past, Ts'ao Hsüeh-ch'in set forth in the beginning of this novel his own purpose and method of writing:

> It seems much better to record the several maidens whom I have seen and heard about personally in the first half of my life. Although

I dare not presume that they are more true to life than the others of the past, yet their deeds and actions would help dissipate the reader's grief and relieve him of boredom. The few doggerel verses in the book could also serve to provoke laughter during mealtime or over a cup of wine. As for the stories of separation and reunion, the emotions of sorrow and joy, the prosperity and decline of family fortune, the numerous occasions and varying circumstances—they are all set forth here in accordance with their cause and effect without my presuming to introduce even slightly any extraneous matter to make them lose reality. (Chapter 1)[21]

Thus, like most Chinese novelists, Ts'ao Hsüeh-ch'in made no effort to build up a plot for plot's sake, but simply wove the variegated threads of life—the trivial and commonplace as well as the spectacular and significant —into a colorful tapestry of supreme artistry and beauty.

An offshoot of the realistic novel is the satirical novel, which, however, is so important that it should be considered as another major type of Chinese fiction. The differences between the two are mainly in aim and emphasis rather than in content, technique, or style. Even their objectives are somewhat similar; thus in a realistic description of the unsavory aspects of domestic and social life, the satire is implied and always present. The satirical novel, however, differs from the realistic in that its assault on the evils of society is much more pronounced and intensive. Its best representative, The *Informal History of the Literati* (translated into English as *The Scholars*),[22] was written probably a few years earlier than the *Dream of the Red Chamber*. It ranks with the others mentioned in this chapter as one of the four great novels of the Ming-Ch'ing period. Space, however, permits only a brief mention of this unique work.

Written by Wu Ching-tzu (1701–1754), himself a member of the intelligentsia, the novel is an unmasking of the shameless behavior of the sham scholars of his time. The author's darts fall especially on the literary snobs, who are parasites of the rich and powerful. The objects of his satire are dual personalities, fawning before their superiors but arrogant in their dealings with those socially inferior. Each puts forth a false front of dignity and righteousness while in fact he is mean and vile. This attack on the literary pretenders is also an attack on officialdom and the examination system, as most of the scholars become officials after passing the examinations. Having thus raised themselves from poverty and obscurity, they display an utter disregard for official decency and, in spite of their professions of Confucian virtue, indulge in the age-old vices of Chinese bureaucracy such as nepotism, graft, and corruption. It should be noted, however, that there are also in the novel a number of good and honest scholars who stand out from the charlatans.

Wu's novel is an exposure of human weakness in general, hypocrisy being its chief target. While the scholars are typical hypocrites, they are equally representative of other follies and foibles. In a delightfully exaggerated and caustic manner is described the deathbed scene of Scholar Yen, a rich but parsimonious man, who purchased his degree by contributing a large sum of money to the Imperial Treasury—a common practice in those days. Scholar Yen had been seriously ill and speechless for three days. Just before his death, the sickroom was crowded with relatives and servants. On a table burned a wick-lighted oil lamp. The dying man was about to breathe his last when he stretched out his hand from the bed sheets and pointed feebly with his two fingers. The meaning of his gesticulation was incomprehensible to those present:

> His nephews and servants all came forward to question him noisily. Some thought it signified two persons; others, two things; still others, two pieces of land. To all these wild conjectures he would simply shake his head to indicate a negative answer. Finally his wife, née Chao, having pushed the crowd apart, went up to him and said: "Dear, I am the only one here who understands your mind. You are upset because it wastes oil to burn two wicks together in the lamp. That's easy! I'll just pick away one of the wicks." After having said this, she went immediately to remove the extra wick. While everyone was looking toward him, Scholar Yen nodded his head, let fall his hand, and immediately gave out his last breath. The whole family began to wail loudly with wide open mouths, and preparations were made to dress him for the funeral, after which they placed the coffin in the central hall of the third courtyard.
>
> (Chapter 6)[23]

Popular as it is, the *Informal History of the Literati* suffers from a basic weakness of the Chinese satirical novel, the lack of organic structure. If other Chinese novelists influenced by the storytelling tradition had a tendency to ramble on in a loose manner, they made at least an attempt to introduce a semblance of unity in their plots. On the other hand, that which strings together the various disconnected episodes in this novel is no more than its central theme mentioned above. The links between the episodes are so weak and ineffectual that the book might as well be divided into a number of separate stories like Thackeray's *Book of Snobs*. The same characteristic is also noticeable in the other satirical novels that flourished toward the end of the Ch'ing period. The appearance of the novel in the form of a travelogue[24] or in serial publications has further impaired the Chinese concept of the structure of fiction. It was not until the introduction of the Western novel in the twentieth century that Chinese writers became aware of the importance of plot-construction and began to learn this art from the literature of the West.

17 : Dramas of the Literati and the People

Chinese drama staged a noticeable comeback in the Ming dynasty with a new form and structure radically different from those of the Yüan. But while dramatic activities continued during the Ming and Ch'ing periods, drama lost its intimate contact with the audience, particularly the common people, and tended to become a type of studio play for a few connoisseurs of *ch'ü* poetry rather than a stage presentation for popular entertainment. This divorce of the drama from the public theater resulted in the rise of playwrights who were interested more in the poetic than the dramatic quality of their works. Little attempt was made to invent new plots or to deal with contemporary events and stories of social import. Instead, the new playwrights concentrated on the portrayal of historical and literary episodes, and in many cases they simply adapted the Yüan plays.

While a great variety of plays were written during the Ming period, differing greatly in length, style and music, the most important type to dominate the dramatic world was the Southern drama, known as *ch'uan-ch'i*.[1] A typical Southern drama is immensely long with an average of forty or more scenes; the songs are chanted by several characters in the play, alternate solo and chorus singing being commonly practiced; instead of the lute used in the Northern drama, the bamboo flute is the chief musical instrument; the language used for the sung and spoken parts is that of the Yangtze region, where the Wu or Soochow dialect becomes later the standard dramatic language.

The prevalence of the Southern drama, however, does not mean the disappearance of the Northern drama, which continued to be cultivated by writers, though sometimes in a modified and adulterated form. An interesting development is the emergence of a type of short play, sometimes in only one scene, in striking contrast with the long *ch'uan-ch'i* drama. A writer often tried both types primarily as a literary tour de force. All in all, this was a period of experimentation in dramatic forms but also of conformity in dramatic language and poetic style, which tended to be ornate and artificial.

Presumably a local product of a crude nature, the Southern drama (see Chapter Eleven) had an origin as old as its Northern counterpart. During the Yüan period it was overshadowed by the brilliance of the Northern drama but it emerged as an important rival of the latter in the early years of the Ming dynasty (second half of the fourteenth century), when the South assumed a greater share of development politically, economically, and culturally. Among the Southern plays of the early period, the most famous is the *Lute Song*, a drama of forty-two scenes, by Kao Ming.[2] Little is known of the author beyond the fact that he was an official-scholar who had obtained the degree of Advanced Scholar in 1345 and who later led a secluded life in the intervening years of war between the Yüan and Ming. His play won high praise from nobility and commoners alike. "The Confucian classics are like the five grains," said the first Ming emperor, "whereas Kao Ming's *Lute Song* is a rare delicacy which no rich and noble family could afford to go without." This encomium from the emperor did not, of course, prevent the play from being enjoyed by the common people as well.

Critics today tend to believe that Kao Ming's *Lute Song* may have been an adaptation of some earlier work by a professional playwright. The story of Ts'ai Po-chieh (Ts'ai Yung) and his wife Chao Wu-niang had been widely known in the folk literature of the Sung-Yüan period. But whereas Ts'ai Po-chieh appeared in popular tales as an ungrateful fellow who deserted his parents and wife, the scholar-hero of the *Lute Song* achieved "complete loyalty and filial piety," as told in the following song in the opening scene of the play:

> The daughter of Chao, a woman of beauty,
> And Ts'ai Yung, an accomplished scholar,
> Had been husband and wife for barely two months
> When the yellow placard from the imperial court
> Everywhere summoned men of worth.
> At his father's behest he went
> Against his will to the spring examination.
> He came out first at the head of the Academy
> And married again, a girl from the Niu family.
> Tied down by fame and wealth he failed to return.
> In a year of drought and dearth
> Died both his father and mother.
> Sad indeed was the occasion!
>
> Sad indeed
> For the daughter of Chao the burden to bear!
> She cut her sweet cloud-like tresses as an offering to her parents-
> in-law.

Carrying the earth wrapped in her mourning dress,
She erected a tomb for their repose.
With the lute to depict her sorrows,
She went straight to the capital.
Filial was Po-chieh,
Virtuous, the Niu woman;
Most grievous was the meeting in his study.
They went to live in a hut near his parents' graveyard,
The man and his two wives,
His paternal dwelling now decorated with insignia by a royal decree.[3]

The moralizing intent of Kao Ming's play is very pronounced. By changing the denouement of the story and the character of Ts'ai Yung as found in popular literature, Kao Ming produced a tragi-comedy of "loyalty and filial piety," featuring a praiseworthy scholar who after a period of deviation from the righteous path because of the allurement of wealth and fame returned finally to the Confucian fold by accepting his first wife of humble origin on an equal status with his second wife, the daughter of a prime minister. This faithfulness to his first wife is matched by his filial act of observing the rites of three years' mourning in a thatched hut beside the paternal graveyard. Such Confucian morality, though extolled by Chinese critics of the past, can win little sympathy from modern readers, least of all from Westerners brought up under a different social system and ethical code.

There are, however, elements of great appeal in this play. Its dialogue and songs are written in a language which matches that of the best Yüan plays in simplicity and beauty. Also like the Yüan drama it has a well-knit plot which holds together fairly well in spite of its great length. Its fine descriptions and memorable scenes have charmed generations of Chinese. While critics may take exception to the all-perfect character of Chao Wu-niang, a paragon of female virtue, she has a great deal of attraction, and some of the most poignant moments in her life are depicted in poetry of enduring beauty. Often quoted is the following song, sung at the time of great distress when she was forced to eat husks so that the limited supply of rice which she had obtained with great difficulty could be served her aged parents-in-law:

Wildly, wildly chaotic is this unbountiful year.
Far, far away is my husband who returns not;
Much, much distressed and impatient are my parents-in-law;
Weak, weakly timid and helpless is my own lonely self.
All my clothes are pawned away,
Not a thread of silk hanging on my body.
Several times I have wanted to sell myself,

But who would care for my husband's parents without the family
    head?
        (Chorus)

When I think about it,
How futile, futilely flitting is our hapless fate,
Difficult to endure!
Real, real indeed are life's dangers and calamities!

Drip, drip down the endless teardrops,
Badly, badly tangled are the threads of sorrow hard to untie;
Bony, bony like a skeleton is this ailing body hard to prop up.
Quivering, quivering with fear are my days and years hard
    to bear!
I would gladly not eat this chaff
But how could I stand this hunger?
If I should eat it,
How could it be swallowed?
Considering all this (oh, bitter!),
Better it would be for me to die first,
So that I would not know the death of my husband's parents.
        (Chorus as in first stanza)

This morning I prepared some rice for my parents-in-law. Not
that I did not want to buy fish and vegetables for them, but I had no
money. Who would have expected that my mother-in-law should
have complained so bitterly about it, suspecting that I had got
something good behind their back? They do not know that what I
have been eating are nothing but chaff and husks. I have to avoid
them since I dare not let them see what I eat. I won't tell them even
if they should complain and blame me to death. Oh, bitter indeed!
How can one swallow these husks? (*Acting as if eating.*)

So much have I sputtered that it hurts my stomach!
My tears fall fast;
My throat is still choked tight. (You, husks!)
You are hulled and pounded,
Winnowed in a sieve, fanned by the wind,
Suffering from endless handling.
You are just like myself, helpless and distressed;
A thousand hardships we have both experienced.
The bitter person eating the bitter fare,
The two bitter ones have met.
Oh, I simply couldn't swallow it!
        (Acting as if eating and spitting)

Chaff and rice,
You were at first mutually dependent;
Who has winnowed you that you fly apart?

One worthless and the other precious,
Like myself and my husband,
Without ever a chance to meet again.
                    (Husband, you are the rice)

But the rice has gone away and is nowhere to be found;
                    (I am just the chaff)

How could human hunger be satisfied with husks?
Now that my husband is away,
What delicious food can I serve my parents-in-law?
                    [*Scene 20*]

Many other songs of considerable beauty are scattered throughout the play. They are mostly sung by Chao Wu-niang in such moments of great emotion as at the death of her parents-in-law, the sale of her hair to raise money for their funeral expenses, the carrying of heaps of earth in her hempen skirt to build their graveyard, her begging and singing with the lute on her way to the capital in search of her husband, and their final reunion in the study of Ts'ai Po-chieh's official residence. Also deeply moving are the following stanzas about her attempt to draw the likeness of her parents-in-law, which she would set up every time she sacrificed to them:

Ever since their death,
I have wanted to visit them, but could not,
Except for a flitting moment of reunion in a dream.
I have tried to draw their likeness, but I could not.
Imagining them dimly in my mind
Has made me shed tears before drawing.
Depict I could not their embittered hearts;
Draw I could not their famished looks;
Portray I could not their wide-open eyes looking for their son.
I could only portray their hair fluttering and soughing,
And their clothes ragged and dirty.
                    (Oh, woe; oh, woe!)

Should I portray them in their best appearance,
They would not look like my parents-in-law at all!

I would like to portray their faces chubby,
But they were famished and thin;
I would like to portray their faces open and broad,
Yet their brows had long been furrowed.
Indeed they would appear ungainly in my drawing,
And that would add to the heaviness of my heart.
I could not picture them as having happy looks and smiling
        faces. (It is not that I don't know how to draw nice pictures,
                but since I went to their house after marriage)

251

Only for the first two months were they care-free,
And for the rest were all sorrowful.

> (Those two months of their happy life
> I have long forgotten. In the last three
> or four years)

I remember only their decaying forms and wilted looks.

> (Their likeness)

Even if their son should keep it,
He would not recognize them as his parents of former
    years.   (Oh, woe; oh, woe!)

But though they cannot be recognized as my husband's
    former parents,
Recognized they must be as my parents-in-law lately deceased.
              [*Scene 28*]

Such fine poetry is rare in the Ming drama, which after the *Lute Song*, does not seem to have made much progress until the rise of the K'un-ch'ü, or K'un-shan Drama, in the sixteenth century. The K'un-ch'ü is a type of Southern drama whose songs were sung to the airs or tunes of the Wu (Soochow) district, where the musician Wei Liang-fu lived and worked to refine the crude music of the native drama. Through his effort the K'un-ch'ü was brought to great perfection and eventual national eminence. Soon afterwards, other Wu musicians and playwrights began to compose songs in the musical patterns set by him. The new kinds of melody took the nation by storm, and in the span of fifty to sixty years, the K'un-ch'ü not only superseded all the other local tunes of the South, of which there were many,[4] but also encroached upon the domain of the *tsa-chü* drama in the North. While the latter continued to be written in the Ming-Ch'ing period, it was mainly as a poetic exercise without much relevance to the theater. Shortly after 1600, the national stage was taken over by the K'un-ch'ü, whose popularity continued for another two hundred years, attaining the height of its development in the seventeenth century.

As a form of Southern drama, the K'un-ch'ü follows in the main the dramatic traditions set by Kao Ming in the *Lute Song*. The difference, if any, lies in the greater harmony between words and melody in the K'un-ch'ü, its elaborate and standardized music scores, and the exclusive use of the Soochow dialect, noted for its sweet, liquid sounds in the singing of the dramatic songs. The language of these songs remains essentially literary. Occasionally some local expressions may find their way into the plays, but they are no more frequent than the Mongol expressions in the Yüan drama. Just as in the Yüan period the Southerners in Hangchow and Soochow became the followers of the Northern drama, so were the Northerners at this time the patrons and admirers of the K'un drama.

Unlike their fellow dramatists in the Yüan period, most K'un-ch'ü writers were prominent literary figures and officials whose biographies appeared in the Ming-Ch'ing dynastic histories.

For these men the desire for fame, not profit, provided the incentive for playwriting. More an intellectual pastime than a professional occupation, the drama was written to convey the author's sentiments, to display his poetic talents, and to win the admiration of his friends, who were at the same time his audience and critics. As a result, some playwrights distinguished themselves as great poets, and others as prosodists and musicians. Least of all were they interested or proficient in the techniques of the theater, the actual staging of their plays, if it ever happened, being left to unknown professionals. Naturally there were exceptional cases of theater men who emerged as playwrights, and of literary writers who managed and directed their own dramatic troupes. Writers of the drama in the Ming period were legion and their production was immense—some twelve hundred titles of Ming plays are known today—but only a few can be mentioned here as representative of the trends noted above.

Probably, the greatest of the Ming dramatists was T'ang Hsien-tsu (1550–1616).[5] The holder of an Advanced Scholar degree (1583), he had an undistinguished and frustrated official career, including a short period of exile in a remote town in southernmost Kwangtung, before his retirement at the age of forty-eight (1598) in his native district, where he spent his remaining years in writing and leading a leisurely scholarly life. Besides a less important earlier work, he wrote four plays known collectively as the "Four Dreams." In this collection, the last two plays exemplify in a Taoist and Buddhist vein the emptiness of fortune and the vicissitudes of life, while the first two are love romances, in one of which, the *Return of the Soul* (or *The Peony Pavilion*), a dream provides an important motive in the plot development. The *Return of the Soul*, generally considered T'ang Hsien-tsu's major work, is the only play for which he invented his own plot, with occasional minor borrowings; all the others are based upon stories from T'ang literary tales.

The plot of the *Return of the Soul*, a long play of fifty-five scenes, revolves round the love story of Liu Meng-mei (Willow Dreaming Plum), a young student, and Tu Li-niang, the daughter of a high official in Nan-an in southern Kiangsi. In a visit to the family garden at the back of the official residence, Tu Li-niang fell asleep and was accosted in a dream by a young scholar, Liu Meng-mei, with whom she had an affair in the Peony Pavilion. Having awakened from her dream, she became lovesick and unconsoled in her longing, until she finally pined away with a broken heart in the seclusion of her maidenly chamber. But before she died, she had a picture painted of herself which she buried under a stone in the garden, where her remains were later interred beside a plum tree. Shortly afterwards, Governor Tu was transferred to a military post in northern Kiangsu. Before the family's departure, provision was made for sacrifices to her spirit tablet in a shrine in the garden. In the meantime, Liu Meng-mei, on his way from Kwangtung to the imperial examination in Hang-chow, fell ill at Nan-an and was given a resting-place at a summer house in the Tu family garden. The discovery of the girl's portrait led to many hours of longing and fond gazing at her lovely form; his wishes were granted, for one night she appeared to him and they renewed the rela-tionship of the dream. At her bidding, the coffin was opened and there she lay alive, as fresh and beautiful as ever.

The couple then left for Hangchow, where Liu Meng-mei took the examination, but there was a delay in the proclamation of its result due to a national crisis caused by the invasion of northern Kiangsu by a rebel leader in the employ of the Jurchen Tartars. Worried by the news of the war that had spread to her father's district, Tu Li-niang sent her husband to look for him, taking her portrait as an identification. By this time, Gov-ernor Tu had already quelled the rebellion through a ruse. In celebration of the victory, his subordinates gave him a feast in the yamen. This happy event, however, was disturbed by the intrusion of Liu Meng-mei, who claimed to be the honor-guest's son-in-law. Having been told previously of the supposed burglary of his daughter's grave, Governor Tu suspected imposture and foul play. Instead of recognizing Liu as his son-in-law, he had him arrested and sent under escort to Hangchow, where Governor Tu himself had an appointment for an audience with the emperor. Upon arriving at Hangchow, Liu Meng-mei was given a sound whipping in the governor's yamen before he was rescued by an official party in search of the scholar who had come out first in the imperial examination. Finally, in an audience before the throne, Liu Meng-mei proved successfully his claims, with the help of his resurrected wife. The play ends, as usual, with official promotion and family reconciliation and reunion.

Like the *Romance of the Western Chamber*, the *Return of the Soul* is noted for its poetic excellence. Compared with its predecessor, it has a more involved plot and a greater variety of scenes and situations. In addi-tion to the dream motive, its supernatural structure is reinforced by a judgment in Hades, which makes possible the release of Tu Li-niang's soul to this world for a visit to the student, and her resurrection after three years in the grave. Some scenes resound with the alarums of war. An uproar in a schoolroom caused by Ch'un-hsiang, Tu Li-niang's de-lightfully impish maidservant, is matched by the farcical entertainment given the Jurchen envoy by the rebel leader and his colorful wife. Great suspense is aroused during the digging up of the girl's grave, at the time of the student's intrusion into his father-in-law's feast, and his subsequent flogging and rescue. While these and the other episodes give variety and zest to the play, the best scenes are those of intense passion delineating the love of the young couple. Critics are especially enthusiastic in their praise of the author's gift in depicting the tender spring-longings of a fair maiden in scenes such as "Dream Startled" and "Dream Quested," and the feeling of sadly seductive melancholy in "Self-portrait" and "Suffering Death"; in creating an atmosphere of weird ghostly beauty in "Spirit Intercourse" and "Phantom Oath." As an illustration of T'ang Hsien-tsu's renowned poetic style are quoted here the following songs sung by Tu Li-niang—the last song alternately by herself and her maid—during her visit to the garden in quest of the dream:

> Most provoking is the spring hue this year.
> No matter how high or low the painted walls,
> The heart of spring wafts in the air and hangs everywhere.
> (*She trips.* Oh!)

> The reclining sow-thistle clutches at the hem of my skirt,
> So hold the flowers a tender spot in a man's heart.
> (Oh, this winding, flowing stream)

> Wherefore did the Jade Lady retrace her steps to the fountainhead
>   of the Peach Blossoms?[6]
> It was for the sight of waters flowing and flowers floating!
> The Lord of Heaven wastes no money to buy flowers;
> Only in our human heart is the sorrow of writing verses on
>   the red petals. (Oh!)

> How ungrateful it is to waste spring time in its prime!
>   (Maid enters saying, "When coming back
>   after the meal, I discovered the young mis-
>   tress had gone away. I could only follow
>   the path to look for her. Oh, young mis-
>   tress, so you are here!)
> (*Maid sings:*)
> Who would have thought that my fair mistress
> Should stand here by this overhanging, flowering tree?
> The morning meal barely over,
> How could you visit the garden alone without a companion?

> (*Tu Li-niang sings:*)
> In front of the painted balustrade,
> Suddenly, I saw, deep in a nook, the mud-carrying swallows;
> So, casually I moved my steps to this lovely garden.

(*Maid sings:*)
Let us turn back!
For a maiden of the inner chamber to be espied by strangers—
It would be no idle joke at all!   [*Scene 12*]

The poet himself has said in the opening song of the play:

I have consumed broad daylight in heart-rending verses;
In this life the sentiments of love are the hardest to tell.

It is this successful utterance in poetry of the sentiments of love—the subject of Tu Li-niang's quest in life and dream, the cause of her death and resurrection, and the driving force of her married life—that gives beauty and unity to the play. On the other hand the play is interspersed with a number of unrelated episodes that distract attention. Another criticism levelled at T'ang Hsien-tsu has been his disregard of the principles of versification and rhyming in the songs. To this accusation the poet retorted: "I would like to say here that I am the one who should know something about the feeling and import of the *ch'ü* songs. It is true that I often became indolent while composing them and dropped a rhyme or two but it is just as well that people strain their necks (literally *throats*) in singing these songs."

Obviously T'ang Hsien-tsu represented one school of dramatists who stressed lyric sentiments and beauty to the neglect of the metrical requirements of the *ch'ü* songs. His contemporary and rival, Shen Ching (1553–1610), was a leader of the prosodic school of Ming drama. While well known as an expert in prosody, Shen Ching was not a great dramatic poet for he lacked the passion and imagination that make good poetry, however melodious his verse may sound and however correctly he observed the metrical rules. His contribution lies in his treatise on the music patterns of the Southern drama, which has since become a classic on the subject, and to which all later writers have turned for guidance in the composition of their songs.

A third group of dramatists consisted of professional men of the theater who possessed a good knowledge of stagecraft but little poetic talent. Most of them were writers of low social status who wrote for a living. A minor and insignificant group in the world of letters, they served nonetheless as a link between drama and the theater. Few of them, however, emerged from obscurity to renown and only a limited amount of their prodigious output has survived the ravages of time.

Chief among them were two Chu brothers (seventeenth century), one of whom, Chu Ku (better known as Chu Su-ch'en) was the author of the *Dream of the Two Bears*, from which is derived the recently revived K'un-ch'ü, *Fifteen Strings of Cash*. Two bears who appeal to a magistrate in a dream to redress their wrongs are actually two brothers with the surname Hsiung or "bear." The plot of this near tragedy is built upon a coincidence involving the two Hsiung brothers, each accused of murder and the theft of fifteen strings of cash (coins). Rats too play an important part in the story, for one death is actually caused by a man's eating a poisoned cake intended for the rats; and the other death, a murder, is committed by a burglar with the nickname, Liu the Rat. Both stories are based upon earlier sources, one of them being taken from the Sung colloquial story mentioned in Chapter Ten. Chu Ku, however, has ingeniously interwoven the two separate episodes into an organic piece full of swift, exciting action. Its interest never flags even though the plot is rather artificial and coincidental in its reliance upon fortuitous happenings. The work of a professional, nonliterary man, the *Dream of the Two Bears* is a typical folk drama, whose dialogue contains numerous crude and vulgar expressions weighted with dialect words.

Finally, in the dramatic works of Li Yü (1611–1680?) are combined the poetic talents of a literary writer, the musical skill of a virtuoso, and the professional knowledge of a man of the theater. The incidents of his life are as interesting as his qualifications as a dramatist. Having failed in the provincial examination for an advanced degree, he abandoned the prospect of an official career for the life of a roving playwright. To support his large household of concubines and sing-song girls—the latter often becoming his concubines in their turn—he travelled widely to seek the patronage of local mandarins, before whom he presented plays of his own composition performed by the girls of his troupe. His slanderers, and there were many, accused him of having corrupted the morals of youth from rich and noble families by exposing them to the lovely sirens of his household, who acted and entertained at the same time.

At one time he made his home on the West Lake in Hangchow, to which he returned in later years, calling himself "The Old Strawhat Man of the Lake." When he was in Nanking, he built the Mustard Seed Garden, from which were issued the famous manuals on painting, though he himself was not their author. His interest in painting as in drama and music made him a true connoisseur of the beaux arts and of the delights of life, which he expounded in a work entitled *A Temporary Lodge for my Leisure Thoughts* (1671). In the first part of the book is summarized much of his experience in the theater. His discourse on topics such as dramatic structure, plot construction, dialogue, action, style, and versification earned him the distinction of being China's first and only drama critic of note. He was chiefly known as the author of numerous plays and stories, and, ironically, no less for a pornographic novel falsely attributed to him.

Li Yü was the most outstanding Chinese writer of well-made plays. He was at his best in the comedy of situation with an intricate plot. His plays such as (1) *The Error of the Kite*, (2) *Female Phoenixes Courting the Male*, (3) *Be Circumspect in Conjugal Relations*, (4) *The Pair-eyed Fish*, (5) *Ordained by Heaven*, are all love comedies with remarkable story interest and stage effect. They are entertaining, inventive, and boldly original in plot and language, qualities which are rare in an age of literary conformity and imitation. The first is a comedy of errors, in which a young scholar has a love tryst with an ugly girl, instead of the beautiful girl of his desire. The confusion is caused not so much by mistaken identity as by the workings of mischievous fate, which sends his kite with a poetic love missive to the wrong girl, thus giving rise to a series of complications, misunderstandings, and surprises. The courtesan, forgotten in drama since the Yüan period, reappears as a resourceful and charming heroine of the second play, in which she and two other girls contend for the hand of the same man and, after many intrigues and quarrels fanned by jealousy, are reconciled to serving him harmoniously together. In the third play, the leading role is played by two courtesans, whose relationships with two scholars, one faithful and the other fickle, change with the vagaries of fortune but end happily in marriage, each with her own lover. For any woman on the verge of yielding too easily to man, the moral of the play is "be circumspect." A supernatural element enters the fourth play in the rescue from drowning of a pair of suicidal lovers, who become a pair of flat fishes in the watery domain; later, upon emerging from the water to terra firma, they are changed back into human beings to live happily ever afterwards.

The most successful of Li Yü's comedies is *Ordained by Heaven*, which combines in a well-constructed and fast-moving plot all the elements of humor, irony, pathos, and fantasy. The dramatic action centers upon the disastrous efforts of Ch'üeh Su-feng, a rich, generous, but horribly ugly man, to get a wife. On the night of their wedding, his bride was so upset and disgusted at the sight of him—one has to remember that in China marriage could be arranged by the go-between without the couple's ever setting eyes on each other—that she fled to his study; there she locked herself in and cut off her hair, as well as her marital ties with him, taking vows to become a nun. The second marriage fared just as badly. The distracted woman, having no place to hide, repulsed the ugly husband by becoming tipsy, and later repaired to the study to join the first wife in religious devotion. His third attempt ended in the suicide of his would-be bride. When his fourth wife threatened to take the same course, he relented and allowed her to share the fate of his first two wives. To commemorate their self-imposed widowhood, the three women raised in their sanctuary a plaque bearing the words "Ordained by Heaven" as a consolation for their unhappy lot, attributing it all to the will of Heaven.

Then the story shifts to the subplot of a war between the government army and rebel forces, the latter consisting of a troop of male warriors and another of female warriors. The male rebels collapsed under the assault of the government soldiers, but the Amazons proved to be more than a match for the imperial army, and many handsome young soldiers became their captives. At this juncture, Ch'üeh Su-feng sent his servant to the battlefront with an offering of large quantities of rice for the starved soldiers who, thus encouraged to renew the fight, ultimately won the war. For his meritorious deed, Ch'üeh Su-feng was ennobled by the emperor. One day as he was washing himself preparatory to the ceremony of receiving the imperial edict, he was suddenly transformed through divine grace into a handsome man, and the three women, casting aside their devotion to religion, began to compete for his affection and a high status in his household.

Li Yü's aim in writing is neither edification nor the expression of personal sentiments and ideas, but entertainment pure and simple. Herein lie his weakness and his strength. His songs do not possess such loftiness of poetic imagination as those of T'ang Hsien-tsu and the others, but he surpasses them in the skillful handling of plot, characterization, and dialogue. A master craftsman, he disdained to borrow from the hackneyed historical and literary sources, and created instead original plots concerned with the lives and incidents of the common people; he delighted in extricating his characters from the predicaments and ludicrous situations in which they were placed. Like Kuan Han-ch'ing of the Yüan period, he was a skilled painter of female characters. As the plays were written for his company of singing girls, it is natural that he should have created for them some immortal roles. Unfortunately, in spite of his significant contributions, the lessons Li Yü taught in both theory and example went unheeded. His plays were looked at askance by the men of letters, and they made little lasting impression on the men of the theater; thus dramatic dialogue, which he had developed to a high degree of sophistication, relapsed once again to its former crude and stereotyped form.

By the time of Li Yü's death, the dramatic movement of the Ming-Ch'ing period had practically spent its force. Mention, however, should be made of two notable achievements that took place before the demise of the K'un drama. The *Palace of Long Life*[7] by Hung Sheng (1646?–1704) and the *Peach Blossom Fan* by K'ung Shang-jen (1648–1718) were both written in the tradition of Chinese poetic drama. The eternal love of the Brilliant Emperor of T'ang and his concubine Lady Yang, a popular but much jaded subject, flames anew in the sweet lyrics of Hung

Sheng's drama, while K'ung Shang-jen presents in a moving historical play a series of tragic episodes from the last years of the Ming dynasty, linked together by the undying love affair of a patriotic scholar and a talented and virtuous courtesan. Although highly acclaimed as two of the best plays of the seventeenth century[8] they were the products of amateurs who happened to have tried their hands at writing drama. While important as landmarks in the history of the Chinese theater, they contributed little to its progress.

In the next century, K'un-ch'ü continued to attract the attention of literary writers and theatrical companies. It also received the patronage of the Manchu emperors, whose dramatic taste was aped by high officials and rich families. But as a form of literature it had reached the end of its development; the bulk of Ch'ing drama was cultivated by lesser talents and consisted of plays to be read rather than acted. This decline came to a head toward the end of the century, and the brilliant performance by a troupe of the best K'un-ch'ü actors before Emperor Ch'ien-lung during his visit to the South in 1784 was but an afterglow that did not last long. The ravaging of Nanking and Soochow by the T'ai-p'ing rebels in the mid-nineteenth century dealt the K'un-ch'ü a final blow from which it never recovered.

The reasons for the fall of the K'un-ch'ü can be enumerated as follows: its local nature as Southern drama; its decline into mere feats of poetic skill; its loss of contact with the people; the inevitable shift of literary taste; and finally, the loss of its economic and cultural base during the T'ai-p'ing Rebellion. One is surprised not so much at its fall after so many years of popularity as at the tenacity and resilience with which it has held the stage, and the continuous fascination it has exerted on Chinese writers, many of whose best plays have been written in this form. Its decline since the early nineteenth century coincided with the rise of the Ching-hsi or Peking theater, which is still popular today.

The Peking theater emerged about a century and a half ago as a reaction against the domination of a local drama that catered only to the interests of the wealthy class. It is essentially a popular theater—by no stretch of imagination can it be called classical—that appeals to an urban audience with a rigid histrionic criterion. Thus, though the plays performed in the Peking theater are mostly imitations and adaptations, the art of acting, including dancing, gesticulating, singing, and elocution, has been perfected in the course of its development. Stage music, which is an integral part of the performance, accompanies the songs and dances in the play; therefore the Peking theater can also properly be called the Peking opera. Instead of great playwrights, it has produced some great actors and singers, whose fame has vied with that of the writers.

While various local dramas had long been current in Peking alongside the prevalent K'un-ch'ü, the beginning of the Peking theater dated from 1790, with the appearance in the capital of several theatrical troupes from Anhwei, presumably to participate in the anniversary celebration of Emperor Ch'ien-lung's eightieth birthday. Noted for their singing of local tunes from Anhwei and Hupeh, these actors mastered at the same time other tunes that were popular in the Peking playhouse, especially those of the Northwest from Kansu and Shansi. Through a process of combination and adaptation of the various tunes, was formed the Peking drama that began to dominate the stage in and outside of the national capital by the mid-nineteenth century.

The Peking performers have introduced a new practice: instead of one long play, a typical bill at a Peking theater consists of a number of selections or scenes from several plays. As the stories of these scenes are generally known to the audience, no difficulty is experienced in understanding or appreciating them. At the same time, the success or failure of a theatrical performance depends not so much on the literary quality of the plays as on music, costume, makeup, and most important of all, the skill of the actors in their respective roles as young scholars, coquettish maidens, aged retainers, generals or ministers with painted faces, and clowns with powdered noses. The art of acting, however, has become so specialized and conventionalized that little freedom or invention is allowed the individual actors, except the most famous ones.

As a whole the literary merit of the Peking drama is minimal compared with that of the Yüan and Ming drama. The bulk of this drama is the work of anonymous hacks and actors with some literary pretensions; it consists mostly of adaptations from older plays, popular novels, and other literary writings. Only rarely are original plays written to dramatize current events of popular interest. Of these very few survive, most being done as scripts without benefit of publication. Hence the Peking theater remains practically an oral, acting tradition, and it is only in recent years that stage versions of certain plays have been printed. Based upon them, it is now quite possible to have a reappraisal of the merits of the Peking drama. But whatever the conclusion may be, it is safe to assert that the plays will be judged less as literary masterworks of lasting value than as popular dramatic pieces that have held spellbound generations of theatergoers down to the present time.

18 : Contemporary Experiments and Achievements

The movement in Chinese literature in the last fifty years has often been called a "renaissance." The epithet is not entirely if its purpose is to imply a parallel with the history of post-Middle Ages western literature. Traditional literature is not dead, and the rebirth of literary force in new forms has not been entirely successful. Nevertheless certain likenesses can be seen between the situation of European literature of the fourteenth-to-sixteenth centuries and the Chinese of our own period. A comparison is especially valid between the social and intellectual backgrounds of the two literatures. For one thing, the monarchism and Confucian dogmatism of the feudal past from which modern China has just emerged is comparable to the twin authority of the Crown and the Church in medieval Europe. Characteristic of both periods are zeal and courage to explore the unknown or to experiment with the new. But China's present display of literary vigor is still hard to assess.

There has been a departure but not a complete break from tradition, and the force that gives impetus to the new literature has come from abroad. At first the Chinese were averse to foreign influences, but their fast disintegrating nation was forced to yield to the powerful military machines of Japan and the West in a series of disastrous wars. These developments had the unexpected effect of arousing Chinese interest in, and admiration for, Western accomplishments in literature and philosophy as well as in science and technology. Translations of Western works, in spite of their tongue-twisting foreign names and unfamiliar terms, were devoured avidly by wild-eyed young intellectuals, with the result that by the second quarter of the present century Westernization had become a fashion in China. A unique feature of contemporary Chinese literature is therefore the all-pervasive influence of the West on forms and techniques, on spirit and ideology. Never before in Chinese history, not even in the period of Buddhist influence, have Chinese authors been exposed so much to the penetration of a culture alien to them.

But if the new Chinese writers were schooled in the literary traditions of the West, their works reflect, nonetheless, the social and intellectual ferment of their own country. Chief among the epoch-making events was the May 4th incident in 1919, which lent stimulus to a nascent cultural movement. Primarily a political protest against the feeble diplomatic efforts of the Peking Government in its negotiations vis-à-vis Japan and the Western powers on the Shantung question, the May 4th Movement had ramifications much broader in scope. The political ardor intrinsic in it spread to other spheres, of which not the least important was literature. And what a dismal picture of China the authors drew in their works: a nation prostrate, morally uprooted and politically disjointed, oppressed by a sanguinary warlord government, and humiliated by foreign powers in war and diplomacy! In their desperate search for a panacea for the nation's ills, these writers introduced all sorts of newfangled foreign ideas, including anarchism and nihilism. It was then that a handful of intellectuals began to advocate Communism, which was destined later to engulf the country. Our discussion here, however, will be limited to the non-Communist literature of the modern period.

Closely interrelated with the political upheavals of the time, Chinese literature has undergone a revolution with important repercussions on language and style, on aim and content. The first call to arms was issued by Hu Shih (1891–1962), later hailed as "the Father of the Chinese Renaissance," in what may be regarded as a revolutionist's manifesto, which he entitled "A Modest Proposal for the Reform of Literature" (1917). His ideas relate mainly to the use in literature of the modern spoken language and of a plain and vigorous style to replace a worn-out literary form fraught with obscure allusions, hackneyed phrases, and stilted epithets. "For this reason," wrote Hu Shih, "I advocate the adoption of colloquial expressions and words in writing poetry and prose. It would be much better to use the living words of the twentieth century than the dead words of three thousand years ago, and to write in the language of the widely read *Tale of the Marshes* and *Journey to the West* than the language of the Ch'in, Han, and Six Dynasties period, which is no longer popular or current."[1] In other essays, charged with the emotions of a youthful crusader, Hu Shih denounced traditional Chinese literature as a dead literature and proposed to create over its grave a living literature of the new age.

Fighting the battle of the literary revolution alongside Hu Shih but for a different purpose, Ch'en Tu-hsiu (1879–1942), one of the founders of the Chinese Communist Party, advocated the creation of a new literature of the people to complete the unfinished business of a "tiger-headed but snake-tailed" political revolution. In the essay "On Literary Revolution" (1917), he wrote:

I am willing to risk the enmity of the pedantic scholars of the whole nation by raising aloft the banner of the "Literary Revolutionary Army" for the relief of my friend. On our banner are writ large the aims and tenets of the Revolutionary Army: (1) to establish a simple lyric literature of the people by overthrowing the polite and snobbish literature of the nobility; (2) to establish a new and earnest literature of realism to supplant the stale and exaggerated literature of classicism; (3) to establish a plain and popular social literature in place of the inept, obscurantist, and cryptic literature of the mountain grove.[2]

Some ten years later, the idea of "Revolution versus Literature" (1926) was further expanded and finalized by Kuo Mo-jo (1892–   ), a leading figure at that time of the literary organization, "Creation Society," in the following words:

Young men! Such being the environment and the time in which we live, if your aim is to be a literary writer—it will be different if you are not going to be one—you have to strain forthwith every nerve-string and to catch up with the spirit of the age. I wish each of you to be a revolutionary writer, not a deserter of the age, for your sake and for the sake of all our people. Complete individual freedom is not to be found under the present system. You shouldn't feel that drinking a few cups of wine constitutes the spirit of romanticism or that the writing of some crooked verse makes you a poetic genius. On the other hand, you should strengthen your life and discern the main currents of literature. You should go to the army, among the people, inside the factory, and into the whirlpool of revolution. You should realize the literature we need is a socialistic and realistic literature that sympathizes with the proletarian classes. Our demands have already been made one with the demands of the whole world. We should urge ourselves to advance boldly with all efforts![3]

In the words of these men are shown the three stages in the Chinese literary revolution and the direction it has taken in the last half-century. It may be said that contemporary Chinese literature, with all its experiments and achievements, is the product of this unrest.

Besides being a university administrator, a diplomat and a statesman, Hu Shih was one of the most versatile scholars in modern China, if not also the most gifted. Steeped in the democratic traditions of the West during his college days in the United States, he was the leader of a school of Chinese thinkers who advocated individualism, pragmatism, and liberalism, for which he received scant acceptance from the authoritarian right and incurred the vehement denunciation of the left. As a pioneer of contemporary literature, his contributions lie not so much in his own creative writings, which are of an experimental nature, nor in his literary research, which has been superseded by later efforts, as in the tremendous influence he exerted on modern writers in the broad field of Chinese culture. His keen and vigorous mind ranged widely over all sorts of intellectual projects but never settled for long on a particular one, with the result that he left unfinished some of his major works on Chinese philosophy and literature. He died at the age of seventy-one, a writer of great renown but unfulfilled expectations.

Except, then, for his role as a literary fighter, "dragging his forty-two centimeter cannon" in the vanguard of the literary revolution, Ch'en Tu-hsiu, a polemicist and political thinker, held only an insignificant position in literature.

Though equally versatile and gifted, Kuo Mo-jo differs radically from Hu Shih in his political creed and literary views. He is the author of voluminous poems, essays, stories, and plays in addition to several historical studies of ancient Chinese society based upon the shell-and-bone inscriptions. In none of these, however, can his achievements be said to be outstanding. His scholarship, otherwise brilliant, is marred by preconceived ideas and brash deductions, while his literary works lack the finer qualities of a conscientious artist. A born romanticist turned Marxist, he has been living, it seems, in an artificial atmosphere where his talents are being frittered away in the service of a totalitarian regime.

In the early years of his life, Kuo Mo-jo appeared on the Chinese literary scene as the author of romantic love tales and songs full of riotous imagination and unbridled passion. His first volume of poems, *The Goddesses* (1921), created a sensation with its bold free verse pervaded by a morbid melancholy prevalent at that time. In "A Lament by the Yellow Sea," he compares himself to a drop of clear spring water that has found its way from his native Mount Omei into the turbulent Yellow Sea, where

> The waves are muddy,
> The eddies deep;
> The taste is salty,
> And the smell foul.
> Tempestuous storms rage
> Without a moment of rest;
> The rolling waves, all filthy,
> Have penetrated and stained the depth of my heart.
> At what time
> Could I regain my purity and lustre?[4]

Such personal lamentation forms a striking contrast to the keen social awareness of his later writings as in the following stanzas from the poem "A Manifesto of Poetry":

Look here, I am so plain and naïve,
Without a shred of ornament.
I love the laborers and farmers,
Their feet bare, their bodies naked.

I too bare my feet and body;
I regard with hatred the rich people:
They are beautiful, they love beauty,
Their bodies adorned with silk, perfume, and jade.[5]

In later years, his creative works consist mostly of historical plays, but on the whole he is more of a poet than a dramatist, his plays being meant for reading rather than for stage performance. As a poet, his accomplishments do not go beyond those of a romantic rebel, "blowing his horn on the rim of the globe."

Another leader of contemporary Chinese literature who has made a substantial contribution to the short story is Lu Hsün (1881–1936), an idol of the literary left-wingers. An author of pungent realistic stories, an irascible satirist, a vitriolic critic, Lu Hsün, who never made the grade as a physician, deftly wielded a literary scalpel, killing his enemies without a trace of blood. When teaching in Peking, he started his literary career with "The Diary of a Madman," borrowing its title from the Russian writer Gogol, though otherwise it is original in content and spirit. The fierce indignation with which he stigmatized the man-eating society of his time, couched in the words of the madman, was the first notable example of social protest in China's new literature. With Confucian morals as the target of his attack, the madman wrote in his diary:

> In ancient times, as I recollect, people often ate human beings, but I am rather hazy about it. I tried to look this up, but my history has no chronology, and scrawled all over each page are the words: "Virtue and Morality." Since I could not sleep anyway, I read hard half the night until I began to see words between the lines, the whole book being filled with two words—"Eat people."[6]

To these modern-day cannibals, Lu Hsün's warning through his mouthpiece is explicit and stern:

> You should change, change from the bottom of your heart. You must know that in future there will be no place for man-eaters in the world.
> If you don't change, you may all be eaten by each other. Although so many are born, they will be wiped out by the real men, just like wolves killed by the hunters! Just like insects![7]

The story ends with a fervent prayer: "Perhaps there are still children who have not eaten men? Save the children!"[8]

266

While equally forthright, Lu Hsün's later stories have a greater narrative interest and give a more realistic representation of life, particularly of the villagers in his native Shao-hsing in Chekiang. Without subjecting these folk to pseudo-psychoanalysis, he was able to enliven his description of them with a genial touch of picturesque local color. A happily deceptive objectivity camouflages his sarcasm, which is readily apparent between the lines. In "The True Story of Ah Q" and other stories, he shows great skill in plot construction and character portrayal. In their economy of incident and style, his works approach more closely the short stories of the West. If it is true that a good story entails the compression of a maximum of life into a minimum of space—a Western concept— "The True Story of Ah Q" falls little short of the ideal.

Since his creation by Lu Hsün, Ah Q, a despicable though harmless odd-jobber in Wei-chuang village, has become an emblem of the seamier traditional Chinese national traits: self-delusion, defeatism, submission to force and authority, boldness in browbeating the weak and helpless. Ah Q typically revels in the joys of his moral "victories":

> If the idlers were still not satisfied, but continued to bait him, they would come to blows in the end. Then only after Ah Q—to all appearances defeated—had his brownish pigtail pulled and his head bumped against the wall four or five times, would the idlers walk away, satisfied at having won. Ah Q would stand there for a second, thinking to himself, "It is as if I were beaten by my son. What is the world coming to nowadays? . . ." Thereupon he too would walk away, satisfied at having won.[9]

Then Lu Hsün remarks caustically: "This may be a proof of the moral supremacy of China over the rest of the world."[10]

Thus, looked down upon by his fellow villagers, worsted in fist fights, unemployed and reduced to petty thievery, and cheated of the "rewards" of the revolution, Ah Q was finally executed by a sham "revolutionary" government as a warning to the public for a robbery that he had not committed. As he was taken in a cart to the execution ground, he sang like a gallows bird: "In twenty years I shall be another. . . ." but his last words were drowned by the crowd, shouting and growling like a pack of wolves.

> At that instant his thoughts revolved like a whirlwind. Four years ago, at the foot of a mountain, he had met a hungry wolf which followed him at a distance, wanting to eat him. He nearly died of fright, but luckily he happened to have an axe in his hand, which gave him the courage to get back to Wei-chuang. But he had never forgotten the wolf's eyes, fierce yet cowardly, gleaming like two will-o'-the-wisps, as if they would bore into him from a distance.

Now he saw eyes even more terrible than the wolf's; dull yet penetrating eyes that seemed to have devoured his words and to be still eager to devour something beyond his flesh and blood. And these eyes kept following him at a set distance.

These eyes seemed to have merged in one, biting into his soul.

"Help, help!"

Ah Q, however, never uttered these words. All had turned black before his eyes, there was a buzzing in his ears, and he felt as if his whole body were being scattered like so much light dust.[11]

In addition to the short stories, on which his fame was built, Lu Hsün left behind an enormous bulk of miscellaneous essays, literary studies, polemic writings, letters, reminiscences, and translations. The last were done for obscure East European writers in his effort to promote "the literature of the weak and small nations." Of his scholarly works, the most highly regarded is A *Brief History of Chinese Fiction* (1925),[12] a pioneer study that remains a classic to this day.

His informal essays are voluminous, but most are random thoughts on the topics of the day and controversies of current interest that have long been forgotten. Nevertheless, despite their generally ephemeral nature, Lu Hsün's writings are alive with his personality and his peculiar brand of irony and humor. As an example of this writer's biting satire, the following parable is quoted:

> I dreamed I was walking in a narrow lane, my clothes in rags like a beggar.
>
> A dog started barking behind me.
>
> I looked back contemptuously and shouted at him: "Bah! Shut up! You fawn on the rich and bully the poor!"
>
> He sniggered. "So sorry," he said, "we are not as good as men."
>
> "What!" Quite outraged, I felt that this was the supreme insult.
>
> "I'm ashamed to say I still don't know how to distinguish between silver and copper, between silk and cloth, between officials and common citizens, between masters and their slaves, between. . . ."
>
> I turned and fled.
>
> "Wait a bit! Let us talk some more. . . ." From behind he urged me loudly to stay.
>
> But I ran straight on as fast as I could until I had run right out of my dream and was back in my own bed.[13]

In Lu Hsün's stories, the dog is a favorite target of the assault he levelled at both political and literary foes. He wrote about the Chao family dog, a cannibalistic accomplice in "The Diary of the Madman," and the ferocious fat black dog that guarded the Convent of Quiet Self-Cultivation in "The True Story of Ah Q"; he also lashed at the lap-dogs that bark every time a man in rags walks past, and at the "pack of mangy curs" for their rushing madly about and whining.

While Lu Hsün's contributions are manifold, he is perhaps greatest as a satirist. He himself defines satire as an expression of truth to be pursued with a positive aim and a genuine passion; on the other hand, "simply convincing one's readers that there is nothing good in the world, nothing worth doing, is not satire but cynicism."[14] Indeed, the role of a satirist is a dangerous one, especially in an age when men of letters have openly or secretly turned into "the teeth and talons of the ruler." Then he continues:

> Nobody wants to be the chief target in a literary inquisition, but so long as man is alive and has some breath left, he will want to work off his feelings under the pretext of laughter. Laughter should not offend anyone, and there is still no law against our citizens' pulling long faces. We can take it then that laughter is not illegal.[15]

Lu Hsün, however, objects to "laughter for laughter's sake"; instead, he chooses to aim his satirical barbs at the men and society of his time.

To summarize, Lu Hsün exemplified in his works the concept of literature as a vehicle for social reform. "Therefore I draw my materials," he wrote, "from among the unfortunate people of a sickly society with the aim of revealing the diseases and pains, and of calling attention to their cures."[16] As a critic and reformer, he clashed with radicals and conservatives alike, lashing out right and left at whoever stood in his way. He was a rugged individualist who belonged to no school, but if he had no qualms about castigating the traditionalists, he at least made friends with the revolutionaries, particularly the young writers who flocked to him for advice or in adoration. In 1930 he became the leader of the League of Left Wing Writers, which served at that time as a front organization for Communist writers and propagandists.[17] Lu Hsün's political affiliation was far from clear. It should be noted, however, that until his death in 1936, he lived constantly under the shadow of persecution by the national government, whereas since 1949 he has been hailed by the Communists as their great proponent!

The path that Lu Hsün cut in contemporary Chinese literature was followed by other authors similarly dedicated to the ideals of a realistic, socialist literature. Only a thin line divided them from Communist writers, who first emerged in the late 1920's. This merely shows that given the society and environment which obtained in these years, any aspiring and patriotic writer would inevitably take the same road, whatever his political creed; and that Communism, instead of being a catalytic agent in literature releasing the latent explosive ideas of the writers, was actually a product of the age, incubated and bred in the pregnant minds of a few intellectuals before it grew and prevailed over the masses.

A major victory of the literary revolution was scored by the fiction writers, chief among whom are Mao Tun (1896–   ), Pa Chin (1904–   ), and Lao Shê (1899–   ). Space, however, permits only a brief mention of their works. Mao Tun, the leader of the Literary Research Association—a rival of Kuo Mo-jo's Creation Society—has carved a career somewhat similar to Kuo's in that he veered to the Left in preCommunist days and was for years a leading cultural official of the new regime. A voluminous writer, Mao Tun has concentrated his creative energy on fiction and contributed at least ten novels and several short story collections. In his trilogy, *Eclipse*,[18] comprising *Disillusion, Vacillation*, and *Pursuit*, delineated the emotional and mental agitation of young Chinese intellectuals sucked helplessly into the seething vortex of revolution: (1) ardor and excitement on the eve of the revolution and subsequent disillusion upon its actual arrival; (2) vacillation at the time of the violent, life-and-death struggle; (3) a desperate but futile pursuit of personal happiness.

Instead of the negative and pessimistic attitude in *Eclipse*, Mao Tun took a more direct and affirmative approach in *Midnight*,[19] his most famous novel. It is a vigorous indictment of the newly emerging upper-class society in metropolitan Shanghai, at that time (around 1930) the financial center of the country. The main plot of the novel revolves around the conflict of two hostile groups—industrialists and comprador-financiers on the one hand; factory workers and revolutionaries on the other. The former are represented by two principal characters: Wu Sun-fu, owner of a silk mill empire, and Chao Po-t'ao, a comprador and stock market speculator; they are flanked by a vast array of other business figures, stockbrokers, factory managers, bourgeois intellectuals such as students and professors, professional people like lawyers and physicians, politicians and army officers. The second, opposing group consists of trade union officials and labor movement agitators. Vividly depicted are the scenes of market speculation and financial manipulation, industrial insolvency and rural depression, labor strikes and peasant uprisings, as well as stories of love, sensuous indulgence, and family complications in the households of the two wealthy protagonists. The novel is heavily weighted on the side of the capitalist-comprador group to the neglect of the so-called revolutionary masses. For this reason Mao Tun has been criticized for his lack of familiarity with the working people, his failure to present a penetrating analysis of the revolution, and his incomplete description of its image, "sometimes even to the point of distortion."[20] Such criticism notwithstanding, *Midnight* is a major novel on Shanghai's multifarious financial and industrial activities in a crucial period of its abnormal, erratic growth.

In the short story trilogy, "Spring Silkworms," "Autumn Harvest," and "Ruinous Winter," Mao Tun turned his attention to the luckless members of the rural community. After much toil and anxiety, they reap a bumper crop of silkworm cocoons only to find that the neighboring silk factories have been closed down because of war; then they have a bountiful autumn harvest that merely induces the city merchants to cut drastically the price of rice; as a finale to the trilogy, they stage in the dull but restless winter months a miniature uprising by killing the village's "Security Corps" members who have tortured an innocent lad. "Spring Silkworms," the best story of the three, gives a masterful characterization of several members of a peasant family, including a rebellious young son who neither shares his father's worries "nor believes that one good crop, whether of silk cocoons or of rice, will enable them to wipe out their debt and repossess their own land. He knows they will never 'get out from under' merely by toil and thrift even if they break their backs in hard work."[21]

A forerunner in the literary race of his time, Mao Tun advocates the theory of literature for life's sake. He feels that literature should reflect social problems and conditions. In his descriptions of the gradual spiritual corrosion of the young intellectuals, the unscrupulous manipulations of the bankers and industrialists, and the bleak wintry forlornness of the country people, he is a faithful chronicler of contemporary China. He too seeks to arouse a class consciousness in his readers and to reaffirm his belief in the inevitability of class strife. In support of Lu Hsün's contention that literature is a weapon of social reform, Mao Tun wrote: "Literature is not intended to provide relief for those who suffer from the ennui of life, or self-intoxication for those who attempt to escape from life, but it performs a positive function of stimulating the human mind. Especially in our age, we hope it will aim to shoulder the heavy responsibility of awakening the masses and giving them strength."[22]

Like Mao Tun, Pa Chin is a prolific writer with seemingly unbounded creative energy. Though a professed anarchist in his early life, Pa Chin shows little political acumen in his writings and even less political experience beyond the role of amateur revolutionist, "who only talks revolution in a comfortable home." When a student at Paris he first started writing to console his young solitary heart. A sentimental and passionate yearning, tempered with some vague revolutionary aspiration, seems to have inspired him at that time. His fluent and impassioned language, his stories of love and revolution, and his characters overflowing with the emotions of youth all accounted for his popularity in the 1930's. A romanticist and idealist at heart, Pa Chin has been swept into a world of socialist realism in which he seems to have found himself as much a stranger as he felt during his stay in France. It is uncertain how well he has adjusted himself to his new situation, but the fact remains that his literary output in recent years has been a mere trickle of the former torrent.

The best known of Pa Chin's novels is the trilogy *Turbulent Currents,* comprising *Family, Spring,* and *Autumn,* which together tell a gigantic story of the disintegration of a once solidly entrenched patriarchal family in the Southwest interior. The complete trilogy is more immense in length and scope than the *Dream of the Red Chamber* and more sophisticated in its treatment of youthful love and rebellion. Its theme is the typical, age-old conflict between the old and young in an extended family with many branches and subbranches living together under one roof; here, parental authority is challenged by the rising generation, and in the course of this struggle occur the many tragedies of unfulfilled love and forced marriage, with the weak and helpless falling victims on the way. But in this novel the flaming passion of youth in its insurrection against family bondage burns much more violently than Chia Pao-yü's. Thus at the end of *Family,* the youngest son, Chüeh-hui, resolutely leaves home for a new life in an unknown world:

> The past seemed like a dream. All that met his eye now was an expanse of deep green water, reflecting trees and hills. On the boat a few sailors plied long sculling oars, singing as they worked.
>
> A new emotion gradually possessed him. He did not know whether it was joy or sorrow, but one thing was clear—he was leaving his family. Before him was an endless stretch of water sweeping steadily forward, bearing him to an unfamiliar city. There all that was new was developing—new activities, new people, new friends.
>
> This river, this blessed river, was taking him away from the home he had lived in for eighteen years to a city and people he had never seen. The prospect dazzled him; he had no time to regret the life he had cast behind. For the last time he looked back. "Good-bye," he said softly. He turned to watch the on-rushing river, the green water that never for an instant halted its rapid advancing flow.[23]

Meanwhile, relentless time continues to lay its heavy hand on those left behind—depraved elders, defiant young rebels, weak, compromising adults —with one catastrophe following another until the final dissolution of the family.

Pa Chin stated his motive in writing the *Family* in the following words:

> What a dreadful nightmare have been those last ten and more years of my life! I read old books in their traditional bindings, sat in the dungeon of Confucian dogma, and saw with my own eyes the struggles and distresses of many people in their confinement beyond the prime of youth, without happiness, forever making needless sacrifices, and suffering ultimately the fate of destruction —not to mention my own agonies! . . . During those years I have buried with my own tears many dead persons who were all hapless victims of a decadent feudal morality, traditional concepts, and the inadvertent, headstrong actions of some two or three people. I left my old-fashioned family as if fleeing from a frightful shadow, without a trace of lingering affection.[24]

This last statement, however, needs modification, for it is actually the lingering memory of his youthful days, together with a sudden new awakening, that prompted him to write this history of a conservative patriarchal family. Insofar as he drew his material from his own experience, the novel, again like the *Dream of the Red Chamber*, may be regarded as autobiographical. Though Pa Chin denied that the young rebel, Chüeh-hui, was his self-portrait, he admitted the similarity of their characters and backgrounds; likewise, his two elder brothers are prototypes of Chüeh-hui's brothers in the novel. Together with their sister and cousins, they represent some distinct youthful types of the modern age, each going his or her own way toward the various destinations of freedom, surrender, or ruin.

Pa Chin's heroes are impelled by a desire to combat destiny—not as if it is an irrevocable predetermined course of events—but in the form of a tyrannical social environment. His villains are the upholders of time-honored traditional beliefs, the artificial systems that obstruct social progress and human development, and the reactionary forces that destroy youth and love. "Not being an artist," he wrote, "I consider writing as a part of my existence. And just as my life is full of contradictions, so are my works. The conflicts between love and hatred, thought and action, reason and emotion . . . these are all interwoven into a net that spreads over my entire career and work. Like my life, my writings have become a painful struggle. Each novel is an outcry in my pursuit of brightness . . . but at the same time the images of misery and suffering fall upon me like lashes on my back."[25] Thus, a nameless spirit has urged him to write incessantly and indefatigably and to give vent to his romantic fury, his belief in the death of the old family and society, and his plea for the salvation of a generation of lost youth.

Practically all the best contemporary Chinese novels were written in the 1930's, the most productive decade of the new literature. In the wake of Mao Tun's *Midnight* (1933) and Pa Chin's *Family* (1933) there appeared in 1938 Lao Shê's *Camel Hsiang-tzu* (known to English readers as *Rickshaw Boy*), often called "the finest modern Chinese novel up to that time."[26] Like Pa Chin, Lao Shê had written his early novels while abroad and under the influence of Western literature—in Lao Shê's case, English fiction. Upon his return to China from England in 1930 his fame as a novelist was already well established. In the intervening years before and after the publication of *Camel Hsiang-tzu*, he was immensely active in writing fiction, producing at the peak of his creativity the trilogy entitled *Four Generations under One Roof* (1946–51), one of the longest novels by a modern Chinese writer. During the Sino-Japanese War he was engaged in patriotic activities as the president of the All-China Writers' Anti-Aggression Association. Under his judicious leadership the Association was able to maintain a united literary front when the united political front was on the verge of breaking up. Today he is one of the very few veteran authors who have become at least not completely sterile in the first two decades of Communist rule.

Lao Shê has been considered modern China's foremost humanist and humorist. In place of Lu Hsün's vitriolic irony, he introduces a genial humor in fiction. Although he can be prankish and mischievous at times in his delineation of the dark aspects of Chinese society, he has found it expedient to play down the miseries of human life with hearty laughter. For this reason he is accused of having diluted with jest and drollery the feelings of righteous indignation against injustice. But actually, the presence of humor is only incidental, at most supplementary, to the central purpose of his novels, which is the assertion of human dignity and social justice. Lao Shê takes his writing seriously, as did most writers of the early literary revolution, but unlike them he draws a line of demarcation between literature and politics, conceiving his task as that of a literary fighter, not a political propagandist. It is this separation of ideology from literature that distinguishes his writings from those of his contemporaries discussed above. Instead of falling into the quagmire of slogans and outcries, Lao Shê succeeds in an artistic and faithful presentation of life, neglected by other writers in their zeal to combat social evils. A conscientious craftsman, Lao Shê seeks to create a dramatic novel with an architectonic plot devoid of unrelated incidents and loose ends, to animate his characters with life and blood, and to introduce an expressive and racy language befitting them.

All these traits are found in *Camel Hsiang-tzu*, a powerful novel with sustained narrative interest and vivid characterization. By adopting the technique of centering a dramatic plot around Hsiang-tzu, its main character, Lao Shê has succeeded in giving intensity to the strains and stresses that beset the life of this humble rickshaw boy, who assumes heroic proportions in the novel. Young, strong, hardworking, and ambitious, Hsiang-tzu has had visions of owning his shiny rickshaw and starting his own happy family, but in the end he finds himself in the clutches of the destructive forces of men and society. He is robbed of his prized rickshaw, bought with sweat and blood; enticed into a marital relationship which can spell only shame and ruin; and forced to tread the downward path that leads ultimately to his becoming a nonentity. After all he is not unlike the common run of rickshaw coolies and the other pitiable creatures dubbed by society its dregs and scum.

The prime of his life has passed by; he has failed to raise a family and make a career of rickshaw-pulling; everything in his life is brought down to the crushed fatalism of, "That's all there is to it." Finally having become a miserable hireling in Peking's colorful wedding and funeral processions, the rickshaw boy, even in this base employment, was unwilling to compete with his equals. Still a tall, burly fellow, he was so reduced in spirit that he would meanly contend with the very old and very young, even with women, for the easiest jobs—he would fight for the opportunity to carry only the lightest objects like the flying-tiger banner or a pair of short and narrow funeral scrolls, unwilling to exert himself with heavier burdens such as the red canopy and the wooden placard bearing the words: "Silence, please."

It should be noted here that the ending of Lao Shê's novel pleased neither his Chinese critics nor his American translator. The former questioned in the words of a workman: "If the rickshaw boy must die like that, what hopes do we have?";[27] whereas the latter changed the author's plot and intention by concluding the English version with an improbable reunion scene between Hsiang-tzu and his harlot-lover, the Little Lucky One, whom he rescues from her deathbed in a house of prostitution.[28] This bit of sentimentality contrasts sharply with the sardonic grin in the last paragraphs of the original novel:

> The face-loving, emulative, dreamy, self-seeking, individualistic, robust, and great Hsiang-tzu! No one knew how many funeral processions he had attended for others, nor was it known when and where he would bury himself, this degenerate, selfish, luckless product of the sickly womb of society, the wayworn ghost of individualism![29]

Lao Shê's intention to bury the ghost of individualism, which haunted him in many of his early novels, is intimated in the words of an old, impoverished rickshaw coolie, once ambitious but now reduced to a skeleton of his former self:

> I know it now! For a hardworking coolie to make a good run of life all by himself is even tougher than to ascend to Heaven. Have you ever watched the grasshoppers? A single one can leap pretty far by itself, but when caught by the kids and tied to a string, it can't even fly off the ground. Nevertheless, once they swarm together and array themselves in a formation—ahem!—in one sweep they can eat up the crops of an entire field without anybody's being able to control them.[30]

This passage has been taken by critics to indicate a new departure in Lao Shě's social and political thought. Actually, it was not until after the triumph of Communism in China that he stated forthrightly his new task and new mission in life:

> Before liberation I was just an isolated individual, cut off from the rest of society. I was a pathetic wisp of down floating between heaven and earth as the wind willed, not knowing where I would end. Now I must strike root among the people; I am no longer an "orphan" but a man with millions of friends. I must learn from them and hope by this means to write something of use to them. In this way I feel I will not have lived in vain.[31]

Thus, according to his own confession, while in the past he wandered alone in darkness without any aim, he is now happy and exhilarated because he has gained "a new lease on life as a writer." The casting off of his burden of individualism—and humanism into the bargain—does not necessarily mean, of course, that he will perform well in his new role as a rider on the "surging tide of the revolution."[32]

A similar fate has befallen another individualist, Ts'ao Yü (1910–   ), a major dramatist of the century. Before his advent, the spoken drama had been striving for recognition and for coexistence with the old Peking drama and the new American movie. Native actors and actresses continued to hold the audience spellbound in the popular Peking theaters while foreign films made considerable strides in popularity in the urban centers of amusement. The realistic spoken drama, recently introduced from Japan and the West by writers of the new literature, fared so badly that it could appear only in the pages of the literary periodicals or at best on the platform of school auditoriums under the sponsorship of student dramatic groups. Among the foreign works fortunate enough to see the footlights were translations of plays such as Ibsen's *Doll's House*, Wilde's *Lady Windermere's Fan*, and Dumas fils' *La Dame aux Camélias*. This state of affairs did not change until the emergence in 1934 of the *Thunderstorm* by Ts'ao Yü, then a student in his mid-twenties.

Ts'ao Yü's best plays such as *Thunderstorm*, *Sunrise*, *Wilderness*, and *The Peking Man* were all written in the six years between 1934 and 1940.

276

With the exception of *Wilderness*, they usually present the degenerate family life of the well-to-do, some belonging to the newly risen group of financier-industrialists, and others to the old gentry class on its way to dissolution. The world of Ts'ao Yü is peopled by licentious, unscrupulous, and decadent members of the two groups. Against them are arrayed the new forces represented by a young miner (in *Thunderstorm*), construction workers (in *Sunrise*), and the Peking Man, symbolic of man's towering primal strength. Human tragedies, however, are caused not so much by the clashes of hostile social forces as by contradictions between antagonistic members of the family, who pay with their lives for a variety of moral transgressions that range from adultery and incest to opium-smoking and heavy drinking. Quite different, *Wilderness* dramatizes a story of persecution, hatred, and revenge in a farming village, where the sins of a dead village despot are visited on his helpless blood relations, from which situation the avenger—a young peasant hero—flees to a dark primeval forest full of nightmarish horrors.

Ts'ao Yü's plays are the best examples of the influence of foreign models on native literature. From Western playwrights he has learned the art of producing the maximum dramatic effect through a skillful combination of realistic dialogue, subtle characterization, and a well-constructed plot interwoven with conflicts, tensions, and suspense. But even if he did borrow his technique from abroad, the content and spirit of his plays are all indigenous and in consonance with the sentiments and ideas of his time. Ts'ao Yü's role, therefore, is that of a creator of effective colloquial plays brought to the limelight of popularity. Once cherished by the intellectuals alone, the new colloquial drama began to gain a greater support from sophisticated urban theatergoers. But Ts'ao Yü's plays have never appealed to the peasants and industrial workers who are the target of the new Communist propaganda. "For this reason, as intimated in his own writings, Ts'ao Yü may have felt rather keenly the changing intellectual climate of the last twenty years and the insecurity of his position in the new literary world of the working masses."[33]

If colloquial drama was late in thriving, colloquial poetry, which was the earliest to be cultivated by writers such as Hu Shih and Kuo Mo-jo, suffered from an arrested development after a brief period of wild, luxuriant growth. This new poetry is a kind of vers libre (without meter and rhyme). Its compensating features are considerable freedom of movement, a broadening of poetic material and scope, and a profusion of novel ideas and expressions. This emancipation from "the shackles of the past," however, was accomplished not without the sacrifice of an age-old poetic art fastidiously cultivated by countless generations of Chinese poets. Western examples have provided modern Chinese poetry with the necessary inspiration, but not the proper technique of writing, because of a basic language barrier in matters of prosody. Thus, in the course of the last few decades, Chinese poets first floundered and then ran riot in all directions, some taking sentimental journeys in fancy's realm, some making detours in the direction of revolutionary signposts, some attaching themselves to the bandwagon of the French symbolists and imagists, while others lagged behind and beat time to the rhyme and rhythm of conventional English poetry, even "dancing in the fetters" of the sonnet. A large number of promising poets, if not the best, have met untimely ends: Hsü Chih-mo (1895–1931) in an airplane accident, Chu Hsiang (1904–1933) in suicide by drowning, Wen I-to (1899–1946) by assassination, all of them "extinct in their refulgent prime."

This picture of modern Chinese poetry may appear too dark for our comfort, but a recent anthology, edited by one who is a poet himself,[34] brings to the reader few rays of hope. It may be said, of course, that the selections are geared to the ideological requirements of the current regime, but on the other hand no one could produce, even if given a free hand, a collection of new Chinese poetry that would have the marks of brilliance.[35] Nevertheless, lest the reader be disheartened by the apparent decline of China's long and great poetic tradition, with whose rise and long life our discussion of Chinese literature has dealt, we append as a conclusion to this book one of the better specimens of contemporary verse, fresh both in content and spirit—however one interprets it:

> From the graveyard of remote antiquity,
> From the age of darkness,
> From beyond the stream of human mortality,
> Shaking with fear the slumberous mountain ranges,
> Like a flaming wheel flying and circling over the sandy hills,
> The Sun rolls toward me . . .
>
> With his blaze undimmed,
> He makes life breathe;
> Tall trees and thick branches dance toward him;
> Rivers and streams rush to him with their mad songs.
> When he comes, I hear
> The hibernating insects and grubs move beneath the earth,
> And the people shout on the broad square;
> The cities from afar
> Summoning him with power, light, and steel.
>
> Then my heart
> Is torn apart by the blazing hand,
> My stale and putrid soul
> Cast aside on the riverbank.
> And I regain my belief in man's rebirth![36]

NOTES
BIBLIOGRAPHY
CHRONOLOGICAL CHART
GLOSSARY
INDEX

Notes

Most of the books cited below can be found in the "Guide to Further Readings." Only those not listed there are here given dates and places of publication.

CHAPTER ONE

1. The best account of Chinese civilization of the Yin and Chou periods can be found in H. G. Creel, *The Birth of China*, reprint ed., (New York, Ungar, 1954).

2. *Analects*, II, 2 (literally, "to have no depraved thoughts.").

3. Ibid., XVI, 13 (literally, "you will have no words.").

4. See Arthur Waley, *The Book of Songs*, Appendix I, "The Allegorical Interpretation," pp.335–337.

5. William Jennings, *The Shi King* (London, 1891), p.200; also James Legge, *The Chinese Classics*, Vol. IV, Pt. II, pp.294–295: "My princely men are arriving."

6. Clement F. Allen, *The Book of Chinese Poetry* (London, 1891), pp. 248–249.

7. Waley, p.191.

8. Bernhard Karlgren, *The Book of Odes*, pp.125–126.

9. Waley, p.170.

10. Karlgren, p.166.

11. These are the first two stanzas in poem No. 174; see Karlgren, p.118 (in this and other poems in this chapter reference is given to Karlgren's book so that the reader can compare the Chinese text there with the present English rendering; however, the translations used here are mine and not from Karlgren).

12. Karlgren, p.245 (No. 280).

13. Ibid., p.24 (No. 38).

14. Ibid., pp.82–83 (No. 128).

15. Ibid., pp.111–113 (No. 168).

16. Ibid., p.66 (No. 103).

17. Ibid., pp.124–125 (No. 180).

18. Ibid., pp.111–113 (No. 168).

19. Ibid., p.185 (No. 234).

20. Ibid., p.72 (No. 112). Karlgren's interpretation of this poem is entirely different, as he used "you" instead of "we."

21. Ibid., pp.161–163 (No. 209).

22. Ibid., pp.96–100 (No. 154).

23. Ibid., p.250 (No. 290).

24. See Marcel Granet, *Festivals and Songs of Ancient China* (London, 1932), pp.11–145.

25. In his note to song No. 15 (No. 56 in Karlgren), Waley, p.29, wrote: "I think that too many of the songs have been explained by M. Granet as being connected with a festival of courtship in which the girls and boys lined up on opposite sides of a stream—a type of festival well known in Indo-China. This song, however, is clearly connected with such a meeting." But even the interpretation of this song is doubtful. Instead of Waley's first line, "Drumming and dancing in the gulley" (p.29), Karlgren, p.37, has "We achieve our joy in the stream valley," and Jennings, p.82, following the standard Chinese interpretation, "His cabin rearing by the mountain stream."

26. Karlgren, p.44 (No. 64).

27. Ibid., p.26 (No. 42).

28. Ibid., pp.88–90 (No. 140).

29. Ibid., pp.50–52 (No. 76).

30. Ibid., p.12 (No. 20).

31. Ibid., pp.58–60 (No. 91). The first two lines of the third stanza are translated here without verb and subject like the original to show that it can be variously interpreted. Karlgren translates: "You come and go hastily, at the look-out tower on the wall," p.59. In Waley: "Here by the wall-gate/ I pace to and fro," p.49. Cf. also L. Cranmer-Byng, *Book of Odes* (London, 1906), "Ah, random and pleasure-drawn,/ To the view tower you are gone," p.39. I am inclined to follow Karlgren and Cranmer-Byng as to meaning and feel that these lines can be translated as follows: "Yet you laze and seek pleasure/ On the watch tower by the city wall."

32. Karlgren, p.90 (No. 143).

33. Ibid., p.17 (No. 30).

34. Ibid., p.56 (No. 86).

35. Ibid., pp.12–14 (No. 23).

36. Ibid., pp.39–40 (No. 58).

37. *Analects*, XVII, 9.

CHAPTER TWO

1. Readers can now enjoy the full magnificence of these southern songs in the excellent translation by David Hawkes, *Chu' Tz'u, the Songs of the South*.

2. Waley, *The Nine Songs; A Study of Shamanism in Ancient China*, p.14. Why the deity should have been so fickle in this and the other cases has not been satisfactorily explained.

3. In Waley's translation he has taken the person driving the red leopards

in 1. 5 as a female shaman in love with a male spirit of the mountain. (Ibid., p.55.) The weakness of this interpretation is that according to it most of the descriptive passages in the song would have been related to the shaman instead of to the Mountain Spirit. Hawkes takes an opposite view of the sex of the spirit (op. cit., p.43). Cf. also other renderings by Yang Hsien-yi and Gladys Yang, *Li Sao and Other Poems of Chü Yüan*, pp.31–32; and Robert Payne, *The White Pony*, pp.90–92.

4. Hawkes, p.36.

5. Hawkes, p.45.

6. Of uncertain authorship, the poem has been attributed to Sung Yü or Ch'ü Yüan. Another poem, *Great Summons*, has also been attributed to Ch'ü Yüan, or to a later Ch'u poet. The two poems are similar in theme and content, the one apparently an imitation of the other. Critical opinions differ on the comparative merits of the two, though it seems there are more splendid descriptions in *Summoning the Soul*, which is also more articulate, than in the other. It is also uncertain whether it is Ch'ü Yüan who summons his own soul, or whether the soul summoned is that of the king of Ch'u by Chü Yüan or that of Ch'ü Yüan by Sung Yü and others.

7. In "Embracing the Sand," the fifth poem in the *Nine Compositions*.

8. "Hsien-ch'ih," *where the sun bathes* (according to the *Huai-nan-tzu*); not the name of a constellation as in Hawkes' note, p.28.

9. I have used Hawkes' version (op. cit., p.92) not only because it is the only complete one available in English, but also because of its excellence.

10. Ibid., p.109.

CHAPTER THREE

1. *Commentary of Tso*, 28th Year of Duke Hsi (632 B.C.). See Legge, *Chinese Classics*, V, 207–212. The King of Heaven, also called the Son of Heaven, is a term of respect for the king; Chung-ni is Confucius; Tsin is the name of a feudal state (in Shansi); the marquis of Tsin referred to here is Duke Wen of Tsin, one of the five hegemonists of the Spring and Autumn period. The word *shou* here translated as "to hunt in winter," may also mean "to make an imperial tour of inspection," or "held a court of reception," as translated by Legge, V, p.207.

2. *Commentary of Tso*, 2nd Year of Duke Hsüan (607 B.C.). Chao Ch'uan was a cousin of Chao Tun. In the original text Chao Tun is also referred to as Chao Hsüan-tzu. Cf. Legge, V, 287–291.

3. *Mo-tzu*, Ch. 17, "Anti-Aggression," Pt. 1. Cf. Lin Yutang, *Wisdom of China and India*, 798.

4. *Mo-tzu*, Ch. 35, "Anti-Destiny" (Princeton, N.J., 1952), Pt. 1. Cf. Fung Yu-lan, *A History of Chinese Philosophy*, tr. by Derk Bodde, I, 86.

5. *Meng-tzu*, Book III, "Teng Wen-kung," Pt. 1, Ch. 4. Cf. Liu, Wu-chi, *A Short History of Confucian Philosophy* (reprinted ed., N.Y., Dell, 1964), pp.71–72.

6. Ibid., Book VI, "Kao-tzu," Pt. 1, Ch. 2; cf. Liu, pp.75–76.

7. Ibid., Book VI, Pt. 1, Ch. 8; cf. Liu, pp.76–77.

8. Ibid., Book IV, "Li Lou," Pt. 2, Ch. 33; cf. Liu, pp.79–80.

9. *Chuang-tzu*, Book I, "Hsiao-yao yu"; cf. Lin Yutang, p.629.

10. Lin., p.630.

11. *Chuang-tzu*, Book II, "Ch'i-wu lun." Cf. Lin, pp.641–642.

12. Cf. Lin, p.643. Chou was the personal name of Chuang-tzu.

13. *Chuang-tzu*, Book I, "Hsiao-yao yu." This quotation is taken from Fung Yu-lan, *A Short History of Chinese Philosophy* (N.Y., 1948), pp.109–110.

14. *Chuang-tzu*, Book II, "Ch'i-wu lun." Taken from Lin Yutang, op. cit., pp.634–635. The translation itself is a masterpiece of imaginative prose.

15. *Hsün-tzu*, Book XXVI, "The Silkworm." Not translated in H. H. Dubs, *The Works of Hsün-tze*.

16. Early Chinese critics such as Pan Ku and Liu Hsieh. See also Arthur Waley, *The Temple and Other Poems*, pp.14–18; J. R. Hightower, *Topics in Chinese Literature*, p.26. The word *fu* has been variously rendered as prose poem, poetic prose, or rime-prose, and is translated here in this book as prose-poetry or prose-poem.

CHAPTER FOUR

1. There are three poems related to the story of Ts'ai Yen's life, all attributed to her. These are (1) a music song accompanied by a reed-leaf whistle of Tartar origin; (2) a song in the style of the verse of Ch'u; (3) a five-word verse poem. The last two poems are both entitled "Sorrow and Indignation." While opinions differ, it seems most likely that the five-word poem, discussed here, is closest to Ts'ai Yen's original. In recent years the poem has aroused a great deal of interest among scholars in Mainland China, but so far it has not received much critical notice in the West.

2. Cf. K'uai Shu-p'ing, "Six Poems of Ts'ao Tzu-chien," *National Peking University Semi-Centennial Papers*, No. 14 (1948), pp.24–31. K'uai gives a very free translation of the poems in a style reminiscent of eighteenth century English poetry. See also Hans H. Frankel, "Fifteen Poems by Ts'ao Chih: An Attempt at a New Approach," *Journal of American Oriental Society*, Vol. 84, No. 1 (March 1964), 1–14. Master Red Pine is a Taoist immortal; the "age of the yellowing hair" denotes longevity.

3. For an English study of their prose-poems, read E. R. Hughes, *Two Chinese Poets; Vignettes of Han Life and Thought*.

4. Also translated as *Records of the Historian*. See Burton Watson, *Ssu-ma Ch'ien, Grand Historian of China*, p.109.

5. S. Y. Teng, "Herodotus and Ssu-ma Ch'ien: Two Fathers of History," *East and West*, New Series, XII, 4 (December 1961), 233–240.

CHAPTER FIVE

1. Written by Ts'ao Ts'ao, founder of the Wei kingdom and father of the poet Ts'ao Chih.

2. Cf. R. H. Van Gulik, *Hsi K'ang and His Poetical Essay on the Lute*, pp.69–70. The Chinese word *ch'in* has been variously translated as zither, lute, or guitar. Here I have consistently used "zither" for *ch'in*, and "lute" for *p'i-p'a*.

3. For instance, in the poem "Harmonizing with Liu Ch'ai-sang."

4. From the poem "Giving up Wine."

5. The fifth poem in the series, "Drinking Wine."

6. Readers can sample his poetry in two recent translations: (1) William Acker, *T'ao the Hermit*; (2) Chang and Sinclair, *The Poems of T'ao Ch'ien*.

7. "Lovely" here is a translation of the word *lien*, which means literally "pitiable." In ancient Chinese, however, the expression *lien* or *k'o-lien* had the connotation of "loveliness."

8. Cf. Waley, *Chinese Poems*, 114–115. During the Six Dynasties period, women daubed or pasted patches on their foreheads for beauty.

CHAPTER SIX

1. It has been estimated that in the *Complete T'ang Poetry*, compiled by imperial order and first published in 1707, there are 48,900 poems by 2,200-2,300 poets.

CHAPTER SEVEN

1. In addition to the eight English versions listed in Martha Davidson, *A List of Published Translations from Chinese into English, French and German*, pp.345–350, items a3755, a3759, a3768, a3781, a3797, a3799, a3814, a3818 (a3824 is same as a3797), there is a ninth English version in Woo Kan Lan, *The Ballad of Everlasting Sorrow* (Shanghai, Sunrise Press, 1933), pp. 21–41; this book also contains English versions by W. J. B. Fletcher (Davidson, a3768) and H. A. Giles (Davidson, a3781), the last wrongly attributed by Woo to the Rev. Mandju.

2. See David Ying Chen, *Li Ho and Keats: A Comparative Study of Two Poets* (Unpublished dissertation, Comparative Literature, Indiana University, 1962).

CHAPTER EIGHT

1. As we have already dealt at length with many *shih* writers of the earlier period, our discussion of Sung poetry, therefore, will have to concern itself mainly with the *tz'u* poets.

2. In the original, "the skies of Ch'u," the Yangtze river region in Central China.

3. Chou Yü is mentioned twice in this song, first as "young man Chou" in this line, and six lines later by his courtesy name, Kung-chin. For the sake of simplicity, I have changed both to "Chou Yü."

4. From the place name, Tung-p'o or East Slope near Huang-chou, where the poet was exiled, is derived the poet's popularly known name, Su Tung-p'o.

The line therefore is ambiguous and can also be translated as "Carousing at night, I, Tung-p'o, am drunk. . . ."

5. Fan's poems have been translated in Gerald Bullett, *The Golden Years of Fan Cheng-ta*, Cambridge (England), 1946.

6. An important school of Sung poetry led by Huang T'ing-chien (1045–1105) and Ch'en Shih-tao (1053–1101). See Ch'en Shou-yi, *Chinese Literature: A Historical Introduction*, pp.380–383.

CHAPTER NINE

1. H. A. Giles, *Gems of Chinese Prose Literature*, p.175.

2. The courtesy name of Mei Yao-ch'en (1002–1060), a well known Northern Sung poet.

CHAPTER TEN

1. The names of these collections, with the number of stories under each, were recorded in the bibliographical section of the *History of the Former Han Dynasty* by Pan Ku.

2. *Yu Hsien K'u*, translated as *The Dwelling of Playful Goddesses* by Howard S. Levy (Tokyo, 1965).

3. See Arthur Waley, *Ballads and Stories from Tun-huang*, pp.249–250.

4. *Ennin's Diary, The Record of a Pilgrimage to China*, trans. by Edwin Reischauer (New York, 1955), pp.298–299. Of Wen-hsü, Ennin wrote "(he) is a Court Priest, a Debater of the Three Teachings, a Reverence Granted the Purple, and a Personal Attendant Priest," p.299.

5. Among the Tun-huang manuscripts in London, Paris, and Peking, three different versions of the story are preserved. Of these, the one in the British Museum, entitled "Great Mu-lien Rescuing his Mother from the Hades," is the longest and the most elaborate in narration and description. A part of this tale, but not the section quoted here, has been translated by Waley, op. cit., pp.216–235.

6. There has been some confusion about the exact classification of the four groups as recorded in the Sung-Yüan sources. The question has been discussed and debated by Chinese literary historians in recent years. The above classification represents the result of my own study and interpretation of the original texts. Cf. Lu Hsün, *A Brief History of Chinese Fiction*, pp.142–143.

7. See next chapter.

8. The poems are omitted in the two English versions by C. C. Wang (*Traditional Chinese Tales*, pp.115–126), and Yang Hsien-yi and Gladys Yang (*The Courtesan's Jewel Box*, pp.11–26).

CHAPTER ELEVEN

1. See Chang Heng's *fu* on Ch'ang-an, the Western Capital, discussed in E. R. Hughes, *Two Chinese Poets, Vignettes of Han Life and Thought*.

2. The term *tsa-chü* was later used to denote an entirely different type of

play, the northern drama of the Yüan period. To avoid confusion, the Sung *tsa-chü* will be called in this book Sung Variety Play and the Yüan *tsa-chü* simply the Yüan drama.

3. See Herbert A. Giles, "Football and Polo in China," *Adversaria Sinica*, No. 4 (1906), pp.87–98.

4. The "tile districts" (*wa-shê* or *wa-ssu*), according to Sung-Yüan writers, were amusement centers where the audience assembles and breaks up at random like heaps of tiles that are loosely put together and that collapse easily.

5. This description is taken from a song sequence, *The Country Cousin Visits a Theater*, by Tu Shan-fu, a 13th century poet, and from an anonymous Yüan play, *Lan Ts'ai-ho*. One of the Eight Immortals, Lan Ts'ai-ho is here represented as the head of a troupe of actors. The Sung term for a theater is *kou-lan*, i.e., "fenced enclosure."

6. Formerly attributed to the Brilliant Emperor, this piece is now believed to have been written by the poet Liang Huang.

7. According to some writers there was a difference between the two in the method of presentation. The Professional Script, it seems, put more emphasis on acting and dancing than on singing. One account states that there were no songs at all in the Professional Script, but this is highly doubtful. What probably happened was that in the performance the singer and the player were two separate persons; the one sang from his seat off the stage while the other performed on the stage.

8. Some scholars have held the view that the word "*yüan*" in *yüan-pen* is an abbreviation of "*hang-yüan*" and that "*hang-yüan*" refers to the house of the courtesans or sing-song girls, where these plays were given. According to this interpretation, a *yüan-pen* is a dramatic script used in the courtesan house and presented by the courtesans. The term "*hang-yüan*," however, has several meanings in the Sung-Yüan period. Although later it came to mean specifically the courtesan house, it originally had the broad meaning of the "professionals" and was so used in a number of instances in Sung stories and Yüan plays. The *yüan-pen* therefore may be more properly translated as "Professional Script."

CHAPTER TWELVE

1. See for instance H. A. Giles, *A History of Chinese Literature*, p.256.

2. For a panoramic description of prevalent social customs and the material environment of Sung China before the Mongol invasion, see Jacques Gernet, *Daily Life in China on the Eve of the Mongol Invasion, 1250–1276* (tr. by H. M. Wright), N.Y., 1962.

3. See Ch. Eleven, p. 165.

4. See James Liu, *Elizabethan and Yuan: A Brief Comparison of Some Conventions in Poetic Drama.*

5. An important anthology entitled *Selections from the Yüan Drama* published by Tsang Mou-hsün in 1616 contains one hundred plays, some of them written in the early Ming period. There are several modern reprints of this work. Another great collection of about 340 Yüan and early Ming plays,

probably the most complete private library of Yüan-Ming drama, was assembled by Chao Mei-chi (1563–1624), a famous book-collector. A photographic reproduction of the entire collection as well as other smaller collections and individual volumes is included in the *Collection of Ancient Text Drama*, Series 4, 1958. These Yüan-Ming plays form an important part of China's literary heritage comparable in merit and value to the romantic verse of Ch'u, the poetry of T'ang, and the *tz'u* lyrics of Sung.

6. In the Sung period, it forms the subject of a twelve-stanza Drum Song to a tune called "Butterfly Loves Flowers," written by Chao Ling-chih, Prince An-ting. Prince Chao, a patron of letters, had as friends such Sung writers as Su Shih and Huang T'ing-chien. He based his composition entirely upon Yüan Chen's story and made no claim to originality. In his preface, Chao Ling-chih testified to the growing popularity of Yüan Chen's romance among scholars, poets, and sing-song girls of his time (eleventh century). The story later found its way into a Sung Variety Play entitled *Ying Ying*, which has been lost.

7. See Liu Wu-chi, "The Original Orphan of China," *Comparative Literature*, V, 3 (Summer 1953), 193–212.

8. This play, translated as *Snow in Midsummer*, and seven others are included in *Selected Plays of Kuan Han-ching*, tr. by Yang Hsien-yi and Gladys Yang.

9. See Roger B. Bailey, *The Chalk Circle in Western Translations and Adaptations* (Unpublished thesis, Comparative Literature, Indiana University, 1962).

10. See Ch. Fourteen.

11. E.g. *Li K'uei Carries Thorns*, by K'ang Chin-chih, tr. by J. I. Crump.

CHAPTER THIRTEEN

1. See Ch. Twelve, pp. 176–177.

CHAPTER FOURTEEN

1. The story of the discovery of Shih's genealogy and epitaph has proved to be a forgery. See Ho Hsin, *Shui-hu yen-chiu* (Studies of the *Marshes*, Shanghai, 1954), pp.27–31.

2. There has been an intensive effort to discredit and denounce Chin Sheng-t'an in recent Mainland China publications; e.g., Ho Man-tzu, *Lun Chin Sheng-t'an p'ing-kai Shui-hu chuan*, (On Chin Sheng-t'an's Comments and Alterations of the *Tale of the Marshes*), Shanghai, 1954.

3. Pearl Buck, *All Men Are Brothers*, 2 vols., 1933, and J. H. Jackson, *Water Margin*, 2 vols., 1937. The only attempt at translating the longer version is F. Kuhn's *Die Raüber vom Liang schan moor*, 1934, which is an abridgment of the 120-chapter edition. For a chapter-by-chapter resume of the 120-chapter version and a translation of the 120th chapter, see Richard G. Irwin, *The Evolution of a Chinese Novel*, Appendix A, pp.117–201.

4. The chapter numbers given here and in the later quotations are those of the complete 120-chapter edition. For comparison, see Buck, op. cit., I, 384–85.

5. A four-line poem is omitted here.

6. Cf. Buck, II, Ch. 42, 765–66.

7. See C. T. Hsia, "Comparative Approaches to *Water Margin*," *Yearbook of Comparative and General Literature*, XI (Bloomington, Indiana, 1962), Supplement, Third Conference on Oriental-Western Literary and Cultural Relations 1962, pp.121–128.

8. Cf. Buck, I, 475.

9. Cf. Buck, I, 96–97.

CHAPTER FIFTEEN

1. The first collection was published originally as *Stories, Old and New, First Series*. The title, *Instructive Words to Enlighten the World*, was probably added and used later, but no complete forty-chapter edition of the book under this title has been found.

2. There are forty stories in the original edition of the first series, but four of them are missing in later editions. Fortunately, a copy of the rare, complete first edition has been preserved in Japan and now reproduced. The twenty-third story in the first series is the same as the twenty-third story in the second series, which, in all the early editions known today, contains thirty-nine stories and a play. This leads to the conjecture that we have yet to discover the original first edition of the second series which may also contain forty stories. As it is, the total number of now extant stories in Ling's two series is actually seventy-eight. See Tien-yi Li, "The Original Edition of the *P'o-an Ching-ch'i*," *Tsing Hua Journal of Chinese Studies*, N.S. I, No. 3 (September 1958), pp. 121–132.

3. An excellent translation of this passage is made by Cyril Birch, *Stories from a Ming Collection*, p.8. I have made here only a few minor changes and one important correction—"every day" for "from childhood days"—the mistranslation caused apparently by the corrupt text which Birch used.

4. Translated into English by Thom R. Sloth as *The Lasting Resentment of Miss Keaou Lwan Wang, a Chinese Tale; Founded on Fact* (Canton, Canton Press Office, 1839).

5. *The Affectionate Pair, or the History of Sungkin, a Chinese Tale*, tr. by P. P. Thoms (London, Black, 1820); "The Tattered Felt Hat" in *The Courtesan's Jewel Box*, tr. by Yang Hsien-yi and Gladys Yang, pp.216–245.

6. There are at least three English versions of this tale: "The Courtesan," tr. by E. B. Howell, in *The Restitution of the Bride and Other Stories*, pp.135–179; "Eastern Shame Girl," tr. by G. Soulié de Morant, in *Chinese Love Tales* (Cleveland, Ohio, 1935), pp.11–41; "The Courtesan's Jewel Box," tr. by Yang Hsien-yi and Gladys Yang, pp.246–271.

7. Ling Meng-ch'u, *Ch'u-k'e p'o-an ching-ch'i* (*Striking the Table in Amazement at the Wonders*, First Series), ed. by Wang Ku-lu (Shanghai, 1957), author's "Preface," p.1.

8. Ling Meng-ch'u, *Erh-k'e p'o-an ching-ch'i* (*Striking the Table in Amazement at the Wonders*, Second Series), ed. by Wang Ku-lu (Shanghai, 1957), Vol. I, author's "Brief Introduction," p.1.

9. Ling Meng-ch'u, *Ch'u-k'e p'ai-an ching-ch'i*, Ch. 11, p.193.

10. Most of the stories in this collection have been translated into Western languages. See Martha Davidson, *A List of Published Translations from Chinese into English, French and German.* (Pt. I: Literature, exclusive of Poetry), pp.35–49.

CHAPTER SIXTEEN

1. One part of this book, also entitled *Journey to the West*, is apparently an abridged version of Wu's novel instead of being its prototype, as has been claimed by some scholars. The other three parts deal with journeys to the north, south, and east, but they are all separate stories unrelated to each other.

2. Cf. Waley, *Monkey*, p.73.

3. Arthur Waley, *The Real Tripitaka* (London, 1952), pp.14–16.

4. By keeping intact the first twelve chapters of the original novel and reducing the other eighty-eight chapters into eighteen in the English version, Waley fails to give in *Monkey* a proper representation of the Chinese work. Most of the episodes in the second half of the novel, including some exceedingly exciting ones, as pointed out by Hu Shih, (*Monkey*, Preface, p.4), are thus left untranslated.

5. Waley, *Monkey*, p.231. A number of poems in the Chinese text are omitted in this translation.

6. *Chung-kuo wen-hsüeh shih* (*A History of Chinese Literature*), a co-operative project by the students of the Classical Literature Section of the Department of Chinese, Fu-tan University (Shanghai, 1958–1959), III, 144.

7. Waley, *Monkey*, p.285.

8. *The Golden Lotus*, translated by Clement Egerton, 4 vols., London, 1939.

9. *Chin P'ing Mei, The Adventurous History of Hsi-Men and His Six Wives* (N.Y., 1947), tr. by Miall from Franz Kuhn's German version, with an introduction by Arthur Waley.

10. For the fascinating legend of its authorship by Wang Shih-chen, an eminent Ming dynasty writer, read Waley's "Introduction," Ibid., pp.ix-xi. Waley's own theory that "Of possible candidates for the authorship of the *Chin P'ing Mei* I personally regard Hsü Wei as the strongest," (Ibid. p.xix) follows a similar Chinese practice of attributing a popular work of literature to some well-known writer of the period without taking into account the important role of the popular storyteller in the development of Chinese colloquial literature from Sung to Ming.

11. Quoted from the 1617 (prefaced) edition. I have used this text, instead of later editions, for its crude simplicity and directness, e.g. instead of "Of course I want to have you," the other editions have "I am just teasing you." See *Golden Lotus*, III, 31–33.

12. While Ts'ao's death date has been established as 1764, there are different suggestions as to his birth date: (1) 1718 by Hu Shih; (2) 1724 by Chou Ju-ch'ang; (3) 1715 by Wu Shih-ch'ang. See Wu, *On the "Red Chamber Dream,"* pp.103–113; 117–118. The difficulty of Wu's date is that it would

make Ts'ao Hsüeh-ch'in almost fifty by Chinese counting at the time of his death, and this does not seem to agree with the primary source of Ts'ao's age, in which he is referred to as having died at forty or in his forties and in which he is compared to the poet Li Ho, who died young. I am more inclined to accept Chou's date and feel that Wu's objections to it are not unsurmountable.

13. Cf. *Dream of the Red Chamber*, translated by Chi-chen Wang, (rev. ed. 1958), p.7. It is omitted in *The Dream of the Red Chamber*, tr. by Franz Kuhn (in German), English tr. by Florence and Isabel McHugh. Both Wang's and Kuhn's versions are incomplete translations of the novel.

14. The earliest extant eighty-chapter handwritten version bears the date 1754, ten years before Ts'ao's death. The comments were made by one of his relatives, probably a paternal cousin. See Wu, xvi–xvii; 20–24, etc.

15. For a discussion of this question, read Wu, pp.267–285, in which Kao's authorship of these forty chapters is reaffirmed; and C. T. Hsia's review of Wu's book in the *Journal of Asian Studies*, XXI, No. 1 (Nov. 1961), pp.78–80. Also read Lin Yutang, "Reopening the Question of Authorship of 'Red Chamber Dream,'" *The Bulletin of the Institute of History and Philology*, XXIX (1958), 327–387, in which Lin takes the view that the last forty chapters are the original work of Ts'ao Hsüeh-ch'in.

16. Last lines of the often quoted "Flower-burial Song" in the novel. Cf. Wang, p.219; it is omitted in Kuhn.

17. Cf. Wang, pp.219–21.

18. Cf. Wang, pp.278–279.

19. Kuhn, pp.578–579; Wang, p.561 (a summary, not a translation).

20. The family name Chia is a homonym of the word meaning "fictitious."

21. Cf. Wang, pp.5–6. Omitted in Kuhn.

22. Translated by Yang Hsien-yi and Gladys Yang (Peking, 1957).

23. Cf. Yang, *Scholars*, p.105.

24. Such as Liu E's *The Travels of Lao Ts'an*, translated by Harold Shadick. Other English versions of the same novel are *Tramp Doctor's Travelogue*, translated by Lin Yi-chin and Ko Te-shun (Shanghai, 1939), and *Mr. Derelict*, translated by Yang Hsien-yi and G. M. Tayler (London, 1948).

CHAPTER SEVENTEEN

1. This term is not to be confused with that for the T'ang literary tales though both have the same romanization and the same Chinese characters.

2. It was translated into French by A. P. L. Bazin in 1841 and into German by Vincenz Hundhausen in 1930; a Broadway adaptation by Sidney Howard and Will Irwin of the Bazin translation was given at the Plymouth Theater, N.Y., on February 6, 1946, and a written version of the Broadway play was published as *Lute Song*, by Kao-Tong-Kia (Chicago, 1954). Kao-Tong-Kia, or Kao Tung-chia, is the courtesy name of Kao Ming. There is also an English translation by Yu Tinn-Hugh, *Memoirs of the Guitar*, (Shanghai, 1928).

3. In this and the following translations, I have used the early Yüan-Ming text as reprinted and edited by Ch'ien Nan-yang (Shanghai, 1960).

4. Important types of local tunes are as follows: (1) I-yang (in Kiangsi), the most popular, spreading widely to Nanking and Peking and as far south as Fukien and Kwangtung; (2) Hai-yen (in Chekiang), the oldest southern tune current in Chekiang; (3) Yü-yao (in Chekiang) also prevalent in Kiangsu and Anhwei.

5. While the date of T'ang Hsien-tsu's death is commonly given as 1617, I have followed as more probable the revised date given by Hsü So-fang, *T'ang Hsien-tsu nien-p'u* (*Chronological Life of T'ang Hsien-tsu*), (Shanghai, 1958), pp.185–186. So here is the interesting coincidence of T'ang's dying in the same year as Shakespeare, to whom he has sometimes been compared.

6. An allusion to the Yüan play, *Entering the Peach Blossom Cave by Mistake*, in which is related the visit of two Taoist scholars to the cave where they encounter two fairy ladies. After staying a year with them, the two men return to their native village only to find that everything at home has changed since their departure, more than a hundred years having lapsed in this world. The play ends with their revisiting the Peach Blossom Cave where they are finally united with the fairies and they themselves become immortals.

7. Also translated as *The Palace of Eternal Youth* by Yang Hsien-yi and Gladys Yang.

8. Another well-known play of the same century, slightly earlier than the two mentioned here, is *The Swallow Letter* by Yüan Ta-ch'eng (1587?–1646).

CHAPTER EIGHTEEN

1. Liu Wu-chi and Li Tien-yi, *Readings in Contemporary Chinese Literature* (New Haven, Institute of Far Eastern Languages, Yale University, 1953), III, 88. (First published in *New Youth*, January 1917).

2. Ibid., III, 91–92. (First published in *New Youth*, February, 1917).

3. Ibid., III, 112–113. (First published in *Creation Monthly*, May 1926).

4. Ibid., I, 100.

5. In *Chung-kuo hsin-shih hsüan* (Selections from New Chinese Poetry), 1919–1949, ed. by Tsang K'e-chia (Peking, 1956), p.22.

6. *Selected Works of Lu Hsün*, I, 11–12.

7. Ibid., I, 19, with slight changes to conform more closely to the Chinese text.

8. Ibid., I, 21.

9. Ibid., I, 84.

10. Ibid., I, 93.

11. Ibid., I, 134.

12. English translation by Yang Hsien-yi and Gladys Yang (Peking, 1959).

13. "The Dog's Retort," in *Selected Works of Lu Hsün*, I, 342.

14. Ibid., IV, 185.

15. Ibid., III, 225–226 (Some changes have been made here based upon the Chinese text).

16. From "How I Came to Write Stories," 1933. My translation differs somewhat from ibid., III, 230.

17. Cf. Huang Sung-k'ang, *Lu Hsün and the New Culture Movement of Modern China*, pp.126–135.

18. The title has been translated as *The Canker* in the English version of Ting Yi's *A Short History of Modern Chinese Literature*, p.189. I have used here C. T. Hsia's translation in his *A History of Modern Chinese Fiction*, p. 141 ff.

19. Translated by Hsu Meng-hsiung and published in Peking, 1957.

20. Ting Yi, *Chung-kuo hsien-tai wen-hsüeh shih lüeh* (A Short History of Modern Chinese Literature), p.303. Omitted in the English translation in Note 18.

21. Mao Tun, *Spring Silkworms and Other Stories*, p.28. Some slight changes have been made in accordance with the Chinese text.

22. Mao Tun, *"Ta chuan-pien ho-shih lai ni"* (When Will Come the Great Transformation?) quoted in Liu Shou-sung, *Chung-kuo hsin-wen-hsüeh shih ch'u-kao* (A History of Modern Chinese Literature, First Draft) (Peking, 1956), I, 130.

23. Pa Chin, *The Family*, translated by Sidney Shapiro, p.321. There are some omissions in the English version which I have not seen fit to restore, for the translation here is actually an improvement over the original style, which is often verbose and padded.

24. Pa Chin, *Pa Chin wen-chi* (Pa Chin's Collected Works), IV, 465, in "A Letter to my Elder Cousin about *The Family*."

25. In a Preface to his *Selected Works*, quoted in Liu Shou-sung, op. cit., II, 317.

26. C. T. Hsia, op. cit., p.187.

27. Ting Yi, op. cit. (English translation), p.174.

28. Lau Shaw, *Rickshaw Boy*, p.384.

29. Lao Shê, *Lo-t'o Hsiang-tzu*, Shanghai, 1947, p.308.

30. Ibid., p.285.

31. Lao Shê, "At Fifty I Learn My Task," in *Chinese Literature*, No. 6 (June 1962), p.105.

32. Ibid., p.104.

33. Quoted from an unpublished article on Ts'ao Yü written by Hsiao Hsia for the Columbia University Project on Modern China, Men and Politics.

34. The same anthology by Tsang K'e-chia, quoted in footnote 5.

35. There are, however, several good anthologies of modern Chinese poetry in English translations, of which the latest is Hsü Kai-yu's *Twentieth Century Chinese Poetry* (N.Y., 1963).

36. Ai Ch'ing, "T'ai-yang" (Sun) in Liu and Li, op. cit., I, 110.

Selected Bibliography of Books in English

A GUIDE TO FURTHER READINGS

I *Introductory Works*

Birch, Cyril, ed. *Anthology of Chinese Literature* (from early times to the 14th century). New York, Grove Press, 1965.

Bishop, John L., ed. *Studies in Chinese Literature*. Cambridge, Mass., Harvard University Press, 1965.

Chai Ch'u and Winberg Chai. *A Treasury of Chinese Literature*. New York, Appleton-Century, 1965.
> A prose anthology including excerpts from fiction and drama.

Ch'en Shou-yi. *Chinese Literature, A Historical Introduction*. New York, Ronald Press, 1961.
> The only comprehensive and systematic survey of Chinese literature, incorporating much of recent scholarship and new knowledge; strong in historical background; some factual errors, repetitions, and misprints.

Feng Yüan-chün. *A Short History of Classical Chinese Literature*. Tr. by Yang Hsien-yi and Gladys Yang. Peking, Foreign Languages Press, 1958.
> Brief, sketchy, but readable.

Giles, Herbert A. *A History of Chinese Literature*. (First ed., London, 1901.) New York, Grove Press, 1958.
> A pioneer work, the first in any language on the history of Chinese literature; adequate in the discussion of traditional poetry and prose, but weak on drama and fiction; historically important in spite of its many faults.

Hightower, James R. *Topics in Chinese Literature*. Cambridge, Mass., Harvard University Press, 1950 (revised, 1953).
> Still the best reference book on the genres and topics in Chinese literature.

Lai Ming. *A History of Chinese Literature*. New York, John Day, 1964.
> A general work that should hardly be called a "history"; contains copious quotations from previously published translations.

Watson, Burton. *Early Chinese Literature*. New York, Columbia University Press, 1962.

294

A fine introduction to early Chinese literature, interpreted in its broad sense to include history and philosophy, from the Chou dynasty to the middle of Later Han (100 A.D.); valuable original translations from the Han *fu*.

II *Prose in Translation*

(1) *Anthologies*

DeBary, William Theodore, Wing-tsit Chan and Burton Watson. *Sources of Chinese Tradition*. New York, Columbia University Press, 1960.
Brief introductions to and excerpts from Chinese historical and philosophical materials, arranged topically and chronologically from antiquity to the modern period; careful translation and editing; useful for background information.
Giles, Herbert A. *Gems of Chinese Literature, Prose*. Shanghai, Kelly and Walsh (second revised ed.), 1923. (Reprint: New York, Paragon, 1964.)
The only important anthology of Chinese essays in English translation; some historical and philosophical pieces but mostly of the belles-lettres type, arranged chronologically according to author.
Legge, James. *The Chinese Classics*. 5 vols. (First ed., Hong Kong, 1861-72.) New York, Oxford University Press, 1961.
Bilingual text; one of the earliest and in some respects still the best translation of the Confucian classics.
———. *The Texts of Taoism*. (Reprinted from *Sacred Books of the East*, vols. 39 and 40, Oxford, 1891.) New York, Julian Press, 1959.
Lin Yutang. *The Wisdom of China and India*. New York, Random House, 1942.
Useful selections from Chinese literature, history, and philosophy.

(2) *Philosophical Works*

Chuang Tzu. *Chuang Tzu, a New Selected Translation (with an Exposition of the Philosophy of Kuo Hsiang)*. Tr. by Yu-lan Fung. Shanghai, Commercial Press, 1933. (Reprint: New York, Paragon, 1964.)
———. *Chuang Tzu, Mystic, Moralist and Social Reformer*. Tr. by Herbert A. Giles. (Second rev. ed., Shanghai, 1926.) London, Allen & Unwin, 1961.
———. *Chuang Tzu: Basic Writings*. Tr. by Burton Watson. New York, Columbia University Press, 1964.
Confucius. *The Analects of Confucius*. Tr. by Arthur Waley. London, Allen & Unwin, 1938.
———. *The Great Learning and the Mean-in-Action*. Tr. by E. R. Hughes. New York, Dutton, 1943.
———. *The Wisdom of Confucius*. Tr. by Lin Yutang. New York, Random House (Modern Library), 1938.
Hsün Tzu. *The Works of Hsüntze*. Tr. by Homer H. Dubs. London, Probsthain, 1928.

———. *Hsün Tzu, Basic Writings.* Tr. by Burton Watson. New York, Columbia University Press, 1963.

Lao Tzu. *The Way and Its Power.* Tr. by Arthur Waley. London, Allen & Unwin, 1935.

———. *The Way of Lao Tzu.* Tr. by Wing-tsit Chan. Indianapolis, Bobbs-Merrill, 1963.

———. *The Wisdom of Laotse.* Tr. by Lin Yutang. New York, Random House (Modern Library), 1948.

Lieh Tzu. *The Book of Lieh-Tzu.* Tr. by A. C. Graham. London, Murray, 1960.

Mencius. *The Book of Mencius.* Tr. by Lionel Giles. London, Murray, 1942.

———. *Mencius.* Tr. by W. A. C. H. Dobson. Toronto, University of Toronto Press, 1963.

Mo Tzu. *The Ethical and Political Works of Motse.* Tr. by Y. P. Mei. London, Probsthain, 1929.

———. *Mo Tzu, Basic Writings.* Tr. by Burton Watson. New York, Columbia University Press, 1963.

(3) *Histories*

Pan Ku. *History of the Former Han Dynasty.* Tr. by Homer H. Dubs. 3 vols. Baltimore, Waverly Press, 1938-55.

Ssu-ma Ch'ien. *Records of the Grand Historian of China.* Tr. by Burton Watson. 2 vols. New York, Columbia University Press, 1961.

Watson, Burton. *Ssu-ma Ch'ien, Grand Historian of China.* New York, Columbia University Press, 1958.

(4) *Literary Criticism*

Liu Hsieh. *The Literary Mind and the Carving of Dragons.* Tr. by Vincent Y. C. Shih. New York, Columbia University Press, 1959.

Lu Chi. *The Art of Letters.* Tr. by E. R. Hughes. New York, Pantheon, 1951.

The above works by Liu and Lu are landmarks in the development of literary criticism in ancient China; important for the discussion of the various literary forms and their writers.

III *Poetry in Translation*

(1) *Anthologies*

Bynner, Witter and Kiang Kang-hu. *The Jade Mountain.* New York, Knopf, 1929. (Reprint: New York, Doubleday, 1964.)
   Translation of the *Three Hundred T'ang Poems,* arranged according to authors.

Candlin, Clara M. *The Herald Wind.* London, Murray, 1933.
   A volume of Sung dynasty poems, some of the *tz'u* type.

Graham, A. C., *Poems of the Late T'ang*. Baltimore, Penguin Books, 1965.

Hart, Henry H. A *Garden of Peonies*. Stanford, California, Stanford University Press, 1938.

Jenyns, Soame. *Selections from the 300 Poems of the T'ang Dynasty*. London, Murray, 1940.

————. A *Further Selection from the 300 Poems of the T'ang Dynasty*. London, Murray, 1944.

These two books by Jenyns constitute another translation of the *Three Hundred T'ang Poems*; the first book is arranged topically.

Kotewall, Robert and Norman L. Smith. *The Penguin Book of Chinese Verse*. England, Harmondsworth, Penguin Books, 1962.

A volume of short lyrical poems, accurately and well translated.

Payne, Robert. *The White Pony*. New York, John Day, 1947.

A systematic anthology of representative Chinese poets from the earliest time to the modern period; quality of the translation done by various hands is uneven; introduction to each poet is more appreciative than critical; some mistranslation and factual errors, otherwise a useful book for beginners.

Rexroth, Kenneth. *One Hundred Poems from the Chinese*. New York, New Directions, 1959.

Waley, Arthur. *Ballads and Stories from Tun-huang*. New York, Macmillan, 1960.

————. *Chinese Poems*. London, Allen & Unwin, 1946.

A collection in one volume of Waley's translations of Chinese poetry, including most of *170 Chinese Poems* (1918), *More Translations* (1919), and *The Temple* (1923); also 28 poems from *The Book of Songs*.

(2) *Individual Works* (arranged chronologically)

Shih Ching. *The Book of Odes*. Tr. by Bernard Karlgren. Stockholm, Museum of Far Eastern Antiquities, 1950.

————. *The Book of Songs*. Tr. by Arthur Waley. London, Allen & Unwin, 1937.

Ch'u Tz'u. *Ch'u Tz'u, The Songs of the South*. Tr. by David Hawkes. London, Oxford University Press, 1959.

————. *Li Sao and Other Poems of Chu Yuan*. Tr. by Yang Hsien-yi & Gladys Yang. Peking, Foreign Languages Press, 1953.

————. *The Nine Songs: A Study of Shamanism in Ancient China*. Tr. by Arthur Waley. London, Allen & Unwin, 1955.

Pan Ku and Chang Heng. *Two Chinese Poets: Vignettes of Han Life and Thought*. Tr. by Ernest R. Hughes. Princeton, Princeton University Press, 1960.

Hsi K'ang. *Hsi K'ang and His Poetical Essay on the Lute*. Tr. by R. H. van Gulik. Tokyo, Sophia University, 1941.

T'ao Ch'ien. *The Poems of T'ao Ch'ien*. Tr. by Lily Pao-hu Chang and Marjorie Sinclair. Honolulu, University of Hawaii Press, 1953.

――――. *T'ao the Hermit; Sixty Poems by T'ao Ch'ien*. Tr. by William Acker. London, Thames & Hudson, 1952.

Wang Wei. *Poems by Wang Wei*. Tr. by Chang Yin-nan and Lewis C. Walmsley, Rutland, Vt., Tuttle, 1958.

Li Po. *The Works of Li Po*. Tr. by Shigeyoshi Obata. New York, Dutton, 1922. (Reprint: New York, Paragon, 1964.)

――――. Waley, Arthur. *The Poetry and Career of Li Po*. London, Allen & Unwin, 1950.

Tu Fu. *Tu Fu, Selected Poems*. Tr. by Rewi Alley. Peking, Foreign Languages Press, 1962.

――――. Hung, William. *Tu Fu, China's Greatest Poet*. Cambridge, Mass., Harvard University Press, 1952.

Po Chü-i. Waley, Arthur. *The Life and Times of Po Chü-i*. London, Allen & Unwin, 1949.

Li Yü. *Poems of Lee Hou-chu*. Tr. by Liu Yih-ling and Shahid Suhrawardy. Bombay, Orient Longmans, 1948.

Su Shih. *The Prose-Poetry of Su Tung-p'o*. Tr. by Cyril D. Le Gros Clark. London, Kegan Paul, 1935. (Reprint: New York, Paragon, 1964.)

――――. *Su Tung-p'o. Selections from a Sung Dynasty Poet*. Tr. by Burton Watson. New York, Columbia University Press, 1965.

Lu Yu. *The Rapier of Lu*. Tr. by Clara M. Candlin. London, Murray, 1946.

(3) *History and Criticism*

Liu, James J. Y. *The Art of Chinese Poetry*. Chicago, Chicago University Press, 1962.
> Valuable as an introduction to Chinese poetry in terms familiar to the Western reader.

Teele, Roy E. *Through A Glass Darkly (A Study of English Translations of Chinese Poetry)*. Ann Arbor, Michigan, 1949.

IV *Drama in Translation*

(1) *Individual Plays and Collections* (arranged chronologically)

Kuan Han-ch'ing. *Selected Plays of Kuan Han-ching*. Tr. by Yang Hsien-yi and Gladys Yang. Peking, Foreign Languages Press, 1958.

Hsi-hsiang chi. *The Romance of the Western Chamber*. Tr. by S. I. Hsiung. London, Methuen, 1935.

――――. *The West Chamber*. Tr. by Henry H. Hart. Stanford, Calif., Stanford University Press, 1936.

Hui-lan chi. *The Story of the Circle of Chalk*. Tr. by Frances Hume from the French version of Stanislas Julien. London, Rodale Press, 1954.

K'an ch'ien nu. *A Slave to Money*. Tr. by Yang Hsien-yi and Gladys Yang. (In *Chinese Literature*, Sept. 1962, pp.53-92.)

Li K'uei fu-ching. *Li K'uei Carries Thorns*. Tr. by J. I. Crump. (In *Occasional*

Papers, I, 38-61, Center for Chinese Studies, University of Michigan, Ann Arbor, 1963.)

Ch'ang-sheng tien. The Palace of Eternal Youth. Tr. by Yang Hsien-yi and Gladys Yang. Peking, Foreign Languages Press, 1955.

Wang Pao-ch'uan. Lady Precious Stream. Adapted by S. I. Hsiung. London, Methuen, 1935.

Arlington, L. C. and Harold Acton. *Famous Chinese Plays.* (Synopses and partial translations of 31 Peking operas and 2 Ming Dynasty *K'un-ch'ü* plays.) Peking, Vetch, 1937.

(2) *History and Criticism*

Liu, James. *Elizabethan and Yuan (A Brief Comparison of Some Conventions in Poetic Drama).* London, China Society, Occasional Papers, No. 8, 1955.

Scott, A. C. *The Classical Theatre of China.* London, Allen & Unwin, 1957. The best book on the Peking opera, its actors, costumes, make-up, musical instruments, and stage conventions.

V *Prose Fiction in Translation*

(1) *Stories and Story Collections* (arranged chronologically)

Wang Chi-chen. *Traditional Chinese Tales.* New York, Columbia University Press, 1944.

The Man Who Sold A Ghost (Chinese Tales of the 3rd-6th Centuries). Peking, Foreign Languages Press, 1958.

The Dragon King's Daughter (Ten Tang Dynasty Stories). Peking, Foreign Languages Press, 1954.

Wang, Elizabeth Te-chen. *Ladies of the Tang (22 Classical Chinese Stories).* Taipei, Heritage Press, 1961.

Yang Hsien-yi and Gladys Yang. *The Courtesan's Jewel Box (Chinese Stories of the Xth-XVIIth Centuries).* Peking, Foreign Languages Press, 1957.

Acton, Harold and Lee Yi-hsieh. *Four Cautionary Tales.* London, Lehmann, 1947.

Birch, Cyril. *Stories from a Ming Collection.* London, Bodley Head, 1958.

Howell, E. Butts. *The Inconstancy of Madame Chuang and Other Stories.* London, Laurie, 1924.

———. *The Restitution of the Bride and Other Stories from the Chinese.* London, Laurie, 1926.

Yu-hsien k'u. The Dwelling of Playful Goddesses. Tr. by Howard S. Levy. New York, Paragon, 1965.

Liao-chai chih-i. Strange Stories from a Chinese Studio. Tr. by Herbert A. Giles. 2 vols. London, Thomas de la Rue, 1880. (Other editions: 1908, 1910, 1925.)

(2) *Novels* (arranged chronologically)

San-kuo chih. Romance of the Three Kingdoms. Tr. by C. H. Brewitt-Taylor. Shanghai, Kelly & Walsh, 1929. (Reprint: Vermont, Tuttle, 1959.)

Shui-hu chuan. All Men Are Brothers. Tr. by Pearl S. Buck. 2 vols. New York, John Day, 1933. (Revised one vol. ed., 1937.)

——. *Water Margin.* Tr. by J. H. Jackson. 2 vols. Shanghai, Commercial Press, 1937. (Reprint: Hong Kong, Commercial Press, 1963.)

——. Irwin, Richard G. *The Evolution of the Chinese Novel: Shui-hu-chuan.* Cambridge, Mass., Harvard University Press, 1953.

Hsi-yu chi. Monkey. Tr. by Arthur Waley. London, Allen & Unwin, 1942. Translation of one-third of the novel, omitting many episodes from Chapters 13-100.

Chin P'ing Mei. The Adventurous History of Hsi-Men and his Six Wives. Tr. by B. Miall from the German version of F. Kuhn. 2 vols. New York, Putnam, 1940. (One vol. ed., 1947.)

——. *The Golden Lotus.* Tr. by Clement Egerton. 4 vols. London, Routledge, 1939. (Reprint: New York, Grove Press, 1954.)

Hung-lou meng. Dream of the Red Chamber. Tr. by Chi-chen Wang. New York, Twayne Publishers (rev. and enlarged ed.), 1958. (First ed., New York, Doubleday, 1929; new abridged ed., Doubleday, 1958.)

——. *The Dream of the Red Chamber.* Tr. by Florence and Isabel Mc-Hugh from the German version of Franz Kuhn. New York, Pantheon, 1958.

There is no complete translation of the novel; both Wang's and Kuhn's versions are partial translations with adaptations and summaries of chapters not translated.

Hung-lou meng. Wu Shih-ch'ang. *On the Red Chamber Dream.* Oxford University Press, 1961.

A textual study of annotated manuscript copies and printed versions; some new light on the biography of the author.

Ju-lin wai-shih. The Scholars. Tr. by Yang Hsien-yi and Gladys Yang. Peking, Foreign Languages Press, 1957.

Lao Ts'an yu-chi. The Travels of Lao Ts'an. Tr. by Harold Shadick. Ithaca, New York, Cornell University Press, 1952.

(3) *History and Criticism*

Bishop, John L. *The Colloquial Short Story in China (A Study of the San-Yen Collections).* Cambridge, Mass., Harvard University Press, 1956.

Buck, Pearl S. *The Chinese Novel. (Nobel Lecture).* London, Macmillan, 1939.

Liu Ts'un-yan. *Buddhist and Taoist Influences on Chinese Novel.* Vol. I: *The Authorship of the Feng Shen Yen I.* Wiesbaden, Otto Harrassowitz, 1962.

Lu Hsün. *A Brief History of Chinese Fiction*. Tr. by Yang Hsien-yi and Gladys Yang. Peking, Foreign Languages Press, 1959.
> A standard book on the subject; original work published in 1923 and not yet superseded.

VI *Contemporary Chinese Literature*

(1) *Poetry*

Acton, Harold and Ch'en Shih-hsiang. *Modern Chinese Poetry*. London, Duckworth, 1936.

Hsu Kai-yu. *Twentieth Century Chinese Poetry*. New York, Doubleday, 1963.

Payne, Robert. *Contemporary Chinese Poetry*. New York, John Day, 1947.

Yu Kwang-chung. *New Chinese Poetry*. Taipei, Heritage Press, 1960.

Kuo Mo-jo. *Selected Poems from the Goddesses*. Peking, Foreign Languages Press, 1959.

(2) *Fiction*

Snow, Edgar. *Living China, Modern Chinese Short Stories*. New York, Reynal & Hitchcock, 1937.

Wang Chi-chen. *Contemporary Chinese Stories*. New York, Columbia University Press, 1944.

———. *Stories of China at War*. New York, Columbia University Press, 1947.

Yuan Chia-hua and Robert Payne. *Contemporary Chinese Short Stories*. London, Transatlantic Arts Co., 1946.

Lao Shê (Lau Shaw). *Rickshaw Boy*. Tr. by Evan King. New York, Reynal & Hitchcock, 1945.

Lu Hsün. *Selected Works of Lu Hsün*. Tr. by Yang Hsien-yi and Gladys Yang. 4 vols. Peking, Foreign Languages Press, 1956-60.
> Translation of most of Lu Hsün's stories in volume I.

Mao Tun. *Midnight*. Tr. by Hsu Meng-hsiung. Peking, Foreign Languages Press, 1957.

———. *Spring Silkworms and Other Stories*. Tr. by Sidney Shapiro. Peking, Foreign Languages Press, 1956.

Pa Chin. *The Family*. Tr. by Sidney Shapiro. Peking, Foreign Languages Press, 1958.

(3) *Drama*

Kuo Mo-jo. *Chu Yuan*. Tr. by Yang Hsien-yi and Gladys Yang. Peking, Foreign Languages Press, 1953.

T'ien Han. *Kuan Han-ching*. Peking, Foreign Languages Press, 1961.

Ts'ao Yü. *Sunrise*. Tr. by A. C. Barnes. Peking, Foreign Languages Press, 1960.

————. *Thunderstorm*. Tr. by Wang Tso-liang and A. C. Barnes. Peking, Foreign Languages Press, 1958.

(4) *History and Criticism*

Hsia, C. T. *A History of Modern Chinese Fiction*. New Haven, Yale University Press, 1961.

Hu Shih. *The Chinese Renaissance*. Chicago, University of Chicago Press, 1934. (Reprint: New York, Paragon, 1963.)

Huang Sung-k'ang. *Lu Hsün and the New Culture Movement of Modern China*. Amsterdam, Djambatan, 1957.

Průšek, Jaroslav, ed. *Studies in Modern Chinese Literature*. Berlin, Akademie Verlag, 1964.

Scott, A. C., *Art and Literature in Twentieth Century China*. New York, Doubleday, 1963.

Ting Yi. *A Short History of Modern Chinese Literature*. Peking, Foreign Languages Press, 1959.
    Translated from the work of a Chinese Communist critic; some changes and omissions in the English text.

VII *References*

Davidson, Martha. *A List of Published Translations from Chinese into English, French, and German*. 2 pts. (Tentative edition). Washington, D.C., American Council of Learned Societies. Pt. I, Literature exclusive of Poetry, 1952; Pt. II, Poetry, 1957.

Giles, Herbert A. *A Chinese Biographical Dictionary*. Shanghai, Kelly & Walsh, 1898. (Reprint: New York, Paragon, 1964.)

Schyns, Joseph, etc. *1500 Modern Chinese Novels and Plays*. Peiping, Catholic University Press, 1948. (Reprint: New York, Paragon, 1965.)

Wylie, A. *Notes on Chinese Literature*. Shanghai, American Presbyterian Mission Press, 1901. (Reprint: New York, Paragon, 1964.)

VIII *Supplement*

Frodsham, J. D. and Ch'eng Hsi. *An Anthology of Chinese Verse, Han Wei Chin and the Northern and Southern Dynasties*. Oxford, Oxford University Press, 1967.

Hsia, C. T. *The Classic Chinese Novel, A Critical Introduction*. N. Y., Columbia University Press, 1968.

Li, Tien-yi. *Chinese Fiction, A Bibliography of Books and Articles in Chinese and English*. New Haven, Far Eastern Publications, Yale University, 1968.

Yoshikawa, Kōjirō. *An Introduction to Sung Poetry*. Tr. by Burton Watson. Cambridge, Harvard University Press, 1967.

Periods of Chinese Literature

Name of Period	Years	Principal Forms	Writers of Most Importance
CHOU	1122?–221 B.C.	Confucian Classics	Confucius (551–479 B.C.)
		Shih Poetry (Four-word verse)	
		Historical Prose	Tso Ch'iu-ming (5th–4th century B.C.)
		Philosophical Prose	Mo-tzu (479?–390? B.C.) Chuang-tzu (369?–286? B.C.) Mencius (370?–290? B.C.) Hsün-tzu (320?–235? B.C.)
		Ch'u Tz'u	Ch'ü Yüan (340?–278? B.C.)
		Fu	Sung Yü (3rd century B.C.)
CH'IN	221–207 B.C.		
HAN	206 B.C.–220 A.D.	Music Bureau Poetry	
		Shih Poetry (Five-word verse)	
		Fu	Ssu-ma Hsiang-ju (179–117 B.C.) Chang Heng (78–139 A.D.)
		Historical Prose	Ssu-ma Ch'ien (145–86? B.C.)
THREE KINGDOMS	221–264 A.D.	*Shih* Poetry	Ts'ao Chih (192–232) Yüan Chi (210–263) Hsi K'ang (223–262)
TSIN	265–316		
SIX DYNASTIES	317–588	Supernatural Tales	
		Shih Poetry	T'ao Ch'ien (365–427) Hsieh Ling-yün (385–433)
		(Four tones)	Shen Yo (441–513)

303

Name of Period	Years	Principal Forms	Writers of Most Importance
SUI	589–618		
T'ANG	618–906	Shih Poetry (Five-word and seven-word verses)	Wang Wei (699–759) Li Po (701–762) Tu Fu (712–770) Po Chü-i (772–846) Li Ho (790–816) Li Shang-yin (812–858) Ssu-k'ung T'u (837–908)
		Tz'u Poetry	Wei Chuang (836–910)
		Neoclassical Prose	Han Yü (768–824) Liu Tsung-yüan (773–819)
		Literary Tales (ch'uan-ch'i)	Po Hsing-chien (d. 826)
		Buddhist Tales (pien-wen)	
FIVE DYNASTIES	907–960	Tz'u Poetry	Li Yü (937–978)
SUNG	960–1279	Tz'u and Shih Poetry	Liu Yung (990?–1050?) Su Shih (1037–1101) Chou Pang-yen (1057–1121) Li Ch'ing-chao (1081–1143) Lu Yu (1125–1210) Hsin Ch'i-chi (1140–1207)
		Neoclassical Prose and Fu	Ou-yang Hsiu (1007–1072) Su Shih
		Vernacular Stories (hua-pen)	
		Variety Plays (tsa-chü)	
		Southern Drama (nan-hsi)	
YÜAN (MONGOL)	1234–1280– 1368	Drama (tsa-chü)	Wang Shih-fu (13th century) Kuan Han-ch'ing (13th century) Ma Chih-yüan (13th century) Po P'o (1226–1285) Kao Wen-hsiu (13th century)
		San Ch'ü Poetry	Kuan Han-ch'ing Ma Chih-yüan Chang K'o-chiu (1265?–1345?) Ch'iao Chi (1280–1345) Liu Chih (13th–14th century)

Name of Period	Years	Principal Forms	Writers of Most Importance
MING	1368–1644	Fiction	Lo Kuan-chung (14th century) Wu Ch'eng-en (1500?–1582) Feng Meng-lung (1574–1646) Ling Meng-ch'u (1580–1644)
		Drama (K'un-ch'ü)	Kao Ming (14th century) T'ang Hsien-tsu (1550–1616) Shen Ching (1553–1610)
CH'ING (MANCHU)	1644–1911	Fiction	Wu Ching-tzu (1701–1754) Ts'ao Chan (1724?–1764) Liu E (1857–1909)
		Drama (K'un-ch'ü)	Li Yü (1611–1680?) Hung Sheng (1646?–1704) K'ung Shang-jen (1648–1718)
		(Peking Theater)	
REPUBLIC	1912–	Poetry	Hu Shih (1891–1962) Kuo Mo-jo (1892–) Hsü Chih-mo (1895–1931) Wen I-to (1899–1946) Chu Hsiang (1904–1933)
		Fiction	Lu Hsün (1881–1936) Mao Tun (1896–) Lao Shê (1899–) Pa Chin (1904–)
		Drama	Ts'ao Yü (1910–)

Glossary of Chinese Words

292, 304

華 陀 Hua T'o 200

話 本 *hua-pen* 154

淮 南 子 *Huai-nan-tzu* 285

黃 巢 Huang Ch'ao 99-100

黃 庭 堅 Huang T'ing-chien 288, 290

黃 州 Huang-chou 108, 111, 287

慧 遠 Hui Yüan 190

湖 南 Hunan 25, 80, 121, 130

紅 娘 Hung Niang 174

洪 昇 Hung Sheng 259

紅 樓 夢 *Hung-lou meng* 228, 302

紅 樓 夢 新 證 *Hung-lou meng hsin-cheng* 241

鴻 門 Hung-men 56

湖 北 Hupeh 24, 108-109, 261

伊 (水) I (River) 130

乙 丑 *i-ch'ou* 36-37

宜 春 I-ch'un 219-220

嶧 縣 I-hsien 234

夷 皋 I-kao 36

弋 陽 I-yang 294

若 木 Jo-mu 31

入 *ju* 65

儒 林 外 史 *Ju-lin wai-shih* 228, 302

開 封 Kaifeng 103, 162, 165

甘 州 Kan-chou 107

康 進 之 K'ang Chin-chih 290

康 熙 K'ang-hsi 119

甘 肅 Kansu 261

高 鶚 Kao E 238

高 明 Kao Ming 248-249, 252, 292

高 監 司 Kao, the Inspector General 250

高 東 嘉 Kao Tung-chia 293

高 文 秀 Kao Wen-hsiu 182

高 東 嘉 Kao-Tong-Kia 293

告 子 Kao-tzu 285

王 嬌 鸞 Keaou Lwan Wang (see Wang Chiao-luan) 291

江 西 Kiangsi 92, 119, 294

江 蘇 Kiangsu 175, 254, 294

楚 懷 王 King Huai of Ch'u 58

可 憐 *k'o-lien* 287

勾 闌 *kou-lan* 289

古 文 *ku-wen* 126

蒯 叔 平 Kuai Shu-p'ing 286

關 漢 卿 Kuan Han-ch'ing 170-171, 178-179, 186, 259, 290, 300, 303

關 羽 Kuan Yü 199, 200, 202

觀 音 Kuan-yin 229

癸 *kuei* 9

崑 *k'un* 252

崑 曲 K'un-ch'ü 252-253, 256, 260-261, 301

崑 崙 K'un-lun 31, 150

崑 山 K'un-shan 252

孔 丘 K'ung Ch'iu 54

孔 融 K'ung Jung 190

孔 尚 任 K'ung Shang-jen 259-260

公 瑾 Kung-chin (see Chou Yü) 287

郭 Kuo 131

郭 沫 若 Kuo Mo-jo 264-265, 270, 277, 303

國 風 *kuo-feng* 12

廣 西 Kwangsi 130, 133

廣 東 Kwangtung 108, 127, 253, 294

貴 州 Kweichow 55

孟 姜 女 Lady Meng Chiang 151-152

湘 夫 人 Lady of River Hsiang 26

楊 貴 妃 Lady Yang 93, 177, 259

洞 庭 湖 Lake Tung-t'ing 26

藍 采 和 Lan Ts'ai-ho 289

蘭 陵 Lan-ling 234

閬 州 Lang-chou 82

老 舍 Lao Shê 270, 274-275, 285, 303

314

Index

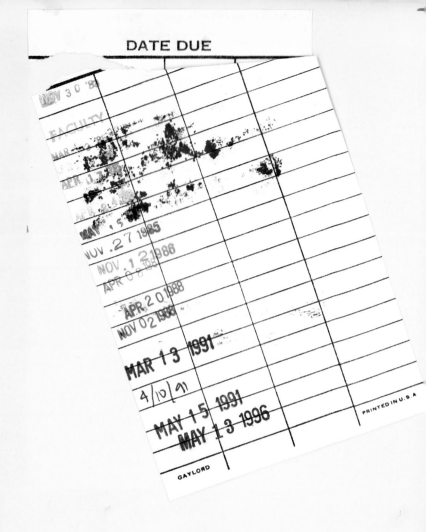